Victims of Progress

John H. Bodley

Fifth Edition

ALTAMIRA
PRESS

A Division of
ROWMAN & LITTLEFIELD PUBLISHERS, INC.
Lanham • New York • Toronto • Plymouth, UK

AltaMira Press
A division of Rowman & Littlefield Publishers, Inc.
A wholly owned subsidary of The Rowman & Littlefield Publishing Group, Inc.
4501 Forbes Boulevard, Suite 200
Lanham, MD 20706
www.altamirapress.com

Estover Road
Plymouth PL6 7PY
United Kingdom

British Library Cataloguing in Publication Information Available

Library of Congress Cataloguing-in-Publication Data

Bodley, John H.
  Victims of progress / John H. Bodley. — 5th ed.
    p. cm.
  Includes bibliographical references and index.
  ISBN-13: 978-0-7591-1148-6 (pbk. : alk. paper)
  ISBN-10: 0-7591-1148-0 (pbk. : alk. paper)
 1. Indigenous peoples. 2. Culture conflict. 3. Acculturation. 4. Social change. I. Title.

  GN380.B63 2008
  305.8—dc22   2007046408

Printed in the United States of America

∞™ The paper used in this publication meets the minimum requirements of American
National Standard for Information Sciences—Permanence of Paper for Printed Library
Materials, ANSI/NISO Z39.48-1992.

Victims of Progress

Contents

Preface and Acknowledgments

Victims of Progress will be a valuable book for courses that stress culture change, modernization, and economic development as they impact indigenous peoples and tribal societies worldwide. Previous editions have also been widely used in introductory general and cultural anthropology courses where the instructor wished to present these topics in depth. Because this book continues to present a particular viewpoint on controversial issues, it often serves as a stimulus for debate. Clear arguments, abundant case material, and ample documentation promote classroom discussion and encourage further reading.

This work assumes that until the rise of indigenous peoples' political organization in the 1970s, government policies and attitudes were the basic determinants of the fate of small-scale tribal societies. It also assumes that governments throughout the world were—and still are—most concerned about the increasingly efficient exploitation of the human and natural resources. The book is informed by my cultural scale perspective which recognizes that many people in the contemporary world, including indigenous peoples, are victims of progress. The development process that increases the scale of culture enriches only some segments of the global culture while it impoverishes many others and depletes ecosystems that all need.

The chapters examine and document the worldwide norms of interaction between industrial nations and tribal societies since 1830. It is an unfortunate record of wholesale cultural imperialism, aggression, and exploitation that involved every major nation, regardless of political, religious, or social philosophy. Although blatant extermination policies have become relatively infrequent, basic native policies and the motives underlying them have changed little since the industrial powers began to expand more than two hundred years ago. Today, however, many hopeful signs are appearing, especially at the international level.

What's New in the Fifth Edition

An updated chapter 10, on the political struggle for indigenous self-determination, includes an extended discussion of developments in Nunavut in the Canadian Arctic, where Inuit peoples have taken political control over a vast territory and gained ownership of extensive territory and natural resources.

An all new chapter 11, "Petroleum, the Commercial World, and Indigenous Peoples," reviews the importance of petroleum as the crucial foundation for the commercial world and includes case studies from the Gwich'in peoples' resistance to oil development in the Arctic National Wildlife Refuge (ANWR) and the legal struggle of indigenous peoples in the Ecuadorian Amazon to mitigate damage caused by oil development and prevent further damage.

Chapter 11 also discusses global warming which is linked to oil development and deforestation, again reviewing both its damaging effects that have already begun in the Arctic and the international struggle that indigenous peoples are waging to reduce the greenhouse gas emissions and to mitigate its affects.

The final chapter now contains an extended discussion of important new international developments on "peoples in voluntary isolation" intended to significantly improve their chances of survival. The adoption of the UN Declaration on the Rights of Indigenous Peoples in 2007 is discussed in this chapter. There is also new discussion of the role of indigenous people in the Arctic Council, especially in relation to global warming. The radical shift away from Aboriginal rights by the liberal government in Australia is also covered, along with the "state of emergency" declared by the Australian prime minister in 2007.

Acknowledgments

The first edition of this work was supported in part by a summer research stipend awarded to me by Washington State University for research during the summer of 1972. In 1980, I was on professional leave at the International Work Group for Indigenous Affairs in Copenhagen to gather new material for the second edition. In London I benefited from discussions with Stephen Corry of Survival International. I am grateful for the many kindnesses extended to me by the IWGIA staff, but I would like to acknowledge my debt especially to the late Helge Kleivan, former director of IWGIA and one of its original founders. His total dedication to the human rights struggle on behalf of indigenous peoples is a continuing source of inspiration.

The third edition benefited from the many readers (too numerous to thank individually) who kindly sent me useful materials and comments over the years. I gained valuable insights during a five-week seminar I attended at the University of Uppsala, Sweden, in 1985, where Kaj Arhem, Hugh Beach, Claes Corlin, and Jan Ovesen were my hosts. In 1986, Ray Barnhardt of the University of Alaska invited me to present a special course on native peoples in Fairbanks and Bethel, which gave me a close view of Alaskan issues. Jerome Bailen of the University of the Philippines in Manila was my host for a brief visit in 1986 to the Philippines, and he helped arrange contacts with indigenous leaders in the Cordillera.

Special thanks go to Napoleon Chagnon, University of California, Santa Barbara; Michael Howard, Simon Fraser University, British Columbia; and Susan H Lees, Hunter College, City University of New York, for their critical reviews of the first draft of the third edition. My thanks also to reviewers of the fourth edition: Anne Buddenhagen, Hofstra University; Susan Lees; Susan Rasmussen, University of Houston; and Neil L. Whitehead, University of Wisconsin–Madison. My wife, Kathleen M. Bodley, assisted with the preparation of the manuscript for the fourth edition.

The fifth edition was inspired by Alan McClare, executive editor of Rowman & Littlefield Publishers, Inc., who suggested that I consider updating *Victims*. I gained new insights on contemporary First Nations issues in Canada from my work as a consultant for the Stl'atl'imx Nation in British Columbia in 2003–2005. In that regard I especially want to thank Grand Chief Saul Terry and his wife, Joanne Drake-Terry; and Chiefs Garry John, and Darryl Peters, and Rodney Louie, Valerie Adrian, Shannon Squire, and Tanya Hoffman. Harvard Ayers, of Appalachian State University, called my attention to the Gwich'in struggle to protect the caribou in the Arctic Refuge, and Luci Beach, executive director of the Gwich'in Steering Committee, reviewed my discussion of the Gwich'in case in chapter 11. I also want to thank the students in my spring 2007 graduate seminar Tribal Peoples and Development Issues—Henry Averhart, Kristina Cantin, Eric Johnson, and Cherri Wemlinger—for sharing ideas and new materials. Thanks also to my WSU colleagues Robert and Marsha Bogar Quinlin for the opportunity to visit the Carib Reserve on Dominica.

A Brief History

The first edition of this book was written in 1972–1974 as a scholarly critique of the ethnocidal national and international policies toward indigenous peoples that still existed during the postwar era of decolonization and economic development. These policies went virtually unchallenged by anthropologists until the late 1960s. My fieldwork with the Asháninka (Campa) in the Peruvian Amazon from 1964 to 1969 convinced me that indigenous peoples were not inevitably doomed to disappear by the advance of globally organized commercial culture. What they needed was the opportunity to defend their resources against outside intrusion, and this required fundamental changes in government policies—and in the way that anthropologists conceptualized the development process. My views on these issues were first presented to an audience of my peers in 1972, through "Tribal Survival in the Amazon," an advocacy paper based on my Asháninka research and published in the first annual document series of the International Work Group for Indigenous Affairs (IWGIA), thanks to the encouragement of Helge Kleivan, then-director of IWGIA. I next wrote "Alternatives to Ethnocide: Human Zoos, Living Museums, and Real People," at the urging of Sol Tax, for the ninth World Anthropology Conference of the International Congress of Anthropological and Ethnological Sciences (ICAES), held in Chicago in 1973. That paper advocated a "cultural autonomy" policy toward indigenous peoples; portions of it appear in chapter 2 of the present edition of *Victims of Progress*, and the portion that appeared as chapter 9 of the first edition is included in the present edition as an appendix. The paper was later published in its original form in two volumes of the proceedings of the World Anthropology Conference (1977, 1978). My ideas on indigenous issues were further shaped in 1978 when Helge Kleivan arranged for me to meet with activist anthropologists in

Denmark and Norway, including many of the founders of IWGIA, during a series of university lectures.

The second edition of *Victims of Progress* appeared in 1982 and reflected the dramatic and unprecedented political mobilization of indigenous peoples throughout the world during the 1970s. It was written in 1980 while I served as a visiting researcher at IWGIA headquarters in Copenhagen, where much of the international action was readily observable. In the second edition, I replaced my original chapter 9, "Alternatives to Ethnocide," with a new chapter, "The Self-Determination Revival," which portrayed indigenous peoples as agents in their own political struggle. I also added a new final chapter on support organizations for indigenous people and discussed various debates among academics and activists over policy issues. In 1976 and 1977, I conducted new field research in the Peruvian Amazon that demonstrated how development pressures led to deforestation and resource depletion for the Shipibo Indians of Peru. This material was published in a monograph (1979), and it also appeared in chapter 8 of the second edition of *Victims of Progress*.

The third edition, published in 1990, documented the increasing gains made by indigenous peoples throughout the world during the 1980s, based in part on my brief visits with the Yupik in Alaska, with the Ifugao in the Philippines, and in aboriginal areas of the Northern Territory in Australia. This edition also reflected the continuing debate among anthropologists and development planners over the formulation of policy toward indigenous peoples. This edition was further influenced by my experiences as a lecturer on indigenous peoples and development issues at universities in Sweden and on many American campuses, including in Alaska during the 1980s. *Victims of Progress* was translated into German in 1983 as *Der Weg der Zerstorung: Stammesvolker und die industrielle Zivilization* and contributed to the growing European debate about indigenous peoples.

In 1986 I was invited to serve on the Tasaday Commission, which met in Manila to hear compelling evidence that the Tasaday were not isolated Stone Age people when they were "discovered" in 1971. In the third edition, then, I presented the Tasaday as an example of a people forced into politically motivated, coerced so-called primitivism, rather than as a case of active avoidance of contact, which is how I presented them in earlier editions.

In 1983 I wrote a critique of a World Bank position paper on indigenous peoples, Robert Goodland's *Tribal Peoples and Economic Development: Human Ecologic Considerations* (1982). The World Bank appeared to advocate my cultural autonomy approach but defined autonomy in such a way that the indigenous peoples' defense of tribal resources seemed weak in the face of internationally funded development projects. I presented my critique at two international conferences in 1983: the Australia–New Zealand Association for the Advancement of Science conference in Perth, and the eleventh ICAES conference in Vancouver, British Columbia. My critique also was presented before a congressional hearing on the World Bank in Washington, D.C. It is discussed in chapter 10 of the third edition, and my full critique is published in *Tribal Peoples and Development Issues: A Global Overview* (1988). In 1984 I was invited to organize a symposium, "Anthropology and the Emerging World Order: The Position of Small-Scale Autonomous Cultures in Latin America," for the annual meeting of the American Association for the Advancement of Science (AAAS) in New York. This symposium provided a forum for Venezuelan anthropologist Nelly Arvelo de Jimenez to discuss the proposed biosphere reserve for the Yanomami.

Subsequently, I further discussed the possibilities for alliances between environmentalists and indigenous peoples in "Umweltschutzer unterstutzen Stammesvolker" (1988), written for German ecologists. During the 1980s environmentalists sometimes uncritically portrayed indigenous people as superior human beings or "ecologically noble savages" to be held up as models of ecological responsibility. I emphasized that indigenous peoples were not perfect human beings who enjoyed perfect health and existed in complete harmony with their natural environments. Moreover, I pointed out that the ecological advantages were well demonstrated by the fact that most of the places slated for reserve status were worth saving precisely because they were territories used and maintained by indigenous peoples. I acknowledged that some indigenous individuals benefited by and even encouraged detrimental development, as anthropologist James Eder (1987) noted. However, the real issue was the increasing resource depletion that typically occurred following development, and the larger political decisions that encouraged the development of tribal lands by outsiders in the first place. To draw further attention to the policy issues at stake and the critical human rights issues involved, I completely rewrote the final chapter of the third edition, drawing on my paper "Realists vs. Idealists: Anthropology and the Politics of Genocide," which was originally written for the 1988 annual meeting of the American Anthropological Association. This final chapter reinterpreted the historic debate over indigenous policy as a split between those arguing for and those arguing against political autonomy for indigenous peoples.

The third edition referred to tribes as "small-scale sovereign nations," but the characterization of indigenous peoples as politically independent, highly egalitarian, and economically self-sufficient referred to the world before the state and did not capture the full significance of the differences in cultural scale produced by the development process.

The fourth edition updated the previous chapter 9, on the contemporary political struggles of indigenous peoples. It also contained a new chapter 1, which introduced the concept of cultural scale to highlight the significance of indigenous peoples in a post–Cold War world dominated by giant transnational corporations, financial markets, and global information networks. Chapter 1 provided a historical context for the modern predicaments of indigenous peoples, surveying events from the Industrial Revolution and early capitalism up to contemporary economic and political situations.

I first presented the cultural scale perspective in a 1991 paper, "Indigenous Peoples vs. the State: A Culture Scale Approach," written for a special conference, "Indigenous People in Remote Regions: A Global Perspective," held at the University of Victoria in British Columbia. The approach was originally developed in 1990 as the organizational structure for *Cultural Anthropology: Tribes, States, and the Global System.*[7] I also presented the cultural scale approach in a 1993 paper, "A Culture Scale Perspective on Intellectual Property Rights of Indigenous Peoples," at a conference ("Intellectual Property Rights and Indigenous Knowledge") held at Lake Tahoe and supported by the National Science Foundation. In 1994 I presented this view in a paper, "Culture Scale, Tribal People, and the Nation State," for the Harry Frank Guggenheim Foundation conference "Peripheral Societies and the State," held in Istanbul, Turkey. I later published this perspective in my essay "A Culture Scale Perspective on Human Ecology and Development" (1994) in *Advances in Human Ecology.*

The cultural scale perspective reflects my increasing recognition that many people in the contemporary world, like indigenous peoples, are victims of progress because the development process that increases the scale of culture enriches some segments of the global culture while it impoverishes many others and depletes ecosystems that we all need. I addressed this side of the victims issue in *Anthropology and Contemporary Human Problems* (1976, 1985, 1996, 2001, 2008) and in my research on social power and scale in America and globally since 1990 (1994, 2003, 2005). Cultural scale is also part of my research project on urban economic elites in eastern Washington State that began in 1995 (1997a, 1997b, 1999a).

1 Introduction: Indigenous Peoples and Culture Scale

Perhaps anthropology's most striking and relevant generalization about small-scale cultures is that they are totally different from both our own global-scale culture and the large-scale ancient civilizations that preceded us. . . . The secret of tribal success is almost certainly related to the absolute small scale of their populations and the relative simplicity of their technology, but the real key lies in the structure of the culture itself. In fact, small-scale cultures represent an almost total contrast to the adaptive strategy and basic cultural design to our own unproven cultural experiment.

-John H. Bodley[1]

INDIGENOUS PEOPLES HAVE BEEN ENGAGED in a political struggle to defend themselves and their resources against encroaching politically centralized societies for at least the past six thousand years, since states first appeared. People living with governments and tribally organized indigenous peoples have contrasting and often opposing ways of life, and they have difficulty being neighbors under the best of circumstances. Historically, indigenous peoples steadily yielded ground against advancing states, but until the beginning of the industrial revolution—barely two hundred years ago—they still effectively controlled much of the world (see figure 1.1). Conquest through colonization by commercially organized societies destroyed millions of indigenous peoples and countless cultural groups. Most surviving indigenous groups lost their political independence and now have only a precarious control over their resources. As of 2006, there were an estimated 350 million indigenous peoples worldwide representing more than five thousand distinct ethnolinguistic groups.[2] Many occupied remote areas that were prime targets for resource development by outside interests (see figure 1.2).

Until recently, scholars in academic disciplines such as anthropology and history observed the destruction of indigenous peoples, sometimes contributing to it with their theories of evolutionary progress. Anthropologists served more directly as agents of colonial governments and thought of indigenous people and their cultures as disappearing objects of study. Humanitarian anthropologists, politicians, and missionaries predicted the total demise of indigenous peoples and attempted to alleviate their suffering with ethnocentric programs of limited protectionism and civilizing "uplift," which effectively denied any opportunity for indigenous people to maintain their independence. The crucial point is that even those who were sympathetic with the "plight"

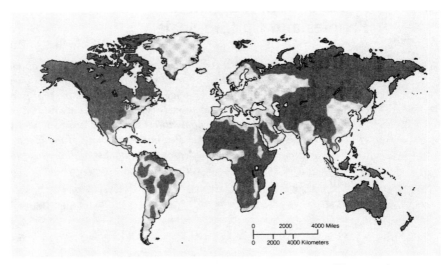

Figure 1.1.   Autonomous Tribal Peoples, Approximately 200 Million People (20 percent of the global population), 1800

of indigenous peoples were not yet willing to either challenge the legitimacy of colonialism or recognize self-determination of peoples and cultural autonomy as basic human rights. However, indigenous peoples did not disappear. They are still defending themselves, and they are appealing to the interna-

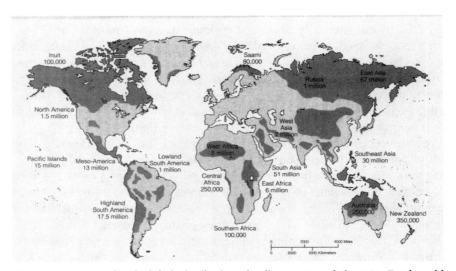

Figure 1.2.   Generalized Global Distribution of Indigenous People in 1997. Total world indigenous population estimated at approximately at 220 million (IWGIA 1997)

tional community for support. New possibilities are emerging as indigenous peoples continue to organize themselves politically and work to expand the concept of human rights to include their own cultural, political, and territorial rights.

Culture Scale, Culture Process, and Indigenous Peoples

Indigenous peoples are unique in the contemporary world because they share a way of life that is focused on family and household, and is organizationally small scale and more sustainable than life in urban-based societies organized by political centralization, market exchanges, and industrial mass production. The scale contrast highlights the uniqueness of indigenous peoples and their societies and cultures, avoiding the ethnocentrism suggested by evolutionary stages of "progress." The scale concept also avoids the romantic notion of the so-called noble savage. Small-scale societies have enormous human advantages, especially because people living in smaller, lower-density populations may be able to enjoy greater democracy, freedom, equality, and security than people living in large, dense populations, where they usually are divided sharply by differential access to vital resources, wealth, and power. In small-scale societies, where all households have assured access to food and shelter and to the rewarding experiences offered by their culture, there is less cultural incentive to accumulate wealth. Likewise, there is little incentive to expand the population and its consumption of resources.

Indigenous peoples share a unique sociocultural system that was the product of millennia of cultural development, culminating in the emergence of fully modern humans at least fifty thousand years ago. The most basic features of this system—maximum social equality and domestic self-sufficiency—exhibited remarkable stability, and small-scale human groups proliferated across the globe and adapted to virtually all biotic communities. Because this small-scale cultural pattern seems to have coevolved with the human species and is concerned primarily with satisfying basic human needs for nutrition and security, it is appropriate to call the process *humanization*. In other words, small-scale cultures are concerned primarily with the biological production and maintenance of human beings and with the cultural production and maintenance of human societies and cultures. The humanization process is shared by all humans and involves at least five cultural aspects that people use to meet their human needs. These are:

- Symbolization (producing abstract concepts)
- Materialization (giving physical form to concepts)

- Verbalization (producing human speech)
- Socialization (producing permanent human societies)
- Enculturation (reproducing culture)

We may call small-scale societies and cultures produced by the humanization process *tribal*, to emphasize the absence of political centralization. This term works well when applied to small-scale societies that existed historically in a world of small-scale societies but becomes problematic when used to describe indigenous peoples today. The term *tribal* is sometimes applied to small-scale societies that retain significant political and economic autonomy, but it has multiple meanings and connotations. Historically, as will be shown in later chapters, *tribes* were often designated by colonial governments as administrative units, with *chiefs* appointed for political purposes. In some areas, *tribe* is used as a self-designation by indigenous peoples living in multiethnic states, although others may reject the term as derogatory or divisive.

The phrase *indigenous peoples* became widely used in the 1970s, and has since been adopted by international organizations including the United Nations. The most accepted formal definition of *indigenous* is "people whose ancestors preceded the state in the territory they occupy." This is, of course, a historical and political definition and says nothing about culture or social scale, even though it connotes "tribal" or "formerly tribal." When I use the term *indigenous peoples*, I mean a group of contemporary people who identify themselves with a specific small-scale society, a unique cultural heritage, and an ancestral territory. In the world before the state, indigenous peoples lived in tribal societies. Mobile tribal foragers operating in a world of foragers are prime ethnographic examples of such small-scale societies. The historic resilience and sustainability of tribal sociocultural systems was threatened and many sorts of changes were introduced by the following processes and events:

15,000 BP: sedentarization and the emergence of village life
12,000 BP: domestication and the emergence of farming and herding
6,000 BP: politicization and the emergence of politically organized large-scale societies
500 BP: commercialization and the emergence of commercially organized global-scale societies

These processes have unfolded over the past fifteen thousand years and have surely changed the context within which small-scale tribal societies operate. For example, among full-time mobile foragers such as Australian Aborigines, control of ritual knowledge and residence in a camp group probably regulated the use of resources more than ownership of territory, whereas knowledge of wild plant resources was no doubt widely shared. By contrast, sedentary villagers and food producers may be more concerned with regulating the use of resources through formal descent structures. Huge cultural differences developed with the emergence of large- and global-scale societies.

Large-Scale versus Small-Scale Society and Culture

Beginning some six thousand years ago, the humanization process was superseded in several parts of the world by the cultural process of politicization, by which a few aggrandizing individuals managed to create centralized political authority and the formal institutions of government. Politicization, a new form of organizing social power, replaced the social equality and domestic self-sufficiency of small-scale societies with political bureaucracy supported by centrally directed production and distribution, taxes and tribute. Politicization quickly made possible the construction of ancient civilizations and conquest empires. These new, more complex societies are a radically different cultural world, which I label the *imperial world* to emphasize the contrast with the earlier tribal world of small-scale autonomous societies. In large-scale imperial societies, central political rulers take production and distribution functions away from households and individuals and promote subsistence intensification, new technology, and population growth to enhance their personal social power.

The earliest pristine states developed out of small-scale tribal societies that were turned into chiefdoms when individual chiefs successfully took political control over more than one local village. The development of chiefdoms was in some respects a more surprising event than the development of states, because the gap between egalitarian tribal societies and rank- and status-conscious chiefdoms is wider than the gap between large chiefdoms and small states. Some tribal societies must have been transformed into chiefdoms and states independently in many different times and places. Others were forced to become chiefdoms and states to defend themselves. More often, tribals were militarily conquered by the rulers of expanding states and were transformed into dependent, tax-paying peasantries.

The rulers of large-scale political societies changed the world in which tribal societies operated. However, rulers were unable to expand everywhere and eliminate all independent tribes, because large-scale societies are costly to maintain and tend to break down. This fact is significant. Ancient civilizations were inherently expansive systems, but because they were politically centralized they were unstable and were characterized by frequent institutional collapses. The large populations and agrarian production systems that sustained them provided the primary energy base of these civilizations, and they quickly reached diminishing returns as subsistence technology and organizational complexity increased. Thus, large-scale societies were restricted to the few regions of the world with the ideal climate, soil, and water to support intensive agriculture. This left vast areas of the world where small-scale societies continued to thrive.

Small-scale societies, in contact with politically organized societies, may put forward temporary representatives to negotiate with or to obtain benefits from the foreigners. Others may promote temporary war leaders. In many regions, important trade contacts brought metal tools and other new objects of wealth that disrupted the system and encouraged the formation of new chiefdoms. However, as long as they retained control over their resources and political autonomy, tribal societies were generally sustainable in spite of—and sometimes because of—their acquisition of new technology.

The Problem of Global-Scale Society and Culture

European elites created a new cultural world in the three centuries after 1500 by replacing feudalism with the institutions of colonialism, market capitalism, and industrialization. The dominant process in this new sociocultural system was commercialization, because the cultural creation of commodities and the related extraction of resources, mass production, large-scale markets, and mass consumption were defining features. The first part of this commercialization process, as detailed by Wallerstein,[3] led rapidly to the emergence of the modern world system. The defining features of capitalism, as described in 1776 by pioneer political economist Adam Smith,[4] include a complex division of labor—involving a few capitalist landlords and manufacturers and a great mass of landless renters and laborers—that promotes the accumulation of capital by means of ever-expanding commercial exchanges. Commercialization has surpassed both humanization and politicization as dominant cultural processes in the world. The expanding commercial economy has created a global society that is many times more complex than any tribal society or ancient civilization.

Economist David Warsh[5] pointed to the ten thousand or so industries recognized by the standard industrial classification code (SIC) of the United States in the early 1980s and argued that the expanding complexity of the economic division of labor in itself "inflates" the cost of living for everyone and must be recognized as a dominant force in the world. The world is now one giant commercial market where, as trend forecasters John Naisbitt and Patricia Aburdene observed, "economic considerations almost always transcend political considerations." [6] Shifting perspective a notch, it is also true that economic considerations must often transcend human considerations. In the commercial world the economy is imagined to have an independent existence, and economic growth is universally recognized as the highest priority for government policy, even when what is good for the economy conflicts with the interests of particular human groups. Furthermore, vast economic power is concentrated in giant corporations that are organizationally far removed from the domestic concerns of individuals and households. From the perspective of individuals within small-scale societies, the commercial world and the commercialization process are relatively inhuman. Unfortunately, the obvious material benefits of commercialization are very unevenly distributed and costly to sustain.

The world dominated by a commercially driven global society is very different from the earlier imperial world, which was balanced between small-scale societies and precapitalist states. As recently as 1800, half the world was still occupied by largely autonomous tribal peoples, but because the commercial world has built-in incentives for expansion, it spread very rapidly— with devastating impact on less complex societies. The following chapters document how tribal peoples throughout the world have experienced genocide and ethnocide along the frontiers of the expanding commercial world during the past two centuries. The previous dynamic equilibrium between tribes and states is now gone. Where tribals have managed to keep their societies relatively intact, they now are threatened with ecocide as the natural resources on which they depend are extracted for use as commercial commodities in the global marketplace. The real problem facing indigenous peoples is that their cultural heritage of community-level resource management, high levels of local self-sufficiency, and relative social equality is the antithesis of how the commercial world was developed and is currently organized.

The intrusion of commercial societies into the tribal world is far more disruptive than contacts with noncommercial, politically organized societies, because commercial societies promote individualism and wealth inequality. Commerce also converts resources into market commodities. These powerful processes are not easily combated by small-scale societies that have not experienced long involvement with market-based societies. The members of tribal societies use many devices to prevent coercive political or economic power from becoming concentrated in any one person or office, because the growth of political power is clearly a threat to social equality and local self-sufficiency. Anthropologist Richard Lee described some of these antihierarchy cultural mechanisms for the San foragers of southern Africa,[7] and Pierre Clastres described them for indigenous groups in Amazonia.[8] There are counterparts in the wealth-leveling mechanisms of peasant communities, such as the image of "limited good" in Latin American peasant societies.[9]

Social Scale and Social Power

Change in social scale requires growth in population and productivity. From the perspective of cultural evolution, though, growth is a unique, usually temporary event as long as a society remains small in scale and as long as social power is organized domestically. During the course of cultural development, the scale of society and social power changed by orders of magnitude that can best be represented on a logarithmic graph as changes in scale in which each level is ten times larger than the previous (see figure 1.3). People have developed three ways to culturally organize the distribution of social power and material living standards: (1) domestically, by means of the household; (2) politically, by means of rulers; and (3) commercially, by means of markets and corporate businesses. Each method fits a different scale of society and produces a distinctive distribution of social power and household living standards. In the world before the state—that is, until approximately seven thousand years ago—social power was directed by autonomous household heads who negotiated within a very small interdomestic society of about five hundred to two thousand people—a society in which no one individual held permanent social power. Power was limited to the members of a household and personal networks of about 150 adults. Power was limited in size because it operated within face-to-face communities, and power seekers were actively rejected if their actions conflicted with community consensus.[10] Culturally, individuals had no power incentive to promote growth to increase power because power had such a culturally limited scope.

Political centralization apparently emerged wherever environmental conditions made it possible for power seekers to overcome the limits to growth imposed by consensus in small-scale societies. The material benefits of growth for political elites were immediately reflected in high levels of domestic luxury. Commercially organized, global-scale societies have emerged since 1790 as a result of changes that removed both cultural and natural limits to growth. Politically organized societies were difficult and costly to maintain. The limits to growth were overcome in late-eighteenth-century Europe when power-seeking elites politically redefined the relationship between commerce and the state in order to make it possible for government officials to support commercially organized power and to promote further growth. Elites then used industrial technology and new energy sources to increase the rate of commercial transactions to generate higher levels of social power for the top ranks through economic growth.

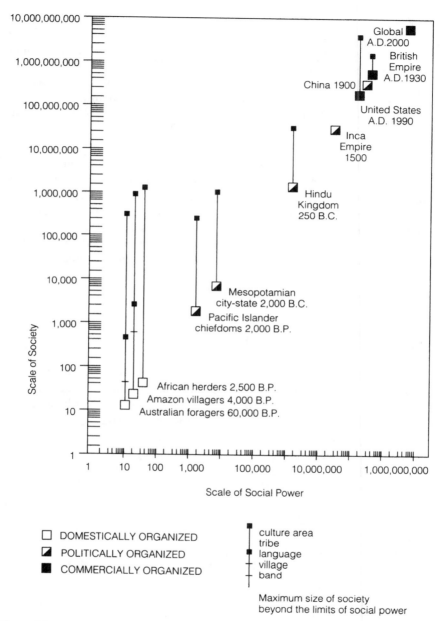

Figure 1.3.

The growth of commercially organized power, as with that of political power, magnified material inequality and impoverished many people. There were actually more impoverished people by the end of the twentieth century than the entire population of the world in 1850. The commercialization of property was a key process in the concentration of social power because, as Adam Smith observed in 1776,[11] people who could not own property were compelled to become renters and wage earners. Commercial elites accumulate social power in the form of money because as a symbol it has infinite growth potential.

An ideology of growth has been a prominent feature of the global-scale commercial culture at least since Smith advocated continual economic progress as the only way to ensure that poor people would accept the inequality that wealth accumulation seemed to require. In the twenty-first century publicly displayed measures of growth, such as gross domestic product values and Dow Jones averages, continue to appear prominently as materializations of growth ideology that sustain social power in the same way that ideological materializations such as statuary and monumental constructions sustained power in ancient civilizations.[12]

Negative Development: The Global Pattern

During the first, preindustrial phase of capitalist expansion, which was under way by 1450, several European powers, including Spain, Portugal, England, and France, gained political domination over large areas of North and South America, the Caribbean, and the islands of the eastern Atlantic. This was the beginning of a colonial process of conquest and incorporation that continued into the twentieth century. By 1800, at the beginning of the Industrial Revolution, preindustrial states still existed in China, Japan, and Africa; traditional kingdoms and chiefdoms in India, the Middle East, and the Pacific Islands still retained considerable autonomy. The great Western colonial powers claimed 55 percent of the world's land area but controlled two-thirds of the world.[13] For the next 150 years, virtually all indigenous territory was conquered by colonizing industrial states, and an estimated 50 million indigenous people died as a result. This process created the modern world system, but it did so at an enormous cost in ethnocide, genocide, and ecocide suffered by the peoples and territories forcibly incorporated into the new global system.

The loss of political autonomy by indigenous peoples occurs when state governments gain enough power over a territory to prevent indigenous groups from acting in their own defense to expel outsiders. This can occur following military conquest, or it can be accomplished by formal treaty signing or some less formal process by which government control is extended over a formerly autonomous indigenous area. In most cases, the relative difference in power between small-scale tribal societies and states is so extreme that the state can impose control over an indigenous territory virtually at will, although it can be a costly and time-consuming process.

The loss of economic autonomy is fostered by political conquest because indigenous groups must maintain control over their resources in order to remain self-sufficient. Drastic depopulation can reduce the economic viability of an indigenous group, but competition with colonists over resources, especially when the land base is reduced by government decree, is often the decisive factor. Any factors that undermine the traditional subsistence base may prompt indigenous peoples to participate in the market economy, whether as wage laborers or in cash cropping. Indigenous peoples may also want to secure some of the manufactured goods, such as metal tools and factory clothing, produced by the world system's industrial centers. However, these "pull" forces in themselves are insufficient to compel indigenous peoples into large-scale participation in the market economy without a strong push. Whenever the subsistence economy remains strong, indigenous people are often poorly motivated target workers, and colonial administrators resort to legal measures such as special taxes and enforced planting laws to force reluctant indigenous peoples into the market economy. Once initiated, involvement in the market economy can become self-reinforcing because wage labor leaves little time for subsistence activities and because cash cropping can degrade the local ecosystem, reducing potential for subsistence production.

Historically, indigenous peoples have not been passive victims of expansion by larger-scale societies. In general, they defended themselves against preindustrial states and empires quite successfully for more than six thousand years. Many tribal societies did, of course, transform themselves into chiefdoms and states in self-defense, but many simply organized temporary military alliances and effectively held the frontier. Often, indigenous peoples sought military hardware such as guns to improve their defense against outsiders.

The most promising recent development was the emergence of the indigenous peoples' self-determination movement during the 1970s. Regional, national, and international organizations of indigenous peoples are now defining their own objectives and pressing their legitimate claims. Political mobilization by indigenous peoples is a hopeful development, and significant gains have been made. However, this phase of the struggle is just beginning. Formal government policies and actual practices must be changed before small-scale indigenous societies can flourish with maximum autonomy. The social science community can support the struggle of indigenous peoples by helping to reduce the ethnocentrism, misunderstandings, and ignorance that underlie many unjust government policies and practices.

Policy Implications

Small-scale societies were successively threatened as the politicization process led to the development of chiefdoms and states and as the commercialization process created a global-scale society based on a global market economy. The policy implications of an anthropological scale and power perspective on indigenous peoples are clear. If the objective is to permit the existence of small-scale societies, then indigenous peoples must be allowed sufficient autonomy and control over their territorial base to maintain their societies and cultures. Such small-scale societies need to be recognized as tiny sovereign nations with well-defined local powers.

Reconstituting autonomous small-scale societies from existing tribal or ethnic minorities would be a complex process, because restoring a viable territorial base often requires major changes in land tenure laws and ownership as well as effective political decentralization. Genuinely autonomous local communities would be in a position to determine their own forms of exchange with the larger politically and/or commercially organized groups surrounding them, but theoretically there is no reason that such culturally very different groups could not coexist satisfactorily. National governments and the global society could treat a self-sufficient indigenous group as a special form of corporation. This would offer an encouraging model for any community that wants a more humane existence within an otherwise increasingly dehumanizing, inequitable, and unsustainable commercial world.

Notes

1. John H. Bodley, 1996, *Anthropology and Contemporary Human Problems*, 3rd ed., Mountain View, CA: Mayfield, 10–11.

2. IWGIA (International Work Group for Indigenous Affairs), 2007. Annual Report 2006, Copenhagen: IWGIA, http://www.iwgia.org/sw17779.asp.

3. Immanuel Wallerstein, 1974, *The Modern World-System: Capitalist Agriculture and the Origins of the European World-Economy in the Sixteenth Century*, New York: Academic Press.

4. Adam Smith, 1776, *An Inquiry into the Nature and Causes of the Wealth of Nations*, vol. 1, London: Strahan & Cadell.

5. David Warsh, 1984, *The Idea of Economic Complexity* (New York: Viking Penguin.

6. John Naisbitt and Patricia Aburdene, 1990, *Megatrends 2000*, New York: William Morrow, 21.

7. Richard B. Lee, 1984, *The Dobe Kung*, New York: Holt, Rinehart and Winston.

8. Pierre Clastres, 1977, *Society against the State: The Leader as Servant and the Humane Uses of Power among the Indians of the Americas*, New York: Urizen Books.

9. George M. Foster, 1969, *Applied Anthropology*, Boston: Little, Brown.

10. Christopher Boehm, 1993. "Egalitarian behavior and reverse dominance hierarchy," *Current Anthropology* 34(3): 227–54.

11. Smith, *Wealth of Nations*.

12. Elizabeth DeMarrais, Luis Jaime Castillo, and Timothy Earle, 1996, "Ideology, materialization, and power strategies," *Current Anthropology* 37(1): 15–31.

13. Grover Clark, 1936, *The Balance Sheets of Imperialism: Facts and Figures on Colonies*, New York: Columbia University Press, 5.

2 Progress and Indigenous Peoples

The Industrial Revolution disrupts and transforms all preceding cultures in West and East alike, and at the same time throws their resources into a common pool.

—A. C. Graham [1]

INDIGENOUS PEOPLES AND THEIR CULTURAL PATTERNS are being drastically impacted as the scale of global society and the market economy continues to expand. For many years most people did not realize that increasing the scale of societies, markets, and economies could actually reduce human well-being by negatively transforming the sociocultural systems and ecosystems that support people. Indigenous people were the first to be negatively impacted by a global growth process that now adversely impacts people everywhere. This book describes the historic experience of indigenous peoples in confrontations with the commercial world, and shows why the impacts have been so destructive. This history reveals serious problems within the global culture itself, but it also shows what can be changed. Understanding the experience of indigenous peoples and their current human rights struggle is a crucial step toward designing a just, truly sustainable, multiethnic global society.

Progress: The Commercial Explosion

In the mid-eighteenth century, the commercialization process and the related technological developments associated with the industrial revolution launched the developing Western nations on an explosive growth in population and consumption called *progress*, which led to an unprecedented assault on the world's indigenous peoples and their resources. In the 250 years since then the world has been totally transformed, many self-sufficient small-scale societies have disappeared, and dramatic resource shortages and environmental disasters have materialized. Now that many researchers are struggling to explain why the global-scale culture seems to be floundering in its own success, anthropologists are beginning to realize that the first and most ominous victims of industrial progress were the several million indigenous people who still controlled more than half the globe in 1820 and who shared a relatively stable, satisfying, and proven cultural adaptation. It is highly significant and somewhat unsettling to realize that the cultural systems of these first victims of progress present a striking contrast to the characteristics of the global-scale society.[2]

The commercialization process was nothing less than an explosion because of the unparalleled scope and the catastrophic nature of the transformations it initiated. Phenomenal increases in both population and per capita consumption rates were the two most critical correlates of commercialization because they quickly led to overwhelming pressure on natural resources.

The acceleration in world population growth rates and their relationship to industrial progress have been well documented. Immediately prior to the industrial revolution, for example, the doubling time of the world's population was approximately 250 years. However, after industrialization was under way, the European population of 1850 doubled in just over 80 years, and the European populations of the United States, Canada, Australia, and Argentina tripled between 1851 and 1900.[3] The doubling time of the world's population reached its lowest point of about 33 years (an annual growth rate of over 2 percent) during the period 1965–1973. By 1986 the global rate of population growth had declined only slightly to 1.8 percent a year. In contrast, clear anthropological evidence shows that small-scale tribal societies grow slowly and use their natural resources conservatively. The relative stability of tribal populations is due only partly to higher mortality rates; the most important cultural factor is that tribal women are empowered to make family-planning decisions. Although small-scale populations have the capacity for growth, and may expand rapidly into empty lands, they are politically and economically designed to operate most effectively at low densities and low absolute size.

The Culture of Consumption

The increased rates of resource consumption accompanying commercialization have been even more critical than mere population increase. Above all else, commercial societies have a culture of consumption, and in this respect they differ most strikingly from small-scale societies. Commercial economies are founded on the principle that consumption must be ever expanded, and complex systems of mass marketing and advertising were developed for that specific purpose. Social stratification in commercial societies is based primarily on inequalities in material wealth and is both supported and reflected by differential access to resources. Commercial ideological systems stress belief in continual economic growth and progress and characteristically measure "standard of living" in terms of levels of material consumption without regard to actual well-being.

Small-scale tribal societies contrast strikingly in all of these aspects. Their economies are geared to the satisfaction of basic subsistence needs, which are assumed to be fixed, and a variety of cultural mechanisms serve to limit material acquisitiveness and to redistribute wealth. Thus, distribution is more important than production. Wealth itself is rarely the basis of social stratification, because nature is the primary wealth, and everyone can generally gain access to natural resources. These contrasts are the basis for the incompatibility between small-scale and global-scale societies and cause problems when indigenous peoples are conquered by commercial societies.

The most obvious consequences of the consumption patterns of tribal societies are that these societies tend to be highly stable, make light demands on their environments, and can easily support themselves within their own boundaries. The opposite situation prevails for societies with a culture of consumption. Almost overnight, the commercially organized nations ate up their own local resources and outgrew their boundaries. This was dramatically apparent in England, where local resources comfortably supported small-scale societies for thousand of years, but after one hundred years of commercial progress the area was unable to meet its basic needs for grain, wood, fibers, and hides. Between 1851 and 1900, Europe was forced to export 35 million people because it could no longer support them.[4] Since 1970 in the United States, where commercial progress has gone the furthest, Americans have been consuming per capita some fifteen times more energy than Neolithic agriculturalists and seven times the world average in nonrenewable resources. They are also importing vast tonnages of food, fuels, and other resources to support themselves.

Tribal peoples typically take only a tiny fraction, often less than 1 percent, of the annual biological production of their territories, whereas the United States consumes the equivalent of 200 percent of its national biological product.[5] Globally, the commercial world consumed the equivalent of 122 percent of the world's biological production. Indeed, few, if any, commercial nations can now supply from within their own boundaries the resources needed to support further growth or even to maintain current consumption levels. It should not be surprising, then, that the "underdeveloped" resources controlled by the world's self-sufficient tribal peoples were quickly appropriated by outsiders to support their own commercial progress.

Resource Appropriation and Acculturation

Historically, in case after case government programs seemingly intended for the progress of indigenous peoples directly or indirectly forced culture change, and these programs in turn were linked invariably to the extraction of indigenous peoples' resources to benefit the national economy. From the strength of this relationship between "progress" and the exploitation of resources, we might even infer that indigenous peoples would not be asked to surrender their resources and independence if industrial societies learned to control their own culture of consumption. This point must be made explicit, because considerable confusion exists in the voluminous culture change literature regarding the basic question of why small-scale societies seem inevitably to be acculturated or modernized by commercial civilization. Historically, the consensus, at least among economic development writers, was the ethnocentric view that contact with "superior" commercial societies causes indigenous peoples to voluntarily reject their own cultures in order to obtain a better life. Other writers, however, seemed curiously mystified by the entire process. An example of this latter position can be seen in anthropologist Julian Steward's summary of a monumental study of change in traditional cultures in eleven countries.[6] Steward concluded that although many startling parallels could be identified, the causal factors involved in the modernization process were still "not well conceptualized."

This inability to conceptualize the causes of the transformation process in simple, nonethnocentric terms—or indeed the inability to conceptualize the causes at all—may be due to the fact that the analysts were members of the culture of consumption that today is the dominant world culture type. The most powerful commercial societies often assumed a natural right to exploit the world's resources wherever they found them, regardless of the prior claims of indigenous populations. Arguing for efficiency and survival of the fittest, early colonialists elevated this "right" to the level of an ethical and legal principle that could be invoked to justify the elimination of any societies that were not making "effective" use of their resources.

Members of expanding commercial societies rationalized as a "natural" evolutionary process the elimination of other societies they considered to be either culturally or racially inferior. They thought such a "natural selection" process was so "inevitable" that nothing could prevent it. For example, in 1915 Paul Popenoe told the scientists assembled in Washington, D.C, for the Nineteenth International Congress of Americanists that the mass destruction of Native Americans following the European invasion was "a process of racial purification of weak stocks." The Indian was "killed off by natural selection." Popenoe declared: "The native succumbed to the process of evolution, and no conceivable kindnesses from their conquerors could have prevented this elimination."[7] Certainly, disease was a major factor in New World depopulation, but it was accompanied by conquest and colonization, which were political processes for which individual decision makers were responsible. Treating ethnocide and genocide as the operation of an immutable scientific law is to mask their underlying political causes.

These old attitudes of social Darwinism are still embedded in our ideological system and were common in the early professional literature on culture change. In fact, as recently as 1971 one development writer declared: "Perhaps entire societies will lack survival value and vanish before the onslaught of industrialization."[8] This viewpoint also appeared in neoevolutionary anthropological theory in the 1960s, as the Law of Cultural Dominance: "That cultural system which more effectively exploits the energy resources of a given environment will tend to spread in that environment at the expense of less effective systems."[9] To speak of a "cultural system" effectively disregards the actual human decision makers who chose to implement the "natural law."

Apart from the obvious ethical implications involved here, upon close inspection all of these theories expounding the greater adaptability, efficiency, and survival value of commercial societies prove to be misleading. Of course, with its culture of consumption, the global-scale society is uniquely capable of consuming resources at tremendous rates, but this does not make it a more effective society than low-energy, small-scale societies, if stability or long-run ecological success is taken as the criterion for "effectiveness." Likewise, the assumption that a given environment is not being exploited effectively by a tribal society may merely reflect the unwillingness of national political authorities to allow local groups to manage their own resources for their own interests. This helps explain why the members of a culture of consumption might consider another culture's tribal resources to be underexploited and to use this as a justification for appropriating them.

"Optimum" Land Use for Hill Tribes

The experience of the Chittagong Hills peoples of East Pakistan (Bangladesh since 1972) provides an excellent example of the process by which commercialization leads to a shortage of resources at the national level and ultimately results in the political conquest and dispossession of indigenous peoples who have preserved their resources more effectively. Along with other parts of the world—thanks to the intervention of commercial nations—East Pakistan had such a severe population explosion that by 1965 population density reached an average of 470 people per square kilometer and the soil resources of the country were being pushed to the limit. As the crunch on resources worsened, the government made dramatic efforts to emulate the economic development route of the developed nations and soon directed special attention to the still largely self-sufficient Chittagong Hills areas, which had managed to remain outside of the cash economy and had avoided major disruptions due to commercial intrusion. The French anthropologist Claude Lévi-Strauss, who visited the area in 1950, found the hill tribes flourishing and observed that the Chittagong Hills "form a kind of anthropological sanctuary."[10] Although the twelve ethnic groups making up the hill tribes were not totally isolated, they had enjoyed considerable political autonomy, especially under British control. However, the areas were beginning to show population growth and subsequent pressure on their own resources due to shortening swidden gardening cycles. But with only thirty-five people per square kilometer, they remained an island of low population density and "underdeveloped" resources in what had suddenly become an impoverished and overpopulated country.

External exploitation of resources in the interests of the national economy initially focused on the forests of the Chittagong Hills. Twenty-two percent of the district was declared a forest "reserve," the provincial government organized a Forest Industries Development Corporation, and in 1953, lumber and paper mills were in operation to facilitate the modern commercial utilization of the region's bamboo and tropical hardwoods. In 1962 the largest river in the area was dammed to supply hydroelectric power to help feed the rising energy demands of East Pakistan's affluent urbanites. In the process, however, 673 square kilometers of the best agricultural land were converted into a lake, further aggravating the land scarcity that was already developing because of earlier disruptions of the population/resources balance and requiring the resettlement and "rehabilitation" of many hill people.

Still dissatisfied with the level of resource exploitation in the Chittagong Hills, in 1964 the Pakistani government enlisted an eleven-member international team of geologists, soil scientists, biologists, foresters, economists, and agricultural engineers to devise a master plan for the integrated development of the area based on what they considered to be optimum land-use possibilities. The team worked for two years with helicopters, aerial photographs, and computers. They concluded that, regardless of how well the traditional economic system of shifting cultivation and subsistence production may have been attuned to its environment in the past, today it "can no longer be tolerated."[11] The research team decided that the hill tribes should allow their land to be used primarily for the production of forest products for the benefit of the national economy because it was not well suited for large-scale cash cropping. The report left no alternative to the Chittagong Hills peoples, as a member of the research team observed: "More of the Hill tribesmen will have to become wage earners in the forest or other developing industries, and purchase their food from farmers practicing permanent agriculture on an intensive basis on the limited better land classes. It is realized that a whole system of culture and an age-old way of life cannot be changed overnight, but change it must, and quickly. The time is opportune. The maps and the basic data have been collected for an integrated development toward optimum land use."[12]

The government policy of "optimum" land use brought immediate disaster for the hill tribes.[13] The U.S. AID-funded Kaptai Dam inundated 253 square miles of the hill tribes' land, including much of the best cultivable land, and displaced 100,000 people. At the same time, the government allowed large-scale entry by Bengali settlers, who practiced plow agriculture and began to further displace the hill tribe people. In 1977 the Bangladeshi military initiated a genocidal extermination policy against the hill tribes. By 1982 some 400,000 Bengali settlers held hill tribe lands and were supported by 30,000 government troops. Two years later, in 1984, international organizations reported that 185,000 hill people had been killed. The Parbattya Chattagram Jana Sanghati Samiti (PCJSS), a guerrilla organization formed to defend the interests of the hill people, proved unable to prevent the slaughter.[14] By 1996, assaults against the hill tribes were continuing, and some 45,000 hill people were living in refugee camps in India, according to Survival International. The PCJSS signed a peace treaty with the central government in 1997.

The Role of Ethnocentrism

Although resource exploitation is clearly the basic cause of the destruction of small-scale populations and their cultures, it is important to identify the underlying ethnocentric attitudes that are often used to justify these exploitative policies. *Ethnocentrism*, the belief in the superiority of one's own culture, is vital to the integrity of any society, but it can threaten the well-being of other peoples when it becomes the basis for forcing irrelevant standards upon another culture. Anthropologists may justifiably take credit for exposing the ethnocentrism of nineteenth-century writers who described indigenous peoples as badly in need of improvement, but they often overlook the ethnocentrism that until recently commonly occurred in the professional literature on economic development. Ironically, ethnocentrism threatens small-scale cultures even today through its support of culturally insensitive government policies.

Ethnocentrism and Ethnocide

Historically, anthropologists were quick to stress the presumed deficiencies of tribal cultures as a justification for externally imposed change or a rejection of proposals that tribals be granted political autonomy. For example, in

1940 British anthropologist Lord Fitzroy Raglan, who later became president of the Royal Anthropological Institute, declared that tribal beliefs in magic were a chief cause of "folly and unhappiness" and the "worst evils of the day." He argued that as long as tribals persist in such beliefs the rest of the world cannot be considered civilized. In his view, existing tribes constituted "plague spots" that threatened to reinfect civilized areas, and the rapid imposition of civilization was the only solution. He declared: "We should bring to them our justice, our education, and our science. Few will deny that these are better than anything which savages have got."[15]

American anthropologist Arthur Hippler echoed Raglan's remarks. Arguing over the merits of tribal autonomy in 1979, he maintained that national religions were superior to the "terrors of shamanism."[16] He found "our own culture" more exciting, interesting, and varied, and better at promoting human potential than "backward" tribal cultures, and he assumed that all tribals would inevitably be drawn to it. Hippler suggested that only internal oppression from tribal elders prevented tribals from "improving" their culture. Not surprisingly, Hippler specifically opposed autonomy proposals for the defense of tribal societies because autonomy would keep people "backward" against their will. Furthermore, he argued that "culture" is an abstraction, not something that can be defended or "saved" from extinction. Thus ethnocide, the destruction of a cultural or ethnic group, could not occur.[17]

Crude Customs and Traditions

Ethnocentrism by culture change professionals, as illustrated in the following example from India, was often a powerful support for coercive government policies directed against tribal peoples. A group of Indian scholars and administrators presented an unsympathetic view of tribal culture in a series of papers and speeches at a seminar on new policy directions for the hill tribes of North East India, which was held in Calcutta in 1966.[18] Some participants in the seminar complained that prior British administrators had committed the fundamental error of placing tribal culture above the "basic need for human progress,"[19] because for a time the hill tribes had attempted to prevent the economic exploitation of the region by nontribal peoples. Throughout the seminar, participants attacked the entire range of traditional culture on ethnocentric grounds. They called the tribal economic system backward, wasteful, and in need of "scientific permanent farming."[20] An Indian professor complained of "crude customs and traditions" and characterized the tribal Garo peoples as being steeped in "primitive ignorance," "tradition-bound," and "static." Participants called for more thorough research to determine whether Garo society could be lifted out of its "morass of backwardness, traditionalism, and pseudo-modernism."[21]

In one paper, curiously entitled "An Outlook for a Better Understanding of Tribal People,"[22] an enlightened tribal member characterized his tribal kin as backward, lacking in culture, and living in darkness. Not only were these people described as cultureless, but according to an educated official they also lacked language: "You see, unfortunately here they do not have a language, what they speak is an illiterate dialect, lacking grammar and orthography."[23]

A few years earlier, an Indian sociologist had supported the conclusion that tribal languages are "merely corruptions of good speech and unworthy of survival." He wanted to see these people adopt the "more highly evolved" Indo-Aryan languages, because he considered the tribal peoples to be nothing more than backward Hindus.[24]

Technological Ethnocentrism

Development writers with tractors and chemicals to sell have expressed more ethnocentrism in their treatment of traditional economic systems than for any other aspect of small-scale tribal societies. These writers automatically assume that small-scale economies must be unproductive and technologically inadequate and therefore consistently disregard the abundant evidence to the contrary. It has long been fashionable to attack the supposed inefficiency of shifting cultivation and pastoral nomadism and the precariousness of subsistence economies in general. But it could be argued that it is industrial subsistence techniques that are inefficient and precarious. Monocrop agriculture, with its hybrid grains and dependence on chemical fertilizers, pesticides, and costly machinery, is extremely expensive in terms of energy demands and is highly unstable because of its susceptibility to disease, insects, and the depletion of critical minerals and fuels. The complexity of the food distribution system in global-scale commercial society also makes it vulnerable to collapse because of breakdowns in the long chain from producer to consumer. In contrast, small-scale systems are highly productive in terms of energy flow and are ecologically much more stable. They also have efficient and reliable food distribution systems.

Cultural reformers almost unanimously agree that all people share our desire for what we define as material wealth, prosperity, and progress and that others have different cultures only because they have not yet been exposed to the superior technological alternatives offered by the global-scale culture. Supporters of this view seem to minimize the difficulties of creating new wants in a society and at the same time make the following questionable and ethnocentric assumptions:

- The materialistic values of commercial societies are cultural universals.
- Small-scale societies are unable to satisfy the material needs of their peoples.

- Commercial goods are, in fact, always superior to their domestically produced, handcrafted counterparts.

Unquestionably, the cultural values of tribal societies represent a rejection
of the materialistic values of the global culture. Yet individuals can be made
to reject their traditional values if outside interests create the necessary conditions for this rejection. Far more is involved here than a mere demonstration of the superiority of commercialization.

The ethnocentrism of the second assumption is obvious. Clearly, small-
scale societies could not have survived for half a million years if they did not
do a reasonable job of satisfying basic human needs.

The third assumption—the superiority of commercial goods and techniques—
deserves special comment because abundant evidence indicates that many of
the material accoutrements of global society may not be worth their real costs,
regardless of how appealing they may seem initially. To cite a specific example, it could be argued that the bow is superior to the gun in some cultural and
environmental contexts, because it is far more versatile and more efficient to
manufacture and maintain. A single bow can be used for both fishing and
hunting a variety of animals. Furthermore, bow users are not dependent on an
unpredictable external economy, because bows can be constructed of local
materials and do not require expensive ammunition. At the same time, use of
the bow places some limits on game harvesting and demands a closer relationship between humans and animals, which may have great adaptive significance. Amazon Indians who adopted shotguns dramatically increased
their hunting yields,[25] but these gains do not entirely offset the extra labor that
must go into raising the money to support the new technology. Furthermore,
the increased hunting efficiency also means that vulnerable species are more
likely to be depleted.

Many of the ethnocentric interpretations of small-scale cultures are understandable when we realize that development writers often mistakenly attribute to them the conditions of starvation, ill health, and poverty, which actually may be related to the inequalities that often accompany industrialization
and commercialization. Self-sufficient tribal societies cannot be considered
underdeveloped. "Poverty" is an irrelevant concept in these small societies,
and poverty conditions do not result from subsistence economies per se.

Tribal Wards of the State

In the past, writers on international law and colonial experts often called on
the wardship principle in an effort to justify harsh government programs of
culture change directed against tribal peoples. This so-called legal principle

reflected the grossest ethnocentrism in that it considered tribal peoples to be incompetent or childlike. It defined the relationship between tribal peoples and the state as that of a benevolent parent-guardian and a ward who must be protected from his or her own degrading culture and gradually reformed or corrected. According to the wardship principle, the state was under a moral obligation to make all tribal peoples share in the benefits of civilization — that is, in health, happiness, and prosperity as defined primarily in terms of consumption.

This legal inferiority of tribal peoples contributed significantly to the speed with which their acculturation or "reform" took place and worked marvelously to satisfy both the conscience and the economic needs of expanding commercial societies.

Placing tribal peoples in the legal category of incompetent or childlike reflected a tendency to view tribal culture as abnormal or sick. This obviously ethnocentric theme runs throughout the colonial literature, in which the civilization process is often described as mental correction, but this same theme continued to appear in the modern literature. Some economic development writers in the 1960s lumped tribal peoples indiscriminately with underdeveloped peoples, referring explicitly to economic underdevelopment as a "sickness," speaking of the "medicine of social change," and comparing change agents to brain surgeons.[26] It appears that the attitudes of some modern cultural reformers were unaffected by the discovery of ethnocentrism.

A Sacred Trust of Civilization

As we have seen, the modern civilizing mission undertaken by governments against tribal peoples was supported by a variety of ethnocentric assumptions, some of which were recognized as principles of international law. Not surprisingly, therefore, prestigious international organizations such as the United Nations initially threw their support behind official attempts to bring civilization to all peoples — whether or not they desired it.

During the second half of the nineteenth century, the colonizing commercial nations began to justify their scramble for foreign territories as a fulfillment of a sacred duty to spread their form of civilization to the world. When the major imperialist powers met in 1884–1885 at Berlin to set guidelines for the partitioning of Africa, they pledged support for the civilizing crusade and promised to assist missionaries and all institutions "calculated to educate the natives and to teach them to understand and appreciate the benefits of civilization."[27] This position was reiterated and took on a more militant tone in article 2 of the Brussels Act of 1892, which called on the colonial powers to raise African tribal peoples to civilization and to "bring about the extinction of barbarous customs." This constituted an internationally approved mandate for ethnocide in the interests of progress.

Whereas such attitudes are perhaps to be expected from colonial nations at the height of their power, they seem inappropriate when expressed by world organizations dedicated to peace and self-determination of peoples. Nevertheless, article 22 of the 1919 League of Nations Covenant gave "advanced nations" responsibility for "peoples not yet able to stand by themselves under the strenuous conditions of the modern world," thereby placing many tribal peoples officially under tutelage as a "sacred trust of civilization." In fact, this sacred trust proved to be a profitable colonial booty for the trust powers, because it gave them the internationally recognized right to exploit the resources of thousands of square kilometers of formerly nonstate territory while making only token allowance for the wishes of the native peoples involved. Under the 1945 United Nations Charter, many of these same tribal peoples were identified as "peoples who have not yet attained a full measure of self-government," and their continued advancement was to be promoted by their guardians "by constructive measures of development."[28] Here again, responsibility for deciding what constitutes tribal peoples' welfare was effectively taken from them and was legally placed in the hands of outside interests. The carefully worded and seemingly nonderogatory phrases "peoples not yet able to stand by themselves" and "non-self-governing" are glaringly ethnocentric and derogatory, because these peoples had governed themselves for thousands of years without the support of politically organized state governments. Of course, they were unable to defend themselves against the incursions of militant, resource-hungry states. But many modern nations exist only at the discretion of more powerful nations, and the UN Charter would not advocate making all militarily weak nations surrender their political autonomy to their stronger neighbors.

Civilization's Unwilling Conscripts

It now seems appropriate to ask the obvious question: How do autonomous tribal peoples feel about becoming participants in the progress of commercial civilization? Because of the power at their disposal, commercial cultures have become so aggressively ethnocentric that they have difficulty even imagining that another lifestyle—particularly one based on fundamentally different premises—could possibly have value and personal satisfaction for the peoples following it. Happily arrogant in their own supposed cultural superiority, many people living in commercial societies assume that those of other cultures may realize their obsolescence and inferiority and may eagerly desire progress toward the better life. This belief persists in the face of abundant evidence that independent tribal peoples are not anxious to scrap their cultures and would rather pursue their own form of the good life undisturbed. Peoples who have already chosen their major cultural patterns and who have spent generations tailoring them to local conditions are probably not even concerned that another culture might be superior to theirs. Indeed, it can perhaps be assumed that people in any autonomous, self-reliant culture would prefer to be left alone. Left to their own devices, tribal peoples are unlikely to volunteer for civilization or acculturation. Instead, "[a]cculturation has always been a matter of conquest . . . refugees from the foundering groups may adopt the standards of the more potent society in order to survive as individuals. But these are conscripts of civilization, not volunteers."[29]

Free and Informed Choice

The question of choice is a critical point because many development authorities have stressed that tribal peoples should be allowed to choose progress. This view was obvious at a 1936 conference of administrators, educators, and social scientists concerning education in Pacific colonial dependencies, where it was stated that choices regarding cultural directions "must lie with the indigenous people themselves."[30] Anthropologists at a later international conference in Tokyo took the same position when they called for "just and scientifically enlightened programs of acculturation which allow the peoples concerned a free and informed basis for choice."[31] Apparently, no one noticed the obvious contradiction between a scientific culture change program and free choice, or even the possible conflict between free and informed. The official position of the Australian government on free choice for the Aborigines in 1970 indicates the absurdities to which such thinking can lead: "The Commonwealth and State governments have adopted a common policy of assimilation which seeks that all persons of Aboriginal descent will choose to attain a similar manner and standard of living to that of other Australians and live as members of a single Australian community."[32]

Those who so glibly demanded choice for tribal peoples did not seem to realize the problems of directly instituting such a choice, and at the same time they refused to acknowledge the numerous indicators that tribal peoples had already chosen their own cultures instead of the progress of civilization. In fact, the question of choice itself is probably ethnocentric and irrelevant to the peoples concerned. *Do we choose civilization?* is not a question that tribal peoples would ask, because they have, in effect, already answered it. They might consider the concept of choosing a way of life to be as irrelevant in their own cultural context as asking a person if he or she would choose to be a tree.

It is also difficult to ask whether tribal peoples desire civilization or economic development because affirmative responses will undoubtedly be from individuals already alienated from their own societies by culture modification programs, and their views may not be representative of their still-autonomous tribal kin.

Other problems are inherent in the concept of free and informed choice. Even when free to choose, tribal peoples would not generally be in a position to know what they were choosing, and they would certainly not be given a clear picture of the possible outcomes of their choice, because the present members of commercial societies do not know what their own futures will be. Even if tribal peoples could be given a full and unbiased picture of what they were choosing, obtaining that information could weaken their freedom to choose, because participation in such an "educational" program might destroy their self-reliance and effectively deny them their right to choose their own tribal culture. An obvious contradiction exists in calling for culture change in order to allow people to choose or not to choose culture change. The authorities at the 1936 conference referred to earlier were caught in just such Alice in Wonderland double-talk when they recommended the promotion of externally directed formal education programs so that people could freely decide whether they wanted their cultures disrupted: "It is the responsibility of the governing people, through schools and other means, to make available to the native an adequate understanding of non-native systems of life so that these can be ranged alongside his own in order that his choices may be made."[33]

Such a program of education might sound like a sort of "cultural smorgasbord," but in fact there is only one correct choice allowed: Tribal peoples must choose progress.

One further problem overlooked in the "free choice" approach is that of the sustainability of industrial progress or of any foreign cultural system in a given cultural and environmental context—even if freely chosen. Should Arctic peoples be encouraged to become nomadic camel herders or to develop a taste for bananas? Can the American "car complex" be sustained on a Micronesian coral atoll of four square kilometers? What will be the long-term effects of a shift from a self-reliant subsistence economy to a cash economy based on the sale of a single product on the uncertain world market? There are inescapable limits to what can constitute a successful human adaptation in a given cultural and environmental setting.

We Ask to Be Left Alone

At this point we will again ask the question posed earlier regarding whether tribal people freely choose progress. This question has actually been answered many times by independent tribal peoples who, in confrontations with the commercial world, have: (1) ignored it, (2) avoided it, or (3) responded with defiant arrogance. Any one of these responses could be interpreted as a rejection of further involvement with progress.

Many of the Australian Aborigines reportedly chose the first response in their early contacts with members of Western civilization. According to Captain Cook's account of his first landing on the Australian mainland, Aborigines on the beach ignored both his ship and his men until they became obnoxious. A. P. Elkin[34] confirmed that this complete lack of interest in white people's habits, material possessions, and beliefs was characteristic of Aborigines in a variety of contact settings. In many cases, tribal peoples have shown little interest in initial contacts with civilized visitors because they simply assumed that the visitors would soon leave and they would again be free to pursue their own way of life undisturbed.

Among contemporary tribal peoples who still retain their cultural autonomy, rejection of outside interference is a general phenomenon that cannot be ignored. The forest foragers of the Congo represent a classic case of determined resistance to the incursions of civilization. Anthropologist Colin Turnbull,[35] who intensively studied the Mbuti foragers in their forest environment, was impressed that these people had successfully rejected foreign cultural domination for hundreds of years. Attempts by Belgian colonial authorities to settle them on plantations ended in complete failure, because the Mbuti were unwilling to sacrifice their way of life in favor of one patterned for them by outsiders whose values were irrelevant to their environment and culture. According to Turnbull, the Mbuti deliberated over the changes proposed by the government and opted to remain within their traditional territory and pursue their own way of life. Their decision was clear: "So for the Pygmies [Mbuti], in a sense, there is no problem. They have seen enough of the outside world to feel able to make their choice, and their choice is to preserve the sanctity of their own world up to the very end. Being what they are, they will doubtless play a masterful game of hide-and-seek, but they will not easily sacrifice their integrity."[36]

Anthropologist Luigi Cavalli-Sforza,[37] who coordinated a series of long-term multidisciplinary field studies of forest foragers, or Pygmies, throughout Africa beginning in 1966, confirmed Turnbull's basic conclusion about their rejection of directed change. He attributes their remarkable two-thousand-year persistence as a distinct people to the attractiveness of their way of life and the effectiveness of their enculturation practices. But like Turnbull, he also cites the importance of the forest itself and the foragers' successful symbiosis with their villager-farmer neighbors. The most critical threat to forest foragers is now deforestation and disruption of their exchange relationships caused by the invasion of new colonists and the development of large-scale coffee plantations.[38] As the forest shrinks, there simply will be no place for Pygmies as forest peoples. Robert Bailey warns: "Unless sufficient areas of forest are set aside, a unique subsistence culture based on hunting and gathering forest resources will be lost in the Ituri [rain forest] and throughout central Africa forever."[39]

Avoiding Progress: Those Who Run Away

Direct avoidance of progress represents what is a widespread, long-established pattern of cultural survival. For example, throughout South America and many other parts of the world, many nonhostile tribal peoples have made their attitudes toward progress clear by choosing to follow the Pygmies' game of hide-and-seek and actively avoiding all contact with outsiders. In the Philippines, a term meaning "those who run away" has been applied to tribal peoples who have chosen to flee in order to preserve their cultures from government influence.[40]

Many little-known tribal peoples scattered in isolated areas around the world have, in fact, managed to retain their cultural integrity and autonomy into the twenty-first century by quietly retreating farther and farther into more isolated refuge areas. As the exploitative frontier has gradually engulfed these stubborn tribes, the outside world periodically has been surprised by the discovery of small pockets of unknown "Stone Age" peoples who have clung tenaciously to their cultures up to the last possible moment. In South America throughout the twentieth century, many different groups, including the Xeta, the Kreen-a-kore in Brazil, various Panoan speakers such as the Amarakaeri and Amahuaca in headwater areas of the Peruvian Amazon, and the Akuriyo of Surinam, were found using stone tools and deliberately avoiding contact with outsiders. In Peru such groups are now officially considered to be living in "voluntary isolation." These determined people are generally peaceful, except when harassed too severely. To avoid contact they prefer to desert their homes and gardens and thrust arrows point-up in their paths, rather than resort to violence. All that even the most persistent civilized visitors usually find—if they do manage to locate the natives' well-hidden villages—are empty houses and perhaps smoldering cooking fires. If a village is disturbed too often, the people abandon the site and relocate in a more isolated place. When, after continuous encroachment, their resource base shrinks to the point that it will no longer support their population and there is no place to which they can retreat, or when violent attacks by civilized raiders and introduced illnesses reduce their numbers to the point that they are no longer a viable society, they must surrender to progress. Most of the groups that we know about have stopped hiding. The most successful groups would have remained completely hidden.

How successfully some of these groups have managed to avoid contact can be seen in the case of the Akuriyo Indians of Surinam. These foraging people were first seen by outsiders in 1937, when a Dutch expedition discovered them while surveying the Surinam-Brazil border. After this brief encounter the Akuriyo remained out of sight for nearly thirty years until American missionaries began to find traces of their camps. The missionaries were determined to make contact with them in order to win them for Christianity, but it was three years before they finally succeeded with the assistance of ten missionized Indians, shortwave radios, and airplanes. They tracked the Akuriyo along their concealed trails through a succession of hastily abandoned camps until they caught up with a few women and children and an old man who, with obvious displeasure, asked the first man who greeted them, "Are you a tiger that you smelled me out?" This small group had been left behind by others who had gone in search of more arrow canes to defend themselves against the intruders. The Indians allowed the missionary party to remain with them only one night. Refusing to reveal either their tribal or their personal identities, they fed and traded with the intruders and then insisted that they leave. The mission Indians sang hymns and tried to tell them about God, but the Akuriyo were unimpressed.

According to the missionaries: "The old chief commented that God must really be good. He said he knew nothing about Him, and that he had to leave now to get arrow cane."[41]

Obviously these people were expressing their desire to be left alone in the most dignified and elegant terms. But the missionaries proceeded to make plans for placing Christianized Indian workers among them and requested "for the sake of this tribe" that the Surinam government grant their mission exclusive permission to supervise further contacts with the Akuriyo. Within a short time contact was reestablished, and the mission was able to encourage about fifty Akuriyo to settle in mission villages. Tragically, in barely two years, 25 percent of the group had died and only about a dozen people still remained in the forest.[42]

Whereas the Akuriyo are an example of a group avoiding contact in a remote area, many other examples can be cited of small tribes that have survived successfully on the fringes of civilized areas. One of the most outstanding of such cases was the discovery in 1970 that unknown bands of Indians were secretly living within the boundaries of the Iguazú National Park in Argentina.[43]

Some observers argue that these cases do not represent real rejections of civilization and progress because these people were given no choice by their hostile neighbors, who refused to share the benefits of civilization, and so they were forced to pretend that they didn't desire these benefits. Critics point out that such people often eagerly steal or trade for steel tools. This argument misses the real point and represents a misunderstanding of the nature of culture change. Stability and ethnocentrism are fundamental characteristics of all cultures that have established a sustainable sociocultural system. Some degree of change, such as adopting steel tools, may well occur to enhance a resilient system and to prevent greater change from occurring.

Cultural Pride versus Progress

The pride and defiance of numerous tribal peoples in the face of forced culture change are unmistakable and have often been commented upon by outsiders. The ability of these cultures to withstand external intrusion is related to their degree of ethnocentrism, or to the extent to which tribal individuals feel self-reliant and confident that their own culture is best for them. The hallmark of such ethnocentrism is the stubborn unwillingness to feel inferior even in the presence of overwhelming alien force.

A case of calm but defiant self-assurance of this sort is offered by a warrior-leader of the undefeated Xavante (Shavante) of central Brazil, who had personally participated in the 1941 slaying of seven men of a "pacification" mission sent by the Brazilian government to end the Xavante's bitter fifty-year resistance to civilization. As further evidence of their disdain for intruders, the Xavante shot arrows into an air force plane and burned the gifts it dropped.[44] After one Xavante community finally accepted the government's peace offers in 1953, the air force flew the chief to Rio de Janeiro in order to impress him with the superiority of the Brazilian state and the futility of further resistance. To everyone's amazement, he observed Rio, even from the air, with absolute calm. He was then led into the center of a soccer field to be surrounded by thousands of applauding fans, and it was pointed out to him how powerful the Brazilian state was and how unwise it was for the Xavante to be at war with it. The chief remained unmoved and responded simply: "This is the white man's land, mine is Xavante land."[45] The Xavante have been militant in defense of their lands since "pacification" and have forcibly expelled settlers and occupied government offices to force the authorities to fulfill their promise of legal protections.[46] Xavante leader Mario Juruna carried the struggle further into the political arena by winning election to Brazil's House of Representatives in 1982. Juruna campaigned effectively for the land rights of Brazilian Indians at both the national and the international level.

The Principle of Stabilization

According to theories of cultural evolution, adaptation, and integration, resistance to change is understandable as a human-directed cultural process. If people gradually adjust the technological, social, and ideological systems of their culture to fit the requirements of sustainable adaptation to a specific environment, other cultural arrangements become increasingly difficult, if not impossible, to accommodate without setting in motion major disruptive changes that will have unpredictable consequences. Resistance to change — whether it be direct avoidance of new cultural patterns, overt ethnocentrism, or open hostility to foreigners — may thus be seen as a significant means of adaptation because it operates as a "cultural isolating mechanism" to protect sustainable societies from the disruptive effects of foreign cultural elements.[47] The resulting "stability" refers to a relative lack of change in the major cultural patterns and does not imply complete changelessness in all the nuances of culture, because people are constantly making small changes in their cultures while keeping the dominant patterns constant. Overall stability is such a fundamental characteristic of cultures that it has been formulated as a general principle: "A culture at rest tends to remain at rest."[48] A corollary of this so-called principle of stabilization states: "When acted upon by external forces a culture will, if necessary, undergo specific changes only to the extent of and with the effect of preserving unchanged its fundamental structure and character."[49]

As change agents are well aware, resistance to change is based not only on the natural resistance or inertia of already established cultural patterns, but also on the realization by the people concerned of the risks of experimenting with unproven cultural patterns. Either the rewards of adopting new ways must appear to be worth the risks, or some form of coercion must be applied. However, change agents convinced of their own cultural superiority tend to overlook the fact that native fears about the dangers of untested innovations may be fully justified. Peoples that reject such unproven cultural complexes as miracle grains, pesticides, and chemical fertilizers may prove in the long run to be wiser and better adapted to their natural environments.

For peoples in relatively sustainable, self-reliant cultures, resistance to change is a positive value. It is only in commercial societies that such emphasis is placed on change for its own sake that, among those who make a profession of promoting change, cultural stability is given a negative connotation and is identified as backwardness and stagnation.

Notes

1. A. C. Graham, 1971, "China, Europe and the origins of the modern science," *Asia Major* 16 (parts 1–2): 178–96, 193.

2. See also John H. Bodley, 2008, *Anthropology and Contemporary Human Problems*, Lanham, MD: AltaMira Press.

3. William Woodruff, 1966, *Impact of Western Man*, London: Macmillan.

4. Ibid.

5. Bodley, *Human Problems*, chap. 2; Jonathan Loh and Mathis Wackernagel, 2004, *Living Planet Report*, Gland, Switzerland: WWF—World Wide Fund for Nature.

6. Julian H. Steward, ed., 1967, *Contemporary Change in Traditional Societies*, Urbana: University of Illinois Press, 20–21.

7. Paul Popenoe, 1915, "One phase of man's modern evolution," *International Congress of Americanists* 19: 620.

8. Denis Goulet, 1971, *The Cruel Choice: A New Concept in the Theory of Development*, New York: Atheneum, 266.

9. David Kaplan, 1960, "The law of cultural dominance," in *Evolution and Culture*, ed. Marshall D. Sahlins and Elman R. Service, Ann Arbor: University of Michigan Press, 75.

10. Claude Lévi-Strauss, 1951, "Social science in Pakistan," *International Social Science Bulletin* 3(4): 825–31.

11. W. E. Webb, 1966, "Land capacity classification and land use in the Chittagong hill tracts of East Pakistan," *Proceedings of the Sixth World Forestry Congress* 3: 3232.

12. Ibid.

13. Wolfgang E. Mey, 1983, "Dammed for progress: About the perversity of state and nation-building in Bangladesh—the Chittagong Hill Tracts Case," symposium paper, *The Fourth World: Relations between Minority Peoples and Nation-States*, XIth International Congress of Anthropological and Ethnological Sciences, Vancouver, BC; Bernard Nietschmann, 1985, "Indonesia, Bangladesh: Disguised invasion of indigenous Nations," *Fourth World Journal* 1(2): 89–126. (reprinted in abridged form in Bodley, 1988a: 191–207); M. Q. Zaman, 1985, "Tribal survival in the Chittagong hill tracts of Bangladesh," *Man in India* 65(1): 58–74.

14. *IWGIA Newsletter*, 1984, 37: 15–17.

15. Lord Fitzroy R. S. Raglan, 1940, "The future of the savage races," *Man* 40:62.

16. Arthur E. Hippler, 1979. "Comment on 'Development in the non-Western world,'" *American Anthropologist* 81: 348–49 (reprinted in Bodley, 1988a).

17. For a point-by-point critique of Hippler's argument, see Gerald Weiss, 1988, "The tragedy of ethnocide: A reply to Hippler," in *Tribal Peoples and Development Issues: A Global Overview*, ed. John H. Bodley, 124–33, Mountain View, CA: Mayfield.

18. Rathin Mittra and Barun Das Gupta, 1967, *A Common Perspective for North-East India*, Calcutta: Pannalal Das Gupta.

19. P. Moasosang, 1967, "The Naga search for self-identity," in *A Common Perspective for North-East India*, ed. Rathin Mittra and Barun Das Gupta, Calcutta: Pannalal Das Gupta, 51.

20. Amit Kumar Nag, 1967, "The society in transition in the Mizo District," in *A Common Perspective for North-East India*, ed. Rathin Mittra and Barun Das Gupta, Calcutta: Pannalal Das Gupta, 90.

21. Parimal Chandra Kar, 1967, "A point of view on the Garos in transition," in *A Common Perspective for North-East India*, ed. Rathin Mittra and Barun Das Gupta Calcutta: Pannalal Das Gupta, 91-102.

22. Hrilrokhum Thiek, 1967, "An outlook for a better understanding of the tribal people," in *A Common Perspective for North-East India*, ed. Rathin Mittra and Barun Das Gupta, 103–9. Calcutta: Pannalal Das Gupta.

23. Suhas Chatterjee, 1967, "Language and literacy in the North-Eastern regions," in *A Common Perspective for North-East India*, ed. Rathin Mittra and Barun Das Gupta, Calcutta: Pannalal Das Gupta, 20.

24. G. S. Ghurye, 1963, *The Scheduled Tribes*, 3rd ed., Bombay: G. R. Bhatkal, 87–190.

25. Raymond B. Hames, 1979, "A comparison of the efficiencies of the shotgun and the bow in neotropical forest hunting," *Human Ecology* 7(3): 219–52.

26. Conrad M. Arensberg and Arthur H. Niehoff, 1964, *Introducing Social Change: A Manual for Americans Overseas*, Chicago: Aldine, 4–6.

27. General Act of the 1884–1885 Berlin Africa Conference.

28. UN Charter, articles 73 and 76.

29. Stanley Diamond, 1960, "Introduction: The uses of the primitive," in *Primitive Views of the World*, ed. Stanley Diamond, New York: Columbia University Press, vi.

30. Felix M. Keesing, 1941, *The South Seas in the Modern World*, Institute of Pacific Relations International Research Series, New York: John Day, 84.

31. Eighth International Congress of Anthropological and Ethnological Sciences, Resolution on Forced Acculturation, 1968, cited in William C. Sturtevant, 1970, "Resolution on forced acculturation," *Current Anthropology* 11(2): 160.

32. Australia Commonwealth Bureau of Census and Statistics, 1970, *Official Yearbook of the Commonwealth of Australia*, no. 56, Canberra, 967.

33. Keesing, *South Seas*, 84.

34. A. P. Elkin, 1951, "Reaction and interaction: A food gathering people and European settlement in Australia," *American Anthropologist* 53: 164–86.

35. Colin M. Turnbull, 1963, "The lesson of the Pygmies," *Scientific American* 208(1): 28–37.

36. Ibid.

37. Luigi Luca Cavalli-Sforza, ed., 1986, *African Pygmies*, New York: Academic Press.

38. Robert Bailey, 1982, "Development in the Ituri Forest of Zaire," *Cultural Survival Quarterly* 6(2): 23–25; John A. Hart and Terese B. Hart, 1984, "The Mbuti of Zaire," *Cultural Survival Quarterly* 8(3): 18–20; Nadene Peacock, 1984, "The Mbuti of Northeast Zaire," *Cultural Survival Quarterly* 8(2): 15–17.

39. Bailey, "Ituri Forest," 25.

40. Felix M. Keesing and Marie Keesing, 1934, *Taming Philippine Headhunters: A Study of Government and of Cultural Change in Northern Luzon*, London: George Alien and Unwin, 87.

41. Ivan L. Schoen, 1969, "Contact with the Stone Age," *Natural History* 78(1): 10–18, 66–67.

42. Peter Kloos, 1977, *The Akuriyo of Surinam: A Case of Emergence from Isolation*, IWGIA Document no. 27, Copenhagen: IWGIA.

43. Miguel Alberto Bartolome, 1972, "The situation of the Indians in the Argentine: The Chaco area and Misiones Province," in *The Situation of the Indian in South America*, ed. W. Dostal, 218–51, Geneva: World Council of Churches.

44. Anonymous, 1945, *Life* 18: 70–72.

45. D. G. Fabre, 1963, *Más Allá del Rio das Mortes*, Buenos Aires: Ediciones Selectas, 34–45.

46. David Maybury-Lewis, 1983, "The Shavante struggle for their lands," *Cultural Survival Quarterly* 7(1): 54–55.

47. Betty J. Meggers, 1971, *Amazonia: Man and Culture in a Counterfeit Paradise*, Chicago: Aldine, 166.

48. Thomas G. Harding, 1960, "Adaptation and stability," in *Evolution and Culture*, ed. Marshall Sahlins and Elman Service, Ann Arbor: University of Michigan Press, 54.

49. Ibid.

3 The Uncontrolled Frontier

The history of the European settlements in America, Africa, and Australia presents everywhere the same general features—a wide and sweeping destruction of native races by the uncontrolled violence of individuals, if not of colonial authorities, followed by tardy attempts on the part of governments to repair the acknowledged crime. . . . Desolation goes before us, and civilization lags slowly and lamely behind.

—Herman Merivale[1]

IF, AS HAS BEEN ARGUED IN CHAPTER 2, tribal peoples are not eager to exchange their basically satisfying cultures for the dubious benefits of the commercial world, we are faced with the problem of explaining how their unwillingness has been overcome. Little "progress" can be made as long as tribal peoples remain autonomous sovereign societies that are both politically and economically self-sufficient. Therefore, the problem is to explain how this autonomy has been broken. In general, it appears that three processes have been weakening tribal resistance and preparing the way for further transformations:

- The uncontrolled frontier
- Military force
- The peaceful extension of administrative control

For analytic purposes, I will distinguish these processes arbitrarily and treat them in separate chapters, even though frequently they may overlap.

The Frontier Process

The initial breakdown of tribal autonomy was accomplished in many areas of the world by the direct action of the countless individual traders, settlers, missionaries, and labor recruiters who, in seeking their own self-interest, dealt directly with indigenous peoples in frontier areas beyond government control.

Many definitions have been proposed for the term *frontier*, but for our purposes those concerned with resource exploitation and the role of the state will be most useful. Ray Billington, for example, defined the frontier as "the geographic area adjacent to the unsettled portions of the continent in which a low man-land ratio and abundant natural resources provide an unusual opportunity for the individual to better himself economically and socially without external aid."[2]

In this definition, the significant point is that frontier resources are considered to be freely available for exploitation by outsiders. Walter Prescott Webb[3] spoke of the frontier as "an area inviting entrance" with its gifts of land and minerals, and, along with many other historians at the time, he explicitly disregarded the aboriginal population. Indeed, a common aspect of the frontier process is the fact that the prior ownership rights and interests of aboriginal inhabitants are considered irrelevant by both the state and the invading individuals. Another aspect of the above definition is that, in frontier areas, individuals are given the opportunity to better themselves without external aid, that is, without any effective legal restraint by the state. This combination of free resources and free enterprise distinguishes the frontier process from the use of military force and from formal native administration, both of which involve direct and effective government control.

Without the restraints of law, individuals used force or deception to ruthlessly and profitably obtain the land, labor, minerals, and other resources they sought. In the process, tribal societies were disrupted, weakened, and embittered—or simply exterminated. There is certainly no mystery to be explained here. It has long been recognized that frontier violence, the dispossession of tribal peoples from their homelands, the destruction of their subsistence bases, the introduction of foreign diseases, the availability of guns and alcohol, and numerous forms of economic exploitation have all directly led to depopulation, apathy, dependence, and detribalization. What is remarkable is the extent of the destruction and the fact that this familiar and uniform pattern has been repeated over the years throughout the world and continues today in some areas where governments either implicitly approve of such actions or are too ineffective to prevent such frontier lawlessness and exploitation.

The main features of the frontier process have been understood at least since the 1836–1837 publication of the one-thousand-page *Report from the Select Committee on Aborigines (British Settlements)*.[4] The fifteen-member committee was commissioned by Parliament to consider measures for the protection of native rights in frontier areas and spent ten months interviewing more than forty settlers, soldiers, politicians, missionaries, and natives from South Africa, Canada, Australia, New Zealand, the South Seas, and British Guiana (now Guyana). Their cautious general conclusion was that frontier contacts had been "a source of many calamities to uncivilized nations. . . . Too often, their territory has been usurped; their property seized; their numbers diminished; their character debased; . . . European vices and diseases have been introduced amongst them, and they have been familiarized with the use of our most potent instruments for the subtle or the violent destruction of human life, viz. brandy and gunpowder."[5]

Furthermore: "From very large tracts we have, it appears, succeeded in eradicating them; and though from some parts their ejection has not been so apparently violent as from others, it has been equally complete, through our taking possession of their hunting-grounds, whereby we have despoiled them of the means of existence."[6]

This committee called on Britain in the strongest terms to end this unnecessary oppression of natives. They did not, of course, reject colonialism itself; rather, they felt that it would be more efficient economically if the process were carried out more humanely. They suggested several specific measures to bring order to the frontier by regulating the use of native labor, prohibiting the provision of alcohol to natives, and the direct purchasing of native lands from natives by individual colonists. However, at the time their evidence and recommendations were not widely accepted. Since then similar official investigations were independently repeated in several countries, the same list of problems was drawn up, and more suggestions made, but frontier abuses did not completely stop. Only in the twenty-first century has frontier violence significantly declined. Considering its prevalence, it seems appropriate to risk "overemphasis" and review here some of the more outstanding regularities characteristic of the uncontrolled frontier since about 1820.

I Didn't Believe It Was Wrong to Kill Indians

The 1836–1837 Select Committee on Aborigines noted in its report that in frontier areas indigenous peoples were being classed as "savages," and it warned ominously that this could result in their being treated as less than human. It is clear from the committee's own published findings that in frontier areas around the world in the 1830s, tribal peoples were indeed considered less than human and were treated accordingly. For example, it was reported that in Canada it had long been considered a "meritorious" act to kill an Indian. Significantly, the Dutch Boers in South Africa felt the same way toward natives, according to a letter received by the committee that stated, "A farmer thinks he cannot proclaim a more meritorious action than the murder of one of these people." Reportedly, in South Africa it was customary for settlers to speak of killing natives with the same indifference applied to shooting partridge, and in fact one settler boasted proudly of personally killing three hundred natives. At the same time, the tattooed heads of New Zealand Maori were being offered for sale as curiosities in Australia.[7]

The committee reported that "many deeds of murder and violence" had been committed by the settlers in Australia, and, in fact, the same violence had continued on the Australian frontier for at least one hundred years, sometimes taking remarkably treacherous forms. In Victoria, Aborigines were known to have been poisoned by arsenic mixed with flour,[8] and strychnine was reportedly used to eliminate Aborigines in western Australia in 1861. In the Northern Territory in 1901, "It was notorious, that the blackfellows were shot down like crows and that no notice was taken."[9] As recently as 1928, thirty-two Aborigines were killed in that area in reprisal for the death of a dingo hunter.[10] Violent anti-Aborigine slogans were again heard in Australia's Northern Territory in the late 1970s as the Aborigines successfully pressed for legal recognition of their land rights.

The frequent attitude of settlers on the American frontier can be summarized by General Philip Sheridan's famous statement, "The only good Indian is a dead Indian," and hardly need be elaborated upon here. However, it is not always remembered that in South American frontier areas the same approach is still being taken, as demonstrated by the reported killing of eleven Pai Tavytere Indians in Paraguay in 1988.[11] In southern Brazil, professional Indian hunters were killing the Xokleng Indians until their final pacification in 1914.[12] In São Paulo, one man claimed to have killed two thousand Kaingang Indians in 1888 by poisoning their drinking wells with strychnine.[13] In the northeast, the Brazilian ethnologist Curt Nimuendaju reported that an entire village of 150 Timbira Indians was wiped out by a band of settlers in 1913. In this case, the murderers were brought to trial but all were acquitted.[14] In nearby Paraguay in 1903, settlers were killing Guayaki Indians and using their bodies to bait jaguar traps.[15] In 1941 it was reported that local settlers still felt that killing Guayaki was not a crime but rather a "praiseworthy action, like killing a jaguar." The rationalization for such violence was that because the Guayaki were not baptized Catholics, they were not human beings.[16]

By 1962, after decades of continual harassment, a Guayaki band of fifty people finally surrendered. It was discovered that every man in the Guayaki group carried bullet wounds received in clashes with the local German colonists, many of whom proudly displayed Guayaki "trophies" in their homes.[17] During the early 1970s German anthropologist Mark Münzel found indications that indiscriminate killings of the Guayaki (now called Aché) were continuing on a scale that he labeled "genocidal."[18] Further investigations carried out in 1978 and 1979, following widespread international protests over the Indian situation in Paraguay, found that the worst abuses had ended.[19]

The Guayaki situation has close parallels in other South American countries. In 1968, shocking news reports came from Brazil of the massacre of several Indian groups, including the Cinta-Larga, and others in Rondônia and

Mato Grosso. In these cases, hired killers used arsenic and dropped dynamite and fired machine guns from light planes. In Colombia anthropologist Bernard Arcand[20] reported that the Cuiva Indians in the llanos were constantly subject to attacks from neighboring cattlemen. He found many Indians bearing bullet scars and was himself fired upon while accompanying them. In 1967, in the same area of Colombia, settlers massacred fifteen Indians and were acquitted in a jury trial because it was considered customary to kill Indians. In his own defense, one of the admitted killers stated, "I didn't believe it was wrong since they were Indians." Even more significantly, another stated: "I killed those Indians because I knew that the government would not reprimand us nor make us pay for the crime that was committed."[21]

This statement raises an important question about the role of the government in the uncontrolled frontier process. Local officials frequently claim that atrocities committed by settlers are beyond the control of any government to prevent, but a closer look at the facts casts doubt upon such claims. Even in 1837 the Select Committee on Aborigines refused to accept this explanation and condemned the indifference and slackness of local authorities, which the committee felt had allowed entire tribes to be exterminated. The committee specifically pointed out that white settlers were seldom punished for their crimes against natives but that courts were thorough in meting out punishment to natives for attempting to defend themselves against settlers. In frontier Australia throughout the nineteenth century, a simple legal mechanism was used to protect whites who openly killed Aborigines: The testimony of surviving Aboriginal witnesses was not admitted because they were "ignorant of the existence of a God or a future state."[22] When the authorities finally took action against known offenders and ordered the hanging of seven whites for massacring twenty-eight Aboriginal men, women, and children in New South Wales in 1838, the murderers protested with a familiar excuse that demonstrated official connivance at such crimes: "We were not aware that in killing blacks we were violating the law or that it could take any notice of our doing so, as it has (according to our belief) been so frequently done before."[23]

Undoubtedly, many of these crimes against tribal peoples would not have been committed, or certainly would not have been committed as openly, if local officials had not cooperated in them. In Brazil in 1968, the evidence for large-scale involvement in Indian massacres by many public officials of the Indian Protection Service was so overwhelming that the organization was abolished. In 1971 in Paraguay, officials of the Native Affairs Department refused to take any action against known Indian hunters or even to conduct investigations into the well-known crimes being committed against the Guayaki.[24] Such official ignorance of frontier crimes, and the general failure of legal processes to protect tribal peoples, suggests that lack of control was a deliberate policy on many frontiers.

Dispossession

Generally, the primary purpose of the killing of tribal peoples was to remove them from the land. In many cases, less violent but equally effective methods were used to accomplish this purpose.

In South Africa in the 1830s, the Select Committee reported that the Boers were in the habit of extending their territory by simply herding their cattle into native territory, destroying native gardens, and taking over natives' houses. The Boers informed protesting natives that complaining would not help them because the government would be unconcerned.[25] One hundred years later, white farmers were still actively dispossessing natives as squatters in the frontier areas of South Africa. The justification for this action was the familiar argument that the natives were merely subsistence farmers and deserved to be treated as squatters because they were not engaged in any "systematic" forms of agriculture. The twentieth-century version of the dispossession process was described in detail by a South African education professor: "When the new owner of the land enters into possession he generally summons a meeting of the squatters, informs them that he is the new owner of the land, announces how many native families he proposes to retain on his property, selects those he desires, and gives the remainder notice to quit at a certain date after they have reaped their crops. The dispossessed natives have the alternative of seeking a new landlord who will receive them as 'labor tenants' or of attempting to find a place in a near-by Native Reserve or of gravitating towards an urban area."[26]

In South America, settlers and ranchers have also applied remarkably similar processes in the twentieth century. Nimuendaju[27] reported that in the Brazilian northeast in the 1930s it was common practice for ranchers to deliberately break down fences and drive their cattle through Timbira gardens in order to force the Indians to abandon their village sites. Dispossessed Indians appealed to the Indian Protection Service and petitioned state and federal government officials for help, but their pleas were ignored. Fifty years later, cattlemen were still driving out the Timbira and even burning their villages with impunity.[28] The continuous construction of Brazil's Trans-Amazon Highway system, begun in 1970, opened Indian territory to ever-increasing frontier pressures driven by the country's enormous social inequality and a national population that grew by nearly 50 percent between 1970 and 1986. The killing of ten Nambiquara Indians in Rondônia by settlers in 1986 is just one example of the continuous destruction.[29]

Other modern examples could be cited from throughout South America, colonial Africa, and the American frontier, but the important point is that all of these cases illustrate that the unwillingness of governments to protect the rights of tribal peoples against the interests of intruding settlers resulted in the natives' dispossession. The problem of land policies is examined in more detail in a later chapter, but at this point it must be emphasized that one primary impact of frontier dispossession has been the disturbance of traditional subsistence patterns, forcing tribal people into participation in the market economy. Dispossessed Aborigines on the Australian frontier and Indians in the American West were unable to feed themselves by hunting and foraging and were forced either to beg food from the missions and government welfare posts or to work for settlers at menial tasks to stay alive. African farmers and herders also experienced severe subsistence hardships when they were pushed off their lands, and, as indicated above, few alternatives were open to them but to labor for whites.

Certainly, direct physical violence has been a prominent frontier process, but it must also be emphasized that the economic exploitation of tribal peoples in an uncontrolled frontier situation has been just as destructive of traditional culture. In the following sections, brief case studies are presented that demonstrate the impact of the rubber trade in the Amazon and the Congo and the labor trade in the Pacific. Finally, the patron system of debt slavery is examined, and an assessment is made of the demographic impact of the frontier on tribal populations.

Atrocities of the Putumayo

World demand for rubber began to rise in the 1870s, after the development of vulcanization, and particularly after 1900, when the automotive industry began to become important. As a result, the price of rubber soared, and the Amazon regions of Brazil and Peru, which were the primary sources of natural rubber, became major new frontier areas as thousands of outsiders arrived to share in the wealth. This initiated a period of frantic economic activity called the rubber boom, which continued until about 1915, when East Indian plantation rubber began to capture the world market. Regular labor was scarce in the Amazon, but because tribal Indians were numerous in many of the rubber zones, they quickly became the backbone of the new extractive industry. The Indians were especially useful because they could be induced to work for cheap trade goods. They were largely self-sufficient and knew the rubber forests perfectly. Best of all, however, the prevailing attitudes of the local government and military officials were highly favorable toward relatively uncontrolled economic exploitation of the Indians, who were considered to be savages in need of civilization.

Given this setting, serious abuses were almost certain to occur. In fact, what followed was the ruthless exploitation and incredibly violent destruction of thousands of people, which must have fully equaled the cruelest periods of the Spanish conquest. The need for Indian laborers in the rubber zones became so great that merely luring them to work with trade goods was not enough, and undisguised slaving activities became institutionalized. Slave raids, popularly known as *correrías*, were commonly reported occurrences even outside the rubber zones and involved armed gangs assaulting isolated Indian settlements, killing the resisting men, and capturing the women and children to be sold as slaves. Not surprisingly, these activities were widely approved as economically advantageous and necessary civilizing measures, as the following commentary by a contemporary Peruvian writer indicates: "It is not strange, then, that there exists the cruel procedure known as *correrías*, which consists of surprising the habitations of some tribe and taking the members of it prisoner. These prisoners are taken to far territories and are dedicated to work. . . . This catechization has the advantage that the individual soon obtains precise concepts of the importance that his personal work has in the commerce of civilized people. . . . In our century, the procedure is cruel and wounds all the fibers of our sensibility; but one must recognize the powerful and rapid help that it lends to civilization."[30]

Under the direction of large corporations such as the British-owned Peruvian Amazon Company, Ltd., a highly profitable system of rubber production was constructed in which a number of regional company officials controlled managers who organized the scattered tribal populations into local sections and directed the actual rubber-gathering activities. Section managers kept records of their Indian laborers and assigned them specific rubber quotas, which had to be carried to the regional administrators at regular intervals. Many of these lower-level company officials, or rubber barons, wielded enormous power and lived lavishly in great houses surrounded by Indian servants and concubines and armed bodyguards. In the Putumayo district of Peru, where some twelve thousand Indians were reported to be working in 1905,[31] it was common knowledge that rubber barons regularly used direct physical violence to increase production. Indians who failed to meet their assigned quotas or who attempted to escape were flogged and tortured or simply shot. Even though these actions occurred openly and were widely reported, the government refused to take any action against known offenders.

Finally, in 1907, an outraged Peruvian, speaking as a private citizen, presented the local court and newspapers with a carefully documented formal denunciation of unspeakable atrocities committed against the Putumayo Indians. The denunciation, which named twenty prominent individuals as responsible, detailed specific crimes of rape, slavery, torture by flogging and mutilation, and mass murder by shooting, poisoning, starvation, and burning—all of which reportedly resulted in the deaths of thousands of Indians. These reports shocked the nation, and the president of Peru called on local officials to make investigations. Because of the involvement of a British company, the matter was even debated in the British Parliament, and Sir Roger Casement was sent to investigate. A local Peruvian judge, Carlos Valcarcel, also conducted his own investigation; soon the testimony of eyewitnesses and the discovery of mass graves and other physical evidence left no doubt that crimes of immense proportion had occurred.[32] The scale of the atrocities is made evident by comparing the estimated pre-1886 Indian population of fifty thousand in the Putumayo district with the estimated population of only ten thousand by about 1910.[33] The precise figure will never be known, but it is certain that thousands of Indians died.

The attitude of the local government officials toward these crimes was continued denial and inaction. The judge who had pursued the case was suspended, and the most prominent of the accused company officials was praised for his talent and financial investment with which he had brought economic progress to the department.[34] In this case, the frontier was being left deliberately uncontrolled.

Heart of Darkness

We have now to record the operations of a System which Conan Doyle has described as the "greatest crime in all history." . . . And it is undeniable that all the misdeeds of Europeans in Africa since the abolition of the over-sea slave trade, pale into insignificance when compared with the tragedy of the Congo. Indeed, no comparison is possible as regards, scale, motive, and duration of time alike.[35]

Events in the Congo closely paralleled—and occurred at the same time as—the situation in the Amazon. But in the Congo, government involvement was more direct and the scale of the atrocities committed was even greater. The Congo Free State, under King Leopold of Belgium from 1885 to 1908, and the adjacent French Congo were based on a system of economic exploitation under which local company officials and government servants were urged to obtain maximum production of rubber and ivory by using whatever means they found most profitable. This exploitation was carried out by government officials under the guise of taxation and by concessionaire companies that were given complete freedom of operation. Officially, of course, murder and slavery were illegal, but in fact they were employed on a massive scale by individuals eager to increase their profits, and here as in the Amazon, the courts seemed unwilling to punish known offenders. Local officials employed government troops to terrorize villagers into greater production, and the concessionaire companies hired undisciplined private armies for the same purpose. Women and children were held captive in special hostage houses to force the men to greater exertions, or were themselves forced to labor in the rubber forests. Villages were burned and looted and entire districts were devastated because if production declined, the population was said to be in a state of rebellion.

As a result of such oppression, disastrous rebellions did occur, subsistence pursuits came to a halt, and disease and starvation became widespread. Although there is no certain estimate of the depopulation occurring as a consequence of all of these conditions, there is no doubt that it was enormous. E. D. Morel, who founded the Congo Reform Movement in England to fight the abusive system, estimated that 8 million people died in the nearly twenty-five years of Free State exploitation alone.[36] He cites an estimate that in one district, six thousand natives were killed and mutilated every six months.[37] Whatever the actual figures, the Congo must have been the scene of some of the worst frontier violence in modern times.

The atrocities set off an outcry in Europe after they were publicized by the Congo Reform Movement and in such books as Morel's *Red Rubber* (1906) and Joseph Conrad's novel *Heart of Darkness* (1971). Eventually a number of official inquiries were conducted, resulting in the annexation of the Congo Free State by Belgium in 1908, which brought the establishment of more normal forms of colonial administration.

"Blackbirding" in the South Seas

> It would be difficult to exaggerate the evil influence of the process by which the natives of Melanesia were taken to Australia and elsewhere to labour for the white man. It forms one of the blackest of civilization's crimes.[38]

From approximately 1860 to 1910, the South Pacific became the scene of frontier violence and exploitation similar to that occurring in the Amazon and Congo. Certainly frontierlike disturbances had arisen earlier in connection with the sandalwood trade, but widespread threats to tribal autonomy did not occur until the American Civil War brought British cotton imports to a halt and stimulated the development of plantations in what was then the British colony of Queensland in Australia, and Fiji.

Unfortunately for the planters, labor was scarce in these areas because white Australians were considered unsuitable for tropical labor, and the native Fijians refused plantation work. Consequently, in 1863 the Queensland planters began sending ships into Melanesia to recruit cheap tribal labor, and the profitable but outrageously exploitative operation known as "blackbirding" became established.

The completely uncontrolled recruiting during the early years relied heavily on deception and often amounted to kidnapping. It was often impossible, for lack of interpreters, to explain the purpose of recruitment to the islanders. Frequently, the islanders were led to believe that they would be away for three months of fun, when actually they were being induced to sign a three-year in-dentured labor contract. Shrewd captains devised a variety of ingenious means to fill the holds of their ships with recruits. In order to lure wary na-tives close enough to be pulled into their boats, they employed the famous "missionary trick," in which they masqueraded as missionaries and even passed out "Bible tracts" that were actually pages from old almanacs. The most direct methods involved ramming canoes to spill their occupants into the sea, or using the "eye drop" trick, which consisted of luring native canoes to the stern of the ship for trade and then dropping heavy pieces of metal to sink them.[39] It is true that islanders sometimes deliberately boarded the re-cruiting ships to obtain trade goods or because they were looking for adven-ture, but force and deception were the prime means of recruitment.

Unwilling natives were often killed accidentally before they could be dragged aboard ship, and it was not uncommon for them to jump overboard and drown while attempting to escape. Further deaths resulted from fighting between recruits when enemies from different islands were thrown together or when mutinous recruits were shot and thrown overboard by the crews. In one case, seventy recruits were killed in this manner.[40] Disease aboard ship also took many lives because of overcrowding, poor food, and inadequate medical attention, and, in some cases, up to half of the recruits died before reaching the plantations.[41] Once on the plantations, the recruits might be sold—rather, their "passage" would be paid by the highest bidder—and they could then look forward to three years of labor, ten to twelve hours a day, six days a week, at an annual wage that was only 5 percent of what low-paid gov-ernment officials earned at that time. Health conditions were little better on the plantations than aboard ship, and annual mortality rates for new recruits sometimes ran as high as 18 percent.[42] Despite all of these outrages, the re-cruiting continued for more than forty years, during which more than sixty thousand natives were legally imported to Queensland alone, and the re-cruiters and plantation owners stoutly defended the process against critics who called it slavery.

However, the open abuses finally became too obvious for the government to ignore completely, and various select committees and royal commissions met in 1869, 1876, 1885, 1889, and 1906 to suggest means of regulating the recruiting process. Strict measures were enacted requiring the licensing of re-cruiters for specific shipments, assigning government inspectors to accom-pany each ship, and specifying how passengers were to be treated and re-quiring that they be informed about what their contracts really meant. In practice, of course, the regulations were often openly defied by the recruiters, and the government inspectors were often incompetent and underpaid politi-cal appointees who retired to their cabins when irregularities occurred. The failure of the many regulations to achieve their purpose was well illustrated by the 1885 Royal Commission, which interviewed 480 natives in Queensland and found that virtually none had been legally recruited.[43]

As usual in frontier situations, the courts tended to move slowly to punish known offenders. This was certainly true with the case of the *Daphne*, a recruiting ship arrested on suspicion of slavery in 1869 off Fiji by Captain George Palmer of the British navy. The ship's bare hold was jammed with one hundred naked, underfed natives who were about to be sold to Fijian planters. It was peculiar that no interpreter was available to question the natives and that the ship's captain was authorized only to carry fifty natives to Queensland and not one hundred to Fiji. The circumstances looked suspicious to Captain Palmer, who was familiar with the African slave trade and was under orders to investigate illegal recruiting activities in the islands. But the Australian courts viewed the situation differently: The natives themselves were not allowed to testify, because as non-Christians they would not be able to take the oath. It was ruled that as long as contracts were involved, whatever occurred could not be considered slavery, and the case had to be thrown out.[44]

Whatever the effects of the unrestricted recruiting in the South Pacific may have been for the individuals involved, the impact on the home villages was devastating. As in the Congo and the Amazon, normal economic, ritual, and social life in the villages was disrupted with a significant proportion of the economically active male population absent, and depopulation resulted from the new diseases introduced and from the increased violence aggravated by the guns and alcohol the natives received from the labor recruiters. Depopulation caused by unrestricted recruiting was recognized as a threat to the labor supply that could not be allowed to continue indefinitely, and colonial governments set strict limits that specified which islands were open for recruiting during which years or seasons.

The Patron System of Debt Peonage

In many of the world's frontier areas, unregulated contacts between isolated tribal peoples and civilized traders were conducted on the basis of an exploitative system of debt peonage, which was certainly less violent than the types of intrusion previously described, but which also resulted in profound tribal disorganization. In many parts of North and South America, Siberia, and India, traders concerned primarily with their own advancement took advantage of tribal peoples in their unfamiliarity with money and their desire for some kinds of trade goods. Following a remarkably uniform pattern everywhere, traders advanced goods to the natives on credit in exchange for furs, rubber, lumber, fish, nuts, labor, or crops, to be delivered in the future. The trick was that by continually advancing more goods, the trader or patron managed the transactions so that the debt was never fully paid, and reaped an extravagant profit by overcharging for the goods advanced and grossly undercrediting for the articles taken in exchange. Individuals were gradually drawn into a relationship of total dependence on the trader and were forced to work harder as they found themselves further in debt and attracted by increasingly more expensive goods. Their difficulties were often complicated by other rules of the system by which debts were inherited and rules that discouraged the use of cash or that prohibited a debtor from dealing with other traders. All of these features of the system opened it to flagrant exploitation, and in many cases the result was a situation resembling slavery.

Comparative research has shown that the long-term effects of the debt peonage system followed a regular pattern even in widely separated areas of the world and generally involved the gradual abandonment of traditional subsistence activities and the weakening of tribal sociopolitical organization until the basic autonomy of tribal culture was destroyed. These regularities were demonstrated clearly by Robert Murphy and Julian Steward in their comparison of the impact of the Amazon rubber trade and the North American fur trade on native peoples.[45]

In other contexts and with minor modification, debt peonage can destroy tribal autonomy by dispossession. This has happened widely in India, where the system known as agrestic serfdom has been used—in spite of government attempts at legislative control—as a means of robbing tribal peoples of their land.

Where this system still exists in the Amazon, the patron himself is often completely dependent on his Indian debtors for their labor and the forest products they supply. However, he still pushes his profits to the limit whenever laws limiting the amount of indebtedness for which an Indian can be held responsible are not enforced. As I observed the practice in the Peruvian Amazon in the 1960s, it was common for patrons to charge Indians double for trade goods and credit them with half of the value of their products. Greedier patrons were known to shift decimal points in their account books and charge up to twenty times the fair market value for specific articles. In one case I recorded, an Asháninka man spent two years cutting valuable mahogany logs for his patron to pay for a twenty-five-dollar shotgun.[46] It is not surprising that such practices undermine both traditional social systems and economic patterns.

Demographic Impact of the Frontier

Wherever the European has trod, death seems to pursue the aboriginal.[47]

Severe depopulation of tribal peoples is a characteristic feature of the frontier process and has been reported by observers from all parts of the world during the past 150 years. As early as 1837, the members of the Select Committee on Aborigines found tribal populations to be declining at alarming rates in areas invaded by British colonists. They noted that the Indians of Newfoundland had been exterminated by 1823 and that the Canadian Cree had declined from ten thousand to two hundred since 1800. They also found "fearful" depopulation in the Pacific, where reportedly the Tasmanians would soon be extinct, and they found that the Australian Aborigines were vanishing from the earth.

In retrospect, it is clear that what the Select Committee was reporting on at that time was only the beginning of a catastrophic decline in tribal populations that continued in most areas of the world for another one hundred years. Table 3.1 indicates the scale of some of this depopulation. According to these figures, tribal populations in lowland South America (east of the Andes and exclusive of the Caribbean) and North America (north of Mexico) were reduced by 95 percent, or nearly 15 million, by 1930. It is noteworthy that in these areas much of this reduction has occurred since 1800 and can be only partly attributed to the Spanish and Portuguese conquests, which decimated large populations in the Orinoco, the lower Amazon, and eastern Brazil and Bolivia prior to 1800. Certainly in North America, with the exception of some

Table 3.1.   World Survey of Tribal Depopulation

	Precontact Population	*Population Lowpoint*	*Depopulation*
North America			
(U.S. and Canada)	7,000,000[a]	390,000[b]	6,610,000
Lowland South America	8,500,000[c]	450,000[d]	8,050,000
Oceania			
Polynesia[e]	1,100,000	180,000	920,000
Micronesia[f]	200,000	83,000	117,000
Melanesia			
Fiji[g]	300,000	85,000	215,000
New Caledonia[h]	100,000	27,000	73,000
Australia[i]	300,000	60,500	239,500
Africa			
Congo[j]			8,000,000
	Estimated Total Depopulation		24,224,500

[a] Thornton, 1987: 30, 32
[b] Thornton, 1987: 30, 32
[c] Denevan, 1976: 291
[d] Dobyns, 1966: 415
[e] Keesing, 1941
[f] Kessing, 1941
[g] Keesing, 1941; Roberts, 1969
[h] Roberts, 1969
[i] Rowley, 1970: 384. More recent estimates place the precontact population as high as 1 million, but such a figure is not yet widely accepted.
[j] Morel in Louis and Stengers, 1968: 123. (Suret-Canale, 1971: 36–37, gives a more liberal estimate of 12 million for the depopulation of the French Congo alone between 1900 and 1921.)

portions of the Southwest, California, and the eastern seaboard, most of the depopulation occurred after 1800. In Polynesia, Micronesia, and Australia, the population has been reduced by approximately 80 percent, or more than 1.25 million, since 1800. If allowances are made for further depopulation in areas not included in table 3.1, such as Siberia, southern Asia, island Southeast Asia, southern Africa, and Melanesia, and if Morel's estimate for the Congo is accepted, it might be estimated that during the 150 years between 1780 and 1930, world tribal populations were reduced by at least 30 million as a result of the spread of global-scale cultures. A more realistic estimate would place the figure at perhaps 50 million. Such an incredible loss has no parallel in modern times and must have been a major factor in the "acculturation" of tribal peoples. This was genocide on a grand scale and was widely recognized as such at the time, as will be shown in chapter 11.

The "population reduction" discussed here is not strictly a record of deaths, because in theory a population could experience increased mortality and show no population decline if fertility rates also increased. There could be many more deaths than those indicated by the "reduction" figures. However, in the case of many tribal groups it is likely that frontier disturbances also caused a decline in fertility.

These population losses have greater meaning when their impact on specific tribal groups is examined, because countless groups were never able to recover from such massive depopulation and simply became extinct, whereas those that did survive were seriously weakened. The speed with which many groups were engulfed by the frontier was a critical factor in the ultimate outcome. The Tasmanians, for example, were reduced by almost 98 percent, from a population of 5,000 to 111, within thirty years. In western Victoria, the Aboriginal population of perhaps 4,000 was reduced to 213 after less than forty years of settlement, and within fifty years anthropologists could find no one who could reliably describe their traditional culture.[48] In California 75 percent of an estimated 85,000 Yokut and Wintun Indians were swept away by epidemic diseases in 1830–1833.[49]

In more recent times there have been reports of rapid rates of decline for many South American tribal groups. In Tierra del Fuego, for example, nomadic Indians such as the Ona and Yahgan, who may have numbered more than 8,000 as recently as 1870, were effectively extinct by 1950. In Brazil alone, an estimated 87 of 230 groups known to be in existence in 1900 were extinct by 1957,[50] and many other surviving groups experienced drastic declines following white contacts. Among the most dramatic cases recorded for Brazil are the Caraja, estimated to number 100,000 in 1845, 10,000 in 1908, and 1,510 in 1939.[51] The Araguaia Kayapo, who numbered 8,000 in 1903, were reduced to 27 by 1929.[52] More recently, the Kreen-a-kore were reduced from 300 to 35 in 1979, just six years after agreeing to establish permanent contact with the national society.[53] Depopulation of this magnitude clearly constitutes a major source of stress for any society, particularly when it occurs in the context of conquest and economic exploitation.

The causes of tribal depopulation have been well understood, at least since the Select Committee's 1837 report designated frontier violence, disease, alcohol, firearms, and demoralization as the principal causes. Ultimately all of these causes can be reduced to the political decisions of national governments to encourage the invasion of tribal territories. However, there were some ethnocentric attempts to attribute depopulation to inherent tribal decadence and racial inferiority and to suggest that civilization merely accelerated a decline that was already occurring. This view was supported by some missionaries and government inquiries and by not a few scholars, such as the historian Stephen Henry Roberts, who spoke vaguely of a "general racial decline, an indefinable malaise of the stock itself."[54] This explanation is no longer regarded seriously by anthropologists and was vigorously rejected years ago by the British anthropologists W. H. Rivers[55] and George Pitt-Rivers,[56] who showed how culture contact was responsible for the depopulation of the Pacific.

The only problem remaining for more recent writers to debate has been the difficulty of assessing which contact factors are the most critical causes of tribal depopulation. Some place special emphasis on the role of disease; others stress the importance of physical violence. Certainly both of these factors were important, but they should not detract attention from other indirect factors, because complex interrelationships and feedback mechanisms are operating among all of the variables leading to depopulation. For example, dispossession often forced enemy groups into intense competition for greatly reduced resources, and the availability of firearms made the resulting conflicts far more destructive than previous conflicts. These increased conflicts, combined with other new disturbances in economic and social patterns (such as those related to debt peonage), often placed new stresses on tribal societies and weakened them to the point that they willingly accepted outside control and welfare. Even depopulation itself is a form of stress that can lead to further depopulation by threatening the subsistence base. Rivers speculated in the 1920s that the sudden total transformation experienced by many tribes caused a form of shock that made people stop producing or desiring children, whereas in some cases they simply died because life was no longer worth living. Although this explanation is now in disrepute, it seems difficult to disprove.

Increased mortality alone does not account for the complete disappearance of so many tribal peoples: Other cultural variables are involved. Ironically, the special adaptive mechanisms of tribal cultures designed to prevent overpopulation, such as abortion, infanticide, and the ideal of a small family, may have actually contributed to depopulation and even extinction when frontier conditions drastically elevated mortality rates. There is little reliable data on this point because the importance of these population-regulating devices has only recently been recognized, but anthropologists have cited these factors to explain the depopulation of the Tapirape in Brazil[57] and the Yap islanders in Micronesia.[58]

Notes

1. Herman Merivale, 1861, *Lectures on Colonization and Colonies*, London: Green, Longman and Roberts.

2. Ray A. Billington, 1963, "The frontier in American thought and character," in *The New World Looks at Its History*, ed. Archibald R. Lewis and Thomas F. McGann, Austin: University of Texas Press, 7.

3. Walter Prescott Webb, 1952, *The Great Frontier*, Boston: Houghton Mifflin, 2.

4. United Kingdom House of Commons, 1837, *Report from the Select Committee on Aborigines (British Settlements)*, Imperial Blue Book no. 7, 425, British Parliamentary Papers.

5. Ibid., 5.

6. Ibid., 6.

7. Ibid., 3–15.

8. Peter Corris, 1968, *Aborigines and Europeans in Western Victoria*, Occasional Papers in Aboriginal Studies no. 12, Ethnohistory Series no. 1, Canberra: Australian Institute of Aboriginal Studies, 153–57.

9. A. G. Price, 1950, *White Settlers and Native Peoples*, London: Cambridge University Press, 107–108.

10. Ibid., 106–14.

11. *IWGIA Newsletter*, 1988, 55/56: 77–78.

12. Jules Henry, 1941, *Jungle People*, New York: J. J. Augustin.

13. Carlos de Araujo Moreira Neto, 1972, "Some data concerning the recent history of the Kaingang Indians," in *The Situation of the Indian in South America*, ed. W. Dostal, Geneva: World Council of Churches, 312.

14. Curt Nimuendaju, 1946, *The Eastern Timbira*, University of California Publications in American Archaeology and Ethnology, vol. 41, Berkeley and Los Angeles: University of California Press, 30.

15. Mark Münzel, 1973, *The Aché Indians: Genocide in Paraguay*, IWGIA Document no. 11, Copenhagen: IWGIA.

16. Miguel Chase-Sardi, 1972, "The present situation of the Indians in Paraguay," in *The Situation of the Indian in South America*, ed. W. Dostal, Geneva: World Council of Churches, 195.

17. Ibid., 197–99.

18. Münzel, *Aché Indians*.

19. David Maybury-Lewis and James Howe, 1980, *The Indian Peoples of Paraguay: Their Plight and Their Prospects*, Special Report no. 2, Cambridge, MA: Cultural Survival.

20. Bernard Arcand, 1972, *The Urgent Situation of the Cuiva Indians of Colombia*. IWGIA Document no. 7, Copenhagen: IWGIA.

21. Anonymous, 1972, "Columbia trial reveals life ('Everyone kills Indians') on plains," *Akwesasne Notes* 4(4): 26.

22. Corris, "Aborigines and Europeans," 105.

23. Price, *White Settlers*, 108.

24. Münzel, *Aché Indians*.

25. UK House of Commons, *Select Committee on Aborigines*, 29.

26. C. T. Loram, 1932, "Native labor in Southern Africa," in *Pioneer Settlement*, ed. W. L. G. Joerg, American Geographical Society, Special Publication no. 14, 170.

27. Nimuendaju, *Eastern Timbira*, 60.

28. Moreira Neto, "Kaingang Indians," 321.

29. IWGIA, 1987, *IWGIA Yearbook 1986: Indigenous Peoples and Human Rights*, Copenhagen: IWGIA, 27.

30. S. Palacios i Mendiburu, 1892, "Conferencia sobre la colonizacion de Loreto," *Boletin de la Sociedad Geografica de Lima* 2: 289–90, my translation, emphasis supplied.

31. Hildebrando Fuentes, 1908, *Loreto—Apuntes Geograficos, Historicos, Estadisticos, Politicos y Sociales*, vol. 2, Lima: Imprenta de la Revista.

32. Carlos A. Valcarcel, 1915, *El Proceso del Putumayo y sus Secretos Inauditos*, Lima: H. La Rosa.

33. Roger Casement, in Walter E. Hardenburg, 1912, *The Putumayo, the Devil's Paradise: Travels in the Peruvian Amazon Region and an Account of the Atrocities Committed upon the Indians Therein*, London: T. F. Unwin, 336–37; Julian H. Steward, 1948, "The Witotoan tribes," in *Handbook of South American Indians*, ed. Julian H. Steward, 749–62, vol. 3, Bureau of American Ethnology Bulletin 143, Washington, DC: Smithsonian Institution.

34. Fuentes, *Loreto*, 113.

35. E. D. Morel, 1906, *Red Rubber*, New York: Nassau Print, 105.

36. E. D. Morel, in Roger Louis and Jean Stengers, 1968, *E. P. Morel's History of the Congo Reform Movement*, Oxford: Clarendon Press, 7.

37. E. D. Morel, 1969, *The Black Man's Burden*, Northbrook, IL: Metro Books, 123.

38. W. H. R. Rivers, 1922, *Essays on the Depopulation of Melanesia*, Cambridge: Cambridge University Press.

39. Edward W. Docker, 1970, *The Blackbirders: The Recruiting of South Seas Labour for Queensland, 1863–1907*, Sydney: Angus and Robertson, 47.

40. Ibid., 82–84.

41. Deryck Scarr, 1968, "Introduction," in *A Cruise in a Queensland Labour Vessel to the South Seas*, by W. E. Giles, Canberra: Australian National University Press, 16.

42. Docker, *Blackbirders*, 205.

43. Ibid., 223–24.

44. George Palmer, 1871, *Kidnapping in the South Seas*, Edinburgh: Edmonston and Douglas.

45. Robert Murphy and Julian Steward, 1956, "Trappers and trappers: Parallel processes in acculturation," *Economic Development and Culture Change* 4: 335–55.

46. John H. Bodley, 1970, *Campa Socio-Economic Adaptation*, Ann Arbor, MI: University Microfilms, 108.

47. Charles Darwin, cited in Merivale, *Lectures on Colonization*, 541.

48. Corris, "Aborigines and Europeans."

49. Sherburne F. Cook, 1955, "The epidemic of 1830–1833 in California and Oregon." *University of California Publications in American Archaeology and Ethnology* 43: 303–26.

50. Darcy Ribeiro, 1957, *Culturas e Linguas Indigenas do Brasil*, Separata de Educacão e Cieñcias Socais no. 6, Rio de Janeiro: Centro Brasileiro de Pesquisas Educacionais.

51. William Lipkind, 1948, "The Caraja," in *Handbook of South American Indians*, ed. Julian Steward, vol. 3, Bureau of American Ethnology Bulletin 143, Washington, DC: Smithsonian Institution, 180.

52. Henry Dobyns, 1966, "Estimating Aboriginal American population: An appraisal of techniques with a new hemispheric estimate," *Current Anthropology* 7(4): 395–449.

53. Shelton H. Davis, 1977, *Victims of the Miracle: Development and the Indians of Brazil*, Cambridge: Cambridge University Press, 69–73; Latin America Political Report, 1979,13(3): 19.

54. Stephen Henry Roberts, 1969, *Population Problems of the Pacific*, New York: AMS Press, 59.

55. Rivers, *Depopulation of Melanesia*.

56. George H. Pitt-Rivers, 1927, *The Clash of Culture and the Contact of Races*, London: George Routledge and Sons.

57. C. Wagley, 1951, "Cultural influences on population," *Revista do Museu Paulista* 5: 95–104.

58. David Schneider, 1955, "Abortion and depopulation on a Pacific island: Yap," in *Health, Culture, and Community*, ed. B. D. Paul, 211–35. New York: Russell Sage.

4   We Fought with Spears

Nothing much is said about the sufferings on our side. Yet we fought with spears, dubs, bows and arrows. The foreigners fought with cannons, guns and bullets.

—F. Bugotu[1]

THE EARLY ANTHROPOLOGISTS WHO STUDIED THE CULTURE change process did not generally place sufficient emphasis on the role of military force in bringing about the initial breakdown of tribal autonomy. According to the authoritative "Memorandum for the Study of Acculturation,"[2] *acculturation* is the result of groups with different cultures entering into "continuous firsthand contact, with subsequent changes in the original cultural patterns of either or both groups." The memorandum indicated that the contact situation could be friendly or hostile, but it gave no hint that force might be a major cause of acculturation. Even some modern anthropology textbooks stress that acculturation often resulted from demands for change coming from tribal peoples themselves, due to their exposure to higher standards of living or the idea of progress—almost as if such "demonstration effects" were the basic cause of culture change.[3] Considered in a different light, giving full credibility to the historical record, ethnocide can, in many cases, be seen as the direct outcome of the defeat of individual tribes in separate engagements in the long war fought between tribal and commercial societies worldwide.

Although it is not appropriate here to present a full review of the history of military actions against tribal peoples, this chapter does emphasize the extent and nature of this military pressure and shows how such pressure has frequently initiated culture change and ethnocide by destroying tribal autonomy.

In many parts of the world, tribal peoples fought back fiercely when their traditional cultures were threatened by outsiders and when they realized that those outsiders intended to impose their will on them. Often tribal peoples were forced into one-sided battles to defend their lives against militarily superior enemies, and in most cases the outcome was never long in doubt when indigenous peoples were fighting against troops armed with modern weapons. Defeat on the battlefield was invariably followed by the surrender of cultural autonomy and the imposition of government administrative control, leading ultimately to further culture change.

In general, two major varieties of military action against tribal peoples can be distinguished: punitive raids and wars. Punitive raids tend to be short-term punishments for specific offenses committed by indigenous peoples, and the intent is merely to establish administrative control. Wars, however, may involve protracted campaigns, often for the purpose of extermination or the forced removal of indigenous populations that are not in themselves of direct economic value. Both approaches have been widely applied and have had profound impacts on tribal culture. These are discussed in the following sections.

The Punitive Raid

The basic purpose of a punitive raid is to impress a tribal population with the overwhelming force at the government's disposal and to thereby gain their "cooperation." It is simply a form of intimidation, always with the threat of greater force in the background, and it normally does not aim at the total annihilation of a people.

The punitive raid has been used widely in New Guinea and throughout the Pacific, where the population of indigenous peoples was too valuable as a source of labor to risk its extermination. The Germans conducted frequent raids in their New Guinea colony and often carried them to excessive lengths. When two white men and eight indigenous laborers were killed by unpacified peoples, the government responded by sending an expedition that killed eighty-one people, destroyed houses and canoes, and carried off women and children as prisoners.[4] Such overreaction was a common feature of punitive raids. In 1928, when two indigenous policemen in Australian New Guinea were killed by the Kwoma in a dispute over the rape of a village woman, the government massacred seventeen villagers in retaliation.[5] By coincidence, in the same year Australian police killed seventeen Aborigines near Alice Springs.[6] Even if these raids were considered a necessary form of retribution for specific "crimes" committed by indigenous peoples, the police seldom made any effort to determine who the guilty parties were or to balance the punishment to fit the crime, let alone understand the real motives for the hostilities.

The French, Germans, British, and Americans often used naval battleships and cruisers in the Pacific to impress recalcitrant islanders. This occurred as late as 1920, when the Americans stopped a revolt in Samoa with naval guns.[7]

The Germans regularly used their warships in New Guinea but did not always gain the intended result. The villagers may have been impressed with the noise, but often they merely returned to their villages when the barrage was over and planted taro in the shell holes.[8]

Punitive raids were also institutionalized in colonial Africa. In South Africa they were known as *commandos* and were often conducted by detachments of armed settlers whose leaders were officially acknowledged by both the government and the military. The usual excuse for a raid was to regain "stolen" cattle, but raids often resulted in the indiscriminate destruction of tribal life and property.

Perhaps the most raided tribal group in colonial Africa was the Nuer of the southern Sudan, who E. E. Evans-Pritchard described in 1930 as arrogant and suspicious. The British usually sent expeditions or patrols against tribes in the Sudan that refused to submit to government administration or that were fighting among themselves. The Nuer were one of the most difficult of such groups to subdue because they refused to be humbled and had abundant land on which to hide. According to the count of one historian, armed force was used against the Nuer and related tribes sixteen times between 1902 and 1932.[9]

Punitive raids caused loss of life and significantly disrupted tribal society. They seriously disturbed the subsistence economy when stored food or gardens were destroyed. Further, the psychological impact of such displays of overwhelming force undermined morale and the self-confidence necessary for tribal autonomy. When these disturbances were combined with the other difficulties characteristic of the uncontrolled frontier, the surrender of tribal peoples to the government becomes understandable.

Punitive raids were not restricted to colonial governments. Such raids were a common tactic of the U.S. Army in the Indian Wars, especially during the 1870s, and were widely applied in Latin America. In Brazil, organized irregular troops, known as *bandeiras*, often punished Indian tribes in the nineteenth century.

Punitive raids also are not a thing of the past. Thanks to modern technology, they can now be conducted more easily and much more effectively. In 1965, newspapers reported that Brazilian air, naval, and ground forces were used against the Marubo, a small Indian tribe in the Brazilian state of Amazonas that attacked settlers who had invaded their territory.[10] At about the same time in the Peruvian Amazon, the Peruvian air force used napalm to punish the Asháninka who were thought to be in support of leftist rebels. The Indonesian government in 1965–1966 used bombing raids and armed patrols to control four thousand "disaffected" Arfak people in West Irian (Indonesian New Guinea), reportedly leaving twelve hundred dead.[11]

Wars of Extermination

Major campaigns and wars of extermination waged against tribal peoples have usually been for the purpose of removing the population so that the territory could be utilized by outsiders to benefit the national economy. The immediate justification for such action, as with punitive raids, has often been the need to protect settlers or colonists from "marauding savages" or to quell tribal rebellions, or it has simply been viewed as a quick means of spreading civilization and progress. In most cases, rebellions and raids by tribal peoples were the direct result of pressures exerted against them by outsiders and could have been prevented if they had been left alone—but that policy was not often economically advantageous to outsiders.

Wars against tribal peoples became extremely frequent throughout the world as European expansion began and reached a high point in the period between 1850 and 1910. It is well known that the Indian Wars in the United States continued almost without respite from 1820 to 1890, but it is not often realized that similar wars were occurring in South America at the same time, sometimes on just as large a scale as in North America. Africa, particularly the southern and eastern regions, was also the scene of almost continual military action during the same period. In Asia, campaigns were conducted against tribal peoples in Formosa by the Japanese, in the Philippines by the Spanish and then by the Americans, in Indochina by the French, and in Burma and Assam by the British. In the Pacific, the Maori Wars of 1860–1872 and the New Caledonia revolt of 1878–1879 were the most significant major military actions. These tribal wars have received relatively little attention in history texts because they were overshadowed by other political and economic events occurring in Europe and America at the same time, but they were nevertheless critical struggles for the peoples most directly involved.

Guns against Spears

> Half measures do not answer with natives. They must be thoroughly crushed to make them believe in our superiority. . . . I shall strive to be in a position to show them how hopelessly inferior they are to us in fighting power although numerically stronger.[12]

Modern weapons gave government forces a distinct advantage, particularly in large-scale battles between troops and indigenous peoples still unfamiliar with the effects of firearms. Conventional forms of tribal resistance were usually futile and often ended tragically, like the Matabele rebellion in Rhodesia in 1896, which was decisively ended when machine gun fire mowed down spear-carrying warriors by the hundreds with "bullets that came like hail in a storm."[13] In many areas, magical as well as empirical defenses were developed by tribal peoples to counteract such weapons. In New Guinea the people invented a special salve that was supposed to deflect bullets.[14] On the American plains, the "ghost dance" shirt was intended to turn bullets into water, and in the Amazon, Asháninka shamans attempted to blow at the bullets as protection. Guerrilla tactics generally proved more effective, however, and better still was the acquisition of firearms.

Although these campaigns were often short, one-sided affairs, tribal peoples were not infrequently capable of stubborn resistance and sometimes struck back major blows against their enemies. In Burma, the British spent more than ten years suppressing rebellious tribesmen,[15] and the Naga were even more resistant, as will be shown. The odyssey of Chief Joseph and the Nez Perce in 1877 is well known, and so is the massacre of General George A. Custer and 264 men of the Seventh Cavalry in 1876. Perhaps even more dramatic was the destruction of more than 800 of the British forces sent against the Zulu in 1879 at Isandhlwana and Rorke's Drift. The soldiers were attempting to teach the Zulu that they were "hopelessly inferior," but in this case spears prevailed against guns. That same year in nearby Basutoland, 300 rebellious Pluthi warriors, armed with a few guns, withstood a siege of their fortified hilltop refuge for eight months against 1,800 soldiers with artillery. The most stubborn cases of resistance often occurred when tribal people were able to obtain firearms from traders and learned to use them before major conflicts broke out. This availability of firearms prolonged the Maori Wars and was an important factor in many other incidents of tribal resistance as well.

The distinction between these wars and the wars Europeans waged among themselves was not merely the usual one-sidedness of the fighting, but rather that their purpose was often the destruction of a way of life and the subjugation, if not destruction, of entire populations. Military defeat of tribal peoples by industrial states involves far more than a mere change in political structure. When the Pluthi were defeated, their cattle and land were immediately taken from them, and their women and children became involuntary laborers for white farmers. In effect, the Pluthi ceased to exist as a distinct tribal entity.

In the postcolonial era since 1945, civil wars have become very common and have often been devastating for tribal peoples, especially in sub-Saharan Africa.[16] For example, the Nuer were also caught up in the Sudanese Civil War of 1955 to 1972 between the Sudan's Islamic government in Khartoum in the north and the non-Islamic peoples in southern Sudan, who sought independence. This conflict resumed in 1983 and continued until a peace agreement was finally signed in 2005. Nearly 2 million civilians died in this conflict, and some 4 million became refugees. Tribal peoples in the Nuba

Mountains and Darfur regions of Sudan have also been devastated by twenty-first-century civil conflicts that have been called genocidal.

In order to more fully illustrate the varied nature of historic military conflicts between modern states and tribal peoples, the following specific examples are examined in greater detail: the defeat of the Indians in southern South America between 1870 and 1885; the Maori Wars of 1860–1872; the resistance of the Naga in Assam; the German extermination campaign against the Herero of Southwest Africa in 1904; and the Japanese method of controlling the Formosan Aborigines from 1902 to 1909.

The Conquest of Fifteen Thousand Leagues

We have six thousand soldiers armed with the latest modern inventions of war to oppose two thousand Indians that have no other defense but dispersion, nor other arms than the primitive lance.[17]

In 1820 most of central Chile and the Argentine pampas were occupied by thousands of autonomous Araucanian and Tehuelche Indians who had successfully held back the frontiers of European settlement during nearly three hundred years of continuous fighting. The Indians fell back, however, when the effects of the commercialization process began to be felt in southern South America and European immigrants began to arrive in greater numbers, bringing new patterns of warfare. By 1883, after a series of major military operations, the Indians were finally defeated, and vast areas of rich agricultural land were opened for the benefit of white settlers. On the pampas, most tribes were virtually annihilated by the military campaigns, but in Chile, after the successful conclusion of the War of the Pacific, seasoned troops turned on the Araucanians and reduced them to disorganized and isolated groups. These Indian wars in southern South America were strikingly similar to those occurring in North America at the same time. Yet their scope and the kind of military force that was required to defeat the Indians are not widely appreciated.

In Argentina by the early 1870s, a semistatic defense system had evolved to protect the expanding agricultural settlements from attacks by dispossessed Indians. The system consisted of a continuous line of ten major forts and nearly seventy smaller forts stretching 1,600 kilometers from the Andes to the Atlantic. The large forts were bastions, each garrisoned by hundreds of soldiers, whereas the smaller were fortifications of walls, moats, and watchtowers, armed with cannon and perhaps ten to twenty troopers. Included in the line were 370 kilometers of walls, and trenches 3 meters wide and 2 meters deep, which were intended to impede the passage of Indian horsemen. Each fort sent daily patrols to the right and left along the line to check for incursions by the Indians. When Indians were detected in the vicinity, cavalry troops were quickly dispatched to intercept them, and if the Indians could be caught, bloody, one-sided battles ensued. In one such action in 1872, the battle of San Carlos, 1,665 cavalrymen clashed with 3,500 Indians. Four soldiers and 200 Indians died. Lances and bolas proved ineffective against repeating rifles and artillery; the Indians' only defense was surprise attacks and rapid flight. This inability to match their enemies' armaments was dramatically apparent in an 1878 incident, when a lone trooper with a rifle killed six Indians and captured nine. Earlier the Indians had successfully held their territory against the advances of soldiers and settlers, but modern firearms rapidly changed the situation. As one Argentine military official described it: "The Remington came, and with the Remington, the offensive, the Indians were finished and the desert was conquered."[18]

The defense network, as described, was actually neither static nor defensive, because it was constantly being moved forward as new land was declared free of Indians. As the Indians surrendered, they were required to sign treaties acknowledging the sovereignty of Argentina and pledging themselves to fight against rebel Indians. Many national leaders were dissatisfied with the relatively slow pace of the advance and openly called for an aggressive war against the Indians. Finally, in 1878, the government approved the "final solution"—a lightning "conquest of fifteen thousand leagues" in which five columns of six thousand soldiers advanced into Indian territory to carry out what President Nicolas Avellaneda called a "great work of civilization" and a "conquest for humanity."[19] Within six months the frontier had been advanced some 640 kilometers until it stood on the south bank of the Rio Negro. More than five thousand Indians were either killed or captured, and the nation's agricultural territory almost doubled at a cost of thirteen soldiers killed.[20] The campaign continued beyond the officially authorized frontier until 1885, when the general in charge of the forces south of the Rio Negro proudly reported the end of the humiliating frontier with the "savages": "Today not any tribe remains in the field that is not voluntarily or forcibly reduced; and if any number of Indians still exist, they are isolated wanderers, without forming groups worthy of consideration."[21]

Indian settlements were indiscriminately destroyed and looted in the campaign, and it appears that many who were not killed were taken captive and removed to uncertain fates, while the women "voluntarily" became wives for the soldiers and settlers. This kind of culture contact had decisive effects. By 1913–1914 little more than one hundred Tehuelche still survived, and by 1925 the Puelche were nearly exterminated.[22] The Argentine Araucanians apparently survived in greater numbers, but their total military defeat left them thoroughly demoralized and willing to accept the authority of the government.

Forcing the Maori into Civilization

And the word of the Maori is, we'll fight for ever, for ever and ever.[23]

In 1840 perhaps one thousand settlers, traders, and missionaries shared New Zealand with at least one hundred thousand Maori who were willing to tolerate the foreigners and even aid them in order to receive new manufactured goods such as muskets. By 1858, due to the usual frontier disturbances, the Maori population had dwindled to about fifty-six thousand, and thanks to rapidly increasing immigration the white population had risen to nearly forty thousand. As the balance swung in its favor, the government felt strong enough to pursue a vigorous policy of Maori land alienation for sale to settlers and land speculators in spite of widespread Maori resistance. As usual in such situations, the colonists demanded the best land for farming and grazing; they rationalized their greed by pointing out that Maori possession of the land was an interference with the industrial and commercial progress of the colony. After all, the land was "the greatest curse the natives have" and taking it from them was "the greatest boon you could confer on them."[24] As early as 1854, the 12,000 colonists in Auckland Province in the North Island had already acquired some 324,000 hectares from the Maori, of which only 3.5 percent was actually being cultivated, and in Wellington Province 6,000 colonists "purchased" 3.6 million hectares from the Maori and were cultivating less than one-tenth of a percent.

These proceedings caused considerable resentment among the Maori, who realized they were being rapidly dispossessed. Calling upon their traditions of warfare and chiefdom-level political organization, and borrowing from the British model, they began uniting to resist further land alienation. In 1858 they elected their own "king," designed flags, and organized troops. Declining Maori customs, such as tattooing, were revived, and there were moves to sever economic ties with the colonists and to demand that they be completely expelled from New Zealand. Soon a general feeling arose on both sides that war was inevitable. In 1860, when the Taranaki Maori passively resisted the work of a survey team preparing to subdivide a large block of their land, the governor of New Zealand declared martial law and called on the military to enforce the government's will. The colonists were eager to teach the Maori a lesson and were confident that the fighting would be short, decisive, and profitable.

In fact, the Maori proved to be formidable opponents, even though their total fighting force could hardly have numbered more than eight thousand men. They managed to fight for twelve years against a force that in 1864 amounted to some twenty-two thousand soldiers, including nearly ten thousand British regulars. The war cost the colony fifteen hundred casualties, including five hundred killed, and a bill of approximately 1.3 million pounds from the Crown to pay for the military operations. The Maori suffered an estimated four thousand casualties in killed and wounded, and in the end were forced to surrender their autonomy because of the greater firepower and overwhelming numbers of the government military forces.[25]

Although Maori resistance did not succeed, it was far stronger than the colonists expected, partly because the Maori were well armed and knew how to use their muskets. They were also skillful at fortifying positions and built numerous redoubts with trenches, rifle pits, and walls with loopholes, parapets, and towers that rivaled those designed by the best-trained military engineers. Maori courage and fighting ability won frequent praise and admiration from their enemies. In the first major campaign in Taranaki in 1860–1861, a force of fifteen hundred Maori besieged the town of New Plymouth and prevented three thousand troops from gaining any significant victories. The common British stereotype of colonial wars, involving a handful of red-coated infantry coolly fighting off hordes of natives, was often curiously reversed in the Maori Wars. In 1864 at Oarakau, three hundred Maori men, women, and children entrenched themselves on a hilltop, where they were surrounded by eighteen hundred soldiers. The Maori, outnumbered six to one, were short of food, water, and ammunition, and were poorly armed, but they refused to surrender. For three days they withstood shellfire and grenades and repulsed four bayonet assaults before thirst forced them to retreat. In the final hours they were so short of ammunition that they were forced to improvise wooden bullets and fearlessly defused grenades thrown at them in order to use the powder. They withdrew in good order, advancing silently and deliberately into the fire of the troops surrounding them, but only a few escaped. In all, more than half were killed, and half of the survivors were wounded.[26] General Duncan Cameron, who led the British troops, spoke in tribute of their courage, and soldiers of the Sixty-fifth Regiment erected a tablet in a local church as a memorial to the Maori who fell at Oarakau.[27]

Naga Resistance in Assam

The Naga hill tribesmen in Assam frustrated British attempts to extend administrative control over them and to end their headhunting and raiding for more than fifty years. Between 1832 and 1851, ten military expeditions were sent against them, inflicting incredible losses, but many of the Naga still refused to surrender their political autonomy.

The first British expedition to enter Naga territory in 1832 consisted of seven hundred well-armed soldiers, but the Naga resisted their advance with every weapon at their disposal and seemed to ignore the devastating effects of gunfire. They yelled and threw spears at the soldiers, rolled rocks on them from the ridge tops, burned grass in their paths, planted punji sticks, poisoned enemy wells, built stockades, and attacked continuously. In the face of such opposition, the British managed only to temporarily occupy and destroy one village before withdrawing.[28] In 1850 another military expedition of five hundred men and four artillery pieces besieged a Naga fortification for sixteen hours before capturing it. The 1851 expedition burned a village when its inhabitants refused to give the soldiers provisions. At first the Naga, who had nothing but scorn for the soldiers' guns and muskets, offered a fierce challenge: "We will fight with spear and shield and see who are the best men."[29]

The British commander eagerly accepted the challenge and promptly attacked the Naga village of 2,000 warriors with 150 soldiers armed with muskets, 2 three-pounder artillery pieces, a mortar, and 800 native allies. The Naga were panic-stricken by the musketry and artillery, and lost 100 killed and another 200 wounded, whereas the soldiers escaped without a single casualty and proceeded to burn the village.

The fighting was not all one-sided, however, because the Naga continued to raid and constantly harassed the soldiers. In 1879 they killed an administrator and thirty-five troops, and six thousand warriors besieged the administrative center for twelve days. In 1879–1880, expeditions sent to punish the Naga suffered more than one hundred soldiers killed.[30]

It gradually became apparent that regardless of how many villages were burned and how many Naga were killed, they remained unhumbled, and it became ridiculously costly to continue punishing them when their territory offered relatively little of economic value. Numerous suggestions began to be made that the Naga be left alone and that all attempts to extend British sovereignty and civilization over them be suspended. In 1854 all British troops were withdrawn, but by 1886, attempts at administrative control were renewed and efforts were under way to build roads and establish economic contacts between the tribesmen and the lowlanders. These less militant efforts were moderately successful, but the Naga continued to resist penetration of their areas by lowlanders and still strongly resented any undue interference in their affairs. After India gained independence in 1947, the Naga openly rebelled again; this time they demanded to be recognized as an independent state. By 1956 they had organized a guerrilla force of fifteen thousand men armed with Japanese weapons hidden during World War II. The Indian army attempted to end the rebellion, but the government was finally forced to make Nagaland a state within the Indian Union in 1963. However, the Naga have continued to fight for independence.[31] Naga resistance was followed by the militarization of their territory. The Indian army still occupies Nagaland and has been accused of many indiscriminate attacks on villagers and other human rights abuses. In the 1980s the army was building roads and opening Nagaland to outside exploitation. Oil was being extracted by at least two oil companies, Indians were invading in greater numbers, and deforestation was becoming a serious problem.[32] Conflict continued in Nagaland into the twenty-first century.

Extermination of the Herero

We tried to exterminate a native race, whom our lack of wisdom had goaded into rebellion.[33]

The Germans founded their protectorate of Southwest Africa in 1884 on the principle that indigenous peoples must step aside and allow Europeans to use both their persons and their land as the Europeans desired. However, in this case they did not bother with any pretense of humanitarian concern for the advancement of what one governor had labeled "the most useless of natives."[34] The three hundred thousand tribal inhabitants of this arid desert region consisted primarily of nomadic cattle herders such as the Khoikhoi and the Bantu Herero, who numbered perhaps one hundred thousand.[35] Unfortunately, their interests in the land were incompatible with German plans. The German administration prepared to use military force against the tribes as soon as settlers began to arrive in 1892, seeking the few areas of valuable grazing land and farmland that were, of course, already occupied by the tribal people. In 1893 an official policy of forced dispossession was initiated when 250 German soldiers and two artillery batteries surrounded a sleeping Hottentot village and massacred sixty men and ninety women and children. In turn, the Herero were attacked in 1896 and were threatened with a "war of extermination" if they refused to surrender their best lands to the settlers and withdraw to the waterless reserves designated for them.[36]

The moral justification for this policy was a simple argument in favor of social Darwinism and economic efficiency, which was explained in 1907 by Paul Rohrbach, leader of the territory's Settlement Commission:

The native tribes must withdraw from the lands on which they have pastured their cattle and so let the White man pasture his cattle on these self-same lands. If the moral right of this standpoint is questioned, the answer is that for people of the culture standard of the South African Natives, the loss of their free national barbarism and the development of a class of workers in the service of and dependent on the Whites is primarily a law of existence in the highest degree. For a people, as for an individual, an existence appears to be justified in the degree that it is useful in the progress of general development. By no argument in the world can it be shown that the preservation of any degree of national independence, national prosperity and political organization by the races of South West Africa would be of greater or even of equal advantage for the development of mankind in general or the German people in particular than that these races should be made serviceable in the enjoyment of their former territories by the White races.[37]

The Herero soon were without grazing land and were virtually cattleless because an epidemic in 1897 carried off two-thirds of their cattle. By 1903 more than half of the remaining cattle had been appropriated by unscrupulous traders. They could tolerate their situation no longer. In 1904 some eight thousand Herero warriors rose against the colonists, and within a few days 150 Germans were killed. Two months after the outbreak of fighting, a Herero chief explained the causes of the war in a letter to the military governor. Speaking bitterly of German abuses, he stated that the war had been started by the whites, and he vowed to fight to the death.

The Germans were well prepared to make good on their earlier threats of a war of extermination. General Lothar Von Trotha was quickly dispatched from Germany and in 1904 surrounded five thousand Herero with an army of fifteen hundred riflemen, thirty field guns, and twelve machine guns. Many Herero escaped in the fighting and were driven into the Kalahari Desert to die of thirst. Von Trotha refused to negotiate and proclaimed that anyone who remained in the country would be shot: "The Herero people must now leave the country, if they do not I will compel them with the big tube [artillery]. Within the German frontier every Herero, with or without a rifle, will be shot. I will not take any more women and children [prisoners], but I will drive them back to their people or have them fired on."[38]

The soldiers ruthlessly carried out these orders for months (even to the extent of deliberately poisoning waterholes), and thousands of Herero died. By 1906 their population had been reduced to twenty thousand landless fugitives. The Khoikhoi also joined in the fighting, but by 1907 the war was officially declared over. It had been a disastrous campaign for the Germans as well. They lost more than sixteen hundred men and had fielded a force of up to nineteen thousand men at an estimated cost of some 23 million pounds. The total indigenous loss in life was estimated at some one hundred thousand, or approximately two-thirds of the labor force, as the Germans viewed it. In the end even Rohrbach, whose policies of land confiscation had directly contributed to the fighting, was willing to admit his "blunder," because "the actual extermination of a race could be politically and economically disastrous."[39]

Advancing the Guard-Line in Formosa

When the Japanese took over Formosa in 1895, some 3 million "civilized" people occupied less than half of the island and the remainder was occupied by 120,000 tribal people. Pressure on the tribal areas was understandable in view of their relatively light population and because of the resources in timber, camphor, gold, and agricultural land contained within them. As soon as the Japanese administration succeeded in putting down the Formosan rebels in 1902, they turned their attention toward controlling the Aborigines and helping them progress toward civilization. The Aborigines were particularly bothersome because they frequently attacked and took the heads of outsiders who approached their frontiers too closely. This made it difficult for the Japanese to extract timber and camphor from Aboriginal territory and virtually excluded the utilization of their agricultural land in the interests of the total economy. According to an official report published by the Formosan Bureau of Aboriginal Affairs,[40] the Japanese developed two methods for dealing with the problem. The first method was called "gradual development" and involved winning Aboriginal cooperation through slow, peaceful penetration. Instead, the Japanese resorted to a second, more direct method, which they called *suppression.*

Suppression of "savages" Japanese-style was similar to the Argentine approach, except the Japanese were able to make use of much more sophisticated weaponry. The approach was to encircle virtually the entire Aboriginal area with a military cordon and then gradually advance toward the center. The cordon itself, called a guard-line, consisted of a line of small guardhouse redoubts situated on ridge tops and paralleled by a road and a wide swath of cleared forest serving as a fire zone. Important innovations included the use of telephone communication, barbed-wire entanglements, electric fences, and land mines, which "have great effect in giving alarm of the invading savages."[41] The Japanese regularly used grenades in fighting and placed field guns in strategic locations where, according to the official report, "one gun is sufficient to withstand the attack of several tribes."[42] In 1909 the guard-line was 493 kilometers long and throughout its length, approximately every 500 meters, guardhouses garrisoned with two to four armed guards were located, and every kilometer-and-a-half there was a special superintendent station.

Like the Argentine line of forts, the Formosan guard-line was never intended to be a permanent frontier between state and tribal areas, but it was to be constantly advanced. The guards regularly conducted patrols and ambushes inside the line and moved the line forward at every opportunity, with or without the consent of the Aborigines. Between 1903 and 1909, seventy-five advances were made, eighteen under "hostile" conditions. Certainly the report was accurate in describing the advance as both "an aggression and progression into the savage territory."[43]

"Punitive expeditions" were frequently sent across the guard-line to punish the Aborigines for their attacks on outsiders. In 1897 one particularly "savage" tribe killed a policeman and a year later killed two more officers at a pacification station. In response, according to the report: "A punitive expedition, consisting of about 5 companies of infantry, was dispatched against this tribe. The Troops destroyed all the dwellings of the tribe. As a result, they surrendered to the Government."[44]

The guards arranged a more elaborate punishment for another tribe that had managed to kill thirty camphor workers and a policeman within its territory in 1906. A special eleven-kilometer guard-line was placed around the area, and the tribe's villages were assaulted from the line while two cruisers bombarded them from off the coast. In this action, six villages and their gardens were destroyed and forty tribal people were killed.

In a typical advancement of the guard-line under hostile conditions—a campaign of 107 days, using 886 fighting men and 1,000 support forces for labor and transport—a tribal area of 222 square kilometers, "containing many camphor and other valuable trees" as well as tribal hunting grounds, was captured. The Aborigines constructed defenses and fought tenaciously, but were finally overcome by rifles and grenades at close quarters. Territory captured in such a manner was immediately made available for outside exploitation, as the Formosan government's report carefully explained: "The territory thus included within the guard-line becomes a peaceful district, where various settlers may engage in the agricultural, timber and camphor industries with greater safety. . . . This act necessarily excites a dislike among the savages, but it intends, by no means, the plundering and destruction of the district occupied by them. It is simply intended to utilize the vast undeveloped territory now held by the Aborigines in the island."[45]

Some measure of the intensity of the resistance in Formosa can be obtained by comparing the figure of 4,341 Japanese and Formosans killed by the Aborigines between 1896 and 1909, with the 500 Europeans killed by the Maori in New Zealand between 1860 and 1872.

Although these case studies of military force against tribals have been historical, many dating from the nineteenth century, the militarization of tribal areas is unfortunately still occurring. Since 1980 military force has supported the invasion of tribal areas by colonists in Bangladesh (cited in chapter 2) and in Indonesian-controlled West Papua, where 14,000 indigenous peoples were reportedly killed during a six-month military operation in 1981–1982 and as many as 150,000 may have been killed between 1963 and 1983.[46] Since 1980 government-sponsored (or condoned) terrorism has been used to suppress indigenous groups in India, the Philippines, Peru, Brazil, Mexico, Guatemala, and Colombia. In many cases, indigenous groups have organized their own guerrilla forces in self-defense, as in the Sudan, West Papua, and the Philippines, or they have been caught between other military forces that have used their territory as a battleground, as, for example, in Southeast Asia, Ethiopia, southern Africa, and Nicaragua.

The arms race has also turned the lands of indigenous peoples into strategic military resources and resulted in their forced expulsion and exposure to nuclear radiation, as in the case of the Bikini islanders in Micronesia. Tribal groups have also been recruited to fight other peoples' battles, as was the case when the U.S. Central Intelligence Agency used Laotian hill tribes against communist forces, and when the South African army used ethnic battalions, some drawn from the Bushmen, in its war against the South West Africa People's Organization (SWAPO), the Namibian independence movement. The war was ended in 1989 by the UN-backed implementation of Namibian independence.

On January 1, 1994, hundreds of indigenous Tzotzil-, Tzeltal-, and Tojolabal-speaking peoples joined the Zapatista National Liberation Army (Ejército Zapatista de Liberación Nacional, or EZLN) in the southernmost Mexican state of Chiapas when it declared war against the Mexican army and the political party ruling the national government. The crucial grievance was rural poverty, exploitation, repression, and the steady loss of indigenous control over land and resources.[47] This was an armed struggle "for work, land, home, food, health, education, independence, liberty, democracy, justice, and peace," according to the Declaration of the Zapatista Army. The rebellion was timed to coincide with the implementation of the North American Free Trade Agreement (NAFTA), which for many Mexican peoples had come to symbolize the domination of global commercial interests over the interests of the rural poor who were struggling to hold on to their lands and resources as their primary means of subsistence. In the first four days of armed struggle, ninety-three people died and the Zapatistas captured three towns and the major city of San Cristobal de Las Casas. The Zapatistas effectively used the Internet to arouse worldwide sympathy for their cause. A cease-fire was established on January 12, but the issues remained unresolved. Direct intervention by many nongovernmental organizations helped minimize reprisals against the Zapatistas by the Mexican army after the initial fighting ended.

Notes

1. F. Bugotu, 1968, "The culture clash: A Melanesian's view," *New Guinea* 3(2): 65–70. Bugotu is speaking of the colonial era in the Solomon Islands.

2. Robert Redfield, Ralph Linton, and M. J. Herskovits, 1936, "Memorandum on the study of acculturation," *American Anthropologist* 38: 149–52.

3. Cecie Starr, ed., 1971, *Anthropology Today*, Del Mar, CA: Communications Research Machines.

4. Stephen W. Reed, 1943, *The Making of Modern New Guinea*, Philadelphia: American Philosophical Society, 136–37.

5. Ibid., 154–155.

6. Charles D. Rowley, 1967, "The villager and the nomad: Aboriginals and New Guineans," *New Guinea* 2(1): 73.

7. Felix M. Keesing, 1941, *The South Seas in the Modern World*, Institute of Pacific Relations International Research Series, New York: John Day, 173.

8. Reed, *New Guinea*, 136.

9. Mohamed Omer Beshir, 1968, *The Southern Sudan: Background to Conflict*, New York: Praeger, 19.

10. James D. Bowman, 1965, "They like white men—broiled" (Associated Press), *Eugene (Oregon) Register-Guard*, October 7, 28.

11. Peter Hastings, 1968, "West Irian—1969." *New Guinea* 3(3): 12–22.

12. Rupert Furneaux, 1963, *The Zulu War: Isandhlwana and Rorke's Drift*, Philadelphia and New York: J. B. Lippincott, 32.

13. John H. Wellington, 1967, *South West Africa and Its Human Issues*, Oxford: Clarendon Press/Oxford University Press, 245.

14. Reed, *New Guinea*, 134.

15. Maran La Raw, 1967, "Toward a basis for understanding the minorities in Burma: The Kachin example," in *Southeast Asian Tribes, Minorities, and Nations*, ed. Peter Kunstadter, Princeton, NJ: Princeton University Press, 131.

16. Human Security Centre, 2005, *Human Security Report 2005: War and Peace in the 21st Century*, New York: Oxford University Press.

17. Julio Anibal Portas, 1967 *Malón Contra Malón: La Solución Final del Problema del Indio en la Argentina*, Buenos Aires: Ediciones de la Flor, 7, my translation.

18. General Ignacio Fotheringham, quoted in ibid., 19, my translation.

19. Lobodon Garra, 1969, *A Sangre y Lanza*, Buenos Aires: Ediciones Anaconda, 433.

20. Portas, *La Solución Final*, 7, 76.

21. General Lorenzo Wintter, quoted in Garra, *Sangre y Lanza*, 522, my translation.

22. John M. Cooper, 1946, "The Patagonian and Pampean hunters," in *Handbook of South American Indians*, ed. Julian H. Steward, vol. 1, Bureau of American Ethnology. Bulletin no. 143, Washington, DC: Smithsonian Institution, 131, 138.

23. Maori answer to the call for their surrender at Oarakau, 1863, in Angus J. Harrop, 1937, *England and the Maori Wars*, New York: Books for Libraries Press, 190.

24. Keith Sinclair, 1961, *The Origins of the Maori Wars*, 2nd ed., Wellington: New Zealand University Press, 4–5.

25. James Cowan, 1922–1923, *The New Zealand Wars*, Wellington: R. E. Owen, Government Printer; Harrop, *Maori Wars*, 196, 312.

26. Cowan, *New Zealand Wars*, 365–407.

27. Harrop, *Maori Wars*, 192.

28. Verrier Elwin, 1969, *The Nagas in the Nineteenth Century*, London: Oxford University Press, 114.

29. Ibid., 142.

30. Ibid.

31. Robbins Burling, 1967, "Tribesmen and lowlanders of Assam," in *Southeast Asian Tribes, Minorities, and Nations*, ed. Peter Kunstadter, 215–29. Princeton, NJ: Princeton University Press.

32. International Work Group for Indigenous Affairs, 1986, *The Naga Nation and Its Struggle against Genocide*, IWGIA Document no. 56, Copenhagen: IWGIA.

33. German Professor Boon, in a lecture to the Royal Colonial Institute of London, 1914, cited in John H. Wellington, 1967, *South West Africa and Its Human Issues*, Oxford: Clarendon Press/Oxford University Press, 204.

34. Robert Cornevin, 1969, "The Germans in Africa before 1918," in *The History and Politics of Colonialism 1870–1914*, ed. L. H. Gann and Peter Duignan, vol. 1: *Colonialism in Africa 1870–1960*, Cambridge: Cambridge University Press, 387.

35. Ibid., 386; George P. Murdock, 1959, *Africa: Its Peoples and Their Culture History*, New York: McGraw-Hill, 370.

36. Wellington, *South West Africa*, 180–88.

37. Ibid., 196.

38. Ibid., 208.

39. Frank R. Cana, 1946, "German South-West Africa," *Encyclopedia Britannica*, vol. 10, 230–31; Cornevin, "Germans in Africa"; Wellington, *South West Africa*, 213.

40. Formosa Bureau of Aboriginal Affairs, 1911, *Report on the Control of the Aborigines of Formosa*, Taihoku.

41. Ibid., 16.

42. Ibid.

43. Ibid., 20.

44. Ibid., 35.

45. Ibid., 20.

46. Fred Korwa, 1983, "West Papua: The colonisation of West Papua," *IWGIA Newsletter* 35/36: 192–97; Bernard Nietschmann, 1985, "Indonesia, Bangladesh: Disguised invasion of indigenous nations," *Fourth World Journal* 1(2): 89–126 (reprinted in abridged form in Bodley, 1988a: 191–207).

47. George Collier, 1994. *Basta! Land and the Zapatista Rebellion in Chiapas*, Oakland, CA: Food First Books.

5   The Extension of Government Control

*The government of any race consists rather in implanting in them ideas
of right, of law and order, and making them obey such ideas.*

—Bronislaw Malinowski[1]

MILITARY FORCE BROUGHT GOVERNMENT CONTROL, which ended the lawless
frontier process and initiated the formal, orderly process of administration.
Such administration was designed to continue exploitation of indigenous peoples through legal means. It was a simple matter to assume political control
over decimated and defeated populations that faced no alternative but sub-
mission. Although governments did not hesitate to use armed force to crush
resistance, in some areas humanitarian concerns prompted the use of peaceful pacification techniques to subdue still-hostile or potentially uncooperative
groups.

By whatever means necessary, governments secured agreements and got
indigenous peoples to sign treaties that surrendered full and final authority for
their lives and that made them submissive wards of the state—whether or not
they understood what this meant. When large populations survived and when
it was in the interest of the state to maintain them with minimal disturbance,
governments devised various systems of indirect rule to ease the impact of
control. Successful rule ultimately depended on census data, elaborate
records, and administrative bureaucracy, but it also required accurate data on
local customs, which were provided by anthropologists working under direct
government supervision or with the support of national and international research institutions.

Aims and Philosophy of Administration

Official statements frequently justified the extension of government control
over tribal populations as an effort to bring them peace, health, happiness, and

other benefits of civilization, but undoubtedly the extension of government control was directly related to protecting the economic interests of non-indigenous peoples moving into formerly exclusive tribal areas. Considering the incompatibilities between the economic and social systems of small-scale and global cultures, it is clear that the small-scale cultures would have to give way and be transformed if the resources of their territories were to be efficiently exploited for the benefit of the world-market economy.

Governments could not allow the frontier process to continue indefinitely, even though it may have been extremely profitable for some individuals, because it was often destructive of local labor and other resources, and, as we have seen, it often led to expensive military campaigns. The maintenance of law and order became a critical concern. If settlers were to successfully acquire land and utilize local labor, the government had to provide security, because unrest and uprisings could quickly sweep away the settlers' economic gains. Economic development of the tribal population itself also became important in many areas, but this will be treated in chapter 8.

Tribal Peoples and National Unity

Many newly independent nations followed an active policy of exerting control over tribal areas in the professed interest of national unity. Economic considerations aside, government authorities see the existence of autonomous tribal populations within the boundaries of the state as a challenge to their authority and a possible invitation to aggression by foreign powers. This has been particularly true where, as is often the case in south Asia, tribal populations occupy remote border areas. Perhaps one of the principal reasons for the efforts of the Indian government to extend its control over the North East Frontier Agency (NEFA) was its proximity to its potential foe, the People's Republic of China, and the rising nationalism of the Naga. From the early days of India's independence in 1947, Prime Minister Jawaharlal Nehru warned other national leaders of the dangers of leaving a political vacuum along the frontier and strongly emphasized the need for full integration of India's tribal populations.

In the 1960s, Ian George Cunnison[2] noted the irritation of governments over the presence of tribal nomads in Asia and Africa, where they were regarded as a stigma, an affront to national pride. This was often the official view until recently. The main complaint was that the lifestyle of the nomad was incompatible with the aims of the state. Nomads do not go to school, cannot easily be reached by state medical services, and are "lawless"—but worst of all, they may regard tribal loyalties above national loyalties.

It remains common for governments to describe tribal peoples as national minorities and, as such, often to speak of them as obstacles to national unity and sources of instability. Newly independent nations have been eager to politically incorporate zones that former colonial governments had left relatively undisturbed, on the theory that such zones had been deliberately perpetuated in order to create division within the country.

In some respects, use of the terms *national minorities* or *ethnic minorities* undermines the legitimate claims of indigenous peoples to local autonomy. Calling a tribal group a "minority" requires an external reference point and needlessly implies inferiority and dependency. Many indigenous political activists, and some modern writers, such as geographer Bernard Nietschmann,[3] refer to tribal or indigenous peoples as "nations," emphasizing the original meaning of the term referring to common language, culture, and territory with an internal social organization. Nietschmann points out that most so-called nation-states are actually composed of many such "nations" that have been arbitrarily forced under the same government administration, often as a legacy of colonialism. Many conflicts around the world are related to efforts of these "ethnic" nations to reassert their independence. Furthermore, as large, composite national governments become increasingly unwieldy, both the desirability and the likelihood of their breaking down into more manageable constituent units increase.[4]

The Transfer of Sovereignty

Most nations throughout the modern period, and indeed many authorities on international law since the beginning of colonial expansion in the sixteenth century, have acknowledged tribal societies as small, independent sovereignties and have recognized that in order to legally govern them, tribal sovereignty would need to be transferred to the state either by conquest or by treaty. Many early Spanish publicists and theologians, such as Franciscus Victoria, Dominic Soto, Bartolomé de Las Casas, and Baltasar Ayala, stressed that non-Christian peoples constituted sovereign "nations." These writers challenged both the validity of European claims to sovereignty based solely on "discovery" and the justice of rights based on conquest. They generally agreed that non-Christian lands were not empty and, therefore, that they were not open to acquisition by Europeans.

Even after the Industrial Revolution had begun and the modern period of colonial expansion was under way, the prevalent opinion among legal authorities continued to recognize the sovereign rights of all peoples living in organized societies, regardless of their level of "civilization." In the nineteenth century this opinion was supported by the French publicists M. P. Pradier-Fodéré, Charles Salomon, Henry Bonfils, and Gaston Jèze; the Italian Pasquale Fiore; and the German August Hefter.

As colonial expansion began to reach a peak in the late nineteenth century, however, important modifications of this position began. By an act of Congress in 1871, the United States declared, contrary to some 350 years of international legal opinion, that it would no longer make treaties with Indian tribes as if they constituted sovereign nations. The French annulled by decree all sovereign rights of traditional rulers in French Equatorial and French West Africa in 1899 and 1904, respectively. Legal authorities quickly fell in line. In 1876 the American lawyer Dudley Field (who helped found the International Law Association in 1873) argued that tribal lands could be acquired by direct occupation. In 1914 the British lawyer John Westlake opined that territorial claims could be recognized only in states that were organized strongly enough to protect the interests of white settlers. In the 1920s other authorities on international law, such as L. Oppenheim and T. J. Lawrence, asserted that tribal societies were not developed sufficiently to be considered sovereign entities and that these territories were therefore outside the family of nations, where they could be legally claimed by any foreign power. In 1889 an Australian legal decision declared Australia to have been *terra nullius*—unoccupied waste territory, legally free for the taking—when it was annexed by Britain in 1788. This approach eliminated the costly inconvenience of paying land claims to dispossessed Aborigines and has also been the implicit policy of many Latin American nations expanding into Indian territory.

The Institute of International Law, meeting in Lausanne, Switzerland, in 1888, rejected the notion that the rights of independent tribes could legally be ignored. It also condemned wars of extermination against tribal peoples, useless severities, and tortures. In spite of these views, it declared that the legal transfer of sovereignty could be carried out by simply extending government control over a region.[5] There was certainly no question at the time of the morality of the procedure as a whole, aside from the details of how it is conducted, and this declaration suited perfectly the needs of colonial administrators.

Treaty Making

> Treaties with aboriginal tribes . . . are made for the purpose of arranging the terms of the guardianship to be exercised over the tribe.[6]

Treaty making as the first step in extending government control was carried out widely in North America and Africa as the frontiers of settlement were extended. Representatives of the governments involved merely located individuals who were assumed to be tribal leaders and obtained their marks on official documents transferring tribal sovereignty to the state and at times also extinguishing their claims to the land. An example of the sweeping powers governments assumed over tribal populations on the basis of such agreements is represented by the following treaty of 1884 between various Bechuanaland (now Botswana) chiefs and the British: "I give the queen to rule my country over white men and black men; I give her to publish laws and to change them . . . to appoint judges . . . and police . . . to arrest criminals . . . to hold them as prisoners . . . to collect money (taxes) . . . to impose fines."[7]

In the terms of the treaty of Waitangi in New Zealand in 1840, an assembly of chiefs ceded "absolutely, and without reservation, all the rights and powers of sovereignty . . . over their respective territories" to the British Crown. German treaties were, if anything, more inclusive: They could involve the transfer of a tribal people's rights to "have their own laws and administration, the right to levy customs and taxes, the right to maintain an armed force," and "all the rights" that Europeans recognize in a sovereign prince.[8] In several areas, the right to make such treaties was delegated by the government to special chartered companies. In Rhodesia (now Zimbabwe), the British South Africa Company, under Cecil Rhodes, obtained an open-ended royal charter from Britain in 1888 that, like sixteenth-century Spanish charters, allowed the company "to acquire by any concession agreement grants or treaty all of any rights interests authorities jurisdictions and powers of any kind or nature whatever, including powers necessary for the purposes of Government and the preservation of public order."[9]

Treaty making often concluded military campaigns as part of a formal surrender ceremony, but even under peaceful conditions, the threat of force was always in the background. It was also not unusual for lavish gifts to be presented to the signing tribal dignitaries, often accompanied by promises of new authority and special privileges to be accorded by the government. It appears that in signing these agreements many tribal leaders either acted largely in their own immediate self-interest or did not really understand the terms and full implications of the treaty and felt themselves under duress. Sometimes tribal leaders recognized the threat to their political independence that such treaties constituted but were unable to resist them. When the Germans approached a Hottentot leader in Southwest Africa in the 1880s with a request that he accept German protection, the leader demanded to know what protection was and from what they were to be protected. He was promised continued jurisdiction over his people if he accepted protection, but he quickly recognized the inconsistency and pointed out that "everyone under protection is a subject of the one who protects him."[10]

Bringing Government to the Tribes

Treaty signing was just a first step in establishing government authority, often intended merely to legitimize sovereign claims to much larger areas. However, regardless of the dominion established over them on paper, tribal peoples remained autonomous until the government physically established contact with them and initiated their political integration into the national polity by:

- Appointing political authorities over them
- Imposing the state's legal-judicial system, including police and imprisonment
- Levying and collecting taxes
- Instituting military recruitment
- Collecting census data
- Extending the national educational system and health services

The methods followed by states to initially break down tribal resistance in order to bring these national institutions to the tribes varied considerably in different parts of the world. But in general, they were well-organized large-scale programs based on the assumption that loyalties were to be developed and tribal hostilities were to be overcome by peaceful means. These efforts thus differed sharply from earlier attempts to overcome resistance by the use of overwhelming military force in raids and wars and could be correctly characterized as peaceful pacification. The new emphasis was on the material benefits that the tribes could gain from cooperation with the government, and gift giving was often a prominent part of the procedure of extending government control. Although the present chapter stresses the role of governments in reducing tribal political independence, it should be noted that tribal peoples themselves have sometimes taken the initiative in establishing peace with governments when they saw it as beneficial to them. The presence of government agents may be used to end intertribal feuding.[11] Perhaps we can best visualize the pacification process by examining several specific examples from various parts of the world.

The Base Camp System in New Guinea

> Soon all villages in Australian New Guinea will have been formally brought under control of the Administration; most of them, in their turn, unwillingly, and resisting what must be, no matter how it is glossed over, an act of conquest.[12]

When the civil administration was established in Australia's Mandated Territory of New Guinea in 1921, a vigorous program for exploration and the peaceful extension of government control was immediately initiated. Material inducements were especially prominent in this procedure, and an important factor in the urgency of the program was the need for supplying the growing demand for laborers on the European copra plantations on the coast. At this time the territory was divided into areas, according to the degree of government influence, to help determine which areas had received the least attention and to map progress as it was achieved. These categories are summarized in the following manner by G. Townsend;[13] they reflect the various degrees of influence and illustrate effectively how control was measured.

1. Complete government control: An area in which an unarmed native policeman could make an arrest and count on the assistance of local villagers.
2. Partial government control: An area in which arrests could be made, but where the local villagers would not necessarily assist.
3. Government influence: An area in which arrests would not be actively resisted and where European lives and property would be safe.
4. Area penetrated by patrols: An area in which "proper contact" still had not been established but where indigenous people offered no opposition.
5. Unknown area.

At the discretion of the government, various areas were declared "uncontrolled areas," and the entry of unauthorized individuals was strictly forbidden in order to prevent the usual frontier difficulties from disturbing the orderly process of peaceful penetration.

To extend control into the latter two categories, the government developed the base camp system. In this system, an armed patrol, well stocked with trade goods and headed by a European patrol officer with perhaps a dozen native police, established a base camp in an area already under government influence. The patrol carefully selected the camp site in order not to indicate special alliance with any particular village, which might have been interpreted as an indication of hostility by neighboring villagers. While the patrol remained in this base camp, various highly prized trade goods, such as steel tools, salt, and cloth, were offered in exchange for food, thus establishing contact with many of the villagers in the surrounding area. At this point the patrol moved out to visit these villages for the first time and requested that the villagers build a rest house to make longer visits possible for the patrol. Townsend indicates that the villagers were not always eager to fulfill this request because they "loathe interference in domestic affairs," but they were usually convinced through the services of an interpreter. When the rest house was completed, the patrol visited for perhaps several days and planted fruit trees for the use of future patrols.

The presence of a government camp distributing valuables in the partially controlled area would eventually attract visitors from the "unknown" areas, who might have arrived fully armed to receive their gifts and then might have departed quickly. They would return, however, and would finally invite the patrol officers to visit their own village to distribute gifts to them directly. The officers would agree to do so on condition that the villagers build a road for them. When the officers visited the new village, they distributed gifts to the villagers and explained (through interpreters) the government's objectives, stressing the material rewards of "belonging to the government." A few months later a feast would be conducted for all of the tribes in the area at government expense, as further proof of goodwill. Peace agreements were negotiated between hostile native groups, and carefully selected native police were brought in to live at strategic points throughout the new area to help enforce the peace and to act as unobtrusive teachers. As soon as possible, *luluais*, or village chiefs, were appointed to serve as intermediaries between the government and the village. Each chief was presented with a red-banded, blue-peaked cap as a badge of honor and a village book that would eventually be filled with census data. Often the chief was assisted by an interpreter-assistant known as a *tultul*, who would be taken to the coast and given several months of training and who might also have served as a medical orderly in the village.

An average base-camp patrol operation lasted about three months and was normally a peaceful, successful procedure. Patrols were under orders not to use firearms except in self-defense, but occasionally trouble broke out and sometimes officers were killed while attempting to arrest participants in inter-tribal fighting. After friendly contact was established and *luluais* and *tultuls* were installed, a patrol officer made annual inspection tours. However, the real measure of successful penetration occurred when the labor recruiters were allowed to operate freely. As Townsend explained: "It is not long before European recruiters of labour work through, and in the next few years each village has members who have worked for white men, and are strong advocates of the white man's Government."[14]

Patrols experienced difficulties in New Guinea when pacifying the head-hunting Sepik River district during the 1920s. In 1924, four European officers and a detachment of thirty police established themselves near the halfway point along the eight-hundred-kilometer river with a twelve-ton patrol boat and began sending out heavily armed patrols. The first patrol to be attacked responded with rifle fire, and thereafter the tribal population resorted to passive resistance. Villagers informed the officers that they had no intention of following their orders and often simply deserted their villages when the patrol boat was sighted. To cope with this problem the officers kidnapped the old men left behind in the deserted villages and housed them in pacified enemy villages near headquarters until they agreed to arrange for communication with the resisters. Within eighteen months, four hundred kilometers of river inhabited by some ten thousand people was declared safe to travel, but "ingrained hostility" still existed. Two years after the establishment of district headquarters, the district officer called a meeting of two hundred men to gain their approval for the government's acquisition of a plot of tribal land to be leased to a mission station. The brief meeting ended when one man made the following statement and everyone filed out: "Several days' journey up the river there is a white man, the District Officer. Several days' journey downstream there is a white man, the missionary. That makes two. Two too many."[15]

The last reported headhunting raid in the Sepik River district occurred in 1927, but the government arrested those involved, hung seven, and imprisoned the rest. The Mokolkol people in New Britain probably were the most difficult case of resistance to pacification efforts anywhere in New Guinea. According to David Fenbury's[16] account, the Mokolkol were a small group of forest nomads who refused trade or any form of peaceful contact with outsiders and occasionally raided their neighbors to obtain steel tools. They occupied a small tract of mountain forest within just eighty air kilometers of Rabaul, the district capital, and were a constant source of embarrassment to the administration. In 1931, a patrol officer approached a Mokolkol village with his police, distributed his "gifts," and sat down to wait for the villagers to receive them. The Mokolkol ran out, grabbed the gifts, and disappeared— only to return four days later to attack the patiently waiting patrol. With this reception, the defeated patrol returned to the coast with two dead and four wounded. Two years later another officer was sent in, but this time with rolls of barbed wire and orders to construct a compound and lock up any "wild men" that he could capture. The Mokolkol played hide-and-seek with the patrol, which was able to capture only four children and three elderly men and women. These captives were taken to Rabaul, but the adults failed to adjust to their new surroundings and soon died. Finally, in 1950, a patrol of fifty-four men stealthily surrounded a village of twenty-seven people that had been located by aerial reconnaissance and rushed in, handcuffing captives. This time two men, one woman, and four children were arrested and taken to Rabaul, where they were successfully indoctrinated in the advantages of cooperation with the government of the Territory of New Guinea.

Throughout Australian New Guinea the process of peaceful penetration continued relentlessly from the 1920s until the granting of independence to Papua New Guinea in 1975, except for an unavoidable pause during World War II. By 1950 some 168,350 square kilometers of territory was not yet fully controlled, but by 1970 only 1,735 square kilometers remained in that category.[17]

Peaceful Pacification in Brazil

The techniques of government penetration used so effectively in New Guinea were first developed in Brazil by Candido Mariano da Silva Rondon, founder of the Indian Protection Service. Officials of the Indian Protection Service worked under the strict motto "Die if necessary but never kill," and during given pacification efforts, perhaps lasting months or even years, they were not allowed to shoot Indians even in self-defense. The usual procedure called for a small team to enter hostile Indian territory and build a house and compound at a strategic location, placing gifts in conspicuous places in hopes of establishing a silent barter system with the indigenous people of the region. In many cases the Indians promptly attacked the team's base, but the house was well shielded with sheet metal, and the Indians' arrows usually had little effect. If the Indians approached too closely, the team was permitted to shoot over their heads to scare them away. Eventually the Indians would decide that the team intended no harm, and direct contact would take place. Pacification was usually followed by resettlement, schooling, and perhaps other forms of supervision by officials at Indian "posts."

In 1967 the Indian Protection Service was reorganized as the National Foundation for the Indian (FUNAI) after disclosure that many of its officials had been involved with wealthy investors in efforts to exterminate tribes that were impeding the development of tribal lands by outsiders. FUNAI continued the pacification techniques developed by the Indian Protection Service and applied them to relocate numerous groups that were in the pathway of highway construction, agricultural efforts, and mineral development in the Brazilian rainforest throughout the 1970s and 1980s. For example, FUNAI used steel axes and knives as gifts to attract and "pacify" the Urueu-Wau-Wau in Rondônia (then a federal territory on the border with Bolivia) in the 1980s.[18]

Unfortunately, in spite of the obvious humanitarian concerns of many of the former Indian Protection Service officials and more recent FUNAI workers, pacification has often had a disastrous impact on tribes that proved unable to adjust to their changed cultural environments.

In other areas of South America, such as Peru and Ecuador, the Summer Institute of Linguistics, a well-organized and equipped group of missionary-linguists, established initial contacts with many isolated and potentially hostile groups in basically the same manner, except that they have been able to make widespread use of airplanes.

Soviet Reconstruction: Red Tents and Red Boats

The tribal peoples of Russia's Far East in Siberia were left virtually undisturbed by the government, and many groups, such as the Chukchi, had no idea that they were part of Russia until rivalry with Americans in nearby Alaska began developing around 1900 and focused special attention on the area. However, an effective policy toward the political incorporation of these peoples did not begin until after the Russian Revolution in 1917, when the new government discovered that the tribal peoples were living outside the Soviet Constitution and were in need of "extreme measures for their salvation" and of "rapid inclusion within the sphere of Soviet authority."[19] In 1924 a special agency called the Committee for Assistance to the Peoples of the Northern Regions (the "Committee of the North") was assigned the task of bringing the tribal peoples into the Soviet system.

The scattered nature of the tribal population and their nomadic habits constantly frustrated efforts at political reorganization. Mobile red tents carried by reindeer or by boats ("red boats") attempted to follow the nomads and offer them political indoctrination, cultural programs, medicine, and education. By special decrees, the tribal populations were exempted from particularly bothersome duties of citizenship, such as payment of taxes, military recruitment, and work levies. "Capitalist" traders were thrown out, and the government became the sole supplier of desirable trade goods. An offensive was launched against traditional tribal leaders who resisted the new program, and they were ousted, to be replaced by clan assemblies. The ultimate aim was the elimination of nomadism and the concentration of the tribal population in settlements for easier administration. Resettlement programs were developed to expedite this end, and thousands of non-native immigrants were brought in concurrently. Stationary "cultural bases," equipped with hospital and veterinary facilities, boarding schools, radios and movie projectors, and model workshops, were established in the most remote areas as inducements to facilitate the resettlement plan.

Tribal "Action Programs" in Southeast Asia

For thousands of years tribal peoples have occupied the hilly interior uplands of Southeast Asia, where they apparently maintained a balance with their environment and a successful symbiosis with the various civilizations on the lowland plains. Although trade and cultural diffusion occurred between the tribal populations and the civilizations surrounding them, the tribes retained their basic autonomy. This tribal independence was possible because the lowland civilizations were ecologically adapted to their own environment and were interested in maintaining the hill tribes as effective buffer zones separating them from neighboring states. Beginning in the 1960s, world political considerations suddenly made the "loyalty" of the hill peoples a matter of major concern for the governments claiming ultimate sovereignty over them, and a variety of programs were devised to win their support peacefully.

Consider, for example, Thailand's hill tribes, which may number some two hundred thousand people. These tribal peoples were not even counted in the nation's 1960 census, and there was no clear government policy on whether they were to be considered citizens.[20] With the rise of antigovernment guerrilla activities, however, Thailand became very interested in the tribal peoples, and by 1967 numerous government agencies were showing a sudden new interest, often developing special programs for them. These organizations included the Provincial Police, the Border Patrol Police, the Ministry of Education, the Ministry of Health, the Ministry of Defense, the Department of Forestry, and the Hill Tribes Division of the Department of Public Health, with its Hill Tribes Research Center and other programs. Considerable international involvement also began in direct support of these national efforts. This included the United States Information Service, the United States Operations Mission, the United States Department of Defense, the Southeast Asia Treaty Organization, UNESCO, the World Health Organization, the Asia Foundation, and at least eleven Protestant missionary organizations and several Roman Catholic orders.

The general intent and organization of these various programs closely parallel the Soviet policy toward Siberian peoples described previously, where the emphasis was on political indoctrination, supported by the rapid provision of bountiful material rewards. Specifically, Thailand's Border Patrol Police Program and the Defense Ministry's Mobile Development Program offer striking parallels to Soviet Red Tent and Culture Base programs. The usual procedure for the border patrol police in carrying out their mission of befriending the hill tribes was to send patrols into the hills in order to persuade the tribal people to build airstrips in exchange for gifts of food, tools, and medical aid. The airstrips were then used to fly in other medical aid and technical assistance. During these visits the people were told "informally" about the national government, and photographs of Thailand's king and queen and the "emerald Buddha," a symbol of the national religion, were distributed. In 1964 the Border Patrol Police removed approximately one hundred young tribal leaders from some forty villages to a district town for technical training and political indoctrination. They were then sent back to their villages as instructors.

The Mobile Development Program also distributed thousands of photographs of the king and queen and the emerald Buddha, but went a major step further with the establishment of model villages in the remote areas of Thailand. Model villages were equipped with schools, TV sets, playgrounds, streetlights, running water, toilets, and medical facilities, and were perhaps even more elaborate than the Soviet culture bases. Critics who suggested that such a lifestyle was inappropriate within the hill tribe context, and that promoting such standards of material consumption might in the long run have a disastrous impact on the people, their culture, and their environments, are answered by Lee W. Huff as follows: "We must also be careful not to underestimate the villager's capacity to change his way of life. Arguments that he does not need, does not want, and cannot get TV, electric power, machinery, and other luxuries may turn out to be shortsighted, in which case the MDUs' [mobile development units] instinct in establishing and supporting the model village concept will look somewhat better in retrospect."[21]

The Political Integration Process

The extension of government control marks a highly significant event in the history of any tribal society, because it means that at this point the society ceases being a politically autonomous "little sovereignty"; it ceases being an autonomous *tribe*, as the term is used here. Upon their official incorporation into the state, tribal peoples must conform to and become integrated with the social and political institutions characteristic of state organization. The tribe is no longer fully responsible for settling disputes and maintaining internal order, and has limitations placed upon its political decision-making processes. At the same time, a new set of problems is created by the need to formally define the relationship between the tribal population and the state government, and with nontribal individuals who now have special interests in the tribal area and its resources.

There has been wide variation in different independent countries and colonial administrations in the extent to which political and legal powers have been delegated to or withheld from tribal peoples. At one extreme is the so-called direct rule system, in which all authority is held by outsiders, whereas at the other extreme is the creation of a political bureaucracy incorporating tribal individuals and extending down to the village level. Many variations on the theme of indirect rule lie between these two extremes, but regardless of which political integration strategy is followed, the result is always profound transformation of traditional tribal organization.

French Direct Rule

According to French colonial theory, control was to be imposed as rapidly as possible over indigenous populations, with virtually no allowances made for incompatibilities between the local sociopolitical organization and the French model. Local officials or canton chiefs were, of course, utilized, because it would have been impossible in many areas to have placed French administrators in every local village (in Africa in the 1920s, 12,500 Europeans controlled more than 15 million indigenous people), but these officials were considered to be government employees, not representatives of traditional cultures.

René Maunier, a member of the French Academy of Colonial Sciences, argued that, in the interests of utility, convenience, prosperity, and justice, it was necessary for the French to abolish the rights of traditional leaders and tribal councils and to replace them eventually with French administrators and French courts, presided over by Frenchmen. In many cases, French authorities denied the legal existence of any tribal social unit above the family. It was felt that in this way the tribe could be remade "to accommodate it to new needs."[22] Direct rule seems to have been a deliberate and well-planned policy, reflecting a fundamental belief in French superiority.

Chiefs appointed by the French in tropical Africa were responsible for the collection of taxes, the requisition of forced corvée labor, forced crop cultivation, military recruitment, the provision of support for visiting dignitaries, and the maintenance of an armed police force. They themselves were subject to imprisonment and corporal punishment for failure to carry out these duties, and, to complicate their situation, often their authority was not recognized by the villagers. Needless to say, this placed these puppet chiefs in extremely uncomfortable positions and led to many abuses.

Under direct rule in French tropical Africa, two legal systems operated side by side. French law and the French court applied to all cases involving indigenous people and Europeans. The *indigenat* system, or indigenous justice, applied to all cases involving only tribal people. In this system at the village level, the canton chief was for a time allowed to judge minor cases and impose fines of up to five days in prison. But in 1912 the chief could no longer impose any fines and could only mediate disputes, and by 1924 full authority was entrusted to Europeans. French administrators operated with full discretionary powers to investigate, arrest, judge, and execute the sentence, and there was no practical means to appeal their decisions. Infractions were defined by the administrator's interpretation of customary law and by decree and included such crimes as "[a]ny disrespectful act or offensive proposal vis-à-vis a representative or agent of authority" or songs, rumors, or speeches "intended to weaken respect for French authority."[23]

French-style direct rule was widely condemned by other colonial authorities, who claimed that it was too harsh on local customs, involved too much government, was too inconsistent and unstable, and, more specifically, deliberately refused to work through the political organization of indigenous peoples.[24]

Indirect Rule

By the 1920s and 1930s, indirect rule came to be widely accepted as the only valid approach to local administration, although as an administrative structure it was often difficult to distinguish from direct rule on more than theoretical grounds. The method was pioneered and developed as both a practical working system and a philosophy by Lord Frederick Lugard during his service as high commissioner among the Islamic rulers of northern Nigeria between 1900 and 1907, and it was propagated through his book *The Dual Mandate in British Tropical Africa*, first published in 1922.[25] Indirect rule involved maintaining and strengthening the rule of traditional local leaders and creating them where they did not exist. Tribes, tribal councils, clans, and villages were generally recognized as legal entities; native courts presided over by indigenous people were encouraged, but with specific limits on their authority. In Lugard's view,[26] one of the primary purposes of indirect rule was the need to prevent the total breakdown of native society and the collapse of all social order, which was being initiated by the arrival of Europeans and would certainly be accelerated by the abuses unavoidably associated with arbitrary direct rule. The demands for recognition of indigenous rights being made by anti-imperialists and humanitarian organizations, such as the Aborigines Protection Society and the Congo Reform Movement, combined with the obvious failures of French direct rule, were probably influential in fostering the acceptance of indirect rule, but practical considerations were undoubtedly paramount.

"Growth from within" was one of the key philosophical concepts behind indirect rule. It was assumed that tribal peoples would thereby be allowed to develop along their own lines, but precisely what this meant was never defined as long as the colonial system remained in place.

More cynical anthropologists, such as George H. Pitt-Rivers,[27] called indirect rule "direct rule by indirect means," and argued that the only difference between the two forms of rule was that direct rule achieved the goal more rapidly and that in the long run detribalization and deculturation occurred either way. Indeed, there is considerable evidence to suggest that indirect rule was designed to preserve tribal political institutions only to the extent necessary to maintain order and to ensure the availability of local labor. In areas where tribal populations were numerically insignificant, indirect rule was usually dispensed with in favor of more efficient or rapid methods. Indirect rule was clearly intended to involve the adaptation of the traditional political system to the political and economic requirements of the state, but this transformation was to be carefully directed.

The system of local administration in preindependence Kenya, as described by M. R. Dilley,[28] is a typical example of indirect rule in operation. In Kenya Colony, according to the guidelines of the Native Authority Ordinance of 1912, authority over the native population at the local level was vested in headmen or councils of elders who were selected by the local people subject to the recommendations of the white district commissioner and the final approval of the governor. Headmen were salaried and were given wide powers to maintain order and see that government regulations were carried out in the local area. In addition to the headmen, native councils existed in each district (sometimes paralleling European-run district councils) composed of native people appointed and presided over by the district commissioner, but with considerable authority to pass resolutions and levy taxes. In addition, native tribunals or courts existed, which in 1932 under the supervision of the administration handled about twenty-five thousand civil cases and seven thousand criminal cases. There were also tribal police at the provincial level.

Systems similar to this were applied by the British throughout Africa. In India, the tribal peoples of the North East Frontier Agency were allowed to form tribal councils that also served as courts with broad powers. Australian New Guinea operated with the headmen, or *luluais*, until 1950 when local government councils were established.

In many areas indirect rule was eventually ended by "independence" in which a native elite, educated by the former colonial rulers, took over the state bureaucratic structure and local appointed headmen were abolished or their jobs became elected positions and dual (native/white) forms of local government were abolished in favor of a single administrative hierarchy.

The Protective Legislation Approach

In the case of tribal peoples who were greatly outnumbered by invading populations and were not themselves useful as sources of labor (such as in lowland South America, North America, and Australia), local administration tended to take the form of a welfare operation. After their traditional cultural autonomy had been destroyed by conquest, or in some cases by treaty, these peoples were treated as incompetent and impoverished citizens to be sheltered in special institutions and managed by special legislation. Canada, for example, provided for the gradual development of some degree of self-government for reservation Indians in its Indian Act of 1869, but the United States did not allow any significant political activity among its Indian population until the Indian Reorganization Act of 1934, which permitted tribal councils. In lowland South America before the formation of truly indigenous political organizations beginning in the 1970s, isolated Indian populations were sometimes technically subject to special protective legislation, and there may be official state organizations, such as Colombia's commissions for Indian protection and welfare, Brazil's National Foundation for the Indian, and Venezuela's National Indigenist Commission—all in principle designed to look after Indian welfare—but there was little deliberate effort to preserve any semblance of traditional sociopolitical structure.

In British India there was a long tradition of protective legislation for tribal peoples in combination with a form of indirect rule. As early as 1855, the Santal Parganas District was declared a nonregulation area, making the general laws of the country inapplicable to it, and it was administered directly by special commissioners with full judicial authority. This approach was extended to other Indian tribal areas by the Scheduled Districts Act of 1874 and the backward tract provisions of the Government of India Act of 1919. Scheduled tribes and tribal areas were designated in the 1950 constitution of independent India, and tribal advisory councils were established under the supervision of the local governors, who could suspend any state laws at their discretion.[29]

Suspension of normal state laws or the creation of extraordinary political arrangements were everywhere viewed as only temporary measures to allow tribal peoples time to gain familiarity and competence with the normal political-legal structures of the state. In many countries, few, if any, boundaries were maintained between the dominant society and the tribal population. In these cases, tribal populations participate in normal state political processes at least theoretically on an equal basis with any other citizen, and there is relatively little in the way of special protective legislation or distinctive administrative structures. This seems to be the approach of many independent African, Asian, and Pacific nations.

An exception to this general pattern is represented by the Soviet Union, which in 1926 began forming national *rayons*, or territorial political units ostensibly representing national minorities. At the lower levels, the *rayons* were composed of clan assemblies and councils patterned after rural soviets, which were councils of delegates organized by workers and soldiers during the revolution. The national *rayons* included clan federations and native executive councils and congresses. This policy of recognizing nationalities or ethnic groups was merely an efficient way of following the larger national policy of helping tribal peoples "develop and consolidate Soviet state structure among themselves in the forms corresponding to the national ways of life of the peoples" and was to be a "gradual transition to the normal territorial system of Soviets."[30] After the disintegration of the Soviet Union 1991, Siberian indigenous peoples began forming their own political organizations. Like the Soviet Union, the People's Republic of China made a similar effort to recognize the existence of national minorities by designating autonomous regions that were to be integral parts of the nation but that enjoyed considerable self-government subject to the approval of the National People's Congress.[31]

Anthropology and Native Administration

Representatives of government have seldom questioned the value of ethnological data for purposes of administration. In modern times practically every nation with expanding frontiers has supported inquiries into the customs of native

peoples in areas of projected or accomplished occupation. . . . Colonization programs, if they have not been dedicated to the destruction of indigenous populations, have necessitated a knowledge of local customs.[32]

Throughout most of the nineteenth century and before indirect rule and other
administrative refinements became widely institutionalized, governments felt
little need to acquire specialized knowledge of the cultures that were being
transformed and eradicated. Gradually, however, it became apparent that such
knowledge could make the task of administration and transformation much
more efficient and effective and that it might even prevent tribal uprisings.
Missionaries and administrators lacked the necessary training, were too busy
with other duties, and were too biased by their roles to obtain reliable scientific data on tribal culture. The assistance of anthropologists was needed.

The United States led the way in 1879 by organizing the Bureau of American Ethnology, which, as its first director, J. W. Powell, explained in his first
annual report, endeavored to produce results of "practical value in the administration of Indian affairs."[33] From about 1890 on, British colonial administrators became increasingly interested in anthropological research.
Many gained some anthropological training at the universities of Oxford and
Cambridge and went on to publish significant monographs. In 1926 the International African Institute was founded with the primary purpose of relating scientific research to the "practical tasks" that were facing Europeans who
were working for the "good" of Africa.[34] Support for this institute came from
virtually all of the major colonial powers, including Great Britain, France,
Belgium, Italy, South Africa, Germany, and the United States, but a great deal
of the research effort of the institute was conducted by British social anthropologists in British colonies. Since the 1920s numerous national and international institutes supported anthropological research in relation to the administration of indigenous groups. Examples of the latter include the South
Pacific Commission, founded in 1948, and the Inter-American Indian Institute, founded in 1940. In addition, many national research institutes have
been founded. Most independent former colonies have also actively supported administration-related anthropological research.[35]

In general, colonial government administrators received the most support
from anthropologists in such areas as sociopolitical organization, law and judicial processes, land tenure, and the general problem of economic development. British anthropologists were ardent supporters of indirect rule, which,
according to Bronislaw Malinowski, was considered by all competent anthropologists to be "infinitely preferable" to direct rule.[36] They also stressed
the functional interrelatedness of culture in their research so that administrators could best evaluate the impact of their policies.[37] Prominent British func-
tionalists such as Bronislaw Malinowski and A. Radcliffe-Brown helped es-

tablish anthropology departments and special training programs for colonial administrators in South Africa and Australia. During their association with colonial governments, anthropologists generally assumed a neutral position in their work and limited themselves to providing data while avoiding direct involvement in policy making. The political implications of applied anthropology in relation to tribal peoples will be discussed further in chapter 12.

Notes

1. Bronislaw Malinowski, 1929, "Practical anthropology," *Africa* 2(l): 22–38.
2. Ian George Cunnison, 1967, *Nomads in the Nineteen-Sixties*, Hull, UK: Hull University.
3. Bernard Nietschmann, 1985, "Indonesia, Bangladesh: Disguised invasion of indigenous nations," *Fourth World Journal* 1(2): 89–126 (reprinted in abridged form in Bodley, 1988a: 191–207).
4. Leopold Kohr, 1978, *The Breakdown of Nations.* New York: Dutton.
5. Alpheus Henry Snow, 1921, *The Question of Aborigines: In the Law and Practice of Nations*, New York: Putnam, 173–201.
6. Ibid., 207–208.
7. M. F. Lindley, 1926, *The Acquisition and Government of Backward Territory in International Law*, London: Longman, Green, 36.
8. Ibid., 38–39.
9. John H. Wellington, 1967, *South West Africa and Its Human Issues*, Oxford: Clarendon Press/Oxford University Press, 241–42.
10. Ibid., 177.
11. For example, see several cases from Melanesia in Margaret Rodman and Matthew Cooper, eds., 1979, *The Pacification of Melanesia*, Association for Social Anthropology in Oceania Monograph no. 7, Ann Arbor: University of Michigan Press.
12. Charles D. Rowley, 1966, *The New Guinea Villager: The Impact of Colonial Rule on Primitive Society and Economy*, New York: Praeger, 63.
13. G. Townsend, 1933, "The administration of the mandated territory of New Guinea," *Geographical Journal* 82: 424.
14. Ibid., 428.
15. Ibid., 431.
16. David Fenbury, 1968, "Those Mokolkols!: New Britain's bloody axemen," *New Guinea* 3(2): 33–50.
17. Ian Grosart, 1972, "Direct administration," in *Encyclopedia of Papua and New Guinea*, ed. Peter Ryan, vol. 1, 266–269. Melbourne: Melbourne University Press.
18. Loren McIntyre, 1988, "Last days of Eden: Rondônia's Urueu-Wau-Wau Indians," *National Geographic* 174(6): 800–17.
19. M. G. Levin and L. P. Potapov, 1964, *The Peoples of Siberia*, Chicago: University of Chicago Press, 490.

20. Peter Kunstadter, ed., 1967, *Southeast Asian Tribes, Minorities, and Nations*, Princeton, NJ: Princeton University Press, 20, 375.

21. Lee W. Huff, 1967, "The Thai Mobile Development Unit Program," in *Southeast Asian Tribes, Minorities, and Nations*, ed. Peter Kunstadter, Princeton, NJ: Princeton University Press, 463.

22. René Maunier, 1949, *The Sociology of Colonies*, vol. 2, London: Routledge and Kegan Paul, 568–69.

23. Jean Suret-Canale, 1971, *French Colonialism in Tropical Africa, 1900–1945*, New York: Pica Press, 331–36.

24. Stephen Henry Roberts, 1969, *Population Problems of the Pacific*, New York: AMS Press, 149–51.

25. Sir F. D. Lugard, 1965, *The Dual Mandate in British Tropical Africa*, London: Frank Cass.

26. Ibid., 214–18.

27. George H. Pitt-Rivers, 1927, *The Clash of Culture and the Contact of Races*, London: George Routledge and Sons, 276–77.

28. M. R. Dilley, 1966, *British Policy in Kenya Colony*, New York: Barnes and Noble, 26–30.

29. Verrier Elwin, 1969, *The Nagas in the Nineteenth Century*, London: Oxford University Press; G. S. Ghurye, 1963, *The Scheduled Tribes*, 3rd ed, Bombay: G. R. Bhatkal.

30. Levin and Potapov, *Peoples of Siberia*, 492.

31. Richard K. Diao, 1967, "The national minorities of China and their relations with the Chinese Communist regime," in *Southeast Asian Tribes, Minorities, and Nations*, ed. Peter Kunstadter, Princeton, NJ: Princeton University Press, 171–73.

32. Homer G. Barnett, 1956, *Anthropology in Administration*, New York: Row, Peterson, 2.

33. J. W. Powell, 1881, *First Annual Report of the Bureau of Ethnology to the Secretary of the Smithsonian Institution 1879–1880*, Washington, DC: Government Printing Office, xiv.

34. Lugard, *Dual Mandate*.

35. Barnett, *Anthropology in Administration*; David Brokensha, 1966, *Applied Anthropology in English-Speaking Africa*, Society for Applied Anthropology, Monograph no. 8; Daryll Forde, 1953, "Applied anthropology in government: British Africa," in *Anthropology Today*, ed. A. L. Kroeber, 841–65. Chicago: University of Chicago Press.

36. Malinowski, "Practical anthropology," 23.

37. Robert Manners, 1956, "Functionalism, realpolitik, and anthropology in underdeveloped areas," *America Indigena* 16(1): 7–33.

6 Land Policies

The land, of course, must be transferred from the hands of the Natives to those of the Whites. . . . So the Natives must give way and either become servants of the Whites or withdraw to the reserves allotted to them.

—John H. Wellington[1]

PERHAPS THE MOST CRITICAL government policies to affect self-sufficient tribal peoples were those relating to their possession of the land. Any modification of the traditional people-land relationship would undoubtedly have a major impact on all aspects of small-scale society. As soon as government control was firmly established and the administrative structures were in operation, officials turned their attention to the problem of defining tribal land rights in order to maximize economic productivity. Although considerable variation existed in different countries, the general effect of the land policies imposed by governments was reduction of the territory available to indigenous populations and modification of their traditional systems of tenure in favor of state-controlled systems. In turn, these results made tribal economic systems and related social and ideological patterns difficult, if not impossible, to maintain. None of these changes was due to mere "contact" and simple diffusion, but rather to deliberate state policy. These policies will be examined in this chapter, but to better appreciate their effects is it necessary to first understand the system of land tenure of small-scale self-sufficient cultures and how those systems contrast with commercial, market-based systems.

The People–Land Relationship

In self-sufficient small-scale cultures, access to land is generally controlled by a complex network of kinship relationships, the principles of which are often incomprehensible to outsiders. It is common to encounter examples of complete misunderstanding of tribal land-tenure systems in the writings of government administrators and colonial experts who felt that native land

rights were always obscure and confused. Tribal land rights are often complex, but some facts do stand out. Typically, group boundaries are well defined and defended against encroachment from neighboring groups. Ownership is vested in the kin group or community, or figuratively in a headperson,
and it is inconceivable that anyone would have the right to permanently alien-
ate land from the group. The concept of ownership at other than the group or
tribal level is quite irrelevant, because land is to be used by individuals and
not owned in the a commercial sense. Access to and use of land is virtually
guaranteed to all tribal members. Even though specific rights are often over-
lapping and subject to numerous conditions, land allocation may remain both
well regulated and flexible. It is very useful to have a variety of cultural
mechanisms of land allocation to help ensure an equitable balance between
land resources and people. Aside from its obvious economic significance, the
land itself often holds important symbolic and emotional meaning for indigenous peoples as the repository for ancestral remains, clan origin points, and
other sacred features in tribal mythology.

Tribal land-use patterns make the concept of waste or unoccupied land as
irrelevant as the concept of private ownership. Pastoralists, shifting agriculturalists, and foragers often exploit their territory in long-term cycles and
leave large areas undisturbed to recuperate before returning to them. Furthermore, not all portions of tribal territory are necessarily exploited in exactly
the same manner, because some zones might be reserved for specialized uses.
These details are, of course, unlikely to be of much consequence to external
policy makers, who were concerned primarily with increasing the cash value
of the land for short-term gains. Intruding government authorities were often
quick to claim ownership over what they interpreted to be wasteland, and in
the process have often undermined the resilient land-use systems developed
by small-scale societies.

Land Policy Variables

It is generally recognized in international law that the aboriginal inhabitants
of a region possess rights in their lands that cannot legally be ignored.[2] This
is acknowledged explicitly in article 11 of the International Labour Organization's Convention 107, which provides that "the right of ownership, collective or individual, of the members of the populations concerned over the lands
which these populations traditionally occupy shall be recognized." [3]

This international convention, which was adopted in 1957, and ILO Convention 169,[4] which replaced it in 1989, is still the primary international standard on tribal land rights. In fact, these rights have not always been recog-

nized, or they have been legally circumvented through a variety of means, as will be shown.

Land laws are often complex, and in any discussion of land policies concerning tribal peoples, several variables must be kept in mind. The land laws may not recognize rights by indigenous peoples, as was the case in Australia until the Land Rights (Northern Territory) Act of 1976, but more often some rights are recognized in some categories of tribal land. These rights and categories must be carefully distinguished because different effects on tribal culture may result. In terms of categories of tribal lands, the state may acknowledge tribal rights to any or none of the following:

- Land traditionally exploited by the tribe
- Land considered necessary to meet the future needs of an expanding or a recovering population
- Land occupied or actively exploited at a given time
- Land with registered title

In addition, legislators must consider whether customary communal tenure will be allowed and how to deal with the problem of land transfers and alienation to outsiders. In theory, any tribal land could be considered inalienable and therefore the permanent possession of the tribe with no provisions for any acquisition by outsiders or the state. But most often governments have assumed responsibility for determining what tribal land can be alienated and for what purposes. It has also been common practice for governments to assume eminent domain over tribal lands with regard to some categories of natural resources, such as minerals, forests, and sometimes game, and to regulate tribal use of these resources accordingly.

The following sections examine historical trends in government land policies as they related to tribal peoples in different parts of the world. The policies of the United States concerning the Indians and Alaska natives are presented in detail as a basis for comparison with the situation in other countries, but in most areas only a brief survey is given. Despite the many divergent details, outstanding parallels throughout the world reside in the fact that governments have restricted the access of tribal peoples to their lands and have actively attempted to destroy customary patterns of land tenure.

The American Reservation System

The right of North American Indians to their lands was recognized in principle since the colonial period. For example, the British Royal Proclamation of 1763 stated that any lands that were not purchased or ceded to the Crown would be reserved as Indian hunting grounds. This principle was reaffirmed by the new American government after the Revolution in the 1787 Ordinance for the Government of the Northwest Territory, which declared: "The utmost good faith shall always be observed towards the Indians; their lands and property shall never be taken from them without their consent; and in their property rights and liberty, they never shall be invaded or disturbed, unless in just and lawful wars authorized by Congress."[5]

Such declarations were probably made in good faith and were apparently taken seriously—at least while the Indians were numerically strong enough to constitute a threat and when there was some danger that they might seek support from foreign governments. As soon as these dangers were no longer a problem and when settlers and speculators began clamoring for new lands, the government forgot these noble promises. There followed a steady reduction of the Indian land base through wars, removals, outright confiscations, and treaties that confined Indians on small reservations against their will.

The first major rejection of the policy of "utmost good faith" occurred with President Andrew Jackson's Indian Removal Act of 1830, which called for the removal of all eastern tribes to "permanent" Indian country in the Great American Desert west of the Mississippi, where it was thought that white men would never be able to settle. Some ninety thousand Indians were removed, but not all tribes left their traditional homelands peacefully. The Florida Seminole fought a war from 1836 to 1842 that cost the United States the lives of fifteen hundred soldiers and 20 million dollars to remove four thousand Seminole. The Cherokee of Georgia also presented a difficult case. They fought removal through the courts and obtained a favorable Supreme Court decision, but President Jackson refused to enforce it and the Cherokee had to surrender 2.8 million hectares to be distributed by lottery to Georgia's white population. Fourteen thousand men, women, and children were then herded into concentration camps and forced by federal troops to march to Oklahoma; four thousand died en route. Unfortunately, not even their newly assigned land in Oklahoma was secure from further dispossession: They had to surrender much of it in a short time as punishment after they sided with the South during the Civil War.

By 1840 a "permanent" frontier had been established by a line on the map and a string of forts running west of the Mississippi from Texas to Canada. Within this Indian country, which extended to the crest of the Rockies and served as a vast buffer zone between the United States and disputed territories in the Far West, the Indians were to be allowed freedom to enjoy their lands. For a short time it appeared that the government intended to deal in the "utmost good faith." Regulations were passed prohibiting the entry of outsiders into Indian country without special permits and outlawing the sale of alcohol to the inhabitants. A few schools and training centers were to be established inside Indian country under the direction of the Bureau of Indian Affairs, created in 1832, and troops were to be used to prevent intertribal conflicts. For the most part, however, the quarter of a million Indians in the area were to be left largely to their own devices. This scheme constituted what must have been the largest tribal "reserve" ever envisioned, and it even held some promise of success. But it was a regrettably short-lived experiment.

When Texas, the Oregon country, and the Southwest passed to American control in 1845, 1846, and 1848, respectively, the Indian country of the plains suddenly seemed to stand in the way of progress, and settlers began to stream across it in great numbers on their way farther west. The government quickly negotiated new land agreements with the tribes, including rights of passage. At the government's invitation in 1851, a general council with thousands of Indians representing many plains tribes was convened at Fort Laramie. In exchange for promises of abundant gifts in the future, the tribes agreed to grant rights-of-way for the Oregon Trail and accepted specific tribal boundaries. This was only the beginning of what was already a familiar process to the eastern tribes. Shortly thereafter, states and territories were carved out of what had been designated permanent Indian country, and all of the tribes were eventually relocated on smaller and smaller reservations.

Land agreements were conducted in a similar manner to the transfers of political sovereignty described in an earlier chapter. Although some writers will perhaps still defend the legality of the transactions and the good intentions of the government, there can be little doubt that coercion—if not outright deception—was often involved and that the Indians lost millions of acres of their best lands against their will. In his account of the plains wars, historian Ralph Andrist acknowledges that, strictly speaking, most Indian land was alienated with Indian consent, but he summarized the conditions under which "consent" was granted as follows: "It was given by tribes which had just been broken in wars, it was given by peoples who had been threatened or cajoled into signing, or misled about what they were agreeing to. It was often consent granted by a minority of the tribe's leaders who had been subverted or liquored up; the Commissioners were never squeamish about hailing the voice of a few as the voice of all if that was the best that could be had. So, when the Indians gave up their land by their own consent, they were usually consenting with a knee in their groin."[6]

Reservations grew smaller and smaller and in many cases became inadequate to support their Indian populations by traditional means. Furthermore, they were often outside traditional homelands. The people were forced to live on sporadic and insufficient government doles of unfamiliar food, and they had to accept the confinement and new regulations imposed on them. From 1789 to 1849, reservations were run by army officers, and even after agents of the Bureau of Indian Affairs took charge, army posts were located on most reservations. Reservations were often unhappy places, and it is little wonder that the government frequently had to resort to force to keep the people on the land assigned to them.

Dull Knife's band of 320 Northern Cheyenne endured what they considered to be the intolerable conditions of their reservation in Oklahoma Indian Territory for a year and a half. Then, in 1878, they attempted to return to their homeland in Montana. After a flight of more than six hundred miles they were recaptured and imprisoned, but they still refused to return to their designated reservation. After being deprived of food and warmth for five days in subzero weather, they attempted to escape again but were surrounded by soldiers and shot down.[7]

In 1946 the government finally acknowledged that Indian grievances over past land deals were still of sufficient magnitude and presented such unique problems that special legal machinery, in the form of the Indian Claims Commission, was created to deal with them. Previously, between 1881 and 1950, 118 Indian land cases had been presented before the United States Court of Claims, but only 34 of these cases recovered damages.[8] The new Indian Claims Commission was more generous toward Indians in terms of the kinds of cases it would hear and the kinds of evidence that could be accepted. A specific category included "fraud, duress, unconscionable consideration, mutual or unilateral mistake" in the treaty signing, or simply the failure of the government to pay as promised, as a basis for claim.[9] Some 247 cases were tried by the commission between 1950 and 1967, and it awarded 250 million dollars in damages as at least partial restitution for past wrongs.

In spite of these belated efforts at compensation, the government had already embarked upon policies that were equally destructive of tribal land rights even before the last Indian wars ended. Indian administrators had long assumed that tribal forms of land ownership constituted an obstacle to progress, and as early as the 1830s an Indian commissioner had maintained that "common property and civilization cannot coexist."[10] These views found expression in the General Allotment Act of 1887, which called for the subdivision of reservations into small plots to be assigned to tribal individuals and held in trust for twenty-five years and then disposed of at the owners' discretion. "Surplus" land remaining after the allotment was purchased by the government and could also be disposed of at will. Indians often vigorously resisted allotment, to no avail, and its effects were devastating. During the period of most active allotment, between 1887 and 1932, more than 60 percent of the 56.7 million hectares then in Indian hands was lost, and the tribes were left with only 20 million hectares of often marginal land.[11]

The integrity of reservation lands was again threatened by implementation of House Concurrent Resolution 108 of 1953, which declared it was the "sense of Congress" that federal supervision of some Indian reservations should be ended, or, as it was more popularly understood, that reservations should be terminated as soon as possible. In this process (which did not differ significantly from allotment except that it was more drastic), many reservations were legally disbanded and their land and other assets divided among their members. Termination proceedings touched off serious controversies on several reservations between those anxious for a quick cash settlement and those who wished to retain their land and tribal status. As in the past, the government was willing to proceed with or without Indian cooperation or approval, but fortunately the termination process was soon abandoned and only a few reservations actually disappeared. In addition to outright termination, Indian lands have been allocated by the Bureau of Indian Affairs in long-term leases to large-scale development corporations for projects such as uranium mining and strip mining of coal.

The Alaska Natives Claims Settlement Act

All aboriginal titles, if any, and claims of aboriginal title in Alaska based on use and occupancy, including submerged land underneath all water areas, both inland and offshore, and including any aboriginal hunting or fishing rights that may exist, are hereby extinguished.[12]

To clear the legal pathway for the construction of the Alaska pipeline following the discovery of oil at Prudhoe Bay in 1968, the U.S. Congress quickly put together formal legislation to permanently "extinguish" all aboriginal claims to the land. The act, passed in 1971 as the Alaska Natives Claims Settlement Act (ANCSA), provided for the payment of 962.5 million dollars in cash and royalties from oil revenues to native corporations set up by the act.[13] The natives were also to receive title to some 162,000 square kilometers of land to be held by regional and village native corporations. In comparison with the land settlements received by Indians in the lower forty-eight states, the Alaska claims settlement might seem like a generous arrangement. The natives, who in 1971 numbered approximately 78,500, or 25 percent of the Alaskan population, received the right to claim approximately 12 percent of the total land area of Alaska, while the nonnative private sector of the state was left with less than 1 percent of the land. State, federal, and local governments accounted for the remaining 88 percent.[14] There were a few catches, however. The Alaskan natives were to be turned instantly into corporate executives and stockholders and were required to use their cash payments and the natural resources of their land holdings to extract cash profits from their native corporations. Furthermore, by 1991, native peoples were able to sell stocks in their corporations to anyone, including outsiders.

By 1983 dissatisfaction with ANCSA and concern over what would happen in 1991 had reached such a point that an indigenous organization, the Inuit Circumpolar Conference, commissioned distinguished British Columbia Supreme Court justice and native rights advocate Thomas R. Berger to review the consequences of ANCSA and make recommendations for possible reforms before 1991. Berger spent nearly two years at this task and interviewed 1,450 witnesses in sixty Alaskan villages before issuing his report.[15] He recommended the transfer of corporate lands to tribal governments and in effect called for native "retribalization"[16] In response to these concerns, in 1988 Congress amended ANCSA to allow the native corporations to restrict the sale of corporate stock, and to allow natives born after 1971 to also become shareholders. The native corporations remained as the primary landholders. In 2004 Congress approved P.L. 108-452, the Alaska Land Transfer Acceleration Act, to complete the final selection and transfer of ANCSA land titles by 2009.[17]

The native corporations have allowed native peoples, as legal landowners, to manage the development of their natural resources themselves in order to create employment opportunities and improved incomes for their native shareholders. For example, in 2006 the Arctic Slope Regional Corporation (ASRC) owned nearly 5 million acres of land, including some valuable subsurface rights, and produced $1.7 billion in revenue, with net income of $206 million through their eleven subsidiary for-profit business corporations. In addition, village corporations in the same area owned more than another million acres. In 1972 the ASRC originally enrolled thirty-eight hundred shareholders, and by 2007, under the revised ANCSA, its numbers had expanded to nearly nine thousand shareholders, including some fifty-three hundred native residents of eight towns and villages.[18] The economic benefits of native ownership are suggested by the 2000 Census figures showing a median household income in the native village of Wainwright of $54,722,[19] which was higher than the $51,571 median for the state of Alaska and well above the median household income of $41,994 for the United States as a whole. Of course living costs are extremely high in these remote Arctic locations.

Reservations and Dispossession in South America

Throughout the Amazon regions of South America, tribal peoples have been driven from their lands by settlers and military action, and until recently the "reservations" established for them either have not been seriously protected by government authorities or have been too small to allow continuation of traditional lifestyles.[20] Thus, the history of land policies closely resembles that in the United States. Like the Indian tribes of the American Great Plains, the Amazonian tribes utilize large areas of land, and, as hunters and shifting cultivators, in many cases they do not remain in a specific locality for more than two to three years. Their land rights have therefore been easily disregarded by governments. National laws that may guarantee Indian land rights on paper have in reality often been only lightly enforced. In the face of continual dispossession, for as long as possible Amazonian Indians merely abandoned their lands and withdrew into more remote areas. The native peoples who most needed land titles and other legal protections were usually unaware of their rights, or else they lacked the means of seeking their enforcement, until they began to form their own political organizations in the 1970s, as will be described in chapter 10.

In the 1850s Brazil's imperial government guaranteed the Indians' rights to the inalienable possession of lands needed for their survival. Under the republic, according to the constitutions of 1891, 1934, 1937, and 1946, this was modified to the extent that Indians were entitled to the possession of lands on which they were "permanently established" on the condition that they did not transfer this land to others. In some states, lands were reserved for Indians under the supervision of the Indian Protection Service, but often the boundaries were not considered inviolable by state governments. In Rio Grande do Sul, for example, tribal reserves that in 1913 had amounted to nearly eighty-one thousand hectares had been reduced to only thirty-two thousand hectares by 1967,[21] through a variety of legal and extralegal means.

The most ambitious Brazilian effort to "reserve" Indian land was begun in 1952, when some eighty-five thousand square kilometers of unexplored territory in Mato Grosso were provisionally declared off-limits to white colonization. However, the local government of Mato Grosso proceeded to let out 75 percent of that area in concessions to land speculators. When the boundaries were finalized in 1961, only some twenty-two thousand square kilometers remained as an Indian reserve designated as the Xingu National Park, but its area was later increased to thirty thousand square kilometers. For many years the Xingu park was left virtually undisturbed as an example of Brazil's ideal Indian policy, but it also became a sanctuary for Indians who were being displaced by the frontier in adjacent areas, and was itself eventually invaded.

Previous legislative efforts to defend Brazilian Indian land rights were seriously undermined by the 1970 Federal Statute of the Indian. This law granted use rights to Indians, but ownership to the federal government, and legalized the physical removal of Indians from their traditional lands for almost any ill-defined reason, ranging from national security and higher national interests to public health concerns or to prevent disturbances occurring when settlers invade Indian lands. In effect, Indians' rights to their lands no longer needed to be respected at all. Even though on paper Brazil's national Indian foundation, FUNAI, has designated millions of hectares as Indian parks and reserves, until recently there has been little serious effort to prevent these areas from being invaded by powerful multinational development interests, highways, ranchers, and settlers.[22] In 1980, the military took control of FUNAI, and the most pro-Indian elements within the organization were removed.[23] Presidential decrees in 1983 and procedural changes initiated by FUNAI in 1986 modified the Federal Statute of the Indian to permit mining on Indian lands and favored land invaders and other special interest groups over Indians.[24] The situation soon began to change in a more positive direction because of international concerns over the rights of indigenous peoples and the destruction of the rainforest. In 1994 FUNAI set up a special agency, Protection for Indigenous Peoples and Lands in the Amazon (Projecto Integrado de Proteção às Populações e Terras Indígenas da Amazônia Legal, or PPTL), to carry out a complete demarcation of Indian lands. This land-titling project was funded in part by the 52-million-dollar Rain Forest Trust Fund in the Pilot Program to Conserve the Brazilian Rain Forest (PPG7), set up by the World Bank in 1992 with donations primarily from Germany, with additional funds from other G-7 countries and the European Union. By 2007 FUNAI reported that 105 million hectares in the Amazon, or 12 percent of the national territory, had been surveyed and registered, or "regularized," as 488 tracts of Indian land, or were in the process of regularization. Another 123 pieces were being studied.[25]

Historically, the actual situation of Indian lands in the Peruvian Amazon was much better than in Brazil. Official land regulations disregarded the forest Indians, who were pushed aside by settlers until 1957, when Supreme Decree No. 3 called for the establishment of native reserves in traditionally occupied areas. The size of reserves was not to be determined with regard to traditional subsistence requirements but, rather, according to a formula that allowed up to ten hectares for each person over five years of age. The long-run policy objective was the introduction of private ownership to specific plots, because, according to the decree, the Indians must share in the benefits of progress and civilization. This began to change in 1974, when Supreme Decree No. 3 was replaced by the Law of Native Communities and in 1975 by the Forest and Wild Fauna Law, which called for the allotment of sufficient lands to native communities to meet their traditional subsistence needs.[26] However, implementation of these laws was initially very slow, and Indian land rights continued to be overridden by corporate development interests.[27] By 2007 many indigenous groups held titles to communal reserves and protected natural areas, and hundreds of communities held deeds to their own community lands, making it possible for them to legally manage their territories and natural resources.

Up to the 1970s, official Bolivian policy made forest Indians the legal equals of any citizen; they were given no preferential treatment regarding land, even though their requirements were unique. They could legally claim title to lands they occupied, but they rarely did so, because the requirements of shifting cultivation did not encourage attachment to any small parcel of land. Consequently, they were subject to dispossession whenever an enterprising colonist applied for a title. The state made no provision for protecting larger tracts of land for Indian hunting grounds or for long-term reuse of swidden plots.[28] This began to change in 1996 with the new Agrarian Law and subsequent movements by landless indigenous peoples to reclaim their territories.

In Colombia an 1890 law provided for the establishment of Indian communal reserves (*resguardos*). However, this did not apply to uncivilized, non-Christian tribal groups, which were given no such rights and instead were placed under the legal guardianship of the Catholic missions delegated to civilize them. By 1961, however, Law 135 allowed reserves to be formed for uncivilized Indians, but unfortunately, either they were not established or they were absurdly small; instead, tribal territories were still considered open for national expansion and colonization. For example, in the llanos in 1970 the Institute of Agrarian Reform reserved 2 hectares of arid savanna for each of 7,000 Guajibo (Guahibo) Indians, and 3,000 to 40,500 hectares were allotted to each of approximately 60 colonists for agricultural development.[29] Through the 1980s Indian groups in Colombia were steadily losing ground, in spite of the creation in 1982 of the National Development Program for Indigenous Populations (Programa nacional de desarrollo de las poblaciones indígenas, or PRODEIN), a government agency ostensibly designed to protect Indians.[30]

In Venezuela, Indian lands were steadily being appropriated by outsiders in the early 1970s.[31] The Agrarian Reform Act of 1960 recognized Indian rights "to hold the lands, woods and waterways which they occupy or which belong to them in those sites where they customarily dwell,"[32] but this law was ineffective because there were no rules for its implementation.[33] Even where community titles were granted to Indians, they were not effectively defended against invasion. This process was going on all over the country and no one seemed to be seriously concerned about puting an end to it. It was only in the last few years that some Indian leaders have been able to request title deeds and legal delimitations of their respective possessions from the appropriate tribunals. Invasion of Indian lands were still common in Venezuela in the 1980s.[34]

Elsewhere in South America, reserves were established in Chile and Argentina, but there, too, the allotment and individualization process was frequently applied. In 1940 only some 1,200 of 4.8 million hectares originally in Araucanian ownership remained under traditional tenure, and the tribal land base had been so reduced that most Araucanians found themselves facing a severe land shortage. Under the Allende government (1970–1973), generous communal reserves were established for the Mapuche, but these were undermined by the Pinochet government by a 1979 decree calling for "the division of the reserves and the liquidation of Indian communities."[35] The first Five-Year Plan in Argentina divided Indian lands into three categories (reservation, *reducción*, and *colonia*) that were actually stages leading to individual ownership on the same basis as that for other citizens.[36] However, a 1984 law provided a basis for reestablishing communal reserves in Argentina.[37]

French Guiana is an overseas territory and France and as such is part of the European Union. While the special Inini Statute was in effect from 1930 to 1968, the Indians of French Guiana enjoyed a favorable land rights situation and were left in undisturbed possession of 90 percent of the country.[38] After 1968 the entire country was divided into twenty-two French communes. In 2007, only two communes, Awala-Yalimpo and Camopi, were occupied exclusively by indigenous peoples.[39] In other areas of the Guianas region, the situation of Indian lands is equally precarious. In Surinam, Indians occupy Crown lands and have no special legal protection, although by 2004 the Organization of American States Division of Sustainable Development was working with indigenous peoples, and in Guyana some reservations have been set up and an Amerindian Land Commission recommended further entitlements of Indian lands in 1969. However, by 1975, plans were under way to inundate the traditional lands of four thousand Akawaio Indians with the Mazaruni hydroelectric project,[40] and the Land Commission recommendations had not been acted upon. Fortunately for the Akawaio, as of 1989 an unresolved border dispute with Venezuela and funding problems were blocking the Mazaruni project.

Tribal Land in Colonial Africa

The pattern of government acquisition of tribal land for the economic benefit of outside interests was unfortunately as common in Africa as in the New World, and was sometimes even more blatant. The principal difference here was that very large tribal populations were involved, often far outnumbering the European colonists. However, except for a few outstanding exceptions such as in British-controlled West Africa, this did not hinder the alienation process.

In French-controlled West Africa, the government declared that all lands for which indigenous peoples had no title belonged to the state. It then proceeded to dispose of such "unclaimed" lands by leasing them with full resource rights to European-owned concession companies for development purposes, whereas it offered token "abandonment indemnities" to dispossessed indigenous peoples. In 1899, 70 percent of French Equatorial Africa was leased to only forty such companies, with one company receiving 140,000 square kilometers. Indigenous people were, of course, free to apply for titles, but they rarely did so (by 1945 fewer than 2,000 out of 16 million had applied), because they either did not feel the need for them or did not want to risk the community conflicts that private ownership would introduce.[41]

The Congo Free State followed a similar course from 1885 to 1908 with its *regime domanial*, which dictated that all "vacant" lands were claimed by the state. *Vacant* in this sense meant all land beyond the immediate vicinity of native villages and gardens. There were no provisions for tribal reserves or for any protection of native land rights beyond the islands of land occupied by villages at any given time, and natives were taxed for exploiting the state-owned resources in the forests surrounding their villages. The government strictly enforced this system, which consequently resulted in the incredible abuses described earlier.

In areas of southern and eastern Africa considered particularly favorable for European settlement, colonial governments set up reserves to concentrate large tribal populations on small poor-quality tracts of land, which served as labor dormitories for the white farmers who cultivated vast holdings of the best land. This situation led to some incredible inequities, as the figures in table 6.1 show. For example, although the indigenous people of Southern Rhodesia constituted 95 percent of the total population, they were left with only a third of the land for their exclusive use.

Table 6.1.   Amount of Land Reserved for Indigenous Populations in Different Countries

	Native Population as Percent of Total Population	*Native Lands as Percent of Total Area*
Beuchuanaland[a]	99+	38
Swaziland[b]	98	48
New Guinea[b]	98	97
So. Rhodesia[c]	95	33
S.W. Africa[a]	87	25
South Africa[d]	80	12
Canada[e]	3	0.2
Chile[f]	2	0.6
United States[g]	0.3	1

[a] Cole, 1966: 526. The British Protectorate of Bechuanaland became the independent republic of Botswana in 1966.
[b] Mair, 1970: 146. Population figures are for 1960; "reserve" land here is actually nonalienated land as of 1967–1968.
[c] Barber, 1967: 1, 7. Figures are for 1970. Southern Rhodesia became independent Rhodesia in 1970 and Zimbabwe in 1980.
[d] Jabavu, 1934, 287.
[e] International Labour Office, 1953: 68, 332. Population as of 1949, land figures 1951.
[f] International Labour Office, 1953: 40, 307. Figures as of 1940.
[g] International Labour Office, 1953: 333, 69. Population as of 1940, land figures 1949.

The poor quality of the African tribal reserves frequently received comment. Writing of the Bantu reserves in southern Africa, Monica M. Cole observed that they were generally poorer than the lands occupied by Europeans and indeed had not attracted European attention. These reserves were also overcrowded and the soil was highly susceptible to erosion, yet with wise management they were potentially productive.[42] John H. Wellington[43] noted that the reserves of Southwest Africa were purposefully located in the zones of lowest rainfall or, as a Herero chief complained in 1922, in deserts "where no human being ever lived before."[44] In Kenya the reserves were structured to allow the Europeans, accounting for less than 1 percent of the population, to have full access to the agriculturally rich uplands that constituted 20 percent of the country and became known as the white highlands.[45] This policy of European priority in the best lands was established early and was spelled out by the colony's first commissioner, Sir Charles Eliot, in the following terms: "The interior of the protectorate is a white man's country, and it is mere hypocrisy not to admit that white interests must be paramount, and the main object of our policy and legislation should be to found a white colony."[46]

Eliot rejected the notion of large reserves because he felt they would retard civilization and perpetuate barbarism and customs that he disapproved of. Instead, he favored a policy of interpenetration for Kenya, which would convert indigenous villages into islands within European estates that would serve as sources of labor. The people were to have full rights to lands they occupied, but here, as elsewhere, the concept of unused land was interpreted to European advantage.

The cattle-herding tribes of Kenya fared particularly poorly under these policies because of their nomadic habits, and, like the North American Indians, they were forced to relocate frequently. The Maasai signed an agreement in 1904 in which they surrendered their finest lands to the whites in exchange for a reserve that would endure "so long as the Maasai as a race shall exist," but seven years later they were forced to move again.[47] No reserve was secure, and any promises of permanence were shattered by the Crown Lands Ordinance of 1915, which "guaranteed" tribal land rights but allowed the governor to cancel any part of a reserve if he decided that the villagers did not need it; additionally, any part could be excluded for railroads and highways or any public purpose. Kenya's tribal peoples in effect became tenants subject to dispossession at the whim of the government.[48]

Land Policies in Asia and the Pacific

In Asia and the Pacific region, almost the entire gamut of land policies is again represented. The harshest, most destructive policies occurred in Australia and areas under French, Japanese, and German colonial control. Meanwhile in New Guinea, Fiji, and Micronesia (under American rule), substantial areas of land remained in native hands if not fully under native control. Where harsh colonial policies were followed in the Pacific, they mirrored the general trends noted elsewhere: An initial period of relatively uncontrolled dispossession was followed by the establishment of reserves or at least stricter controls on the alienation process, and finally, individual title registration schemes were imposed that undermined communal tenure systems and resulted in further alienation.

In some respects, Australia represents a special case because the entire continent was occupied by hunter-gatherers and the government recognized neither the sovereignty nor the land ownership rights of these Aborigines. No land treaties or compensation payments were ever made to formalize their dispossession. Given the widespread practice in other areas of acknowledging native rights only in obviously occupied land, it is surprising that the government declared all of Australia to be "unoccupied wasteland" and therefore state property. This was done in spite of the abundant testimony of early observers who were well aware of Aboriginal land ownership and use practices. Anthropologists have even argued that every part of Australia was claimed by Aborigines and was exploited up to its maximum carrying capacity. According to Joseph B. Birdsell, "There were no empty or unclaimed spaces."[49] Australia had been occupied for perhaps forty to fifty thousand years before the arrival of Europeans, and this was plenty of time to develop effective land tenure systems. The European invaders realized that these traditional systems conflicted with the system they wished to impose and chose to ignore them. The Aboriginal reserves that were eventually established in Australia were almost afterthoughts, left largely to the discretion of the local state governments. Such reserves were usually in the least desirable locations, remained government property, and were never considered to be for the exclusive, undisturbed use of Aborigines. Until the Aboriginal Land Rights Act (Northern Territory) of 1976 (see chapter 10), the Australian government seemed convinced that ownership of land by Aborigines must be on exactly the same basis as for any other "citizen" of Australia—that is, by individual title[50]— and it stubbornly refused to acknowledge the legitimacy of aboriginal claims. The official position as of 1970 was clearly stated by the federal minister for the interior: "The Government believes that it is wholly wrong to encourage Aboriginals to think that because their ancestors have had a long association with a particular piece of land, Aboriginals of the present day have the right to demand ownership of it."[51]

The situation of aboriginal land rights began to change rapidly in 1972 with the election of a new Australian government and the granting of some land holdings to Aborigines under the Land Rights Act. However, by 1980 the old government was again in power and it was clear that corporate mineral development would again have priority over aboriginal claims.

In New Caledonia the French dealt with the indigenous peoples in a straightforward manner. In 1855, the government assumed the exclusive right to handle land transactions involving natives and nonnatives, and claimed all land that they considered to be unoccupied. In 1868 it introduced native reserves as a temporary measure pending full native acceptance of individual titles. As European planters became more interested in the island, the reserves proved to be too generous, and in 1876 a ruling known as the Confinement Decree was passed that, like the Indian Removal Act in the United States, called for the removal of indigenous peoples and their relocation on smaller, often already occupied reserves. The people resisted the removal process, which had to be postponed until 1895, when it set off a rebellion that killed some two hundred Europeans and one thousand indigenous people. When the rebellion was quelled, many of the defeated rebels were deported to small islands, and others were forced to agree to voluntary renunciations of their lands in exchange for promises of annuities to be paid to the chiefs. Some villages were moved as many as three times in a single year and were sometimes even burned down by military authorities who were overly eager that the land arrangements be followed. By 1883 roughly 90 percent of the island had been taken out of native hands.[52]

In New Zealand the Maori were guaranteed by the 1840 Treaty of Waitangi with the British "the full, exclusive, and undisturbed possession of their lands and estates, forests, fisheries, and other properties which they may collectively or individually possess."[53]

As in America, the British respected in principle Maori rights of land ownership, but they pursued a steady policy of land "purchase" by government land agents, who were not always scrupulously fair in their dealings. The main difficulty faced by the government agents was that of determining whether all individuals with claims to a given piece of land were indeed willing to sell and that they fully understood the transaction. It became obvious when fighting broke out in 1860 that the Maori felt that their land rights were not being properly respected. The familiar problem, as Keith Sinclair noted in a careful understatement, was that "the chief aim of land policy was to benefit the Europeans."[54]

After most of the fighting had stopped in 1865, the government established the Native Land Court to continue the registration and alienation process in a more orderly manner. By 1940 the Maori had surrendered some 94 percent of their 1840 holdings in spite of—or perhaps because of—government "protection." Furthermore, thanks to the individualization policy, much of the land remaining in Maori ownership quickly became so fragmented as to be almost useless. This reduction in land base was particularly serious because the Maori population had been increasing since 1896 and had nearly tripled by 1940. Subsequently, the alienation process slowed (only forty-six hundred hectares were transferred to Europeans in 1958–1959) and the government attempted to consolidate fragmented individual Maori holdings, but little land remained under the traditional tribal system. The modern Maori have faced the unpleasant threat of an increasing population and a decreasing land base.[55] The Maori have continued a political struggle for control of their lands, but by 1987 they controlled less than 5 percent of their original holdings and their claims were still unrecognized. However, there were mechanisms in place, such as the Waitangi Tribunal, that suggesting that the government was moving in a more favorable direction on the land question.[56]

Australian land policy in preindependence New Guinea markedly contrasted with the government's policy toward the Aborigine in Australia. When the protectorate was declared over Papua New Guinea in 1884, indigenous peoples were assured that "evil-disposed men will not be able to occupy your country, to seize your lands or take you away from your homes."[57] The native title was recognized here and in the Mandated Territory from the beginning, as in New Zealand, and here too the government assumed exclusive control of the alienation process. This time, however, there seemed to be genuine concern that enough land be reserved for native use to protect their future interests (and to preserve the labor supply), and relatively little land was actually alienated. By 1967–1968, only about 3 percent of the total land area of what was then the Trust Territory of New Guinea and the Territory of Papua had been alienated—but, of course, this figure includes much of the most valuable land, and in some areas indigenous peoples were forced into overcrowded reserves. The government also embarked upon a policy of registering individual titles because, as usual, it was believed that communal tenure would not offer a satisfactory basis for economic development. In its 1964–1965 report, the Papua New Guinea administration expressed its policy aims as follows: "The ultimate long-term objective is to introduce throughout the Territory a single system of landholding regulated by the Territorial Government and providing for secure individual registered titles after the pattern of the Australian system."[58]

Since 1975 independent Papua New Guinea has allowed local communities to retain traditional patterns of communal ownership, but this has not prevented environmental damage by large-scale multinational mining and lumbering activities on traditional lands,[59] or the overriding of communal land rights by influential local political leaders.[60]

The Dutch were so protective of native land rights in their half of New Guinea and did so little to encourage colonization that by 1953 little more than two thousand hectares had been alienated. This changed after the Indonesians took control in 1963 and, in typical colonial fashion, claimed all unoccupied land for the state and proceeded to introduce Javanese settlers into once exclusively tribal areas.[61] Officially, this was part of Indonesia's transmigration program, which was designed to eradicate overpopulation and poverty in Java by moving people to the presumably underpopulated outer islands of Sumatra, Kalimantan, Sulawesi, East Timor, and West Irian (West Papua, the former Dutch New Guinea). By 1985 transmigration was considered to be the centerpiece of Indonesian development plans and called for the resettlement of at least 20 million Javanese.[62] In the process, the land rights of the indigenous inhabitants have been largely ignored, and they are being displaced by incoming settlers. Indonesia has used military force to overcome local resistance, especially in West Papua and East Timor.

In many of the smaller Pacific islands of Micronesia and Polynesia, where the land area is severely limited, colonization was usually rigidly controlled. However, colonial governments sometimes still sought to discourage communal tenure practices and replace them with individual tenure in hopes of facilitating cash-cropping activities and settling land disputes. Unfortunately, the result here, as elsewhere, was often serious fragmentation of the land or its concentration in the hands of a few, even though alienation was not usually a threat.

In both independent and colonial Asia, there has been a general tendency not to create special reserves for tribal peoples. In India, Bangladesh, Thailand, and Malaysia, forest areas are claimed by the state, and in several cases forest reserves have been created in which tribal peoples are allowed to remain only by special permission and under special conditions. By 1987, shifting cultivators and foraging peoples in Malaysia, especially Sarawak, were being dispossessed by hydroelectric projects and lumbering operations.[63]

The land regulations of 1947–1948 that were applied to the hill tribes of the North East Frontier Agency of India were unusually generous in that they allowed tribal communities full rights to the lands they normally cultivated in their shifting cycles and even recognized that villages might move within a general area without abandoning rights to the land.[64] In other areas of India, tribal peoples lost large amounts of land when they failed to register titles or when their temporarily abandoned plots were claimed by settlers in spite of the special provision for tribal and scheduled areas. In Bangladesh no lands were reserved for tribal peoples; instead, their use rights were "protected" and, as we have seen, were subject to government controls. The American administration in the Philippines specifically rejected the notion of tribal reserves, preferring instead to issue individual titles to tribal land. Later, the independent Philippine government created some small reserves that were to be allotted to individuals as they became sufficiently assimilated.[65] In Indochina the French claimed all hill tribe areas as Crown lands and opened them for colonization. They specified that areas claimed by tribal peoples could not be purchased by outsiders, but these areas could be leased for ninety-nine years.[66] In Thailand, tribal peoples were presumably on equal terms in regard to land with other citizens. This "no special policy" policy was probably one of the simplest ways to accomplish the goal of replacing tribal peoples and their tenure systems with what the government considered to be more productive populations and ownership systems.

Notes

1. John H. Wellington, 1967, *South West Africa and Its Human Issues*, Oxford: Clarendon Press/Oxford University Press.

2. Gordon Bennett, 1978, *Aboriginal Rights in International Law*, Occasional Paper no. 37, Royal Anthropological Institute of Great Britain & Ireland.

3. International Labour Organization, 1957, Convention concerning the Protection and Integration of Indigenous and Other Tribal and Semi-Tribal Populations in Independent Countries, Geneva, http://www.ilo.org/ilolex/english/subjectE.htm#s20 (accessed July 6, 2007).

4. International Labour Organization, 1989, Convention concerning Indigenous and Tribal Peoples in Independent Countries, Geneva, http://www.ilo.org/ilolex/cgi-lex/convde.pl?C169 (accessed July 6, 2007).

5. Harold E. Fey and D'Arcy McNickle, 1970, *Indians and Other Americans: Two Ways of Life Meet*, New York: Harper and Row, 56.

6. Ralph K. Andrist, 1969, *The Long Death: The Last Days of the Plains Indian*, New York: Collier Books, 8.

7. Ibid., 320–30; Fey and McNickle, *Indians and Other Americans*, 34–36.

8. Nancy Oestreich Lurie, 1957, "The Indian Claims Commission Act," in *American Indians and American Life*, ed. George E. Simpson and J. Milton Yinger, The Annals of the American Academy of Political and Social Science (May), vol. 311, Philadelphia: American Academy of Political and Social Science, 57.

9. Ibid., 62.

10. Fey and McNickle, *Indians and Other Americans*, 72.

11. Ibid., 84.

12. ANCSA (Alaska Natives Claims Settlement Act), P.L. 92-203, sec. 4b.

13. Robert Arnold, 1978, *Alaska Native Land Claims*, Anchorage: Alaska Native Foundation.

14. Alaska Department of Natural Resources, Division of Forestry, n.d, *Who Owns/Manages Alaska?* Poster, http://plats.landrecords.info/images/who_owns_alaska_poster.jpg (accessed July 7, 2007).

15. Thomas R. Berger, 1985, *Village Journey: The Report of the Alaska Native Review Commission*, New York: Hill and Wang.

16. Ibid., 158.

17. Nathan Brooks, 2005, The Alaska Land Transfer Acceleration Act: Background and Summary, Library of Congress, Congressional Research Service, http://www.lbblawyers.com/RL32734.pdf (accessed July 6, 2007).

18. Arctic Slope Regional Corporation, http://www.asrc.com/stock/stock.asp (accessed July 7, 2007).

19. United States Bureau of the Census, Census 2000, table DP-1, Profile of General Demographic Characteristics: 2000, Wainwright ANVSA, AK, http://censtats.census.gov/data/AK/280027735.pdf (accessed July 2, 2007).

20. Roger Plant and Søren Hvalkof, 2001, *Land Titling and Indigenous Peoples*, Sustainable Development Department Technical Paper Series, Washington, DC: Inter-American Development Bank.

21. Carlos de Araujo Moreira Neto, 1972, "Some data concerning the recent history of the Kaingang Indians," in *The Situation of the Indian in South America*, ed. W. Dostal, Geneva: World Council of Churches, 319.

22. Shelton H. Davis, 1977, *Victims of the Miracle: Development and the Indians of Brazil*, Cambridge: Cambridge University Press; Anna Presland, 1979, "An account of the contemporary fight for survival of the Amerindian peoples of Brazil," *Survival International Review* 4(1): 14–40.

23. Shelton H. Davis, 1980, "Brazilian Indian policy: The present situation," *ARC Bulletin* 3: 2–3.

24. Andrew Gray, 1987, *The Amerindians of South America*, Report no. 15, London: Minority Rights Group, 19.

25. FUNAI, Fundação Nacional do Índio, 2007, *Povos Indígenas: As terras-Situação Atual*, http://www.funai.gov.br/index.html (accessed July 8, 2007); World Bank, 2002, *Brazil Rain Forest Pilot Program Success Story 2: Innovative Project Contributes to Regularizing Indigenous Lands in the Amazon*, http://www.worldbank.org/rfpp/docs/SS2%20engl.pdf (accessed July 8, 2007).

26. Alberto Chirif, 1975, "En torno a la titulacion de las comunidades nativas y a los recursos forestales y de fauna silvestre," in *Marginacion y Futuro, Sistema Nacional de Apoyo a la Movilizacion Social, Direccion General de Organizaciones Rurales, Serie: Communidades Nativas*, 66–76. Lima: Sistema Nacional de Apoyo a la Movilizacion Social, Direccion General de Organizaciones Rurales.

27. *Cultural Survival Newsletter*, 1980, 4(3): 9–10.

28. Heinz Kelm, 1972, "The present situation of the Indian populations in non-Andean Bolivia," in *The Present Situation of the Indian in South America*, ed. W. Dostal, Geneva: World Council of Churches, 165–67.

29. Bernard Arcand, 1972, *The Urgent Situation of the Cuiva Indians of Colombia*, IWGIA Document no. 7, Copenhagen: IWGIA; Victor D. Bonilla, 1972, "The destruction of the Colombian Indian groups," in *The Situation of the Indian in South America*, ed. W. Dostal, 56–75, Geneva: World Council of Churches; Gonzalo Castillo-Cardenas, 1972, "The Indian struggle for freedom in Colombia," in *The Situation of the Indian in South America*, ed. W. Dostal, 76–104, Geneva: World Council of Churches.

30. Andrew Gray, 1987, *The Amerindians of South America*, Report no. 15, London: Minority Rights Group.

31. Esteban E. Mosonyi, 1972, "The situation of the Indian in Venezuela: Perspectives and solutions," in *The Situation of the Indian in South America*, ed. W. Dostal, Geneva: World Council of Churches, 48.

32. Walter Coppens, 1972, *The Anatomy of a Land Invasion Scheme in Yekuana Territory, Venezuela*, IWGIA Document no. 9, Copenhagen: IWGIA.

33. Nelly Arevalo de Jimenez, 1972, "An analysis of official Venezuelan policy in regard to the Indians," in *The Situation of the Indian in South America*, ed. W. Dostal, Geneva: World Council of Churches, 38.

34. IWGIA, 1986, *IWGIA Newsletter 1985*, 42: 198–204; 1987, *IWGIA Yearbook 1986: Indigenous Peoples and Human Rights*, 23; 1988, *IWGIA Yearbook 1987*, 23.

35. Gray, *Amerindians of South America*, 17.

36. International Labour Organization, 1953, *Indigenous Peoples: Living and Working Conditions of Aboriginal Populations in Independent Countries*, Studies and Reports, New Series no. 35, Geneva, 463.

37. Gray, *Amerindians of South America*, 17.

38. J. Hurault, 1972, "The 'Francization' of the Indians," in *The Situation of the Indian in South America*, ed. W. Dostal, 358–70, Geneva: World Council of Churches.

39. Fédération des Organisations Autochtones de Guyane, http://www.coica.org /en/members/foag.html (accessed July 7, 2007).

40. Gordon Bennett, Audrey Colson, and Stuart Wavell, 1978, *The Damned: The Plight of the Akawaio Indians of Guyana*, Survival International Document no. 7, London: Survival International.

41. Raymond L. Buell, 1928, *The Native Problem in Africa*, 2 vols, New York: Macmillan, 1033; Jean Suret-Canale, 1971, *French Colonialism in Tropical Africa, 1900–1945*, New York: Pica Press, 20, 255–61.

42. Monica M. Cole, 1966, *South Africa*, London: Methuen.

43. John H. Wellington, 1967, *South West Africa and Its Human Issues*, Oxford: Clarendon Press/Oxford University Press.

44. Ibid., 279.

45. Robert A. Manners, 1967, "The Kipsigis of Kenya: Culture change in a 'Model' East African tribe," in *Contemporary Change in Traditional Societies*, ed. Julian Steward, Urbana: University of Illinois Press, 1:283.

46. Sir F. D. Lugard, 1928, "The International Institute of African Languages and Cultures," *Africa* 1(1): 1–12, 324.

47. Edward W. Soja, 1968, *The Geography of Modernization in Kenya*, Syracuse Geographical Series, no. 2, Syracuse, NY: Syracuse University Press, 19.

48. M. R. Dilley, 1966, *British Policy in Kenya Colony*, New York: Barnes and Noble, 251–60.

49. Joseph B. Birdsell, 1971, "Ecology, spacing mechanisms, and adaptive behavior in aboriginal land tenure," in *Land Tenure in the Pacific*, ed. Ron Crocombe, Melbourne: Oxford University Press, 334.

50. See discussion by Rowley and Pittock: Charles D. Rowley, 1971, *The Remote Aborigines*, Vol. 3, Aboriginal Policy and Practice, Canberra: Australian National University Press; A. Barrie Pittock, 1972, *Aboriginal Land Rights*, IWGIA Document no. 3, Copenhagen: IWGIA.

51. Cited in Pittock, *Aboriginal Land Rights*, 17.

52. Alain Saussol, 1971, "New Caledonia: Colonization and reaction," in *Land Tenure in the Pacific*, ed. Ron Crocombe, 227–45, Melbourne: Oxford University Press.

53. M. F. Lindley, 1926, *The Acquisition and Government of Backward Territory in International Law*. London: Longman, Green, 345.

54. Keith Sinclair, 1961, *The Origins of the Maori Wars*, 2nd ed., Wellington: New Zealand University Press, 44.

55. International Labour Organization, *Indigenous Peoples*, 301–302, 555–56; New Zealand Department of Statistics, 1960, *The New Zealand Official Year-Book*, Wellington: R. E. Owen, Government Printer, 467–71.

56. IWGIA, 1988, *IWGIA Yearbook 1987: Indigenous Peoples and Development*. Copenhagen: IWGIA, 42–43.

57. Lucy Philip Mair, 1970, *Australia in New Guinea*, Melbourne: Melbourne University Press, 135.

58. Australia Department of Territories, Report for 1964–1965, 43.

59. Colin De'Ath and Gregory Michalenko, 1980, "High technology and original peoples: The case of deforestation in Papua New Guinea and Canada," *Impact of Science on Society* 30(3) (reprinted in Bodley, 1988a, 166–80); David Hyndman, 1988, "Melanesian resistance to ecocide and ethnocide: Transnational mining projects and the Fourth World on the island of New Guinea," in *Tribal Peoples and Development Issues: A Global Overview*, ed. John H. Bodley, 281–98, Mountain View, CA: Mayfield.

60. Lawrence S. Grossman, 1983, "Cattle and rural economic differentiation in the highlands of Papua New Guinea," *American Ethnologist* 10(1): 59–76.

61. Ron Crocombe and Robin Hide, 1971, "New Guinea: Unity in diversity," in *Land Tenure in the Pacific*, ed. R. Crocombe, Melbourne: Oxford University Press, 314–15.

62. Mariel Otten, 1986, *Transmigrasi: Indonesian Resettlement Policy, 1965–1985*, IWGIA Document no. 57, Copenhagen: IWGIA.

63. *IWGIA Yearbook 1986*, 43; *IWGIA Yearbook 1987*, 53.

64. Verrier Elwin, 1959, *A Philosophy for NEFA*, 2nd ed., Shillong, India: J. N. Chowdhury, 65.

65. International Labour Organization, *Indigenous Peoples*, 550; Felix M. Keesing and Marie Keesing, 1934, *Taming Philippine Headhunters: A Study of Government and of Cultural Change in Northern Luzon*, London: George Allen and Unwin, 163–70.

66. Gerald C. Hickey, 1967, "Some aspects of hill tribe life in Vietnam," in *Southeast Asian Tribes, Minorities, and Nations*, ed. Peter Kunstadter, Princeton, NJ: Princeton University Press, 752.

7 Cultural Modification Policies

Cultural realities can be changed rapidly by governmental action if . . .
massive, expensive, and highly organized coercive action is used.

—Ron Crocombe[1]

UP TO THIS POINT, we have seen historically how governments destroyed the political autonomy of tribal populations and gained control of tribal lands. Although these actions were certain to bring about profound "acculturation," the almost total transformation of tribal cultures seemed assured when these actions were combined with programs designed to eliminate all unique aspects of tribal culture and to bring about their full integration into national societies. Tribal peoples throughout the world have faced this situation, and it is a testimony to their courage and determination and the remarkable resilience of their cultures that so many groups have survived and have regained much of their cultural autonomy, as will be shown in chapter 10.

From their positions of coercive power and authority, government administrators, their agents, and missionaries methodically set about to destroy small-scale cultural patterns in the name of progress, to make the people more amenable to the interests of commercial elites and the production of short-term financial gain. Every area of small-scale culture—from language to marriage customs and religion—came under attack by various crusading agencies and individuals anxious to reform and improve them. Any native custom that seemed immoral, offensive, or threatening was instantly abolished by decree, whereas other customs that were considered barriers to progress were abolished outright or steps were taken to suppress them. Native offenders who continued the then-illegal customs were fined, jailed, or subjected to various forms of corporal or capital punishment until they respected the new laws. However, despite all of the forces brought against them, many customs proved difficult to eradicate and were often carried on covertly for years.

Forced cultural modification can be approached from many angles, several of which have already been discussed or alluded to. This chapter describes the general attitude of governments and social scientists toward the subject and surveys the range and intensity of cultural modification practices in different countries with an emphasis on the colonial period, from approximately 1830 to 1950. (Economic development constitutes a special category of cultural modification and will be treated in a separate chapter.)

These Are the Things That Obstruct Progress

> The political autonomy, economic habits, religious practices, and sexual customs of organized native groups, in so far as they threaten European control or offend Western notions of morality, must be abandoned.[2]

Once the state embarks upon a policy of integrating small-scale cultures (and, as we have seen, this path is almost always taken), administrators must make policy decisions regarding how to deal with the many diverse elements of a small-scale culture that do not mesh easily with the commercial state. The opening quote suggests that given enough force, governments could completely destroy any small-scale society's cultural diversity with massive cultural modification programs. However, such a rapid course has generally not been economically desirable, and governments usually have been more selective in their destruction of tribal culture.

In the mid-nineteenth century, Herman Merivale,[3] in his lectures on colonization, provided some guidelines for government administrators interested in the control of native customs. Objecting to what he considered to be the misguided philanthropy of some individuals who would leave tribal peoples alone except in matters directly involving Europeans, he discussed tribal customs in terms of three categories: (1) "violations of the eternal and universal laws of morality"; (2) "less horrible," but still "pernicious," customs; and (3) "absurd and impolitic" customs that were not directly injurious.

The first category included such practices as cannibalism, human sacrifice, and infanticide, all of which, according to Merivale, must be suppressed. As we shall see, most authorities have agreed that a category for "immoral" customs should be established, but there have been some different interpretations about which customs belonged in it. Merivale's second category was even less clearly defined. It included a variety of cultural traits that were considered to be "incompatible with civilization," many of which he felt should also be suppressed, although other authorities felt they would best be eliminated by gradual enlightenment rather than by outright force. Merivale's ethnocentric approach to the problem was apparent in his general conclusions: "It will be necessary, in short, that the colonial authorities should act upon the assumption that they have the right in virtue of the relative position of civilized and Christian men to savages, to enforce abstinence from immoral and degrading practices, to compel outward conformity to the law of what we regard as better instructed reason."[4]

This basic directive has been implicitly followed up to the present by government authorities throughout the world, although the "law" of "better instructed reason" has not always held the same meaning, and the question of which cultural traits should be modified is still being debated in some cases.

In general, states have suppressed headhunting and all forms of tribal feuding and warfare, along with cannibalism (including endocannibalism, the ritual eating of a people's own dead), infanticide, euthanasia, execution, and whatever was interpreted to be slavery. These traits all fall under the "inhumane or grossly immoral" category,[5] even though many, such as warfare and execution, are often institutionalized by states. It seems reasonable to assume that such traits are prohibited more because they represent challenges to state authority rather than because they are universally recognized as immoral. A good case could in fact be made in support of many of these "immoral" traits on moral grounds. Euthanasia, for example, is now openly advocated by some physicians. Also, the category of prohibited customs has been expanded to include almost every conceivable trait of small-scale cultures. For example, by 1844, government authorities in New Zealand were likely to prevent anything done by the Maori that could be considered "inconsistent with good order and with the progress of civilization."[6] In practice, throughout the British Commonwealth tribal peoples were legally subjects of the crown and were expected to behave accordingly. They could retain their traditional cultures as long as they were compatible with "justice, humanity and good government."[7]

Many aspects of tribal kinship and social organization have been attacked as crimes against public order, shocking and injurious, cruel, or simply as obstacles to progress. A partial list of such traits that have been condemned at various times includes transfer of bridewealth, infant betrothal, the levirate (the practice by which a man marries his brother's widow), polygamy, secret societies, and kinship duties in general. The extended family in particular has been criticized as an inappropriate "drag on economic development" and a "serious obstacle to economic progress,"[8] but it is doubtful that direct efforts have ever been made to abolish extended family kinship.

The Indian government attempted to soften its policy of assimilation by taking care not to disturb traditional tribal customs as long as they were considered to be proper.[9] In the North East Frontier Agency, where greater liberality toward tribal cultures was followed than in other regions of India, it was standard practice for government administrators to prohibit the usual traits that offended against "law and order or the universal conscience of mankind." Such traits came to include anything that was clearly "impoverishing" the population, as well as "cruel" forms of animal sacrifice.[10]

French policy toward cultural modification was summarized by the French authority on colonial science, René Maunier, who explained that anything incompatible with French economic interests must be abolished: "Let us say that the French must—or think they must—abrogate the customary law of the colonies when it threatens to interfere with security or prosperity."[11]

This approach was combined with an assimilation theory that attempted to replace everything native with things French and gained for the French the title of "cultural imperialists," for the "wholesale attempt to impose an outside culture upon another people."[12] This was, of course, no different in fact from the policies of every other major nation, but at that time the French were very blatant and at least seemed to be less sympathetic toward indigenous cultures than, for example, were the British.

In the American dependencies, government directives regarding small-scale culture were as ambiguous and open-ended as in other areas. A circular issued in 1932 by the Philippine Bureau of Non-Christian Tribes urged government officials to respect cultural practices that were "not contrary to law, morals, and good customs" but reaffirmed that tribesmen were still to be assimilated as rapidly as possible.[13]

According to Isaac Schapera, by the 1930s, South Africa was following the adaptationist policy as the most reasonable and economical means of "facilitating the transition to assimilation."[14] This policy assumed that tribal culture might be allowed to persist where necessary, but administrators and missionaries did not always agree on this point. Native customs were recognized by the courts if they were not "repugnant to elementary ideas of justice and humanity" or "illegal"![15] Here as elsewhere, this policy gave local officials considerable room for independent action, and attitudes toward tribal culture varied widely even among the country's scholars. In his discussion of the "native problem," the South African economist W. H. Hutt called for sympathetic understanding of native culture but stressed that assumptions regarding the necessity or permanence of any traits should be avoided.[16] His conclusion on the matter was that probably the entire culture would have to "go": "Fortunately there is now almost universal agreement that the 'cattle cult,' animal sacrifices, the doctoring of land [magic], and many other obviously effete primitive customs and taboos must go. What is not so readily admitted is that with them must also go the native mode of life and probably the language which was adapted to that life."[17]

In New Guinea the Germans prohibited whatever they considered to be antisocial, whereas the Australian mandate government declared on the positive side that its policy would be to improve the moral and physical environment of village life and to introduce "healthy forms of amusement." This policy resulted in the natives being forced to abandon everything threatening or offensive to Europeans; it extended to the extreme that in the 1930s a person who used "obscene" language could end up in court.[18] By the late 1960s, the Australian administration in Papua New Guinea was still prohibiting religious practices thought to be "repugnant to the general principles of humanity," illegal, or "not in the best interest of a child." There were also official complaints that cultural diversity presented "obstacles to orderly social change" and that "adherence to custom can hinder progress."[19]

The cultural modification policies of the independent, modernizing nations have sometimes been more sweeping in their destruction of tribal culture than were the earlier colonial authorities, particularly where they have followed the ruthless prescriptions of development experts such as economist Robert Heilbroner, who recommended the following measures to help transform "tradition-bound" societies into "modern" societies: "Nothing short of pervasive social transformation will suffice: a wholesale metamorphosis of habits, a wrenching reorientation of values concerning time, status, money, work; and an unweaving and reweaving of the fabric of daily existence itself."[20]

It seems that anything remotely considered an obstacle to progress might have been slated for elimination by the new leaders of developing nations acting on the advice of development specialists. Guy Hunter, one such expert who wrote widely on the development problems of Africa and Asia, listed a number of "nonadaptable" African tribal institutions, such as tribal organization, matrilyny, and shifting cultivation, which he felt were unsuitable in a modernizing society and presumably should be abandoned.[21] In a similar manner, Denis Goulet, another development writer, lumped "chattel marriages" (implying bridewealth exchanges), along with infanticide as incompatible with human rights and positively harmful impediments to development, and therefore considered them to be expendable cultural traits.[22] Almost in the same breath Goulet observed that the African value system based on cattle might also be "doomed to disappear." Paradoxically, Goulet earlier complained that in such matters social engineers lacked "clear universal directives" and faced "perplexing questions" over "which cultural peculiarities are to be allowed and which eliminated."[23] Such problems are unavoidable when individuals attempt to program a way of life for people in alien cultures.

Social Engineering: How to Do It

When a change that is to be applied to the common man, usually a village peasant, has been agreed upon by a member of the ruling elite and the overseas specialist, the problem is how to convince this common man to accept the new ideas without using force.[24]

It is no easy task for an outsider to get people to change their pattern of doing things.[25]

Designating which aspects of small-scale culture to eliminate and selecting suitable replacements are relatively simple problems compared with the difficulties of executing such decisions. During the early period of colonial expansion, governments allowed most of their cultural modification work to be carried out by "natural" frontier processes, or they resorted to direct military or police force to suppress "illegal" customs, while the remaining unsuitable customs were attended to by missionaries. Naked force has been widely applied against tribal cultures and continues to be used even at the present time because of the speed and apparent efficiency of its results. In the late 1960s, the Ugandan government, for example, abolished a bothersome hunting-and-gathering culture virtually overnight when it loaded the entire population of Ik into trucks and drove them out of their homeland.[26] More commonly, direct coercion has been used to suppress specific aspects of a traditional culture that have been declared illegal. Maunier explained the French approach to this kind of legal abolition or "civilization by legislation" as follows: "Such and such an act may be absolutely, totally, unreservedly forbidden."[27] Later in this chapter, numerous examples of such use of direct force in culture change are presented, but indirect force, or "social engineering," will be discussed first because, since the 1960s, it has become far more common and deserves special treatment.

In the post–World War II decolonization period, with its emphasis on self-determination of peoples, the use of force in culture change has generally been frowned upon by international agencies and social scientists concerned with human rights. Although the 1948 United Nations Declaration of Human Rights does not specifically mention forced culture change programs, it does state in article 22 that everyone is entitled to the realization of the "cultural rights indispensable for his dignity and the free development of his personality," and forced change could certainly threaten such rights. This interpretation was affirmed, enlarged upon, and made directly applicable to indigenous peoples by the International Covenant of Human Rights, adopted by the UN General Assembly in 1966, which states unequivocally in its convention on civil and political rights that "in those states in which ethnic, religious, or linguistic minorities exist, persons belonging to such minorities shall not be denied the right, in community with the other members of their group, to enjoy their own culture, to profess and practice their own religion, or to use their own language."

Any program of directed culture change imposed upon a "target" population against the people's will would almost unavoidably violate these rights, and in principle at least such programs are usually rejected by social engineers. In

1968 the Permanent Council of the International Congress of Anthropological and Ethnological Sciences acknowledged that force was still being widely used and unanimously passed a resolution on forced acculturation that called upon governments to respect the Declaration of Human Rights.

Applied anthropologists have in general rejected the use of any change techniques that the target or recipient population might interpret as coercive, in part because, as Ward Goodenough explained, "[w]e have scruples against attempting to impose blueprints on others,"[28] but perhaps more importantly because it was long realized that force did not always achieve permanent results. Even Maunier[29] warned that force often generated resistance and caused undesirable cultural traits to go underground. Goodenough was concerned with the same problem and felt that, from a strictly "practical" viewpoint, successful "reform" could not depend on external force, because "the truth is that to accomplish purposive change in another usually requires the other's cooperation." Cultural modification then becomes "helping others to reform themselves." Goodenough specifically rejected the notion that force might still be involved even when it may not be directly perceived by the target group, and he stated flatly that his book outlining how change agents can gain the "cooperation" of their targets was not a book on "how to get other people to do what you want and like it."[30] A closer look at the general techniques of social engineering as it developed in the early postwar period suggests otherwise.

Margaret Mead, in her discussion of culture change in Manus Island, New Guinea, was convinced that tribal peoples there were eager for change, and she too seemed unwilling to recognize how force could possibly be involved in the "modernization" process. As she stated: "We do not conceive of people being forcibly changed by other human beings. We conceive of them as seeing a light and following it freely."[31]

Such firm conviction that if cooperation is gained force is not involved is perhaps understandable in change agents convinced of the desirability of the changes sought. Indeed, to many change experts, the ends appeared to justify the means, regardless of the likelihood that outsiders might make ethnocentric judgments concerning "benefits" and in spite of the unpredictability of the long-term effects of change. This reckless attitude seemed to be expressed in the formal code of ethics adopted by the Society of Applied Anthropology (SfAA) in 1963, which spoke of the need for respecting the "dignity and general well-being" of target peoples, but which was silent on the specific issue of the use of force and appeared to condone it under the proper circumstances. Action that might adversely affect the "lives, well-being, dignity and self-respect" of targets was considered unethical, unless efforts are made to minimize such adverse side effects and unless such action was thought to be beneficial.[32] In other words, as long as your intentions were good, whatever techniques achieved the desired results most effectively were considered acceptable. Since the 1960s there has been an enormous shift in the attitude of applied anthropologists toward the peoples studied and their culture. Not only are applied anthropologists now ethically required to fully disclose their goals, methods, and sponsors to the peoples studied, but Point 2 of the SfAA's current Statement of Ethical and Professional Responsibility clearly states: "To the communities ultimately affected by our activities we owe respect for their dignity, integrity, and worth. We recognize that human survival is contingent upon the continued existence of a diversity of human communities, and guide our professional activities accordingly. We will avoid taking or recommending action on behalf of a sponsor which is harmful to the interests of the community."[33]

Today professional applied anthropologists could not ethically participate in the *indirect* manipulation of tribal peoples, but such techniques have had a long history under colonialism. Maunier advised French colonial authorities that it was generally more advantageous to "conditionally" eliminate undesirable customs through such measures as taxation, licensing, or other forms of control. The secret was to make the change imperceptible: "If reform is necessary, it ought to be carried out after preparation and with due consideration, leaving the subject people under the illusion that their old traditions will be maintained, even if they are in fact being gradually, unobtrusively, progressively, modified—as is necessary. That seems to be sound psychology."[34]

Elsewhere Maunier observed that there are "thousands of ways" of achieving culture change against the real wishes of the natives. In addition to the general method of regulating without directly abolishing customs, Maunier described what could be called the enlightenment approach, in which "reform" was sought by convincing argument, example, and education—all aimed at showing how inferior were native ways and how advantageous it would be for the inhabitants to abandon them in favor of superior French ways. The formal education approach will be examined more closely in another section, but here it can be pointed out that the creation of dissatisfaction as a stimulus for change has been widely recommended by modern change experts. Goulet suggested that traditional peoples must be shocked into the realization that they are living in abnormal, inhuman conditions as psychological preparation for modernization.[35] In Goodenough's view: "The problem that faces development agents, then, is to find ways of stimulating in others a desire for change in such a way that the desire is theirs independent of further prompting from outside. Restated, the problem is one of creating in another a sufficient dissatisfaction with his present condition of self so that he wants to change it. This calls for some kind of experience that leads him to reappraise his self-image and reevaluate his self-esteem."[36]

Applied anthropologists had no secret weapons for achieving culture change: Their recommendations, as they evolved during the 1960s, were usually in the form of common sense advice or sound psychology, based on an understanding of the culture to be modified and embodying proven methods of persuasion. For example, in addition to the obvious tactic of tampering with self-images, change agents were advised to:

- Involve traditional leaders in their programs
- Work through bilingual, acculturated individuals who have some knowledge of both the dominant and the target culture
- Modify circumstances or deliberately tamper with the equilibrium of the traditional culture so that change will become imperative
- Attempt to change underlying core values before attacking superficial customs

The change agent was furthermore advised to gain the respect and confidence of the indigenous people, to manipulate traditional attitudes toward status and prestige to his or her advantage, to make certain that the modifications sought are actually possible, and to time modifications carefully.[37] The judicious employment of material rewards or "benefits" was perhaps one of the strongest change strategies because these may be offered to the target group "when it performs in a manner prescribed by the agent of change," not unlike pigeons being taught to peck at appropriately colored disks.[38]

While anthropologists trained and advised change agents, they were able to use their specialized knowledge of social structure, value systems, and the functional interrelatedness of culture to identify both the "barriers" to change and the "progressive forces" within a specific target culture.[39]

Clearly, the change strategies just outlined did not rely on the direct use of force, but in terms of the larger context of most change programs, coercion was almost always implicit. Change was being deliberately initiated by outsiders. In the final analysis, blueprints were being handed down from above by individuals and agencies in the dominant culture that were making the policy decisions for a submissive target culture that ultimately had no power to resist. The critical problems were that not only were basic human cultural rights being threatened, but the changes themselves, though they may have been well intentioned, all too often were tragically destructive. The ethical problem that later anthropologists questioned was what George M. Foster called the "rationale" for directed culture change programs: "that technical experts can and should evaluate the practices of other people and decide which ones should be modified."[40]

When "other people" are people with a radically different culture, and when they are ultimately powerless to resist such change programs, the rationale does need to be reconsidered. The earlier views of seemingly well-informed anthropologists on the appropriateness and value of particular cultural practices were sometimes dangerously wrong. For example, A. P. Elkin, for many years the principal authority on Australian Aborigines, understood the intricacies of aboriginal beliefs in totemic ancestors and sacred sites, but Elkin was also a Christian minister and felt that such beliefs were wrong. He argued that Christianity and science should replace Aboriginal reverence for sacred sites. He thought that for their own benefit, Aborigines needed to be convinced that "their own spiritual life and the future of natural species is not bound up with the integrity of particular spots on the earth's surface."[41] In fact, the Aborigines were right—their spirituality and the future of their natural resources were tied to the integrity of their sacred sites, but it was more than forty years before the Australian government acknowledged this point. Since the Land Rights Act of 1976 (see chapter 10), sacred sites have been the foundation of the Aborigines' struggle to regain control of their lands.

The following sections present specific examples of cultural modification policies in action against tribal peoples in different parts of the world. Education policies in colonial settings and American Indian schools are briefly examined, and both direct and indirect change strategies are illustrated with cases involving government attempts to destroy shamanism and ceremonial activities, desert pastoral nomadism, the East African cattle complex, and swidden agriculture.

Education for Progress

> People must learn to be scientific and progressive in outlook instead of living by ancestral laws and long-tried rules of thumb.[42]

In many countries, especially under colonialism, schooling has been the prime coercive instrument of cultural modification and has proved to be a highly effective means of destroying self-esteem, fostering new needs, creating dissatisfaction, and generally disrupting traditional cultures without empowering people to take control over the conditions affecting their daily lives. As representatives of the prestige and power of the dominant society, teachers assumed positions of authority over students, overshadowing parents and traditional tribal leaders. But even more important, schooling conflicted with the education that children gain from participation in their own societies and cultures. Tribal cultures generally require mastery of a specialized knowledge of the natural environment, as well as special training in folklore, religion, ritual, technology, and other skills. The years that children are required to spend studying the dominant culture's textbooks are in direct competition with the normal enculturation process. Furthermore, schooling deprives the traditional community of the important contribution that children often make to the subsistence economy. Ian Cunnison reported that children of Sudanese tribal "nomads who spent as little as two years in schools returned to their homes without the skills needed of cattle herders, and they also became physically too 'soft' to readapt to the demands of traditional life. This example no doubt overstates the incompatibility between formal schooling and effective participation in subsistence pursuits, but this issue is too often overlooked."[43]

Under colonial conditions, schooling was often a direct means of cultural modification. According to Raymond Buell,[44] in French colonial schools two basic subjects were taught. The first was morale, which aimed at instilling French ideals of "good habits, cleanliness, order, politeness, respect, and obedience." French was the second subject and the principal language of instruction, whereas in some colonies all use of native language in schools was forbidden by decree. Lessons included "simple ideas of France and the French people," and advanced students were instructed in the meanings of such terms as *justice, respect, altruism, charity, pity*, and *compassion*—all of which were presumed to be unfamiliar concepts. The most important lessons were the need for loyalty to France and the importance of cooperating with French interests. Schoolchildren were taught to despise their own traditions and cultures in a direct and ethnocentric manner, as illustrated by the following excerpt from a French reader designed in 1919 for use by French West African schoolchildren: "It is . . . an advantage for a native to work for a white man, because the whites are better educated, more advanced in civilization than the natives, and because, thanks to them, the natives will make more rapid progress . . . and become one day really useful men. . . . You who are intelligent and industrious, my children, always help the Whites in their task. This is a duty."[45]

In the colonial government schools of Italian East Africa, tribal children were taught discipline, respect, and obedience—to Italian authority. With amazing ethnocentrism, teachers also proceeded to teach tribal boys arts and crafts and how to farm, while girls were taught how to cook native food! Italian textbooks, described as "didactic aids adapted to the attitudes and capacities of the natives," contained such choice readings as:

I am happy to be subject to the Italian government and I love Italy with the affection of a son.

or simply:

Help me, oh God, to become a good Italian![46]

For many years in the United States the government delegated the formal education of Indian children to missionaries such as Stephen Riggs, whose attitude toward Indian culture was summarized by his 1846 statement that "*as tribes and nations the Indians must perish and live only as men!*"[47] Boarding schools were considered one of the best means of destroying Indian culture because here even very young children could be almost permanently separated from the influences of their parents. Mission teachers imposed haircuts, Western dress, new English names, and rigid schedules on their charges, and they emphasized religion and manual labor.

A similar approach to missionary boarding schools was applied in South America. For example, the Salesian boarding school of La Esmeralda, which was opened in 1972 in Venezuela for the Yanomamo and Makiritari Indians, was apparently operated with little regard for the traditional culture. Children were kept within the school's walled-in compound, often against their wills. Their hair was cut, their clothing was changed, and they were given Spanish names. Outside observers reported that the children complained of the restrictions, lack of food, homesickness, ridicule of their traditions, and being beaten. They also frequently attempted to run away.[48]

In the Peruvian Amazon in 1964, I found Seventh-day Adventist missions promoting profound changes among the Asháninka. The Adventists forbade polygyny, shamanism, drinking manioc beer, dancing, body ornaments, and the eating of a long list of fish and game considered "unclean." These prohibitions struck at the very core of Asháninka culture, but at that time the missions went even further by discouraging use of the Asháninka language in the schools. In contrast to this ethnocentric and colonizing approach, beginning in the 1980s indigenous leaders, anthropologists, and many educators have made competence in indigenous language and culture, as well as competence in the national language, the goal of formal bicultural, or intercultural education for indigenous students. For example, AIDESEP,[49] an indigenous organization operating in the Peruvian Amazon, began an intercultural bilingual teacher training and primary education program in 1985 to replace missionary-focused programs. By 2007 this program, FORMABIAP,[50] was working with fourteen indigenous groups and had trained more than two thousand teachers. FORMABIAP also emphasizes a practical understanding of contemporary realities of national politics, economy, and society, so that graduates of the training program can become future indigenous leaders.[51]

Eliminating Shamanism

Government authorities and missionaries often singled out tribal curers and shamans for negative attention because they seemed to represent direct challenges to Western medicine and Christianity and because they were thought to symbolize traditional culture in opposition to progress. More recently, as cross-culturally sensitive indigenous leaders and anthropologists have moved into decision-making positions in development agencies, these attitudes have begun to change. Some of the most successful health programs have combined traditional curers and indigenous knowledge of herbal medicines with Western biomedical practices to help improve health conditions in indigenous communities. PSI, the indigenous health program begun in the Peruvian Amazon by AIDESEP[52] in 1994, is a good example of this intercultural approach. PSI was funded in part by the Nordic Agency for Development and Ecology (NORDECO) in Denmark. When the PSI pilot program was completed in 2000, it was reaching 119 indigenous communities and included a training program to support community level health coordinators.[53]

Respect for indigenous culture was not easily won, and could be easily lost, because it is so vulnerable to national politics and the power of the state. One of the strongest antishaman campaigns was carried out during the Stalin era, especially before World War II, by the Soviet Union in the Soviet Far East, where shamans were classified along with other tribal leaders (or ruling cliques) as wealthy "exploiters" and "parasitic groups" who "battled bitterly against the new regime and actively attempted to sabotage its projects."[54] According to Soviet officials, shamans played an extremely negative role in small-scale cultures, in part because they made "wasteful" animal sacrifices and were the principal exponents of an "outdated religious ideology," but also because they apparently led the resistance to Soviet schools, medical centers, "culture bases," and collective farms. One shamanistic activity that must have been particularly frustrating for Soviet authorities was the continuing effort of the shamans to regulate the tribe's resource exploitation practices by enjoining hunting and fishing on some days and even prohibiting the killing of specific animals. Clearly, in Soviet eyes, shamans were a "reactionary, counter-revolutionary force."[55]

An offensive was launched against the shamans in which they were arrested and exiled or forced to publicly renounce their activities. The local representatives of the League of the Militant Godless were enlisted to gather information on shamans and to generally conduct antireligious propaganda among the tribes. As part of the campaign, efforts were also made to replace shamans with what Walter Kolarz refers to as the "Lenin-Stalin Cult."[56] The government circulated poems and folk tales in which Lenin and Stalin were represented as all-powerful solar deities capable of defeating all evils, in hopes of overshadowing the role of shaman. The extravagant nature of these tales is well represented by the following quote from "Sun of the People," a story that was designed for the hunting and fishing Nanai: "Nobody can equal the strength of that hero [Stalin]. His eyes see everything that goes on on earth. His brain knows all that people think. His heart contains the happiness and the woe of all peoples. The depth of his thought is as deep as the ocean. His voice is heard by all that inhabit the earth. Such is the greatest of the very greatest in the whole world."[57]

What shaman could compete with that kind of power and authority?

Shamans and the practice of tribal religions in general also came under similar attacks in other parts of the world. Speaking of Bantu shamans in South Africa, Schapera stated that their influence was unhealthy and that they constituted a "powerful obstacle to progress" because of their "almost fanatical" conservatism.[58] He felt that the best way to eliminate their influence and their belief in witchcraft and magic would be through "the effective teaching of scientific principles."

In nearby Rhodesia (now Zambia and Zimbabwe), witchcraft and some forms of divination were outlawed by the Witchcraft Regulations of 1895 and the Witchcraft Suppression Act of 1899. The latter act, which was vigorously enforced in the 1960s, provided medieval punishments of up to seven years' imprisonment and/or thirty-six lashes for anyone proved to be "by habit and repute a witch doctor or witch finder"[59] or for the use of charms to locate lost or stolen articles. The law also declared that anyone receiving money for any "exercise of so-called witchcraft or the use of charms," or who gave any instruction or advice on the subject, would be punished for fraud.

In New Guinea, curers were often regarded as illegal and were not infrequently prosecuted for practicing their art. Medical doctors sometimes attempted to shame and embarrass them by using modern drugs and even imposed medical attention on unwilling patients, who sometimes had to be literally dragged into operating rooms because of their fear of foreign practitioners.[60]

Every Ceremony Must Go

Conspicuous ceremonial activities or particularly unusual customs were very often candidates for elimination, because even if colonial authorities did not define them as contrary to "universal morality," they were certain to be considered obstacles to progress.

From 1884 to 1933, U.S. laws forbade "pagan" Indian ceremonies that the Indian Bureau felt would inhibit the spread of Christianity. The Sun Dance ceremony of the Plains Indians, which was their highest expression of tribal unity and identity, was specifically outlawed, presumably because it involved physical ordeals that the U.S. government considered immoral. In 1926 the leaders of Taos Pueblo in New Mexico were jailed for participating in illegal religious ceremonies described as pagan, horrible, sadistic, and obscene. Efforts were even made to prevent Pueblo youth from being initiated in traditional tribal fashion.[61]

The French acted with characteristic thoroughness in areas under their jurisdiction. In the Marquesas in the 1850s, tattooing, singing, dancing, and performance of the traditional religion were abolished at one sweep.[62] The Dutch treated ceremonies more cautiously than did the French. In the Celebes, ceremonies "which could be vested with a Christian mantle" could remain, but this sometimes required some special engineering such as changing the dates on which some ceremonies would take place, renaming them, and so on.[63]

In New Guinea, missionaries took it upon themselves to speed culture change by destroying "pagan" ceremonial art and burning down spirit houses.[64] Missionaries in Assam forbade singing, dancing, and the wearing of all distinctive ornaments by their Naga converts, and government schools went even further by not allowing pupils to wear flowers in their hair.[65] In the Naga case, the missionaries' rationale for their action was simple, as Verrier Elwin explains: "As religion plays a part in every Naga ceremony and as that religion is not Christianity, every ceremony must go."[66]

Whereas missionary efforts to clothe natives are notorious, it is often forgotten that government efforts in the same direction have often been just as vigorous and even harder for tribal people to ignore. For example, a local government order in Burma in 1957 prohibited hill tribe people from wearing their traditional red cane belts and specified how wide their loincloths were to be, as well as the length of women's skirts.[67] By royal decree in 1881 the Spanish attempted to force Philippine hill tribesmen in northern Luzon to wear breeches and coats in the presence of government officials.[68] It was also common practice for government edicts to require the distribution of clothing to native labor forces and to insist that it be worn.

Even the simple dignity of burial according to the forms prescribed by their traditional cultures was sometimes denied tribal peoples. In 1918 and 1922 the American administration in the Philippines passed laws requiring the tribespeople to bury their dead in a specific fashion in approved cemeteries. In order to eliminate lengthy processes of smoking and tending of the bodies, regulations specified that burial must take place within forty-eight hours.[69] Practices involving platform burials or secondary burial have almost always been prohibited. Even the normally liberal-minded Dutch authorities refused to allow tribal peoples in the Celebes to clean the bones of their dead.[70] Tribal peoples in New Guinea protested bitterly when medical researchers and government coroners desecrated their dead against their wishes, and as recently as 1968 riot police were called out to prevent native "interference" with official autopsies.[71]

It may seem incredible that any society would accept so much interference in their lives, but once government control was firmly established over a tribal population there was little alternative but conformity, at least with conspicuous customs. However, before government authority was complete the situation was different. For example, in Assam a British survey party and escort totaling some eighty men was massacred by the Wancho in 1875 after the people had been ridiculed for their peculiar burial practices and when a chief's tomb was desecrated.[72] In New Guinea in 1904, ten missionaries were killed in a single incident when they attempted to outlaw polygyny.[73] It seems that formerly autonomous tribal peoples did not always welcome interference even after control was established and that they managed to keep many aspects of their cultures alive covertly in the face of constant government efforts at suppression.

Settling Nomads

> In the corridors of international agencies and the desert capitals, the cry goes up, "How do we settle the nomads?"[74]

The pastoral nomads of North Africa, the Middle East, and southwest Asia have evolved a successful ecological adaptation to extremely arid conditions and for thousands of years have maintained a stable symbiotic relationship with their sedentary "civilized" village neighbors.[75] Few small-scale societies in other parts of the world have made such a satisfactory adjustment to both civilization and their natural environment. However, since 1945 this adaptation has been increasingly threatened because governments have set about to solve what they considered to be the nomad problem by abolishing the nomadic way of life. The "problem" of nomads is that their mobility makes it difficult for governments to impose controls over them and that they seem to place tribal loyalties above national loyalties. Furthermore, there are sometimes misleading official complaints that nomadism is wasteful and that nomads infringe on the rights of settled farmers. Some writers have explained that nomadism constitutes a "challenge to the orderly mind" of the government administrator eager to do something to improve the "wretched" living conditions of the nomads.[76] This is perhaps closer to the truth than other perspectives. Writing in the late 1960s, Cunnison boiled down all of the charges against nomads into one: "incompatibility with the aims of a modern state and the modern world."[77] This means, of course, that most states refuse to compromise and will not recognize either the special contribution that nomads make to the national economy or their special needs. Actually, nomads efficiently exploit vast arid lands in the only way that the peculiar ecological conditions of many of these areas will probably ever allow, and as a result nomads are often better fed and wealthier than village agriculturalists.

Governments generally followed the "solution" to the nomad "problem," which called for converting all nomads into sedentary villages. In some countries this was expressed as clear government policy, such as in Syria, where the 1950 Constitution declared, "[T]he government shall endeavor to sedentarize all nomads."[78] Some degree of continuous sedentarization has probably always been a necessary part of the nomadic adaptation and has even included some nomadization of the sedentary population, but in the second half of the twentieth century the process was drastically accelerated by deliberate government action. Certainly the pacification of the desert, which ended intertribal feuding and raids, served to weaken tribal political organization but would not in itself destroy the nomadic way of life. More significant have been government settlement schemes involving outright propaganda programs on the virtues of settled life and the drilling of wells, land allotments, and schooling. These direct measures have been facilitated by the roads and trucks that have replaced camel caravans and by the oil companies that have made extensive use of nomad labor. Governments are fighting powerful ecological and cultural forces, however, and they may not be entirely successful without the use of even greater coercion. In 1960 nearly 7 million people in the Sahara, Arabia, and Southwest Asia were estimated to still be following a nomadic life.[79] In 1987 IWGIA estimated that there were 21 million nomads or pastoral peoples in North and East Africa and southwest Asia.[80]

Nomadism in general (and the Arab Bedouin form in particular) has been highly romanticized in the Western world, but fortunately this has not prevented anthropologists from defending the nomadic way of life. Some social scientists, however, have supported the prevailing government policies of assimilation. For example, Mohamed Awad, who in 1960 participated as chairman of UNESCO's executive board in the UN-sponsored international symposium "The Problem of the Arid Zone," in no way questioned the need to settle nomads and reported optimistically that converting them to a sedentary life was not impossible, although he cautioned that the process would be slow and that "no initiative can be expected from the nomads themselves." He felt that the initiative must come from the governments concerned, and he recommended that the end should be achieved as rapidly as possible, whether the motives were humanitarian, political, economic, strategic, or administrative.[81] Interestingly, several other participants in the symposium felt that total elimination of the nomadic way of life was undesirable and would result in the impoverishment of the people involved. They made the then-radical suggestion that governments might attempt to cooperate with the nomads.

Combating the Cattle Complex

Closely paralleling the drive to settle the desert nomads were the efforts of some East African governments to end the seminomadism of tribal cattle herders and to convert them into settled village farmers or isolated ranchers with "improved" herds. These societies are characterized by a so-called cattle complex because subsistence, kinship organization, politics, religion, folk-lore, and personal identity and worth all center on cattle.[82] The great value placed on cattle extends to the point that the loss of a person's favorite cow might be cause for suicide. Much to the frustration of colonial administrators, undisturbed African cattle herders were almost totally self-sufficient and found that very little from the outside world was of any use to them. This, of course, made it difficult to replace their cattle values with equally compelling money values and in general made their overall lifestyle difficult to modify. Although administrators complained of the poor quality of tribal cattle, an-thropological researchers repeatedly emphasized that African pastoralists were interested in cattle for subsistence purposes, not for marketability. Their herds were designed to support as many people as possible, and the system was not an inefficient, irrational, and wasteful use of natural resources, as many development experts and government planners supposed. It simply was, and remains where the system still operates, a specialized and resilient economic system based on principles in complete opposition to those under-lying cattle raising in an industrial society.[83] Any highly successful economic system is bound to be persistent.

The Karimojong of northeastern Uganda represent a specific case of one such East African cattle-herding society that was subjected to intensive government-directed pressure to abandon their nomadic lifestyle and modify their cattle complex. According to Neville Dyson-Hudson,[84] pressure for change began for the Karimojong in 1921, when the British established a civil administration after several years of military patrolling during which "chiefs" had been appointed. In rapid succession, missionaries, a poll tax, and controls on population movement were introduced, and administrative boundaries were drawn in disregard for traditional cultural groupings. Perhaps most seri-ously, the tribe was prohibited from using its normal dry-season grazing ar-eas without special permission from the district commissioner, and anyone making unauthorized moves was subject to a fine of four head of cattle or im-prisonment. Movement between settlements, which had helped distribute the population, was prohibited, and the administration itself freely moved com-munities about to suit its own purposes. The Karimojong often openly defied the new orders in spite of the punishments that were meted out, and in 1923 they even speared to death one of the government-appointed chiefs who had attempted to prevent their annual cattle movements. Restrictions on cattle and population movement were followed by measures to reduce the number of cattle and "improve" their quality so the cattle would be suitable for market. The administration urged the Karimojong to sell their cattle and raise cash crops instead. As a further inducement, entire regions traditionally used as pasturage were closed to the Karimojong and opened to use by the neighbor-ing tribes. In addition, the administration organized cattle markets and initiated inoculation programs for cattle. These actions only caused further resentment, and the Karimojong responded by hiding their herds and refusing to sell. They were particularly disturbed when some of their inoculated cattle died and correctly assumed that their way of life was being attacked by a government that "eats our cattle."

On the basis of his study of the Karimojong, Dyson-Hudson concluded (along with numerous other observers) that pastoral societies are "generally slow and difficult to change." By 1958, after facing nearly forty years of deliberate cultural modification policies, the sixty thousand Karimojong had managed to maintain their basic value system intact, even to the extent that they still engaged in cattle raiding against neighboring groups. Karimojong raiding and intergroup violence continued into the twenty-first century, amplified by government intervention and the availability of automatic weapons.[85]

In nearby Kenya, the government-sponsored Konza Scheme was designed in 1947 as a pilot program to convert the nomadic Maasai into settled ranchers, but it failed to overcome traditional pastoral values. Ten families were settled on individually fenced plots that were provided with wells, dams, and dipping tanks, but they refused to sell their cattle, retained their social ties with their nomadic kin, and within ten years had completely undermined the scheme.[86]

More direct action was taken by Tanzania, an independent country with an avowed goal of blending socialism and African culture. Perhaps recognizing the difficulties of changing pastoralists when the cattle complex remained intact, they attempted to force the Barabaig to stop herding cattle and to settle down as gardeners. The government program included a ban on traditional dress and forced "reeducation" of tribal youth, and was pushed so vigorously that George Klima, who conducted anthropological research in the area, concluded that "[a]ll of these changes and more will eventually destroy the traditional life-ways the Barabaig have created over the centuries. Another island of cultural diversity will have disappeared into oblivion."[87]

Unfortunately, the result of such modification policies meant far more than merely the loss of cultural diversity, but, as will be shown in chapter 9, it also brought social, economic, and environmental disaster. Forced modification of the subsistence practices of cattle-herding peoples has been carried out in the name of environmental protection, but evidence that such practices are degrading the environment seems questionable and other factors may well be at work.[88] Cattle herders such as the Maasai have been excluded from some areas that they used traditionally because conservationists believed cattle herding was incompatible with the maintenance of wildlife. Such incompatibility seems unlikely, however; the value of maintaining "pure wilderness" for tourism was probably the real objective for government planners.[89]

Weaning from the Axe

Shifting, or swidden, agriculture came under government attack almost as frequently as pastoral nomadism. Swidden agriculture involves cutting and burning a small opening in the forest, cultivating it for two years or so, and then allowing the forest to regrow. Within fifteen to twenty-five years the same plot may be cleared and planted again. To administrators it appears to be a wasteful process, but in most tropical forest environments under aboriginal conditions it has proved to be a sound and stable form of adaptation to the severe limitations shallow soils and heavy rainfall place on agricultural activities. Like nomads, shifting agriculturalists tend to be independent, self-sufficient peoples, characterized by frequent population movements, and their entire cultures are often neatly integrated with their agricultural cycles. None of these features fits neatly with the interests of government planners.

The Baiga of India, who have been described by Elwin,[90] exemplify the kinds of pressures that governments have used in many countries to destroy the swidden lifestyle. In 1868, in the interests of both civilizing the Baiga and opening their forests for commercial exploitation, the government declared that the Baiga had no occupancy rights in their forests and completely forbade shifting cultivation in some zones. To enforce the new laws, crops were destroyed, and, since hunting and fishing were also important components of the Baiga subsistence system, they too were declared illegal by the Game Act, which prohibited even the killing of hares. The bows and arrows the Baiga were no longer allowed to carry were confiscated and burned by officials, whereas outsiders who could purchase licenses were allowed to hunt within Baiga territory. In Elwin's estimation, forbidding shifting cultivation was equivalent to taking food from Baiga mouths and thus constituted a direct assault on their entire culture. Under some administrators the policy was softened to a gradual "weaning" from the axe because, as an official report complained in 1893, the Baiga insisted on clinging "like a spoilt child to their axe and fire."[91] Axes were taxed and the Baiga were permitted to continue their traditional farming practices only in carefully selected reserve zones considered to be useless for any other purpose. Even within these reserves, the government attempted to make the Baiga take up sedentary plow agriculture on individually allotted plots, and outsiders were brought in to farm reserve land as examples for the Baiga. These efforts were supplemented by attempts to remove some Baiga tribespeople and integrate them with sedentary villagers, where they could be supplied with plows, seed, land, and bullocks. Some successes were claimed, but many Baiga chose to flee rather than give up their traditional culture. Weaning from the axe also caused the population to plummet from some fifteen hundred individuals in 1891 to a low of six hundred in 1939, and those who survived faced poverty and destitution.

Notes

1. Ron Crocombe, 1971, "Land Reform: Prospects for Prosperity," in *Land Tenure in the Pacific*, ed. R. Crocombe, 375-400. Melbourne: Oxford University Press, 380.

2. Stephen W. Reed, 1943, *The Making of Modern New Guinea*, Philadelphia: American Philosophical Society, xvii.

3. Herman Merivale, 1861, *Lectures on Colonization and Colonies*, London: Green, Longman and Roberts, 502–3.

4. Ibid.

5. M. F. Lindley, 1926, *The Acquisition and Government of Backward Territory in International Law*, London: Longman, Green, 374.

6. Alpheus Henry Snow, 1921, *The Question of Aborigines: In the Law and Practice of Nations*, New York: Putnam, 204.

7. Lindley, *Backward Territory in International Law*, 375, emphasis mine.

8. Peter T. Bauer and Basil S. Yamey, 1957, *The Economics of Under-Developed Countries*, Cambridge Economic Handbooks, Chicago: University of Chicago Press, 64, 66.

9. L. A. Krishna Iyer and L. K. Bala Ratnam, 1961, *Anthropology in India*, Bombay: Bharatiya Vidya Bhavan, 227.

10. Verrier Elwin, 1959, *A Philosophy for NEFA*, 2nd ed., Shillong, India: J. N. Chowdhury, 224, 250–51.

11. René Maunier, 1949, *The Sociology of Colonies*, London: Routledge and Kegan Paul, 2:501–2.

12. Raymond L. Buell, 1928, *The Native Problem in Africa*, 2 vols., New York: Macmillan, 77.

13. Felix M. Keesing and Marie Keesing, 1934, *Taming Philippine Headhunters: A Study of Government and of Cultural Change in Northern Luzon*, London: George Alien and Unwin, 33.

14. Isaac Schapera, 1934, *Western Civilization and the Natives of South Africa*, London: George Routledge and Sons, x–xii.

15. Ibid., emphasis mine.

16. W. H. Hutt, 1934, "The economic position of the Bantu in South Africa," in *Western Civilization and the Natives of South Africa*, ed. I. Schapera, 195–237. London: George Routledge and Sons.

17. Ibid., 209–10.

18. Stephen W. Reed, 1943, *The Making of Modern New Guinea*, Philadelphia: American Philosophical Society, xvii, 138–39, 176–77.

19. Australia Department of Territories, Report for 1967–1968, 3, 8,10–11,19.

20. Robert L. Heilbroner, 1963, *The Great Ascent: The Struggle for Economic Development in Our Time*, New York: Harper Torchbooks, 53.

21. Guy Hunter, 1967, *The Best of Both Worlds: A Challenge on Development Policies in Africa*, London: Oxford University Press, 72.

22. Denis Goulet, 1971, *The Cruel Choice: A New Concept in the Theory of Development*, New York: Atheneum, 326.

23. Ibid., 268–70.

24. Conrad M. Arensberg and Arthur H. Niehoff, 1964, *Introducing Social Change: A Manual for Americans Overseas*, Chicago: Aldine, 68.

25. Ibid., 87.

26. Colin M. Turnbull, 1972, *The Mountain People*, New York: Simon and Schuster.

27. Maunier, *Sociology of Colonies*, 2:504.

28. Ward H. Goodenough, 1963, *Cooperation in Change*, New York: John Wiley and Sons, 16.

29. Maunier, *Sociology of Colonies*, 513.

30. Goodenough, *Cooperation in Change*, 16–17.

31. Margaret Mead, 1961, *New Lives for Old*, New York: New American Library, 19–20.

32. Society for Applied Anthropology, 1963, "Statement on ethics of the society for applied anthropology," *Human Organization* 22: 237.

33. Society for Applied Anthropology, 2007, Statement of Professional and Ethical Responsibilities, http://www.sfaa.net/sfaaethic.html (accessed July 9, 2007).

34. Maunier, *Sociology of Colonies*, 513.

35. Goulet, *Cruel* Choice, 25–26.

36. Goodenough, *Cooperation in Change*, 219.

37. Arensberg and Niehoff, *Manual for Americans Overseas*; George M. Foster, 1969, *Applied Anthropology*, Boston: Little, Brown; Goodenough, *Cooperation in Change*; Garth N. Jones, 1965, "Strategies and tactics of planned organizational change: Case examples in the modernization process of traditional societies," *Human Organization* 24(3): 192–200.

38. Jones, "Strategies and tactics."

39. Foster, *Applied Anthropology*, 120.

40. Ibid., 136.

41. A. P. Elkin, 1934, "Anthropology and the future of the Australian Aborigines," *Oceania* 5(1): 7.

42. Jones, "Strategies and tactics."

43. Ian Cunnison Cunnison, 1966, *Bagara Arabs: Power and Lineage in a Sudanese Nomad Tribe*, Oxford: Clarendon Press, 40–41.

44. Buell, *The Native Problem*, 55.

45. Moussa et Gi-gla, *Histoire de deux Petits Noir*, cited in Buell, *The Native Problem*, 63.

46. Roland R. De Marco, 1943, *The Italianization of African Natives: Government Native Education in the Italian Colonies 1890–1937*, Teacher's College, Columbia University Contributions to Education no. 880, New York: Columbia University Press, 36, 40.

47. Emphasis in original, cited in Robert F. Berkhofer, 1965, *Salvation and the Savage: An Analysis of Protestant Missions and American Indian Response, 1787–1862*, Lexington: University of Kentucky Press, 7.

48. Jacques Lizot, 1976, *The Yanomami in the Face of Ethnocide*, IWGIA Document no. 22, Copenhagen: IWGIA.

49. Asociación Interétnica de Desarrollo de la Selva Peruana, Interethnic Development Association of the Peruvian Forest, http://www.aidesep.org.pe/ (accessed July 10, 2007).

50. El Programa de Formación de Maestros Bilingües de la Amazonía Peruana,, Bilingual Teacher Training Program of the Peruvian Amazon, http://www.formabiap.org/ (accessed July 10, 2007).

51. Lucy A. Trapnell, 2003, "Some Key Issues in Intercultural Bilingual Education Teacher Training Programmes—as seen from a teacher training programme in the Peruvian Amazon Basin," *Comparative Education* (39)2: 165–83.

52. Programa de Salud Indígena, Indigenous Health Program, Asociación Interétnica de Desarrollo de la Selva Peruana, Interethnic Development Association of the Peruvian Forest, http://www.aidesep.org.pe/index.php?id=20,155,0,0,1,0> (accessed December 11, 2007).

53. Søren Hvalkof, 2004, *Dreams Coming True: An Indigenous Health Programme in the Peruvian Amazon*, Copenhagen: NORDECO.

54. M. G. Levin and L. P. Potapov, 1964, *The Peoples of Siberia*, Chicago: University of Chicago Press, 10, 497–98.

55. K. Kosokov, 1930, *Voprosu o Shamanstve v Severnoy Azii* [On the question of shamanism in northern Asia], Moscow, cited in Walter Kolarz, 1954, *The Peoples of the Soviet Far East*, New York: Praeger, 76.

56. Kolarz, *Soviet Far East*, 79–80.

57. Ibid., 80.

58. Schapera, *Natives of South Africa*, 33–34.

59. Witchcraft Suppression Act of 1899, articles 4 and 8, cited in J. R. Crawford, 1967, *Witchcraft and Sorcery in Rhodesia*, London: Oxford University Press (for International African Institute).

60. John Ryan, 1969, *The Hot Land: Focus on New Guinea*, New York: Macmillan, 41.

61. John Collier, 1947, *The Indians of the Americas*, New York: W. W. Norton, 233–34, 256.

62. Maunier, *Sociology of Colonies*, 500–1.

63. A. C. Kruyt, 1929 "The influence of Western civilization on the inhabitants of Poso (Central Celebes)," In *The Effect of Western Influence on Native Civilizations in the Malay Archipelago*, ed. B. Schrieke, Batavia: Java Royal Batavia Society of Arts and Sciences, 7–8.

64. Ryan, *The Hot Land*, 68.

65. Verrier Elwin, 1939, *The Baiga*, London: John Murray, 512; *Philosophy for NEFA*, 196, 220.

66. Elwin, *Philosophy for NEFA*, 220. Elwin, of course, did not advocate this.

67. F. K. Lehman, 1963, *The Structure of Chin Society: A Tribal People of Burma Adapted to a Non-Western Civilization*, Illinois Studies in Anthropology no. 3, Urbana: University of Illinois Press, 211.

68. Keesing & Keesing, *Philippine Headhunters*, 67–68.

69. Ibid., 238–39.

70. Kruyt, "Influence of Western civilization," 6.

71. Ryan, *The Hot Land*, 41.

72. Elwin, *Philosophy for NEFA*, 250.

73. Ryan, *The Hot Land*, 65.

74. Ian George Cunnison, 1967, *Nomads in the Nineteen-Sixties*, Hull, UK: Hull University, 10.

75. Brian Spooner, 1973, *The Cultural Ecology of Pastoral Nomads*, Modules in Anthropology, Reading, MA: Addison-Wesley, 1973.

76. O. Brémaud and J. Pagot, 1962, "Grazing lands, nomadism and transhumance in the Sahel," in *The Problems of the Arid Zone*, Paris: UNESCO, 320.

77. Cunnison, *Nomads*, 9.

78. Constitution of Syria, 1950, article 158.

79. Mohamed Awad, 1962, "Nomadism in the Arab lands of the Middle East," in *The Problems of the Arid Zone*, 325–39, Paris: UNESCO; Fredrik Barth, 1962, "Nomadism in the mountain and plateau areas of South West Asia," in *The Problems of the Arid Zone*, 341–55, Paris: UNESCO; R. Capot-Rey, 1962, "The present state of nomadism in the Sahara," in *The Problems of the Arid Zone*, 301–10, Paris: UNESCO.

80. IWGIA, 1988, *IWGIA Yearbook 1987*, Copenhagen: IWGIA.

81. Awad, "Nomadism," 336.

82. Robert M. Netting, 1977, *Cultural Ecology*, Menlo Park, CA: Benjamin/Cummings.

83. Rada Dyson-Hudson and Neville Dyson-Hudson, 1969, "Subsistence herding in Uganda," *Scientific American* 220(2): 76–89; J. Terrence McCabe, 2004, *Cattle Bring Us to Our Enemies: Turkana Ecology, Politics, and Raiding in a Disequilibrium System*, Ann Arbor: University of Michigan Press.

84. Neville Dyson-Hudson, 1962, "Factors inhibiting change in an African pastoral society," *Transactions of the New York Academy of Sciences*, series 2, vol. 24, 771–801.

85. Sandra J. Gray, 2000, "Memory of loss: Ecological politics, local history, and the evolution of Karimojong violence," *Human Organization* 59(4): 401–18.

86. William Allan, 1965, *The African Husbandman*, New York: Barnes and Noble, 322–24.

87. George J. Klima, 1970, *The Barabaig: East African Cattle Herders*, New York: Holt, Rinehart and Winston, 112.

88. K. M. Homewood and W. A. Rodgers, 1984, "Pastoralism and conservation," *Human Ecology* 12(4): 431–41 (reprinted in Bodley, 1988a, 310–20). See also chapter 9.

89. Kaj Arhem, 1985, *The Maasai and the State: The Impact of Rural Development Policies on a Pastoral People in Tanzania*, IWGIA Document no. 52, Copenhagen: IWGIA.

90. Verrier, *The Baiga*.

91. Ibid., 119.

8 Economic Globalization

In other words, it is now held that economic development can be induced or even imposed, the goals being determined by governments who become responsible for the coordination and planning deemed necessary to attain them.

—A. B. Mountjoy[1]

GIVEN THE FUNDAMENTAL IMPORTANCE of economic patterns in all cultures, and considering the extreme contrasts between small- and global-scale economies, the economic incorporation of small-scale societies into the global market economy is a critically important phenomenon. A tribal society may surrender its political autonomy but can still continue to be culturally distinct if it is allowed to retain its self-sufficient subsistence economy and if it remains unexploited by outsiders. The nature and degree of a small-scale society's participation in the commercial world is best determined by the people themselves and on their own terms. Only in this way can economic self-sufficiency and cultural autonomy be safeguarded and the "price of progress" be minimized.

Economic experts widely assume that the global economic domination of all smaller-scale systems is *development* in the usual meaning of the word— that is, "a process of natural evolution or growth." But in fact, outside coercion and deliberate manipulation have usually been necessary both to destroy small-scale economies and to carefully channel their conversion into the global market-oriented economy. Development has become an ethnocentric concept, based on assumptions of progress and inevitability, but it might better be replaced by a more accurate and less ethnocentric term such as *transformation*. This is a human problem when outside-directed socioeconomic transformations actually reduce the well-being of people and make local and regional sociocultural systems less resilient and sustainable.

In many areas of the world, the initial breakdown of small-scale economies began under the coercive pressure of the policies of colonial governments designed to develop native labor resources or to promote cash cropping for the benefit of the colonists. These efforts were successful in initiating widespread migratory wage labor and many forms of marginal production for the market economy, but most small-scale societies still managed to retain many of their characteristic features, including partial self-sufficiency and low levels of consumption. Following World War II, government pressures on small-scale economies greatly intensified as a result of a new worldwide campaign for rapid economic growth. Under the technical and financial assistance of the leading industrial countries, nations everywhere attempted to raise their GNPs and initiate self-perpetuating economic growth. Professional development experts, including economists, anthropologists, sociologists, geographers, agriculturalists, and other specialists from various countries and the United Nations, all turned their attention to indigenous peoples, who, because of their "backward" cultures, were considered to be major obstacles to national and international economic goals. These experts devised elaborate programs to bring unwilling indigenous peoples fully into national economies, to further raise their agricultural productivity and per capita cash incomes, and to promote whatever socioeconomic transformations planners deemed necessary to achieve these goals.

In this chapter, the primary concern is to examine the attitudes of government officials and development writers toward this kind of economic development directed at self-sufficient indigenous peoples. Emphasis is given to the strategies employed and the obstacles encountered. The purpose is to demonstrate that indigenous peoples have not always been enthusiastic recipients of commercial economic values and techniques, but rather that their participation in the global market economy has often been brought about by government-supported compulsion, persuasion, and deliberately altered circumstances. The consequences of this economic transformation will be examined in the following chapter.

Forced Labor: Harnessing the Heathens

The natives must be induced to work.[2]

Throughout Africa, Asia, and the Pacific, the economic pursuits of European colonists depended almost entirely upon native labor, but as these new areas were opened, government administrators and colonists soon realized to their dismay that indigenous peoples were neither willing nor eager to labor for the newcomers. Undisturbed tribal societies usually are relatively well-integrated, self-contained, satisfying systems, and their members cannot be expected to suddenly begin working for the material rewards of an alien society without some form of compulsion.

Many governments openly indulged in direct compulsion in the form of corveé, or forced, labor. In British colonies it was common practice to demand an annual period of labor from villagers, sometimes for up to a month of road construction work. In the Dutch Celebes, nearly two months of labor per year were required of indigenous peoples. This was considered to be a tax and was justified in terms of its effectiveness for dealing with cashless small-scale economies.

The force involved in the recruitment of labor by the blackbirders was described in chapter 3, but by the 1880s, when New Guinea was being opened for settlement after the Queensland labor trade had subsided, both German and Australian government officers engaged in their own kidnapping of labor recruits. Stephen W. Reed assures us that this was done primarily in cases of undisturbed villages that refused to supply recruits and where kidnapping seemed to be the only way of "breaking the ice." We are told that trickery was used more often than force and that the procedure would only resemble slavery if done too often. In some instances, small groups of highland Papuans were flown by the government to work in coastal plantations, but this operation was not very successful because the recruits soon wanted to return home and suffered high mortality rates in the strange environment. In its 1923 report to the League of Nations, the Australian mandate government of New Guinea defended such labor policies with the novel argument that if they were not forced to work, the natives were likely to die out from lack of exercise!

The French made liberal use of forced labor in both Africa and Indochina. The Fifteen-Year Plan for the economic development of French West Africa received a major boost by a decree in 1926, creating a conscript labor force that allowed three years of labor per person toward the construction of highways, railroads, irrigation works, and other development projects. Such measures became necessary when the indigenous population proved unwilling to volunteer for year-round labor at incredibly low wages, sometimes thousands of miles from home, and in the face of high mortality rates. The extent of this corveé labor force was staggering. For example, in 1923 nearly 5 million person-days of free labor were reportedly employed in Senegal. Conditions were so poor in some areas that annual death rates in the labor forces sometimes ran as high as 60 percent.[3] Elsewhere in Africa, forced labor was used extensively by the Congo Free State, where a 1903 decree called for forty hours of labor a month from each native in exchange for a token wage.

At best, corveé labor was a traumatic introduction for indigenous peoples to the benefits of labor in the market economy; at worst it was an inhuman and destructive form of slavery. However, clear evidence for the apparent necessity of the procedure can be seen in the fact that the world community did not officially outlaw corvée labor until 1957—long after it had served its purpose.

In that year, the International Labour Organization formally abolished corveé labor in member nations, regardless of whether it was justified as a means of education, labor discipline, or economic development.

Learning the Dignity of Labor: Taxes and Discipline

> Under all circumstances the progress of natives toward civilization is only secured when they shall be convinced of the necessity and dignity of labour; and therefore I think that everything we reasonably do to encourage the natives to work is highly desirable.[4]

Even where direct corveé labor was not practiced, indigenous people were still coerced into the labor force by other means and were often subjected to rigid discipline so that they would not fail to learn the dignity of labor. The most popular and effective form of indirect compulsion was taxation. There were head taxes, poll taxes, even dog taxes, all payable only in cash, which in turn was obtainable only through labor or cash cropping. In many cases, the primary purpose was not to obtain revenue for the state directly; rather, it was to create an artificial need for money and to thereby force reluctant recruits to seek labor in the mines, on the farms and plantations of the colonists, or in the towns, or to take up cash cropping. This is clearly indicated by official government statements and by contemporary observations but is also confirmed by the manner in which these taxes were applied. For example, in Australian New Guinea the head tax did not apply to anyone who had already signed up as an indentured laborer. South African scholars had no doubts about the purposes of the various taxes that their government directed at the Bantu. As W. H. Hutt observed in 1934: "The poll tax and hut tax to which natives are subjected have been used as a means of forcing them into the European economic system."[5]

He felt that the more "backward" a given tribe proved to be, the greater the pressure must be in order to overcome the people's reluctance to join the labor force. The poll tax itself was initiated around 1900 and demanded the equivalent of up to two months of annual labor for all male tribe members over age eighteen. A jail sentence awaited those who failed to pay up. Significantly, this tax applied only to indigenous people and recognized their adulthood three years earlier than that of Europeans, but it was defended as a relatively mild and effective device: "As the natives were often reluctant to leave their homes, a little gentle pressure was brought to bear upon them by the introduction of a poll tax. This measure quite effectively stimulated their desire for earning the white man's money."[6]

Merely forcing indigenous people to obtain a cash income was not sufficient to convert them into permanent full-time employees, because they frequently responded to these pressures by becoming unenthusiastic "target workers" who returned to their villages when they had earned enough to pay their taxes or to purchase a few specific items. Further "instruction" was needed in the dignities of labor, and sympathetic governments readily provided concerned European planters and miners with laws allowing various forms of corporal punishment to correct the "negligence" and "ignorance" of their native employees (see figure 8.1). In German Southwest Africa, the Imperial Ordinance of 1896 prescribed imprisonment in irons and other forms of corporal punishment for workers if their employers found them guilty of "continued neglect of duty and idleness" or "unwarranted desertion" from their places of work. German law did not consider deaths resulting from such "fatherly correction" to be murder, but it did recognize that the villagers might not understand such subtle distinctions.[7] In German New Guinea, European plantation owners could obtain a special disciplinary license permitting them to administer floggings to their employees "for sufficient cause."

The Chief Registrar of Natives,   N.A.D. Form 54/____
NAIROBI.
COMPLAINT OF DESERTION OF REGISTERED NATIVE.

Native's Certificate No. _____ Name _____

The above native deserted from my employ _____
(date)
He was engaged on _____ on _____days verbal contract
(date)   _____ days written contract

at _____
(place)

I wish to prosecute him for this offence and hereby agree to appear as a witness or to produce evidence if and when called upon.

_____
Signature of Employer.

Address _____
_____

Date _____

Figure 8.1. Imposed laws in Kenya in 1922 attempted to teach indigenous workers "the dignity of labor." It was a crime for such workers to quit work without authorization. (W. McGregor Ross, 1927, *Kenya from Within*. London: George Allen & Unwin Ltd.)

Under the Australians, punishments for labor offenses were strictly a government prerogative and officially took place only after trial in the district courts, which seemed particularly dedicated to this problem. Reed reports that in 1937–1938 nearly half of all district court cases involved handing out two-week jail sentences to workers accused of deserting or neglecting their duties.[8]

All of these measures have been stoutly defended by apologists for the colonial system as fulfilling the necessary responsibilities of a civilized guardian over a childlike ward. The American legal authority Alpheus Snow[9] pointed out that indigenous people simply lacked the acquisitive drive characteristic of civilized people, and that doing virtually anything to correct this mental deficiency is permissible and even a moral duty of the state.

Creating Progressive Consumers

> The Australian Government's expenditure on general administration, social services and education helps to raise consumption levels and thus assists the growth of local commercial enterprises.[10]

One of the most significant obstacles blocking native economic "progress" was the ability of the people to find satisfaction at relatively low and stable consumption levels with low ecological footprints and the fact that their cultures were self-sufficient. Independent indigenous peoples with viable economies often expressed little desire to obtain any foreign manufactured goods except those of immediate practical utility, such as metal axes, knives, and mirrors. Demand for these simple utilitarian articles often initiated specific changes in day-to-day life but did not mean a rejection of indigenous culture. Therefore, this demand was often not powerful enough to ensure transformation. Outsiders quickly realized that if indigenous peoples could somehow be made to reject the material satisfactions provided by their own cultures and if they could be successfully urged to desire more and more commercial goods, they would become more willing participants in the cash economy.

Raising consumption levels was not as simple as it might seem. As pointed out previously, acquisitiveness is not a universal trait, and small-scale cultures have developed numerous means of limiting the overaccumulation of material goods. Special pressures were necessary to overcome these built-in defenses against alien material goods and standards of value. The first and most obvious pressures for increased consumption of foreign goods were brought about by disturbances in small-scale socioeconomic organization that accompanied the uncontrolled frontier and the end of the group's political autonomy. Forced labor, depopulation, reduced land base, loss of indigenous food sources, and taxation all helped create a dependency on external goods. When these factors were combined with the ready availability of such goods—whether given out by missionaries and government welfare posts or offered by traders—increasing demand was almost certain to follow. Naturally, government development projects that have pushed new communication networks into formerly isolated areas and that have encouraged or even subsidized the work of commercial agents have contributed to increased demand for manufactured goods. It seems doubtful, however, that the mere availability of these goods, in the absence of the disturbances accompanying this availability, would be sufficient to create significant demand for them. Many proponents of the demonstration effects theory would argue just the opposite—attributing the disturbance and breakdown of small-scale societies largely to their demands for the superior goods of global-scale societies. But it would seem equally valid and certainly less ethnocentric to assume that these new demands were more symptomatic of disruptions that were already in progress, rather than their immediate causes.

Since the establishment of administrative control, governments have been able to manipulate conditions to unobtrusively stimulate new needs within small-scale societies almost at will through such means as community development programs and formal schooling. Schools controlled by central governments or foreign missionaries have served the double function of creating new needs and preparing individuals for their roles as consumers. Ivan Illich[11] has argued that this double function is one of the primary purposes of schools, even in highly commercialized societies.

Promoting Technological Change

Governments around the world have been engaged in a massive effort to replace crops, livestock, and productive techniques of small-scale cultures with what development experts consider to be superior crops, livestock, and techniques. What makes this phenomenon so different from "natural" diffusion is that the recipients, or target peoples, are not generally allowed to pick and choose what suits them. Choices are made by distant officials who are concerned primarily with increasing the production of a specific region. The task of implementing those decisions is delegated to local administrators, extension agents, and applied anthropologists, who must present tangible results within specified program timetables. Not only are the choices made by outsiders who have their own goals in mind, but the technologies themselves are usually the products of foreign environments and cultures and in many cases must still be considered experimental even in their countries of origin.

Accepting novel technologies in most cases must mean abandonment of economic self-sufficiency, which is not always easy to promote. Many of the innovations are, in fact, tailored specifically to the needs of the world market. Accepting such innovations often means also accepting a variety of related innovations and an ever-increasing dependence on the world economy. Growing a miracle hybrid grain may require expensive applications of purchased chemical fertilizers and pesticides, and the grain seed itself may need to be purchased again each year. Cash crops may also undermine self-reliance in other, less obvious ways. In many areas under the influence of government-directed agricultural development programs, all of the productive land in entire regions may be transformed from subsistence farming to production of a nonfood cash crop. Such a transformation means, of course, that people who were formerly feeding themselves directly must now purchase their food from external sources by selling their crops. In less extreme cases, some subsistence farming may be carried on, but substantial amounts of imported food still must be purchased. An unforeseen hazard in cash cropping is that it is often difficult to return to full self-sufficiency if crops fail or if world-market prices fall—and tropical monocrops are particularly vulnerable to both of these problems.

Indigenous peoples' frequent resistance to technological change can thus be readily appreciated. The uncertain benefits of new crops and techniques must be weighed carefully against the certain loss of both economic independence and reliable subsistence pursuits, as well as against the unknown hazards involved in any experiment with complex cultural and natural systems. Unfortunately, governments have pushed innovations with little appreciation of the problems involved. In many areas, they have imposed new crops by direct force. New Guinea, for example, resorted to a Compulsory Planting Ordinance in 1919, requiring villagers to plant a specified number of coconut palms under penalty of fines or jail sentences. Coffee planting was forced by both the Spanish in the Philippines and the Dutch in the East Indies, and forced planting was common practice in many other colonial countries. Since the postwar emphasis on increasing agricultural production under way since the 1950s, reluctant indigenous peoples have been cajoled and harassed by eager agricultural extension agents and have been plied with free seeds and special subsidies in order to overcome their justified caution.

In the following sections, three specific case studies illustrate the argument presented in the preceding sections. The first case involves the initial efforts of Dutch colonial administrators to force a self-sufficient, autonomous tribal population into the world-market economy. In the second case, the Zande Scheme, a colonial government is shown using a massive and coercive development scheme designed to introduce a new cash crop after the establishment of administrative control and initial involvement with a cash economy. The final example is an extended treatment of the noncoercive methods employed by the American administration of Micronesia to introduce American standards of consumption to small subsistence-oriented societies in which local resources will not support such developments. Although these three examples by no means represent the full range of development strategies, they do illustrate several major historic trends.

Dutch Colonial Development in the Celebes

A brief case study of how Dutch colonial administrators prepared the way for the "healthy" development of the Toradjas, indigenous peoples of the Poso district in central Celebes (now Sulawesi, a large Indonesian island), is an example of classic colonial development techniques designed to force an unwilling population into the world economy. According to A. C. Kruyt,[12] when mission efforts began in 1892 the Dutch government deemed the Toradjas completely incapable of progress without outside intervention. Kruyt found and described several of the basic stabilizing features of small-scale societies in full operation among the Toradjas. He concluded that because of these features, "development and progress were impossible"—the Toradjas were "bound to remain at the same level." Toradja society was cashless and there was neither desire to earn money nor unfulfilled needs for which it might be required. Wealth-leveling mechanisms, such as reciprocal kinship obligations, religious sacrifices and feasting, and special values on generosity, helped maintain the balance.

Mission work in this relatively undisturbed setting proved a dismal failure. The Toradjas were entirely self-satisfied and quite uninterested in converting to any new religion, in sending their children to the mission schools, or in planting coconuts and coffee as cash crops. Obviously, drastic measures were required to break through their "wall of conservatism." In 1905 the Netherlands Indies government brought the Poso region under administrative control, using armed force to crush all attempts at resistance. In rapid succession headhunting was stopped, a head tax was imposed, roads were built with conscript labor, and the entire Toradja population was forcibly removed from their traditional hilltop homes where they had grown dry rice and were relocated along the new roads in the lowlands where tribespeople were persuaded to grow wet rice for their own good.

The Toradjas were understandably resentful and bewildered by these actions, especially when their mortality rates suddenly soared and they found themselves being punished continually by the administration for offenses that they did not understand. They turned to the missionaries for help, became "converted," and began sending their children to school. Eventually they were cultivating their own coconut and coffee plantations and began to acquire the appropriate new *needs* for such goods as oil lamps, sewing machines, and "better" clothing. Within twenty years the self-sufficient tribal economy had been replaced by deliberate government action. However, in spite of the enormous changes to which they have been subjected, the Toradjas have retained their strong ethnic identity and cultural distinctiveness.

The Zande Development Scheme

The Zande Development Scheme, which has been described in detail by Conrad C. Reining,[13] represents a massive economic development effort aimed at raising the cash income and agricultural productivity of a subsistence-oriented indigenous population after the usual colonial development techniques proved too slow and ineffective. The scheme deserves special attention as a pioneer effort at the directed economic transformation of a small-scale society and as an illustration of how even well-intentioned development plans may often be executed with coercion and little regard for the real wishes of their "targets."

Prior to extensive European intervention, the Azande were a large population of shifting cultivators and hunters living in the isolated southwest corner of the Sudan in self-sufficient, dispersed homesteads and recognizing the political authority of local chiefs. The termination of Azande political autonomy in 1905 and the initial administrative assaults on their subsistence economy followed the familiar pattern. To establish "law and order," the British disbanded warrior groups, collected firearms, outlawed the manufacture or possession of shields, and, according to the Azande, banned the smelting of iron. The traditional authority of chiefs was limited, and they were converted into government agents under indirect rule.

After civil administration began in 1911, the entire Azande population was relocated along roads constructed by conscript native labor. Ostensibly, the move was designed to prevent people from living in tsetse fly zones, but it was also intended to facilitate administration. This first major disturbance of the indigenous ecological balances was quickly followed by other "improvements." In the interest of conservation, the Azande were forbidden to locate their swiddens in the most favored locations in the gallery forests along the streams, and indigenous hunting techniques were seriously restricted or forbidden. Participation in the cash economy was stimulated by a head tax introduced in the 1920s. At that point, deliberate efforts at economic development were pushed no further, although the importation of manufactured goods by licensed traders and missionary education were encouraged. Further development seemed frus-

trated by the region's extreme isolation and lack of significant natural resources for the world market. In spite of the disturbances already introduced,
the Azande remained largely self-sufficient subsistence farmers. They had developed a taste for a limited range of consumer goods offered by the traders,
but they were content to obtain these by selling wild honey, beeswax, and wild
peppers. They remained uninterested in augmenting this meager cash income
by migratory wage labor because, it was said, they were too fond of their own
country and did not want to leave it. When prices on their limited salable resources fell or when the price of the foreign goods rose too high, they readily
returned to their own goods. According to Reining, the Azande had not yet
passed the point of no return in their economic involvement with the commercial world and could easily have reverted to full self-sufficiency. Unfortunately, administration planners had other ideas.

In the late 1930s, the government began to favor expanded economic development—regardless of cultural and environmental "barriers"—and exper-
iments were begun with cotton as a possible cash crop for the Azande. In
1938 J. D. Tothill, an agricultural development specialist, was appointed to
conduct research and make policy recommendations. Within five years, he
presented his views to the administration in the form of a memorandum entitled "An Experiment in the Social Emergence of Indigenous Races." He
called for the conversion of the Azande into "happy, prosperous, literate communities . . . participating in the benefits of civilization" through the cultivation of cotton and the establishment of factories to produce exportable products on the spot.[14] Tothill's plans found support in the government, although,
of course, no one apparently thought of consulting the Azande themselves,
and in 1944 the civil secretary urged the governor-general's council to approve an intensive economic development policy for the entire southern Sudan. Blaming the region's "backwardness" on "tribal apathy and conservatism," he made an appeal to the wardship principle as a justification for
renewed efforts and stated with familiar ethnocentrism: "We have a moral obligation to redeem its [the southern Sudan's] inhabitants from ignorance, su-
perstition, poverty, malnutrition, etc."[15]

By 1946 a modified scheme for the total economic transformation of the
Azande was under way. A small industrial complex was built that included
spinning, weaving, cotton oil and soap mills, an electrical power station, a
water system, and a dairy. All of these industrial plants were to be operated
by fifteen hundred Azande workers, who would be trained and supervised by
Europeans and northern Sudanese. Telephone lines, improved motor roads,
and concrete bridges soon spread across the landscape.

The scheme was envisioned and entirely directed by British planners, and
the Azande, who had not been consulted at any point, were called upon to

furnish labor for the initial construction at the rate of approximately 1,000 men a month for nearly seven years. Every man in the district was required to work at least one month per year for pay of from $0.85 to $1.30 a month! The administration decided that the cotton planting could be most efficiently regulated by introducing a carefully laid-out, geometrically precise settlement pattern that would allow the Azande to live in an "accessible and rational manner, not as beasts in the wilderness." Consequently, over a five-year period 50,000 Azande families—nearly the entire district population of some 170,000 people—were removed from their roadside locations (where they had been placed thirty years earlier) and distributed along a grid of sixteen-hectare individual household plots covering thousands of square kilometers of dry scrub forest. Plots were arbitrarily assigned by a clerk escorted by police, with no regard for the desire of individual Azande to live near their kin, and restrictions were imposed against any future moves.

The key to the entire scheme was the growing of cotton, but this presented some difficulties because the Azande were not interested in growing cotton. Deliberate efforts were made to train Azande merchants and to supply them with consumer goods, because planners believed that what the Azande lacked was a "realization of what money can do for them." The planners felt that as soon as the Azande had learned to desire money they would become eager cash croppers. However, along with these deliberate attempts to increase consumerism, direct compulsion was felt to be necessary. This compulsion took the form of forcing anyone who refused to plant or properly cultivate cotton to do a month of public-works labor on the roads as punishment. When yields declined as a result of low prices and dissatisfaction occurred over food shortages that were caused by this new stress on normal subsistence activities, the number of cotton "defaulters" and the frequency of punishment increased accordingly.

In the face of this degree of direct compulsion, and with a social-engineering scheme of this magnitude, it seems incredible that the planners were motivated by the best intentions, but this seems to be the case. In 1948 the chairman of the project's board of directors reiterated in a memorandum that the underlying purpose of the Zande Scheme was "to bring progress, prosperity, and the reasonable decencies and amenities of human existence to the Azande."[16] Herein, of course, lay the difficulty. Outsiders applied their own ethnocentric judgments on what should constitute progress, prosperity, decency, and amenities, and then proceeded to impose this blueprint on a totally different culture, assuming that the noble ends justified the apparently drastic means. While the scheme was in progress, the administration operated under the incredible illusion that the Azande culture was being respected, whereas it was in fact being eliminated. According to the district commissioner's platitudes: "The object throughout has been to interfere as little as possible with the people's own way of life."[17]

It appears that the Zande Scheme did succeed somewhat in raising production, income, and consumption levels in the short run. These successes were apparently illusory, however, because as soon as the independent Sudanese government was instituted, a new team of development experts was called in to submit further recommendations for the entire southern Sudan. Their report, submitted in 1954 to the Development Branch of the Ministry of Finance and Economics, concluded that greater agricultural output was needed to provide steady improvement in the standard of living. What was needed were new crops, improved techniques, mechanization, better marketing, and so on. By 1960 an all-new Ten-Year Development Plan was under way.

In 1965, some twenty years after the first development project was begun and halfway through the Ten-Year Plan, a Sudanese journalist, Beshir Mohammed Said,[18] reported enthusiastically that the standard of living in Zandeland was higher, consumption of sugar had doubled in just nine years, there were no naked people left, Azande women were dressed in the fashionable northern Sudanese style, and everyone had bicycles and lived in clean houses equipped with beds and mattresses. And Said reported that, best of all, there were now swarms of children everywhere! A more cynical observer might well have wondered who would be setting the development goals for the burgeoning next generation and how long Zandeland's shallow lateritic soils and the Azande themselves could support their newly attained standard of affluence.

Like the Nuer, the Azande were also caught up in the Southern Sudan Civil War of 1955–1972 and 1983–2005. During the war many Azande peoples fled the country, and all of the agricultural developments introduced by the Zande Scheme were disrupted. Some 2 million people died in the civil war, and those who remained were severely impoverished. The southern Sudan gained considerable autonomy under the terms of the 2005 peace agreement, and USAID supported reconstruction by contracting through private development organizations such as Citizens Network for Foreign Affairs (CNFA), based in Washington, D.C.[19] Foreign investment capital quickly began flowing in, but the emphasis shifted to petroleum development. It is uncertain how the Azande people will fare as large-scale externally funded agricultural and forestry developments begin in their territory.

Purchasing Progress and Dependency in Micronesia

Micronesia represents another outstanding example of the close relationship between government policy and the transformation of a traditional subsistence economy. In contrast to the Zande Scheme, in which overt coercion was an integral part of development strategy, in Micronesia the transformation has been readily accomplished without coercion. Instead, it involved a lavish distribution of material rewards by a wealthy government and by massive spending on administration, education, and special development programs. By the late 1960s many Micronesians who only a few years earlier were participants in presumably satisfying indigenous societies, and who were self-sufficient in food and material needs, were consuming costly imported goods in the American style. The Micronesian subsistence economy was undermined in favor of dependence on a cash system in a manner that is perhaps unique but that dramatically magnifies the general processes involved in the "development" of small-scale economies around the world.

The Micronesian environment imposes several rigid limitations on economic activity, one of the most obvious being the severe limitation on land area, combined with vast distances and extreme isolation. There are approximately two thousand islands, with a total combined land surface of only 1,864 square kilometers, scattered over 7.7 million square kilometers of ocean—an area roughly the size of the United States. Many of these islands are low coral atolls, and agricultural potential on even the largest islands is limited. A further complication is the fact that the region is swept regularly by devastating typhoons. This seemingly unpromising environment has been populated by a rich variety of self-sufficient cultures for more than a thousand years and has been in contact with the commercial cultures for some 450 years. Spain, Germany, Japan, and the United States have successively claimed political control over the islands, but thanks to the area's isolation and because relatively few of Micronesia's limited resources have found a place on the world market, the indigenous economies have been only slightly disturbed by foreign influences until recently. There were some efforts under the German administration, beginning in 1899, to promote copra plantations, but major efforts at economic development did not occur until the Japanese took control in 1914.

Under the Japanese, the typical colonial pressures were applied to bring the native Micronesians into the economy. All "unoccupied" land was claimed by the government, and the best areas were opened to Japanese colonists or developed as sugar plantations. Micronesian dances, which the Japanese considered vulgar, and kava drinking were suppressed; more than half of the Micronesian children were placed in schools to learn Japanese and "ethics"; all males older than sixteen years were required to pay a head tax; and subsidies were offered for the planting of coconuts. In spite of these inducements, indigenous people still proved to be unwilling laborers. The economic development that did occur during this period was centered on the larger islands and was undertaken largely by the Japanese colonists, who outnumbered Micronesians by 1937. Except for a general increase in copra production, the outlying islands were relatively undisturbed.[20]

World War II brought large-scale devastation to Micronesia because many of the islands had been fortified by the Japanese and bitter fighting was necessary to dislodge them. The U.S. Navy assumed administrative control in 1945, and the pattern for large-scale intervention in the lives of the people was soon reestablished. In 1946, within a few months after gaining control, the navy launched a major survey of Micronesia's economic potential in order to guide the military administration in the formulation of policy. The survey was undertaken by twenty-three specialists from the United States Commercial Company, a branch of the Foreign Economic Administration, and included anthropologists, geologists, nutritionists, geographers, economists, botanists, and agronomists. According to Douglas Oliver, who edited a summary of the final report, the astonishing objective of the survey was "the sobering one of attempting to prescribe a way of life for people who have no effective voice in deciding their own destinies."[21]

The report clearly recognized that the administration was assuming ultimate power over the lives and welfare of the indigenous population and would, in effect, shape their cultures after whatever pattern the administrators chose. It contained a curious mixture of caution over the dangers involved in manipulating other cultures and of blatantly ethnocentric and even contradictory recommendations. According to the report, the indigenous cultures were still intact and represented "more or less delicately balanced adaptations to specific sets of environmental and historical factors and could be badly unbalanced by unwise forced changes."[22] It was stressed that the population should be helped to return to its prewar economic self-sufficiency and that the government should not attempt to attract Micronesians to settle in administrative centers for government convenience, because this was contrary to their indigenous ecological patterns and would threaten their self-reliance. The report also indicated that some of the more isolated areas might not even need permanent administrators.

It seems obvious in retrospect that at this point the administering authorities had an opportunity to permit a resumption of an essentially indigenous way of life, free even of the modifications introduced by the Japanese. The aboriginal cultures were familiar with the disruption and devastation of typhoons and were therefore equipped with traditional patterns for dealing with the kinds of problems presented by the war's destruction. Some segments of the population undoubtedly missed the foreign luxuries made possible by the massive Japanese colonization, but everywhere proven patterns of subsistence and technology were being resumed. Even people who had become familiar with motor-driven boats were repairing and rebuilding their sailing canoes. Inspired by premature speeches and naval authorities promising "liberty," the people of Ponape returned enthusiastically to their traditional subsistence activities and feasting. According to William R. Bascom,[23] who conducted anthropological research on Ponape, such speeches caused the people to ignore their copra plantations and served only to "retard" economic development.

It soon became apparent that the policy makers were not considering a return to cultural autonomy; rather, these cultures were to be remade and reformed, this time according to American ideals.

After just four months of fieldwork, the team of experts of the United States Commercial Company Economic Survey proceeded to lay the groundwork for policy decisions that would completely transform cultures that possessed the accumulated knowledge of a thousand years of successful adaptation to a unique and complex environment. Micronesian culture was to be replaced by foreign cultural patterns that policy makers assumed would provide a more satisfying way of life. With colossal ethnocentrism, reinforced by ignorance of the complexities of Micronesian culture, these "experts" made judgments in the light of their own misplaced values and recklessly proceeded to prescribe a way of life for an entire people.

The basic assumptions of the survey team were apparent in the report, which spoke of economic reform and the need to establish an expanding economy and an expanding population.[24] The indigenous people were described as impoverished because they were not enjoying the standards of consumption of luxury goods established by the Japanese, and it was repeatedly emphasized that these foreign goods were now necessities. A taste for such exotic foods as rice, flour, canned meat, and cheese had been cultivated among the conscript labor forces at military camps. Because some of these conscripts were anxious to continue eating these foods, *the foods had to be supplied*—regardless of expense or sustainability issues. One member of the survey later advised that new "needs" should be deliberately promoted among Micronesians: "Acquaintance with new ideas should be encouraged and desires to try new articles or products should in general be facilitated."[25] Apparently no one recognized the incompatibility between self-sufficiency and dependence on foreign foods and consumer goods.

According to the team's report, traditional Micronesian gardening practices were undeveloped by American standards and native food was monotonous, bland, and not well balanced, even though no signs of nutritional deficiency could be found. The report stated that the people were not eating enough fruit and that for their own benefit they should learn to grow vegetables, "in spite of the present native resistance to a vegetable diet."[26] The team felt that agricultural advisers should be provided to teach the population "elementary practices of horticulture," even though it should have been obvious that perhaps the indigenous people might have had more to teach the advisers about such basics as plant varieties and their special requirements, soil conditions, growing seasons, and so on. Along with dietary changes, new crops, and new gardening techniques, the experts recommended that, where possible, every family should be provided with a cow, two pigs, and as many chickens as they wanted. This was surprising in view of the fact that the traditional economy was already solidly based on ample *marine* protein sources. Pigs and chickens were not needed (and there was little to feed them), and cattle, having pasturage requirements, were absurdly out of place in an area as short of land as Micronesia.

The report piously affirmed, almost as a self-evident truth, that economic change in Micronesia was inevitable, implying that the people were bringing it on themselves and that it could therefore not be prevented: "Micronesians will, for better or worse, continue to expand their participation in western systems. In the kind of world we live in, that is inevitable, and no one but a nostalgic antiquary would imagine otherwise."[27]

Curiously, however, the report ominously warned that the "inevitable" changes "must occur gradually and voluntarily."[28] Administrators were advised not to use force; rather, the people were to be directed, not compelled, into proper economic patterns. As the report explained: "Much can be accomplished positively if natives are led rather than pushed into channels which are intended for their economic benefit."[29]

In spite of this strange double-talk, Oliver explicitly noted in his conclusions that Micronesians would probably not "be permitted the absolute freedom of choice to decide their own destinies." Obviously, the government was deciding what was to be inevitable and was deliberately setting about to create the conditions under which the inevitable new economic style would be chosen. In one remarkable passage in a report full of paradoxes, the team of experts recommended that Micronesians should be made to think they were choosing freely even though they really were not: "Attempts to bring about economic reform in conformance with western modes of living, before the natives are ready to make the changes, would undermine their faith in our avowed intentions. Natives should be given the opportunity of learning about and considering cultural alternatives, but the desire for change should come from within the society. No penalties in any form should be invoked for refusal to accept a proposed change over which they were told they had a free choice."[30]

When the administration of Micronesia was transferred in 1951 to civilian authorities of the U.S. Department of the Interior (under the United Nations Trust Territory agreements), the newly appointed high commissioner proclaimed to the natives that "your existing customs, religious beliefs, and property rights will be respected," but this proved to be as misleading as the navy's promise of liberty.[31] In the same proclamation, the high commissioner also promised an administration based on "applied science," and the tone of the annual administrative report for 1951–1952 leaves no doubt that *respect* was being pushed aside by the need for *advancement.* Although there was talk of "gradual evolution," and it was claimed that "no pressure has been used to force the native Micronesians to discard their customs in favor of western institutions," there were complaints that the "divisive effect of ethnocentricity must be overcome" and that a more democratic form of government with a broader outlook was being carefully created through "well-nurtured growth . . . , education and civil guidance by administrative officials."[32] The ethnocentrism referred to in the report was, of course, the Micronesians' belief in the superiority of their own institutions, not the ethnocentrism of government officials who, after all, were dealing in applied science to further a natural evolutionary process.

In the economic field, subsistence activities were to be fostered, but it was felt that the "fullest possible development of land resources" was impeded by traditional land tenure practices. The official program for Micronesian economic advancement followed the lines recommended by the 1946 survey and overflowed with extravagant promises and American values. Everything was to be improved—more and better, better and greater. Production would be increased, new practices and superior crops would be introduced, and the environment would be dealt with more effectively.[33] In effect, one thousand years of Micronesian cultural development was declared obsolete, and applied science was to miraculously replace it. In the eyes of the administration, the traditional culture was simply standing in the way of a better life.

Within two years, the administration's development strategy was taking shape. The territory's natural isolation would be ended by the introduction of radio communication and a modern air and sea shipping network. The reluctance of Micronesians to abandon their traditional way of life would be overcome by large doses of administrative advice and education, and the natural limitations on economic growth imposed by the restricted resource base would be circumvented by the massive importation of American dollars in the form of wages for indigenous government employees. In 1953, 15 percent of the native population of fifty-seven thousand was enrolled in schools. This figure included thirteen hundred high school and college students who were preparing for government employment and acquiring firsthand experience in American standards of consumption at schools in Guam, Hawaii, and the U.S. mainland. By 1954 the success of the program was already becoming apparent in the fact that more than twelve hundred Micronesians were on the administration's payroll, two hundred cars were in the hands of local people, and 1.3 million dollars worth of imports were now flowing into the islands. An annual government operating budget of nearly 6 million dollars was needed to support these activities, but only 1.6 million dollars could be obtained in revenue from local resources. The remainder was appropriated as a direct subsidy from the federal government.[34]

The motivation for this policy of creating native dependency on the government seems to have resulted largely from the government's desire to strengthen its dominance in the region in order to retain it as a strategic military resource, rather than from any real need for the area's other meager resources. The exploitation of Micronesia by the American military did not end with the war. In 1946 the navy removed the 170 Marshallese residents of Bikini Atoll and relocated them on other islands so that nuclear bombs could be exploded over and under the lagoon in Operation Crossroads.[35] By 2007, radioactive decontamination was still ongoing, and resettlement of Bikini was still not possible, but the lagoon was being used for diving tours.[36] Guam was used as a base for B-52 bombers during the Vietnam War, and Kwajalein Atoll in the Marshall Islands was targeted for test nuclear missiles fired from California.

By 1958, the American administration was even prouder of the success of its development strategy. Micronesian houses were more substantial, power-boats were being purchased more widely, and government officials could point to some 500 private vehicles, 275 radios, and various other electric appliances as evidence of an increased standard of living. However, some isolated pockets of cultural resistance still remained. Improvement in the remote islands was slower and less evident, necessitating more education and greater effort:

> In such remote areas the basic problem is one of educating the local inhabitants to the need for or desirability of improvement and the development of local means to accomplish such improvements.
> Further improvement of living standards can be accomplished throughout the Territory. . . . The policy and programs of the Administration are planned and intended to develop an awareness and understanding of community needs and the desirability of improvement, and to develop local community resources and means to a maximum extent to achieve the improvement desired.[37]

For ten years the pace of development input from the administration increased, steadily but gradually, until the annual budget stood at approximately 7.4 million dollars. Micronesians were now consuming more than 60 dollars' worth of imported goods per capita annually, while exports of island resources remained at approximately their prior levels. It was obvious that the value of exports had reached an absolute ceiling even by the mid-1950s, but apparent economic growth continued as more and more Micronesians were placed on the government payroll and more capital improvements were made. Clearly, dependency was growing and the indigenous culture was being gradually overwhelmed in a tide of dollars and foreign consumer luxuries.[38] If at this point the world price of copra had fallen, and if the government payroll had been drastically reduced, several thousand impoverished Micronesians would have been left to fend for themselves. In that case, if enough of the indigenous culture had survived in the outlying islands, it would have been possible for the people to return to self-sufficiency. The government, however, had no intention of reducing its development efforts and actually had even greater things in store.

In 1962 the government more than doubled its spending in Micronesia to facilitate more rapid development and to "meet the needs of the Micronesian people." Official reports explained that this represented a major shift in the administration's commitment to Micronesia,[39] but this was a careful understatement. A massive, all-new development machine was being cranked into motion, fueled by a seemingly endless stream of American dollars. By 1965 government spending had tripled the pre-1962 annual levels and was still climbing, until the projected 1973 budget reached an incredible 78.6 million dollars—more than eleven times the pre-1962 levels! Between 1962 and 1972, the administration spent some 397.4 million dollars, much of this directed toward what was called an accelerated emergency program to upgrade and speed development of essential public services, including schools, transportation, communication, and power plants. The results of some of this money could be seen immediately in the realm of education, where by 1972, 80 percent of the public elementary schools met American standards—approximately eighty square meters of working space and concrete and metal to replace coral floors and thatch.

In a dramatic rejection of earlier policy emphasizing self-reliance, the territory was opened to U.S. capital investment by presidential decree in 1962 to stimulate new economic activity for the "maximum economic and cultural benefit of all Micronesians."[40] Progress based on local resources and capabilities was no longer adequate: "The government recognizes that outside capital and expertise, particularly for large-scale, sophisticated enterprises, are needed for maximum efficiency and profit."[41]

The subsistence economy was now out: "The Administration continues to seek means to promote development of the economy of Micronesia so that it will become geared to a world money economy and thus, its subsistence aspects will become supplemental."[42]

An enormous tide of exotic material wealth was beginning to engulf the islands, but the official administration position was that these changes would be good and they would be voluntarily chosen. According to the 1972 report to the United Nations, the "Administering Authority . . . encourages Micronesians to voluntarily integrate into their own culture useful features of other civilizations to enable them to lead more meaningful and rewarding lives in today's changing world."[43]

Predictably, the "useful features" were all drawn from American civilization and represented the material trappings that Americans considered essential for a "more meaningful and rewarding" life. In a remarkable exercise in self-deception, the administration observed that it would permit only those foreign investments that would contribute to the territory's overall economic well-being "without adversely affecting the existing social and cultural values and ethnic conditions of the district."[44]

Evidence of progress suddenly began to appear throughout the territory in direct proportion to government spending and foreign investment. Jetports sprang up on Truk, Ponape, and Majuro, and by 1972 Continental Airlines was operating tourist hotels on three islands. Nearly 7,000 private motor vehicles were now spilling over 960 kilometers of roads, and 26 million dollars' worth of imported food, clothing, gasoline, machinery, and other consumer goods were pouring in. There were 415 licensed commercial business outlets where there had been only 54 in 1958. Electric power plants were in place or were being installed for a total capacity of 30,000 kW; 22 movie houses were in operation, 1 television and 8 radio stations were broadcasting, and an estimated 50,000 radios were in private homes and cars.

A multitude of special programs and new institutions were needed to channel native participation in these developments. A massive effort at the recruitment, training, and placement of future civil servants was soon under way to help swell the government payrolls even further. In 1972 there were already more than fifty-seven hundred native employees in the government receiving some 18 million dollars in salaries, and more than six hundred natives were enrolled in special training programs designed to increase incomes. These programs were sponsored by the U.S. federal government under Public Service Careers Project and Public Employment Program, the United Nations, the South Pacific Commission, and the World Health Organization. Credit unions, the Small Business Administration loan program, and the Economic Development Loan Fund were all "making it easy to borrow money for useful purposes."[45] Useful purposes included such diverse but thoroughly American enterprises as the establishment of cattle ranches, laundromats, jewelry and upholstery shops, car rentals, and the purchase of outboard motors and motorcycles. In 1972 the Economic Development Loan Fund alone had made more than 1 million dollars' worth of direct and guaranteed loans, and 3 million dollars' worth of applications were pending.

To help overcome the last remnants of resistance in the remaining backward areas, in 1966 the Peace Corps was called in for community development work. In its peak year, seven hundred volunteers were on duty teaching English, organizing self-help programs, advising on business matters, promoting increased agricultural production, and spending money. As an underdeveloped, impoverished region, Micronesia also qualified for a number of federal War On Poverty programs, and soon there were federally funded Community Action programs, Head Start programs, Economic Opportunity Office programs, special scholarships, workshops, and a bewildering array of other "opportunities," plus a Neighborhood Youth Corps and a special Grant-in-Aid program. As a final touch, the most isolated communities were visited every year by Santa Claus, the supreme cultural hero of American materialism, who air-dropped free consumer goods on needy children, courtesy of the U.S. Navy and Air Force based on Guam.

Beginning with the creation of the Commonwealth of the Northern Mariana Islands in 1976 as a U.S. territory, the United Nations Trust Territory administration of Micronesia has been replaced by other political arrangements. In 1978 the Marshall Islands became a constitutional republic[46] and the Caroline Islands formed the Federated States of Micronesia. Local political autonomy has not yet overcome Micronesia's problems, and the United States continues to exert a powerful influence by taking advantage of Micronesian economic dependency. For example, between 1980 and 1983 the Palauan people voted four times to keep the self-governing Republic of Palau a nuclear-free zone, thus excluding U.S. ships that might be carrying nuclear weapons, but the United States refused to accept this decision.[47] In recognition of Palau's opposition to nuclear weapons, the government of Palau was awarded an alternate Nobel Peace Prize in 1983.[48]

Tourism and Indigenous Peoples

> The economic, technical and cultural marginalisation of tourism exposes cultural minorities to discontinuity, disturbance, divergence, even disintegration, and usually to a dangerous dependency.[49]

The development of tourism cited in the previous example about Micronesia involves a larger issue that has affected indigenous peoples throughout the world: the exploitation of indigenous territory and culture as exotic tourist attractions and symbols of national identity. This topic has been examined in detail by anthropologists,[50] but in this section only a few major points will be raised. Tourism in the impoverished world is a product of global economic inequality and often disproportionately favors a few special-interest groups.

Furthermore, it often leads to distorted national development and obscures the realities of exploitation.

Tourism involving indigenous peoples can be attacked on several grounds, as the Pierre Rossel quote, above, indicates. First, indigenous peoples are "marginalized" by tourism, or made to feel like inferior outsiders, when they must interact with wealthy outsiders who flaunt their economic, technological, and cultural superiority. They also are marginalized in that they often have no direct control over the tourist trade, cannot set prices, and enjoy only a small proportion of the profit from tourism. In extreme cases, such as with the Yagua Indians in the Peruvian and Colombian Amazon,[51] tour organizers have set up artificial villages and relocated native groups for the convenience of tourists. Indians are then coerced into maintaining an ethnographically "primitive" image and must perform on cue to be observed and photographed. The Tasaday in the Philippines, who were "discovered" in 1971, appear to have been deliberately set up to be exhibited as primitive cave dwellers to make the Marcos administration appear to be a benevolent protector of tribal groups. These sorts of "human zoos" can be readily identified as demeaning and exploitative, but in many cases the detrimental impact of tourism may be less obvious. For example, where large numbers of backpacking trekkers hike into "authentic" indigenous areas, they may unwittingly degrade the environment, increase pressure on local resources, distort local value systems by the sudden injection of cash into the economy, and create internal inequalities and dependency because only a few indigenous people are able to benefit from the trekkers' presence. More serious consequences of tourism have occurred when indigenous groups, such as the Maasai in East Africa, have been removed from their own lands to allow tourists greater access to observe wildlife.

Tourism officials and tourist agencies sometimes defend cultural tourism as a form of cross-cultural education in which members of dominant, urban, commercial societies gain knowledge of and respect for indigenous peoples. This may be true under some conditions, but more often tourism creates and maintains illusions about exotic cultures. Tourists are escorted about and insulated from unpleasant truths. Often they return home believing themselves to be "experts" on the peoples they visited, but knowing little about the larger realities of land rights, discrimination, and economic exploitation.

The cultural tourism industry is not entirely negative, however. Where indigenous peoples are able to control the conditions of their interaction with tourists, set prices, and obtain a fair share of the profits, a modest income from tourism can help these groups maintain economic self-sufficiency. Where native groups have retained ownership over territory within national parks, such as in the Kakadu National Park in the Northern Territory of Australia, they may be able to combine cultural tourism and wildlife tourism in beneficial ways. Indigenous peoples can market their arts and crafts while educating the public about contemporary tribal realities. The critical element is that indigenous peoples must be allowed to control their own cultural and territorial resources.

Notes

1. A. B. Mountjoy, 1967, *Industrialization and Underdeveloped Countries*, Chicago: Aldine, 28.

2. Report to the League of Nations for 1923, Australian Trust Territory of New Guinea, in Stephen W. Reed, 1943, *The Making of Modern New Guinea*, Philadelphia: American Philosophical Society, 179.

3. Raymond L. Buell, 1928, *The Native Problem in Africa*, 2 vols., New York: Macmillan, 937–1044.

4. Joseph Chamberlain, 1926 speech to the House of Commons, in John H. Wellington, 1967, *South West Africa and Its Human Issues*, Oxford: Clarendon Press/ Oxford University Press, 250.

5. W. H. Hutt, 1934, "The economic position of the Bantu in South Africa," in *Western Civilization and the Natives of South Africa*, ed. I. Schapera, London: George Routledge and Sons, 212–13.

6. W. M. Eiselen, 1934, "Christianity and the religious life of the Bantu," in *Western Civilization and the Natives of South Africa*, ed. I. Schapera, London: George Routledge and Sons, 71.

7. Wellington, *South West Africa*, 230–31.

8. Reed, *The Making of Modern New Guinea*, 143, 177.

9. Alpheus Henry Snow, 1921, *The Question of Aborigines: In the Law and Practice of Nations*, New York: Putnam, 163.

10. Australia Department of Territories, Territory of Papua, *Report for 1967–1968*, 24.

11. Ivan Illich, 1970, *Deschooling Society*, vol. 44, World Perspectives, New York: Harper and Row.

12. A. C. Kruyt, 1929, "The influence of Western civilization on the inhabitants of Poso (Central Celebes)," in *The Effect of Western Influence on Native Civilizations in the Malay Archipelago*, ed. B. Schrieke, 1–9, Batavia: Java Royal Batavia Society of Arts and Sciences.

13. Conrad C. Reining, 1966, *The Zande Scheme: An Anthropological Case Study of Economic Development in Africa*, Evanston, IL: Northwestern University Press.

14. Ibid., 143.

15. Mohamed Omar Beshir, 1968, *The Southern Sudan: Background to Conflict*, New York: Praeger, 55.

16. Reining, *The Zande Scheme*, 156.

17. Ibid., 108.

18. Beshir Mohammed Said, 1965 *The Sudan, Crossroads of Africa*, Chester Springs, PA: Dufour Editions, 141.

19. USAID/Sudan, 2005, Annual Report FY 2005, http://pdf.usaid.gov /pdf_docs/PDACD881.pdf (accessed July 11, 2007); Citizen Network For Foreign Affairs, Agricultural Market and Enterprise Development (AHMED) Project, http://www.cnfa.org/page.cfm?pageID=158 (accessed July 11, 2008).

20. Paul H. Clyde, 1935, *Japan's Pacific Mandate*, New York: Macmillan; Midori Nishi, 1968, "An evaluation of Japanese agricultural and fishery developments in Micronesia during the Japanese mandate 1914–1941," *Micronesia* 4(1): 1–18.

21. Douglas L. Oliver, ed., 1951, *Planning Micronesia's Future: A Summary of the United States Commercial Company's Economic Survey of Micronesia*, Cambridge: Harvard University Press.

22. Ibid., 8.

23. William R. Bascom, 1965, *Ponape: A Pacific Economy in Transition*, Anthropological Records 22, Berkeley and Los Angeles: University of California Press, 15.

24. Oliver, *Planning Micronesia's Future*.

25. Bascom, *Ponape*, 53.

26. Oliver, *Planning Micronesia's Future*, 13–19.

27. Ibid., 85–86.

28. Ibid., 8.

29. Ibid., 91.

30. Ibid., 91.

31. U.S. Department of the Interior, Office of Territories, 1953, *Report on the Administration of the Trust Territory of the Pacific Islands (by the United States to the United Nations) for the Period July 1, 1951, to June 30, 1952*, Proclamation No. 2, 79–80.

32. Ibid., 13–14.

33. Ibid., 26–31.

34. U.S. Department of the Interior, Office of Territories, 1954, *Annual Report, High Commissioner of the Trust Territory of the Pacific Islands to the Secretary of the Interior (for 1953)*; U.S. Department of State, 1955, *Seventh Annual Report to the United Nations on the Administration of the Trust Territory of the Pacific Islands (July 1, 1953, to June 30, 1954)*, Washington, D.C., statistical tables.

35. Robert Kiste, 1974, *The Bikinians: A Study in Forced Migration*, Menlo Park, CA: Cummings; Jack Niedenthal, 2001, *For the Good of Mankind: A History of the People of Bikini and their Islands*, Majuro, Republic of the Marshall Islands: Micronitor/Bravo Publishers.

36. Bikini Atoll Web site, http://www.bikiniatoll.com/ (accessed July 11, 2007).

37. U.S. Department of State, 1959, *Eleventh Annual Report to the United Nations on the Administration of the Trust Territory of the Pacific Islands (July 1, 1957, to June 30, 1958)*, 90–91.

38. James G. Peoples, 1978, "Dependence in a Micronesian economy," *American Ethnologist* 5(3): 535–52. (A detailed examination of dependency on the island of Kosrae.)

39. U.S. Department of State, 1973, *Twenty-Fifth Annual Report to the United Nations on the Administration of the Trust Territory of the Pacific Islands (July 1, 1971, to June 30, 1972)*, 41.

40. U.S. Department of State, 1964, *Sixteenth Annual Report to the United Nations on the Administration of the Trust Territory of the Pacific Islands (July 1, 1962, to June 30, 1963)*, 49–50; 1973, *Twenty-Fifth Annual Report*, 54.

41. U.S. Department of State, *Twenty-Fifth Annual Report*, 54.

42. Ibid., 45.

43. Ibid., 93.

44. Ibid., 54.

45. Ibid., 56.

46. Holly M. Barker, 2004, *Bravo for the Marshallese: Regaining Control in a Post-Nuclear, Post-Colonial World*. Belmont, CA: Thomson/Wadsworth.

47. IWGIA, 1983, *IWGIA Newsletter* 34: 91–92.

48. IWGIA, 1983, *IWGIA Newsletter* 35/36: 161–65.

49. Pierre Rossel, 1988, *Tourism and Cultural Minorities: Double Marginalisation and Survival Strategies*, IWGIA Document no. 61, Copenhagen: IWGIA, 13.

50. *Cultural Survival Quarterly*, 1982, 6(3); N. H. Graburn, 1976, *Ethnic and Tourist Arts: Cultural Expressions from the Fourth World*, Berkeley and Los Angeles: University of California Press; Rossel, *Tourism and Cultural Minorities*; V. L. Smith, ed., 1977, *Hosts and Guests: The Anthropology of Tourism*, Philadelphia: University of Pennsylvania Press.

51. J. P. Chaumeil, 1984, *Between Zoo and Slavery: The Yagua of Eastern Peru and Their Present Situation*, IWGIA Document no. 49, Copenhagen: IWGIA; Annemarie Seiler-Baldinger, 1988, "Tourism in the upper Amazon and its effects on the indigenous population," in *Tourism: Manufacturing the Exotic*, ed. Pierre Rossel, 177–193, IWGIA Document no. 61, Copenhagen: IWGIA.

9 The Price of Progress

In aiming at progress . . . you must let no one suffer by too drastic a measure, nor pay too high a price in upheaval and devastation, for your innovation.

—René Maunier[1]

UNTIL RECENTLY, GOVERNMENT PLANNERS have always considered economic development and material progress beneficial goals that all societies should want to strive toward. The social advantages of progress—as defined in terms of increased incomes, higher standards of living, greater security, and better health—are thought to be positive, universal goods to be obtained at any price. Although one might argue that indigenous peoples should not be forced to sacrifice their own cultures and autonomy to obtain these benefits, government planners historically felt that the loss of cultural autonomy would be a small price to pay for such obvious advantages.

In earlier chapters, evidence was presented to demonstrate that autonomous indigenous peoples have not chosen progress to enjoy its advantages and that the real reason governments have pushed progress upon them was to obtain resources, not primarily to share the benefits of progress with indigenous peoples. It was also shown that the price of forcing progress on unwilling recipients included the deaths of millions of indigenous people, as well as their loss of land, political sovereignty, and the right to follow their own lifestyle. This chapter does not attempt to further summarize that aspect of the cost of progress, but instead analyzes the specific effects of the participation of indigenous peoples in the global economy. In direct opposition to the usual interpretation, it is argued here that the benefits of progress are often both illusory and detrimental to indigenous peoples when they have not been allowed to control their own resources and define their relationship to the market economy.

Progress and the Quality of Life

One of the primary difficulties in assessing the benefits of progress and economic development for any culture is that of establishing a meaningful measure of both benefit and detriment. It is widely recognized that standard of living, which is the most frequently used measure of progress, is an intrinsically
ethnocentric concept that relies heavily upon indicators that lack universal
cultural relevance. As a less ethnocentric alternative, the Happy Planet Index,
which uses self-reported life satisfaction levels, life expectancy, and ecological footprint to rank nations, shows that some of the smallest, least developed
nations rank as the happiest.[2] Vanuatu, the "happiest" country in the world,
had just over two hundred thousand people in 2007, and a per capita GDP of
under three thousand dollars. More than half (65 percent) of the population
derived its living from the subsistence sector.[3] A top ranking on Happy Planet
Index requires high satisfaction, good life expectancy, and a very small ecological footprint. Such factors as GDP and per capita income may be especially irrelevant measures of actual quality of life for autonomous indigenous
peoples. For example, in its 1954 report, the Trust Territory government indicated that since the Micronesian population was still largely satisfying its
own needs within a cashless subsistence economy: "Money income is not a
significant measure of living standards, production, or well-being in this
area."[4] Unfortunately, within a short time the government began to rely on an
enumeration of specific imported consumer goods as indicators of a higher
standard of living in the islands, even though many tradition-oriented islanders felt that these new goods symbolized a reduction of their quality of
life.

   A more useful measure of the benefits of progress might be based on a formula for evaluating cultures devised by Walter R. Goldschmidt.[5] According
to these less ethnocentric criteria, the important question to ask is: *Does
progress or economic development increase or decrease a given society's stability or its ability to satisfy the physical and psychological needs of its population?* This question is a far more direct measure of quality of life than are
the standard economic correlates of development, and it is universally relevant. Specific indication of this standard of living could be found for any society in the nutritional status and general physical and mental health of its
population, incidence of crime and delinquency, demographic structure, family stability, and the society's relationship to its natural resource base. We
might describe a society that has high rates of malnutrition and crime and one
that degrades its natural environment to the extent of threatening its continued existence as having a lower standard of living than another society in
which these problems do not exist.

Careful examination of the data, which compare on these specific points the former condition of self-sufficient indigenous peoples with their condition following their incorporation into the world-market economy, leads to the conclusion that their standard of living is often lowered, not raised, by economic progress—and often to a dramatic degree. This is perhaps the most outstanding and inescapable fact to emerge from the years of research anthropologists have devoted to the study of culture change and modernization. Despite the best intentions of those who have promoted change and improvement, all too often the results have been poverty, longer working hours, much greater physical exertion, poor health, social disorder, discontent, discrimination, overpopulation, and environmental deterioration—combined with the destruction of the small-scale culture.

Diseases of Development

> Perhaps it would be useful for public health specialists to start talking about a new category of diseases. . . . Such diseases could be called the "diseases of development" and would consist of those pathological conditions which are based on the usually unanticipated consequences of the implementation of developmental schemes."[6]

Economic development increases the disease rate of affected peoples in at least three ways. First, to the extent that development is successful, developed populations suddenly become vulnerable to all of the chronic "lifestyle" diseases suffered almost exclusively by "advanced" peoples,[7] including diabetes, obesity, hypertension, and a variety of circulatory problems. Second, development disturbs existing environmental balances and may dramatically increase some bacterial and parasite diseases. Finally, when development goals prove unattainable, an assortment of poverty diseases may appear in association with the crowded conditions of urban slums and the general breakdown in small-scale socioeconomic systems.

Outstanding examples of the first situation can be seen in the Pacific, where some of the most successfully transformed small-scale societies are found. In Micronesia, where development has progressed more rapidly than perhaps anywhere else, the population doubled between 1958 and 1972. However, the number of patients treated for heart disease in the local hospitals nearly tripled, the incidence of mental disorders increased eightfold, and by 1972 hypertension and nutritional deficiencies began to make significant appearances for the first time.[8]

Although some critics argue that the Micronesian figures simply represent better health monitoring due to economic progress, rigorously controlled data from Polynesia show a similar trend. The progressive acquisition of modern degenerative diseases was documented by an eight-member team of New Zealand medical specialists, anthropologists, and nutritionists, whose research was funded by the Medical Research Council of New Zealand and the World Health Organization. These researchers investigated the health status of a genetically related population at various points along a continuum of increasing cash income, modernizing diet, and urbanization. The extremes on this acculturation continuum were represented by the relatively traditional Pukapukans of the Cook Islands and the essentially Europeanized New Zealand Maori; the busily developing Rarotongans, also of the Cook Islands, occupied the intermediate position. In 1971, after eight years of work, the team's preliminary findings were summarized by Dr. Ian Prior, cardiologist and leader of the research team, as follows: "We are beginning to observe that the more an islander takes on the ways of the West, the more prone he is to succumb to our degenerative diseases. In fact, it does not seem too much to say our evidence now shows that the farther the Pacific natives move from the quiet, carefree life of their ancestors, the closer they come to gout, diabetes, atherosclerosis, obesity, and hypertension."[9]

In Pukapuka, where progress was limited by the island's small size and its isolated location—some 480 kilometers from the nearest port—the annual per capita income was only about 36 dollars and the economy remained essentially at a subsistence level. Resources were limited and the area was visited by trading ships only three or four times a year; thus, there was little opportunity for intensive economic development. Predictably, the population of Pukapuka was characterized by relatively low levels of imported sugar and salt intake and a presumably related low level of heart disease, high blood pressure, and diabetes. In Rarotonga, where economic success was introducing town life, imported food, and motorcycles, sugar and salt intakes nearly tripled, high blood pressure increased approximately ninefold, diabetes increased two- to threefold, and heart disease doubled for men and more than quadrupled for women. Meanwhile, the number of grossly obese women increased more than tenfold. Among the New Zealand Maori, sugar intake was nearly eight times that of the Pukapukans, gout in men was nearly double its rate on Pukapuka, diabetes in men was more than fivefold higher, and the incidence of heart disease in women was more than sixfold greater than that of women on Pukapuka. The Maori were, in fact, dying of "European" diseases at a greater rate than the average New Zealand European.

Government development policies designed to bring about changes in local hydrology, vegetation, and settlement patterns and to increase population mobility, and even programs aimed at reducing some diseases, have frequently led to dramatic increases in disease rates because of the unforeseen effects of disturbing the preexisting order. Charles C. Hughes and John M. Hunter[10] published an excellent survey of cases in which development led directly to increased disease rates in Africa. They concluded that hasty development intervention in relatively balanced local cultures and environments resulted in "a drastic deterioration in the social and economic conditions of life."

Self-sufficient populations in general have presumably learned to live with the endemic pathogens of their environments, and in some cases they have evolved genetic adaptations to specific diseases, such as the sickle-cell trait, which provided immunity to malaria. Unfortunately, however, outside intervention has entirely changed this picture. In the late 1960s, the rate of incidence of sleeping sickness suddenly increased in many areas of Africa and even spread to areas where the disease had not formerly occurred, due to the building of new roads and migratory labor, both of which caused increased population movement. Forest-dwelling peoples such as the Aka in central Africa explicitly attribute new diseases such as AIDS and Ebola to the materialism associated with roads and new settlements.[11]

Large-scale relocation schemes, such as the Zande Scheme, had disastrous results when natives were moved from their traditional disease-free refuges into infected areas. Dams and irrigation developments inadvertently created ideal conditions for the rapid proliferation of snails carrying schistosomiasis (a liver fluke disease), and major epidemics suddenly occurred in areas where this disease had never before been a problem. DDT-spraying programs have been temporarily successful in controlling malaria, but there is often a rebound effect that increases the problem when spraying is discontinued, and resistant strains of the malarial mosquitoes are continually evolving.

Urbanization is one of the prime measures of development, but it is a mixed blessing for most small-scale cultures. Urban health standards are abysmally poor and generally worse than in rural areas for the former villagers who have crowded into the towns and cities throughout Africa, Asia, and Latin America seeking wage employment out of new economic necessity. Infectious diseases related to crowding and poor sanitation are rampant in urban centers, and greatly increased stress and poor nutrition aggravate a variety of other health problems. Malnutrition and other diet-related conditions are, in fact, one of the characteristic hazards of progress faced by indigenous peoples and are discussed in the following sections.

The Hazards of Dietary Change

The diets of indigenous peoples are admirably adapted to their nutritional needs and available food resources. Even though these diets may seem bizarre, absurd, and unpalatable to outsiders, they are unlikely to be improved by drastic modifications. Given the delicate balances and complexities involved in any subsistence system, change always involves risks, but for indigenous people the effects of dietary change have been catastrophic. The benefits of traditional subsistence-based diets are dramatically demonstrated by the negative health effects explicitly connected with the "Nutrition Transition," the shift to diets based on highly processed commercial foods.[12] This negative process was first identified as a complex of conditions called the Saccharine Disease, caused by a reduction in dietary fiber associated with the shift to refined commercial foods.[13]

Under normal conditions, food habits are remarkably resistant to change, and indeed people are unlikely to abandon their traditional diets voluntarily in favor of dependence on difficult-to-obtain exotic imports. In some cases it is true that imported foods may be identified with powerful outsiders and are therefore sought as symbols of greater prestige. This may lead to such absurdities as Amazonian Indians choosing to consume imported canned tuna fish when abundant high-quality fish is available in their own rivers. Another example of this situation occurs in tribes where mothers prefer to feed their infants expensive and nutritionally inadequate canned milk from unsanitary, but high-status, baby bottles. The high status of these items is often promoted by traders and clever advertising campaigns.

Aside from these apparently voluntary changes, it appears that more often dietary changes are forced upon unwilling indigenous peoples by circumstances beyond their control. In some areas, new food crops have been introduced by government decree or as a consequence of forced relocation or other government policies designed to end hunting, pastoralism, or shifting cultivation. Food habits have also been modified by massive disruption of the natural environment by outsiders—as when sheepherders transformed the Australian Aborigines' foraging territory or when European invaders destroyed the bison herds that were the primary element in the Plains Indians' subsistence patterns. Perhaps the most frequent cause of diet change occurs when formerly self-sufficient peoples find that wage labor, cash cropping, and other economic development activities that feed resources into the world-market economy must inevitably divert time and energy away from the production of subsistence foods. Many indigenous peoples in transforming cultures suddenly discover that, like it or not, they are unable to secure traditional foods and must spend their newly acquired cash on costly and often nutritionally inferior manufactured foods.

Overall, the available data seem to indicate that the dietary changes that are linked to involvement in the world-market economy have tended to reduce rather than raise the nutritional levels of the affected peoples. Specifically, the vitamin, mineral, and protein components of their diets are often drastically reduced and replaced by enormous increases in starch and carbohydrates, often in the form of white flour and refined sugar.

Any deterioration in the quality of a given population's diet is almost certain to be reflected in an increase in deficiency diseases and a general decline in health status. Indeed, as indigenous peoples have shifted to a diet based on imported manufactured or processed foods, there has been a dramatic rise in malnutrition, a massive increase in dental problems, and a variety of other nutrition-related disorders. Nutritional physiology is so complex that even well-meaning dietary changes have had tragic consequences. In many areas of Southeast Asia, government-sponsored protein supplementation programs, which supplied milk to protein-deficient populations, caused unexpected health problems and increased mortality. Officials failed to anticipate that in cultures where adults do not normally drink milk, they no longer produce the enzymes needed to digest it, resulting in milk intolerance.[14] In Brazil, a similar milk distribution program caused an epidemic of permanent blindness by aggravating a preexisting vitamin A deficiency.[15]

Teeth and Progress

There is nothing new in the observation that savages, or peoples living under primitive conditions, have, in general, excellent teeth. . . . Nor is it news that most civilized populations possess wretched teeth which begin to decay almost before they have erupted completely, and that dental caries is likely to be accompanied by periodontal disease with further reaching complications.[16]

Anthropologists have long recognized that undisturbed indigenous peoples are often in excellent physical condition. And it has often been noted specifically that dental caries and the other dental abnormalities that plague global-scale societies are absent or rare among indigenous peoples who have retained their diets. The fact that indigenous food habits may contribute to the development of sound teeth, whereas modernized diets may do just the opposite, was illustrated as long ago as 1894 in an article in the *Journal of the Royal Anthropological Institute* that described the results of a comparison between the teeth of ten Sioux Indians and a comparable group of Londoners.[17] The Indians, who were examined when they came to London as members of "Buffalo Bill's Wild West Show," were found to be completely free of caries and in possession of all their teeth, even though half of the group was over thirty-nine years of age. The Londoners' teeth were conspicuous for both their caries and their steady reduction in number with advancing age. The difference was attributed primarily to the wear and polishing caused by the Indian diet of coarse food and the fact that they chewed their food longer, encouraged by the absence of tableware.

One of the most remarkable studies of the dental conditions of indigenous peoples and the impact of dietary change was conducted in the 1930s by Weston Price,[18] an American dentist who was interested in determining what contributed to normal, healthy teeth. Between 1931 and 1936, Price systematically explored indigenous areas throughout the world to locate and examine the most isolated peoples who were still living relatively self-sufficiently. His fieldwork covered Alaska, the Canadian Yukon, Hudson Bay, Vancouver Island, Florida, the Andes, the Amazon, Samoa, Tahiti, New Zealand, Australia, New Caledonia, Fiji, the Torres Strait, East Africa, and the Nile. The study demonstrated both the superior quality of aboriginal dentition and the devastation that occurs as modern diets are adopted. In nearly every area where traditional foods were still being eaten, Price found perfect teeth with normal dental arches and virtually no decay, whereas caries and abnormalities increased steadily as new diets were adopted. In many cases the change was sudden and striking. Among Inuit (Eskimo) groups subsisting entirely on traditional food he found caries totally absent, whereas in groups eating a considerable quantity of store-bought food, approximately 20 percent of their teeth were decayed. This figure rose to more than 30 percent with Inuit groups subsisting almost exclusively on purchased or government-supplied food and reached an incredible 48 percent among the native peoples of Vancouver Island. Unfortunately for many of these people, modern dental treatment did not accompany the new food, and their suffering was appalling. The loss of teeth was, of course, bad enough in itself, and it certainly undermined the population's resistance to many new diseases, including tuberculosis. But new foods were also accompanied by crowded, misplaced teeth, gum diseases, distortion of the face, and pinching of the nasal cavity. Abnormalities in the dental arch appeared in the new generation following the change in diet, while caries appeared almost immediately even in adults.

Price reported that in many areas the affected peoples were conscious of their own physical deterioration. At a mission school in Africa, the principal asked him to explain to the native schoolchildren why they were not physically as strong as children who had had no contact with schools. On an island in the Torres Strait the aborigines knew exactly what was causing their problems and resisted—almost to the point of bloodshed—government efforts to establish a store that would make imported food available. The government prevailed, however, and Price was able to establish a relationship between the length of time the government store had been established and the increasing incidence of caries among a population that had shown an almost 100 percent immunity to them before the store had been opened.

In New Zealand, the Maori, who in their aboriginal state are often considered to have been among the healthiest, most perfectly developed of peoples, were found to have "advanced" the furthest. According to Price: "Their modernization was demonstrated not only by the high incidence of dental caries but also by the fact that 90 percent of the adults and 100 percent of the children had abnormalities of the dental arches."[19]

Malnutrition

Malnutrition, particularly in the form of protein deficiency, has become a critical problem for indigenous peoples who must adopt new economic patterns. Population pressures, cash cropping, and government programs have all tended to encourage the replacement of previous crops and other food sources that were rich in protein with substitutes high in calories but low in protein. In Africa, for example, protein-rich staples such as millet and sorghum are being systematically replaced by high-yielding manioc and plantains, which have insignificant amounts of protein. The problem is increased for cash croppers and wage laborers whose earnings are too low and unpredictable to allow purchase of adequate amounts of protein. In some rural areas, agricultural laborers have been forced systematically to deprive nonproductive members (principally children) of their households of minimal nutritional requirements to satisfy the need of the productive members of the household. This process has been documented in northeastern Brazil following the introduction of large-scale sisal plantations.[20] In urban centers, the difficulties of obtaining nutritionally adequate diets are even more serious for tribal immigrants because costs are higher and poor quality foods often are more tempting.

One of the most tragic, and largely overlooked, aspects of chronic malnutrition is that it can lead to abnormal brain development and apparently irreversible brain damage; chronic malnutrition has been associated with various forms of mental impairment or retardation. Malnutrition has been linked clinically with mental retardation in both Africa and Latin America,[21] and this appears to be a worldwide phenomenon with serious implications.[22]

Optimistic supporters of progress will surely say that all of these new health problems are being overstressed and that the introduction of hospitals, clinics, and other modern health institutions will overcome or at least compensate for all of these difficulties. However, it appears that uncontrolled population growth and economic impoverishment will likely keep most of these benefits out of reach for many indigenous peoples, and the intervention of modern medicine has at least partly contributed to the problem in the first place.

The generalization that global-scale culture frequently has a negative impact on the health of indigenous peoples has found broad empirical support worldwide,[23] but these conclusions have not gone unchallenged. Some critics argue that the health of indigenous peoples was often poor before modern-ization, and they point specifically to low life expectancy and high infant mortality rates.[24] Demographic statistics on self-sufficient indigenous peoples are often problematic because precise data are scarce, but they do show a less favorable profile than that enjoyed by many global-scale societies. However, it should be remembered that our present life expectancy is a recent phenom-enon that has been very costly in terms of medical research and technologi-cal advances. Furthermore, the benefits of our health system are not equally enjoyed by all members of our society. We could view the formerly high in-fant mortality rates as a relatively inexpensive and egalitarian small-scale public health program that offered the reasonable expectation of a healthy and productive life for those surviving to age fifteen.

Some critics also suggest that certain indigenous peoples, such as the New Guinea highlanders, were "stunted" by nutritional deficiencies created by their natural diet, which was "improved" through "acculturation" and cash cropping.[25] Although this argument suggests that the health question requires careful evaluation, it does not invalidate the empirical generalizations already established. Nutritional deficiencies undoubtedly occurred in densely popu-lated zones in the central New Guinea highlands. However, the specific case cited above may not be widely representative of other indigenous groups even in New Guinea, and it does not address the facts of outside intrusion or the inequities inherent in the contemporary development process.

Ecocide

> "How is it," asked a herdsman . . . "how is it that these hills can no longer give pasture to my cattle? In my father's day they were green and cattle thrived there; today there is no grass and my cattle starve." As one looked one saw that what had once been a green hill had become a raw red rock.[26]

Progress not only brings new threats to the health of indigenous peoples, it also imposes new strains on the ecosystems upon which they must depend for their ultimate survival. The introduction of new technology, increased con-sumption, reduced mortality rates, and the eradication of all previous controls have combined to replace what for many indigenous peoples was a relatively stable balance between population and natural resources with a new system that is unbalanced. Economic development is forcing ecocide on peoples who were once careful stewards of their resources. There is already a trend toward widespread environmental deterioration in indigenous areas, involving re-source depletion, erosion, plant and animal extinction, and a disturbing series of other previously unforeseen changes.

After the initial depopulation suffered by many indigenous peoples during their engulfment by frontiers of national expansion, their populations began to experience rapid growth. Authorities generally attribute this growth to the introduction of commercial medicine and new health measures and the termination of chronic intergroup violence, which reduced mortality rates, as well as to new technology, which increased food production. Certainly all of these factors played a part, but merely reducing mortality rates would not have produced the rapid population growth that most indigenous areas have experienced if traditional birth-spacing mechanisms had not been eliminated at the same time. Regardless of which factors were most important, it is clear that all of the natural and cultural checks on population growth have suddenly been pushed aside by culture change, while indigenous lands have been steadily reduced and consumption levels have risen. In many areas, environmental deterioration due to overuse of resources has set in, and in other areas such deterioration is imminent as resources continue to dwindle relative to the expanding population and increased use. Of course, population expansion by indigenous peoples may have positive political consequences, because where they can retain or regain their status as local majorities, they may be in a more favorable position to defend their resources against intruders.

Swidden systems and pastoralism, both highly successful economic systems under former conditions, have proven particularly vulnerable to increased population pressures and outside efforts to raise productivity beyond its natural limits. Research in Amazonia demonstrates that population pressures and related resource depletion can be created indirectly by official policies that restrict swidden people to smaller territories. Resource depletion itself can then become a powerful means of forcing indigenous people into participating in the world-market economy—thus leading to further resource depletion. For example, Foley C. Benson and I[27] showed how the Shipibo Indians in Peru were forced to further deplete their forest resources by cash cropping in the forest area to replace the resources that had been destroyed earlier by the intensive cash cropping necessitated by the narrow confines of their reserve. In this case, some species of palm trees that had provided critical housing materials were destroyed by forest clearing and had to be replaced by costly purchased materials. Research by Daniel R. Gross and others[28] showed similar processes at work among four indigenous groups in central Brazil and demonstrated that the degree of market involvement increases directly with increases in resource depletion.

The settling of nomadic herders and the removal of prior controls on herd size have often led to serious overgrazing and erosion problems where these had not previously occurred. There are indications that the desertification problem in the Sahel region of Africa was aggravated by programs designed to settle nomads. The first sign of imbalance in a swidden system appears when the planting cycles are shortened to the point that garden plots are reused before sufficient forest regrowth can occur. If reclearing and planting continue in the same area, the natural patterns of forest succession may be disturbed irreversibly and the soil can be impaired permanently. An extensive tract of tropical rain forest in the lower Amazon of Brazil was reduced to a semiarid desert in just fifty years through such a process.[29] The soils in the Azande area are also now seriously threatened with laterization and other problems as a result of the government-promoted cotton development scheme.[30]

The dangers of overdevelopment and the vulnerability of local resource systems have long been recognized by both anthropologists and indigenous peoples themselves, but the pressures for change have been overwhelming. In 1948 the Maya villagers of Chan Kom complained to Robert Redfield[31] about the shortening of their swidden cycles, which they correctly attributed to increasing population pressures. Redfield told them, however, that they had no choice but to go "forward with technology."[32] In Assam, swidden cycles were shortened from an average of twelve years to only two or three within just twenty years, and anthropologists warned that the limits of swiddening would soon be reached.[33] In the Pacific anthropologists warned of population pressures on limited resources as early as the 1930s.[34] These warnings seemed fully justified, considering the fact that the crowded Tikopians were prompted by population pressures on their tiny island to suggest that infanticide be legalized. The warnings have been dramatically reinforced since then by the doubling of Micronesia's population in the fourteen years between 1958 and 1972, from 70,600 to 114,645, while consumption levels have soared. By 1985 Micronesia's population had reached 162,321.

The environmental hazards of economic development and rapid population growth have become generally recognized only since worldwide concerns over environmental issues began in the early 1970s. Unfortunately, there is as yet little indication that the leaders of nations in transformation are sufficiently concerned with environmental limitations. On the contrary, governments are forcing indigenous peoples into a self-reinforcing spiral of population growth and intensified resource exploitation, which may be stopped only by environmental disaster or the total impoverishment of the indigenous peoples.

The reality of ecocide certainly focuses attention on the fundamental contrasts between small- and global-scale systems in their use of natural resources. In many respects the entire "victims of progress" issue hinges on natural resources, who controls them, and how they are managed. Indigenous peoples are victimized because they control resources that outsiders demand. The resources exist because indigenous people managed them conservatively. However, as with the issue of the health consequences of economic globalization, some anthropologists minimize the adaptive achievements of indigenous groups and seem unwilling to concede that ecocide might be a consequence of cultural change. Critics attack an exaggerated "noble savage" image of indigenous people living in perfect harmony with nature and having no visible impact on their surroundings.[35] They then show that indigenous groups do in fact modify the environment, and they conclude that there is no significant difference between how indigenous peoples and global-scale societies treat their environments. For example, Charles Wagley declared that Brazilian Indians such as the Tapirape "are not 'natural men.' They have human vices just as we do. . . . They do not live 'in tune' with nature any more than I do; in fact, they can often be as destructive of their environment, within their limitations, as some civilized men. The Tapirape are not innocent or childlike in any way."[36]

Anthropologist Terry Rambo demonstrated that the Semang of the Malaysian rainforests have a measurable impact on their environment. In his monograph *Primitive Polluters*,[37] Rambo reported that the Semang live in smoke-filled houses. They sneeze and spread germs; breathe and thus emit carbon dioxide. They clear small gardens, contributing "particulate matter" to the air and disturbing the local climate because cleared areas proved measurably warmer and drier than the shady forest. Rambo concluded that his research "demonstrates the essential functional similarity of the environmental interactions of primitive and civilized societies"[38] in contrast to a "noble savage" view, which, according to Rambo, mistakenly "claims that traditional peoples almost always live in essential harmony with their environment."[39]

This is surely a false issue. To stress, as I do, that small-scale indigenous societies tend to manage their resources for sustained yield within relatively self-sufficient and resilient subsistence economies is not to portray them as either childlike or "natural." Nor is it to deny that tribal societies "disrupt" their environment and may never be in absolute "balance" with nature.[40] The crucial point is that the total consumption of natural resources, or ecological footprint, of self-sufficient tribal peoples in their territory is minuscule in comparison to the ecological footprint of commercial societies. For example, the Asháninka use only 0.24 percent of the biological potential of their territory, whereas Americans in 2001 were using the equivalent of nearly 200 percent. The elevated American consumption rate was only possible because of their use of fossil fuels and reliance on global trade.[41]

The ecocide issue is perhaps most dramatically illustrated by two sets of satellite photos taken over the Brazilian rainforests of Rondônia.[42] Photos taken in 1973, when Rondônia was still a tribal domain, show virtually unbroken rainforest. The 1987 satellite photos, taken after just fifteen years of highway construction and "development" by outsiders, show more than 20 percent of the forest destroyed. The surviving Indians were being concentrated by FUNAI into what would soon become mere islands of forest in a ravaged landscape. It is irrelevant to quibble about whether indigenous peoples are noble, childlike, or innocent, or about the precise meaning of balance with nature, carrying capacity, or adaptation; the fact is that for the past two hundred years rapid environmental deterioration on an unprecedented global scale has followed the wresting of control of vast areas of the world from indigenous peoples by resource-hungry commercial societies. The reality is that nearly 80 percent of the world's primary forest (tropical, temperate, and boreal) is gone.[43] It is also no accident that the areas with the richest and/or best-preserved ecosystems in the world are occupied by indigenous peoples.

Deprivation and Discrimination

> Contact with European culture has given them a knowledge of great wealth, opportunity and privilege, but only very limited avenues by which to acquire these things.[44]

Unwittingly, indigenous peoples have had the burden of perpetual relative deprivation thrust upon them by acceptance—either by themselves or by the governments administering them—of the standards of socioeconomic progress set for them by the commercial world. By comparison with the material wealth of commercial societies, small-scale societies become, by definition, impoverished. They are then forced to transform their cultures and work to achieve what many economists now acknowledge to be unattainable goals. Even when the modest GDP goals set by economic planners for the impoverished nations during the "development decades" that began in the 1960s were met, the results were hardly noticeable for most of the indigenous people involved. Population growth, environmental limitations, inequitable distribution of wealth, and the continued rapid growth of national societies have all meant that both the absolute and the relative gap between the rich and poor in the world is steadily widening. In 2000 the top 10 percent of the world's households held 71 percent of household net worth in purchasing power parity dollars, measured in standard commercial values.[45] Viewed from the bottom up, the four hundred wealthiest Americans held more personal wealth than 2.5 billion people in the poorest eighty-one countries in the world.[46] In a world this divided, the prospect that indigenous peoples will actually be able to attain the levels of resource consumption to which they are being encouraged to aspire is remote indeed, except for those few groups that have retained effective control over strategic mineral resources.

It is of course quite incorrect to consider indigenous people "impoverished" when they enjoy cultural autonomy with full ownership over their territories. Elsewhere I have estimated income and wealth for an Amazonian tribal society represented by the Asháninka by imputing dollar values to the time households expend for maintenance and reproduction of society and culture, treating the expenditure as the value of an annual social product.[47] These calculations yield an income equivalent to $14,185 per capita in standard market exchange values, which is comparable to Portugal's per capita GDP. If Asháninka social product were treated as a 5 percent annual return on their social and cultural capital, each household would be worth 1 million dollars. Including the capitalized value of nature's services provided by the amount of rainforest needed to sustain the area forest required to support the Asháninka would raise average household wealth to between 20 and 50 million dollars.

Indigenous peoples may feel deprivation not only when the economic goals they have been encouraged to seek fail to materialize, but also when they discover that they are powerless second-class citizens who are discriminated against and exploited by the dominant society. At the same time, they are denied the satisfaction of cultural autonomy when it has been lost in the process of globalization. Under the impact of major economic change, family life is disrupted, previous social controls are often lost, and many indicators of social anomie, such as alcoholism, crime, delinquency, suicide, emotional disorders, and despair, may increase. The inevitable frustration resulting from this continual deprivation finds expression in the cargo cults, revitalization movements, and a variety of other political and religious movements that have been widespread among indigenous peoples following their disruption by the economic globalization process.

Notes

1. René Maunier, 1949, *The Sociology of Colonies*, London: Routledge and Kegan Paul, 2:725.

2. Nic Marks, Saamah Abdallah, Andrew Simms, and Sam Thompson, 2006, *The Unhappy Planet Index: An Index of Human Well-Being and Environmental Impact*, London: New Economics Foundation.

3. CIA, World Factbook, https://www.cia.gov/library/publications/the-world-fact-book/index.html (accessed July 11, 2007).

4. U.S. Department of the Interior, Office of Territories, 1953, *Report on the Administration of the Trust Territory of the Pacific Islands (by the United States to the United Nations) for the Period July 1, 1951, to June 30, 1952*, Annual Report on the Administration of the Territory of the Pacific Islands, 44.

5. Walter R. Goldschmidt, 1952, "The interrelations between cultural factors and the acquisition of new technical skills," in *The Progress of Underdeveloped Areas*, ed. Bert F. Hoselitz, Chicago: University of Chicago Press, 135.

6. Charles C. Hughes and John M. Hunter, 1972, "The role of technological development in promoting disease in Africa," in *The Careless Technology: Ecology and International Development*, ed. M. T. Farvar and John P. Milton, Garden City, NY: Natural History Press, 93.

7. World Health Organization, 2003, *Diet, Nutrition and the Prevention of Chronic Diseases*, Report of a Joint WHO/FAO Expert Consultation, WHO Technical Report Series 916, Geneva: WHO.

8. U.S. Department of State, 1959, *Eleventh Annual Report to the United Nations on the Administration of the Trust Territory of the Pacific Islands (July 1, 1957, to June 30, 1958)*; U.S. Department of State, 1973, *Twenty-Fifth Annual Report to the United Nations on the Administration of the Trust Territory of the Pacific Islands (July 1, 1971, to June 30, 1972)*, statistical tables.

9. Ian A. M. Prior, 1971, "The price of civilization," *Nutrition Today* 6(4): 2.

10. Hughes and Hunter, *Careless Technology*.

11. Barry S. Hewlett and Bonnie L. Hewlett, 2007, *Ebola, Culture and Politics: The Anthropology of an Emerging Disease*. Belmont, CA: Wadsworth/Thompson.

12. Adam Drewnowski and Barry M. Popkin, 1997, "The Nutrition Transition: New Trends in the Global Diet," *Nutrition Review* 55(2): 31–43; Barry M. Popkin, 1998, "The nutrition transition and its health implications in lower-income countries," *Public Health Nutrition* 1(1): 5–21.

13. T. L. Cleave, 1974, *The Saccharine Disease*, Bristol, UK: Wright.

14. A. E. Davis and T. D. Bolin, 1972, "Lactose intolerance in Southeast Asia," in *The Careless Technology: Ecology and International Development*, ed. M. T. Farvar and John P. Milton, 61–68. Garden City, NY: Natural History Press.

15. George E. Bunce, 1972, "Aggravation of vitamin A deficiency following distribution of non-fortified skim milk: An example of nutrient interaction," In *The Careless Technology: Ecology and International Development*, ed. M. T. Farvar and John P. Milton, 53–60. Garden City, NY: Natural History Press.

16. Earnest A. Hooton, 1945, "Introduction," in *Nutrition and Physical Degeneration: A Comparison of Primitive and Modern Diets and Their Effects*, by Weston A. Price, Redlands, CA: Author, xviii.

17. Wilberforce Smith, 1894, "The teeth of ten Sioux Indians," *Journal of the Royal Anthropological Institute* 24: 109–16.

18. Weston Andrew Price, 1945, *Nutrition and Physical Degeneration: A Comparison of Primitive and Modern Diets and Their Effects*, Redlands, CA: Author.

19. Ibid., 206.

20. Daniel R. Gross and Barbara A. Underwood, 1971, "Technological change and caloric costs: Sisal agriculture," *American Anthropologist* 73(3): 725–40.

21. F. Monckeberg, 1968, "Mental retardation from malnutrition," *Journal of the American Medical Association* 206: 30–31.

22. Ashley Montagu, 1972, "Sociogenic brain damage," *American Anthropologist* 74(5): 1045–61.

23. Axel Kroeger and Franchise Barbira-Freedman, 1982, *Culture Change and Health: The Case of South American Rainforest Indians*, Frankfurt am Main: Verlag Peter Lang (reprinted in Bodley, 1988a: 221–36); K. R. Reinhard, 1976, "Resource exploitation and the health of western arctic man," in *Circumpolar Health: Proceedings of the Third International Symposium, Yellowknife, Northwest Territories*, ed. Roy J. Shephard and S. Itoh, 617–27, Toronto: University of Toronto Press (reprinted in Bodley, 1988a: 211–20); R. Wirsing, 1985, "The health of traditional societies and the effects of acculturation," *Current Anthropology* 26: 303–22.

24. Robert B. Edgerton, 1992, *Sick Societies: Challenging the Myth of Primitive Harmony*, New York: Free Press.

25. Glenn Dennett and John Connell, 1988, "Acculturation and health in the highlands of Papua New Guinea," *Current Anthropology* 29(2): 273–99.

26. J. D. Rheinallt Jones, 1934, "Economic condition of the urban native," In *Western Civilization and the Natives of South Africa*, ed. I. Schapera, 159–92. London: George Routledge and Sons.

27. John H. Bodley and Foley C. Benson, 1979, *Cultural Ecology of Amazonian Palms*, Reports of Investigations, no. 56, Pullman: Laboratory of Anthropology, Washington State University.

28. Daniel R. Gross et al., 1979, "Ecology and acculturation among native peoples of Central Brazil," *Science* 206(4422): 1043–50.

29. F. L. Ackermann, 1964, *Geologia e Fisiografia da Região Bragantina, Estado do Para*, Manaus, Brazil: Conselho Nacional de Pesquisas, Instituto National de Pesquisas da Amazonia.

30. Mary McNeil, 1972, "Lateritic soils in distinct tropical environments: Southern Sudan and Brazil," in *The Careless Technology: Ecology and International Development*, ed. M. T. Farvar and John P. Milton, 591–608. Garden City, NY: Natural History Press.

31. Robert Redfield, 1962, *A Village That Chose Progress: Chan Kom Revisited*, Chicago: University of Chicago Press/Phoenix Books.

32. Ibid., 178.

33. Robbins Burling, 1963, *Rengsanggri: Family and Kinship in a Garo Village*, Philadelphia: University of Pennsylvania Press, 311–12.

34. Felix M. Keesing, 1941, *The South Seas in the Modern World*, Institute of Pacific Relations International Research Series, New York: John Day, 64–65.

35. Thomas N. Headland, 1997, "Revisionism in ecological anthropology," *Current Anthropology* 38(4): 605–30.

36. C. Wagley, 1977, *Welcome of Tears: The Tapirape Indians of Central Brazil*. New York: Oxford University Press, 302.

37. A. Terry Rambo, 1985, *Primitive Polluters: Semang Impact on the Malaysian Tropical Rain Forest Ecosystem*, Anthropological Papers no. 76, Ann Arbor: Museum of Anthropology, University of Michigan.

38. Ibid., 78.

39. Ibid., 2.

40. John H. Bodley, 1997c, "Comment on 'Revisionism in ecological anthropology' by Thomas N. Headland," *Current Anthropology* 38(4): 611–13.

41. John H. Bodley, 2008, *Anthropology and Contemporary Human Problems*, Lanham, MD: Altamira Press, 73–76.

42. William Albert Allard and Loren McIntyre, 1988, "Rondonia's settlers invade Brazil's imperiled rain forest," *National Geographic* 174(6): 772–99, 780–81.

43. United Nations Food and Agriculture Organization, 2006, *Global Forest Resources Assessment 2005: Progress towards Sustainable Forest Management*, FAO Forestry Paper 147, www.fao.org/forestry/site/32039/en (accessed December 11, 2007).

44. Ron Crocombe, 1968, "Bougainville! Copper, R. R. A. and secessionism," *New Guinea* 3(3): 39–49.

45. James B. Davies, Susanna Sandstrom, Anthony Shorrocks, and Edward N. Wolff, 2006, *The World Distribution of Household Wealth*, Helsinki, Finland: World Institute for Development Economics Research.

46. John H. Bodley, 2008, *Anthropology and Contemporary Human Problems*, Lanham, MD: Altamira Press, chap. 7.

47. Allen Johnson, 2003, *Families of the Forest: The Matsigenka Indians of the Peruvian Amazon*, Berkeley and Los Angeles: University of California Press; John H. Bodley, 2005, "The Rich Tribal World: Scale and Power Perspectives on Cultural Valuation," presentation, Society for Applied Anthropology Annual Meeting, Santa Fe, New Mexico; *Contemporary Human Problems*, chapter 2.

10 The Political Struggle for Indigenous Self-Determination

Our plea to the world is to help us in our struggle to find a place in the world community where we can exercise our right to self-determination as a distinct people and as a nation.

—Mel Watkins[1]

THE PREVIOUS CHAPTERS have presented a rather gloomy picture for small-scale indigenous societies worldwide. Throughout, indigenous peoples have appeared largely as passive victims, except for scattered episodes of armed resistance. It might, therefore, be easily assumed that their situation was hopeless. Indeed, until quite recently many observers confidently predicted the impending extinction of all self-sufficient tribal peoples, but such a judgment would be premature. In recent decades the widespread availability of electronic communications has made it possible for indigenous peoples to politically organize for self-defense on a scale never before possible. The consciousness of sharing a common identity can now develop among peoples who previously might never have talked to more than a few hundred people in a lifetime. By politically mobilizing, indigenous peoples have successfully captured the attention of governments and international agencies, including the United Nations, and have made their well-being a prominent human rights and social justice issue.

During the 1970s self-identified indigenous peoples began organizing new institutions and political structures to enable them to peacefully negotiate with national governments to secure their right to exist as independent societies. Ideally, such accommodations would be characterized by political "self-determination" that would allow indigenous people to control their small-scale societies, their natural resources and territories, and their cultural ways of life as a basic human right. As indigenous people define it, self-determination would mean a return to full local political, economic, and cultural autonomy. As we shall see, this need not mean isolation from the metropolitan commercial world, but rather that indigenous peoples would be allowed to control their own affairs on their own terms within their own territories. As the preceding chapters have shown, self-determination of this kind was lost by most small-scale societies worldwide in the push for "progress."

The present self-determination revival by indigenous peoples raises such critical questions as *Who are indigenous peoples? What are their objectives, and how can they be realized?* Perhaps the most important questions are *How do indigenous people self-identify?* and *How do they organize their social, political, and economic institutions?* These issues are especially important to-day because many conflicting groups are clamoring for recognition, for con-trol of resources, and for self-determination. This conflict creates a situation in which the human rights of indigenous peoples may continue to be over-looked and their just claims could be again ignored. The present chapter con-siders these questions in detail and explores the historical development of the new political relationship between indigenous peoples and national govern-ments and international organizations since 1945.

Who Are Indigenous Peoples?

The term *indigenous peoples* is used extensively as a self-designation by in-dividuals and organizations involved in this political struggle. For many peo-ple it replaces, or is interchangeable with, the expression *tribal peoples*. In-digenous peoples have been sometimes justifiably reluctant to define themselves because, in the past, governments often used "legal" definitions to divide and manipulate them. However, the self-identity of indigenous people has now become a central element in their political struggle for social and cultural survival. The most obvious answer to the question *Who are indige-nous peoples?* is that they are whoever they say they are. For example, UNIPA, an indigenous organization representing the sixteen thousand Chibchan-speaking Awá people in the southwest corner of Columbia and ad-jacent Ecuador posted their "identify and life plan" on its Web site in 2007 as follows: "Awá Identity: We, the +nkal Awá people, 'people of the Montaña, of the forest,' we base our existence, origin, identity, knowledge, and auton-omy on the forest where we have been able to structure our way of life ac-cording to the natural environment, building cultural practices transmitted from generation to generation, consolidating the particulars of our culture, based on our Ancestral Territory, and continually fighting to consolidate a strong people with cultural identity in support of autonomy."

The Awá "life plan" was simply: "To live in our territory and improve life . . . fortified by our own thought, living together under principles of unity, ter-ritory, autonomy, and cultural identity, and who maintain relations of respect with nature and with other peoples. Our practices of justice, education, health, and production are fundamentally in accord with our cultural reality."[2]

This is a very clear and eloquent self-description of an indigenous society, emphasizing attachment to territory, identity, and culture; however, governments require formal definitions. The World Council of Indigenous Peoples (WCIP), one of the first international indigenous organizations, passed a resolution at its second general assembly in 1977 declaring that only indigenous peoples could define indigenous peoples. The WCIP noted as a partial definition that indigenous peoples were descendants of the earliest populations in an area, but they did not control the national government.[3] Historical priority and lack of political power highlights the justice of the indigenous cause, but legal authorities need more guidance.

Granted that indigenous status depends on self-identification, most international organizations use formal definitions of indigenous people that draw on the "working definition" developed by José R. Martínez Cobo[4] for his massive *Study on the Problem of Discrimination against Indigenous Populations*. Cobo carried out his work from 1972 to 1986 as Special Rapporteur of the Sub-Commission on Prevention of Discrimination and Protection of Minorities of the UN Commission on Human Rights. His indigenous people "working definition" was highly flexible, but contained the following optional criteria:

Indigenous communities, peoples and nations are those which, having a historical continuity with pre-invasion and pre-colonial societies that developed on their territories, consider themselves distinct from other sectors of the societies now prevailing on those territories, or parts of them. They form at present non-dominant sectors of society and are determined to preserve, develop and transmit to future generations their ancestral territories, and their ethnic identity, as the basis of their continued existence as peoples, in accordance with their own cultural patterns, social institutions and legal system.

This historical continuity may consist of the continuation, for an extended period reaching into the present of one or more of the following factors:

a) Occupation of ancestral lands, or at least of part of them;
b) Common ancestry with the original occupants of these lands;
c) Culture in general, or in specific manifestations (such as religion, living under a tribal system, membership of an indigenous community, dress, means of livelihood, lifestyle, etc.);
d) Language (whether used as the only language, as mother-tongue, as the habitual means of communication at home or in the family, or as the main, preferred, habitual, general or normal language);
e) Residence on certain parts of the country, or in certain regions of the world;
f) Other relevant factors.

On an individual basis, an indigenous person is one who belongs to these indigenous populations through self-identification as indigenous (group consciousness) and is recognized and accepted by these populations as one of its members (acceptance by the group).

This preserves for these communities the sovereign right and power to decide who belongs to them, without external interference.[5]

Cobo's working definition is clearly compatible with the statements of self-identification consistently and repeatedly issued by indigenous people organizations. In 1995 the United Nations Working Group on Indigenous People adopted a more concise set of principles that should be "taken into account" by any definition of indigenous peoples used in a formal context:

(a) priority in time, with respect to the occupation and use of a specific territory;

(b) the voluntary perpetuation of cultural distinctiveness, which may include the aspects of language, social organization, religion and spiritual values, modes of production, laws and institutions;

(c) self-identification, as well as recognition by other groups, or by State authorities, as a distinct collectivity; and

(d) an experience of subjugation, marginalization, dispossession, exclusion or discrimination, whether or not these conditions persist.[6]

The concept of *indigenous peoples*, defined by these lists of criteria, is for the purpose of implementing measures to protect the human rights of indigenous peoples and to make restitution for past injustices that they continue to experience. These criteria say nothing about specific cultural characteristics. For example, the agreement between the Inuit and the Canadian government that established Nunavut in 1999 officially referred to the Inuit as "all those members of the aboriginal people, sometimes known as Eskimos, that has traditionally used and occupied, and currently uses and occupies, the lands and waters of the Nunavut Settlement Area." The agreement further states in article 35 that "Inuit are best able to define who is an Inuk [a single Inuit person]," and specifies that a designated Inuit organization will establish an enrollment list of Inuit for the purposes of the agreement. Aside from being alive, Canadian, and self-identified as Inuit, a qualified person must be Inuk by Inuit custom and be associated with the territory.[7]

There is no justification for claims that the indigenous people concept lacks intellectual rigor or is racist.[8] Indigenous people who recognize common ancestry as important are not by definition racist, because they define kinship culturally, not biologically, and they commonly practice adoption and admit to their societies whoever they chose to admit. However, national governments have sometimes imposed racist tribal membership criteria. *Indigenous peoples* is now the most widely accepted global term for the small-scale societies we are concerned with in a human rights context. Other generic terms have gained wide regional acceptance by some indigenous peoples but have been rejected elsewhere in the world. The term *Indian* is now widely accepted in the Americas, but the Eskimo peoples now prefer to call themselves Inuit and have never considered themselves to be Indians. Native Americans have tribal governments, and the term *tribal* is accepted by many indigenous peoples in Amazonia and the Philippines but may be rejected elsewhere.

Of course, the real issue is not the label used but the underlying common identity among indigenous peoples, and their just claims to territory and cultural identity. The formal definitions ignore the specifics of indigenous culture and society that matter to indigenous people. The cultural details that matter to indigenous people are the scale- and social-power-related details that support household, community, and the humanization process, but these are internal matters. When leaders from diverse indigenous cultures meet each other for the first time, they recognize that they share the same basic culture in spite of their often conspicuous, but superficial, differences. As will become apparent in the case studies later in this chapter, indigenous peoples throughout the world independently say the same things when they describe the elements that make them different from the dominant societies surrounding them. The first shared trait that is invariably mentioned is their relationship to the land. As Julio Carduño, a Mexican Indian leader, declared at the First Congress of South American Indian Movements held in Cuzco in 1980: "Perhaps what most unites us is the defense of our land. The land has never been merchandise for us, as it is with capitalism, but it is the support for our cultural universe."[9]

We have noted repeatedly in other chapters that land is held communally by indigenous peoples. Community land cannot be sold, even though there may be many different systems for regulating individual access and even individual ownership. Native leaders often state that their land system is equitable and that no exact parallel to it exists in any industrial nations, socialist countries included. Indigenous peoples are also united in opposition to technologies and development projects that they consider destructive and unnecessary. They consider themselves more sensitive to the need to protect their land from environmental deterioration than are those who would take the land from them. This view was presented by Carduño at the Cuzco conference in the following terms: "There can be no economic interest superior to the necessity of preserving the ecosystem; we do not want a bonanza today at the cost of a desolate future."[10]

There are other shared features of the social and political systems of indigenous peoples that present sharp contrasts to those of other national systems, minority groups, or political parties. Leaders of the emerging indigenous peoples' self-determination movement see their own societies as classless, community-based, egalitarian, and close to nature. On the other hand, they see the societies around them as highly stratified, centralized, individualistic, antinature, and highly secular. These opposing constellations of traits do, in fact, pinpoint the most crucial differences anthropologists recognize between the idealized small-scale cultures and commercially organized nation-states.[11] Some anthropologists might argue that no society was ever really egalitarian and that all contemporary small-scale societies have irrevocably lost whatever ideal features they may once have possessed, but today's indigenous leaders do not agree.

Certainly, not all indigenous peoples accept the idealized view of their own culture, nor do they necessarily all support the self-determination movement. Many individuals may find the personal rewards potentially available in the dominant society to be more attractive than life in a relatively self-sufficient small society. It is significant, however, that those who are prominent in the self-determination movement usually have had extensive experience and opportunities in the dominant commercial society but have rejected it in favor of their own culture, which they consider to be superior. An example of this attitude was demonstrated by a Bolivian Indian leader when he attempted to explain to a journalist in Amsterdam why the Indian movement rejected Marxism. To make his point, he outlined general differences between Indian and Western social systems and discussed the advantages of Indian methods of wealth and power regulation, concluding: "We think that this [Indian method] is an original way of solving the problem of individual wealth accumulation and political power at the same time, but it seems absurd to Westerners. We want to conserve our institutions not only because they are ours, but also because we consider them just."[12]

The Initial Political Movements

What we want is to have the tools to run our own lives and to participate as equals in the greater life of Canada as a whole. The principal tools are, simply, reasonable Inuit land claims settlements and a Nunavut territorial government.[13]

In the past, government officials, missionaries, anthropologists, and other experts endlessly debated the best policies for indigenous peoples. The usual solution was to recommend integration into the dominant society, perhaps somehow blending "the best of both worlds." The indigenous people themselves were seldom consulted, because either no one thought the people knew what was best for themselves or no one was seriously concerned about their real desires. However, it is now apparent that indigenous leaders of the self-determination movement do have a clear conception of who indigenous peoples are. They also know what needs must be accommodated if their societies and cultures are to remain a viable alternative to the perceived deficits of the commercial world. The specific objectives of different indigenous groups may vary widely according to local conditions, as will be seen in the case studies that follow, but self-determination is the common theme, and control over traditional lands is always an overriding objective.

There have been many cases in the recent past in which indigenous peoples approached government officials with well-reasoned proposals that would permit their cultural autonomy and continued well-being. However, such proposals were seldom accepted. For example, in 1975, representatives from thirty-four Guajibo communities in the Colombian llanos presented the government with a formal petition for the establishment of a reserve measuring twenty thousand square kilometers for the forty thousand Guajibo, the indigenous residents of the region. They argued that not only did they know how to take care of the land, but they also had a rightful claim to it, unlike the twenty colonists who had illegally moved in. They also rejected a previous recommendation for a series of small Guajibo reserves, because such fragmentation would have facilitated their eventual destruction.[14]

Creating Nunavut

One of the most comprehensive recent agreements negotiated by indigenous peoples was the establishment of the Inuit-governed Canadian territory of Nunavut in 1999 in combination with the comprehensive settlement of Inuit land claims signed in 1993. In this exceptional case most of the demands of the indigenous group were met. The negotiation process began in 1976 when the Inuit Tapirisat of Canada presented the Canadian government with a proposal for the establishment of a special territory to be known as Nunavut, which means "our land" in the Inuit language. Nunavut would consist of the nearly 2 million square kilometers of land that the Inuit had never surrendered by treaty, where the Inuit continued to be the dominant inhabitants. The Inuit wanted full ownership of some 648,000 square kilometers and exclusive hunting and fishing rights over the remainder. They also proposed that they should, as the majority population, control the regional government as well as the regulation of any resource development of Nunavut. Such ownership and control would ensure their primary objective of self-sufficiency.

In their 1982 letter to the provincial prime ministers of Canada, the Inuit Committee on National Issues (ICNI) eloquently presented their position on the constitutional guarantees they required as the minimum conditions for the recognition of their basic rights and to set the stage for the creation of Nunavut. Specifically, they wanted the following principles to be protected:

   i. The collective recognition of the aboriginal peoples as distinct peoples in Canada due to our occupation of our lands since time immemorial, including the protection of our cultures, histories and lifestyles, and flowing from this principle:
  ii. The recognition of our political rights to self-governing institutions (structures) of various kinds within the Canadian Confederation; and
 iii. The recognition of our economic rights to our lands and waters, their resources and their benefits, as a base for self-sufficiency and the development of native communities and families, including the protection of our traditional livelihoods.[15]

In 1982 the Inuit voted overwhelmingly in a plebiscite in favor of the establishment of Nunavut as a politically separate Inuit territory. Shortly thereafter, the Nunavut Constitutional Forum (NCF) and the Canadian federal government agreed in principle to the establishment of Nunavut.[16] The forum made it clear that what they were seeking was not an ethnically or racially based political division, but rather a division based on peoples who were permanent residents of a natural region and who practiced a self-sufficient economy based on renewable resources. Additional and more detailed proposals for the design of Nunavut were presented by Inuit representatives at a constitutional conference held in 1983, in which the Inuit emphasized that Nunavut was to be a form of self-government within the Canadian federal tradition. Final agreements on the specific boundaries of Nunavut were not completed until 1988. Nunavut Territory became official in April 1999 (see figure 10.1). At that time Nunavut contained 26,000 people, 85 percent of whom were Inuit, and a total of 770,000 square miles (1,993,530 km²), an area larger than Mexico. The Inuit received a cash settlement of 840 million dollars over 14 years, as well as mineral rights to 14,000 square miles (35,250 km²), and direct title to 136,000 square miles (352,104 kilometers), which was substantially more than the Alaska natives received in their claims settlement.[17]

Nunavut is a small nation within a nation, with its own government, the Government of Nunavut, which has a full complement of government agencies, including a premier, seven ministerial departments, and a nineteen-person assembly to represent three regional communities. Nunavut also sends a representative to the Canadian Parliament. A special organization, Nunavut Tunngavik Inc. (NTI), manages the land and resources collectively owned by the Inuit and promotes Inuit well-being generally, according to the terms of

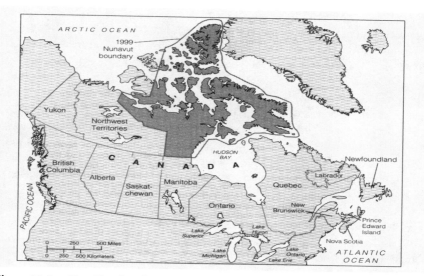

Figure 10.1.   Map Showing the Final Boundaries of Nunavut Effective April 1, 1999
Original base map from *Vort land, vort liv* (Our Land, Our Life) by Helge Kleivan, Institute for Eskimology, Copenhagen University, no. 3, 1976. It also appears in IWGIA Newsletter 34 (1983): 31.

the Nunavut Land Claims Agreement Act. The NTI also issues the annual "State of Inuit Culture and Society" report[18] and maintains a registry of Inuit-owned business corporations operating in Nunavut.[19]

Nunavut is a unique experiment in which indigenous peoples are attempting to create a truly sustainable society in the commercial world based on social and cultural principles that proved successful in the tribal world. A formal Nunavut Economic Development Strategy was issued in 2003 by the newly formed Sivummut Economic Development Strategy (SEDS) Group, a coalition of some twenty Inuit organizations convened by the Nunavut Economic Forum (NEF). The SEDS Group's goal was "a high and sustainable quality of life," to be achieved "without compromising the unique culture, values, and connections to the land that have supported Inuit society over countless generations."[20] The Nunavut Development Strategy emphasizes sustainability and self-reliance, environmental stewardship, traditional knowledge, and social equity based on four principles: cultural integrity, determination and realism, community control, and cooperation and coordination.[21] The Inuit envision a mixed economy that balances a wage and salary sector with a strong "land-based economy" drawing on natural resources. Hunting, fishing, and foraging are dominant features of Inuit culture and identity, but also provide at least half of Nunavut's food and are important sources of income.[22]

Nunavut's development goals are more achievable because Nunavut is a small-scale society. There are only 28 communities, averaging just 820 persons. Iqaluit, the capital, is the largest settlement, with an Inuit population of 2,956 in 1999. In 1995 there were about 100 Inuit-owned commercial businesses, most very small, operating in the territory, but by 2007 there were 243 businesses. Nunasi Corporation, headquartered in Iqaluit, produced revenues of over 200 million dollars (U.S.) in 2005, and was probably the largest Inuit business in Nunavut. Nunasi is collectively owned by all the Nunavut Inuit.[23] Nunasi owns a holding company, NorTerra, jointly with the Inuit of the Western Arctic. In turn, NorTerra owns Canadian North, an airline operating Boeing 737 jetliners in the arctic; the Northern Transportation Company Limited, (NTCL), which operates maritime shipping in the Canadian Arctic; and Weldco-Beales (WBM), a heavy equipment manufacturing company with plants in Alberta, British Columbia, and Washington State. The political and commercial development of Nunavut is certainly a dramatic transformation of Inuit society and culture as it existed a century ago, but many problems remain to be resolved.[23]

Kuna Self-Determination

In rare cases indigenous peoples have successfully been able to force governments into accepting their own forms of self-determination and coexistence with the commercial world. In 1925 the Chibchan-speaking Kuna Indians were able to take advantage of the relative political and military weakness of the Panamanian government and declared themselves an independent nation. The Kuna fought a brief armed rebellion before the government compromised with them in 1930 and accepted the Kuna plan for the establishment of an autonomous Kuna territory, which came into effect in 1938.[25] This territory is known today as the Comarca Kuna, or Kuna Yala, and the lands within it continue to be held communally by the resident Kuna, who in 2005 officially numbered more than thirty-six thousand people occupying their own territory of more than five thousand square kilometers of tropical forest and the adjacent Eastern Caribbean marine ecosystem.[26] The greater Kuna world includes two more recently formed *comarcas*, the Comarca Kuna Madungandi (1996), and the Comarca Kuna Wargandi (2000).

Self-determination means that indigenous people run their own affairs and control the conditions of their lives, their society, and their culture. This is what the Kuna have been able to do. They are a politically organized territory, a small nation with their own internal government, which the Panamanian government treats administratively as the equivalent of a province with unique internal structures. As part of Panama, Kuna Yala has two electoral circuits and elects two deputies to the National Assembly. Within Kuna Yala the Kuna are subject to the political authority of three senior political leaders, the *Saila Dummagen*, who head the Kuna General Congress, an assembly of representatives from each of the forty-nine villages. The General Congress convenes every six months, and each village also has a local congress that meets frequently. In 1995, in response to the legal requirements of the "dominant" Panamanian society, the Kuna formalized in writing their Kuna Norms, or Fundamental Law, which was approved by all Kuna communities after some ten years of deliberation.[27] The Norms explicitly make Kuna language, cultural norms, and cosmology the centerpiece of Kuna Yala's organizations, proceedings, and policies. The objective of the Norms is, as Cacique Harmodio Vivar declared, "the unity of our people" based on Kuna language and culture.[28] The Fundamental Law contains an anthropological definition of Kuna culture as "an integrated and coherent system of values, institutions, history, religion, language, customs and traditions that form the foundation of the identity of the Kuna people, and that manifests itself through its philosophy, socio-political arts and system, which was created and developed by the Kuna over the centuries."[29]

Article 6 of the Kuna Norms declares that the accords adopted by the congresses "can not be contrary to fundamental social, cultural and religious values." A separate organization, the General Congress of Kuna Culture, is the highest authority on the culture and has the duty to protect, conserve, defend, promote, and add to the history, tradition, religion, and ethical and social values of the Kuna people.[30] The entry of outsiders, including researchers and religious missionaries, is limited by Kuna officials. The primary language of instruction in the territory is Kuna, but education is intercultural and bilingual.

The Fundamental Law is emphatic about the collective and traditional nature of the Kuna land tenure system: Kuna Yala "is the collective property of the Kuna people, whose acquisition, exploitation, utilization, and profit will be carried out collectively, in conformity with customary norms and practices. . . . [These lands] cannot be alienated, nor leased under any title, neither temporarily, or permanently. Property rights acquired by natural or legal persons before this law came into affect shall be null and void."[31]

Significantly, among the functions of the Kuna General Congress are "to protect and conserve the ecosystems and establish the rational use of natural resources." These protections are applied comprehensively to forests, soils, waters, flora, fauna, freshwater and marine species, and all biodiversity. All endangered species are protected against large-scale exploitation, and there are special provisions for off-seasons, and special protected areas. All mining activities or mining concessions are subject to approval by the General Congress.[32] Defense of Kuna territory and resources is clearly a prime political objective, and they have successfully surveyed their southern border along the continental divide and have removed invading settlers. Much of the original forest cover of Kuna Yala and the adjoining indigenous *comarca* of Embera remains intact, and the recorded deforestation rate within these territories of less than 0.2 percent a year from 1992 to 2004 was the lowest in the country.[33] This was an order of magnitude lower than the national deforestation rate of 1.1 percent, and far lower than the highest provincial rate of nearly 4 percent. First Kuna Cacique Gilberto Arias explains the positive Kuna environmental record: "The forest is our life and our existence. In the forest we find our food, our medicines, our housing and our knowledge. How can they think that we, the indigenous people, could destroy our life, destroying forest? We have used the forests for a truly sustainable development, only taking what we needed."[34]

The Political Struggle

In many respects, the problems confronting indigenous peoples are political power and human rights problems: Indigenous peoples can be overwhelmed because they lack the political power to adequately defend themselves against dominant societies and to promote their human rights to self-determination and sociocultural development. Unfortunately, the obvious solution of seeking political power is not as easy as it might seem. In the past, peoples without governments have sometimes consolidated in self-defense against invading states, transforming themselves into states, only to lose their unique cultural identity in the process. Fortunately, stateless societies have devised many ingenious ways of regulating political power to maintain internal social justice and viability. Today, indigenous peoples are designing political structures that permit the consolidation of a power base to successfully confront states without sacrificing their egalitarian and communal characteristics. On the other hand, small-scale societies are often numerically weak and face the difficult task of combining within ethnically different, previously hostile neighboring groups to form larger political entities. To further complicate matters, they must win allies in the dominant society and even internationally. Regardless of the difficulties, in recent years there has been a steady emergence of regional, national, and international indigenous political organizations that have been working with increasing success for the self-determination of indigenous peoples.

Indigenous political organizations can accomplish many critical tasks. Perhaps the most important task is the dual role of keeping the traditional heritage strong and organizing often widely dispersed and demoralized peoples into a united force to confront the common external threat. Acting in concert, indigenous peoples can press their demands with much greater visibility and effectiveness. Simply bringing local cases to national and international attention is an important function because many of the most serious assaults on indigenous peoples are illegal, according to national legislation, and may be violations of widely recognized international human rights agreements. Under the embarrassing glare of international publicity, national governments have, in some cases, been forced to take action on behalf of indigenous peoples. It is also likely that most of the recent improvements that have taken place in official policies have been a direct result of the steadily increasing political power of indigenous peoples.

The unifying role of indigenous political organizations is often carried out at periodic local and regional assemblies where common problems are discussed and resolutions are passed. Many organizations have increasingly come to rely on their own published newspapers, magazines, newsletters, and Web sites. Some groups operate their own radio broadcasting systems and have gained control over their own formal educational institutions. Indigenous political organizations vary widely in the details of their structures and exist at different levels. Some may be small, local groups representing single homogeneous ethnic groups. Others are regional federations, perhaps united on the basis of a more remote cultural heritage. Many countries have national organizations of indigenous peoples.

Although the basic objectives of these new political organizations are remarkably similar throughout the world, the context of the political struggle varies considerably from country to country. This makes it difficult to generalize about strategies and prospects. In order to give a clearer picture of the complexities of this ongoing struggle, case studies will be presented in the following sections to illustrate historic examples from Ecuador, Colombia, Canada, Australia, and the Philippines. These cases by no means exhaust the field; a multitude of other important indigenous political organizations, particularly in North, Central, and South America, are not discussed here. The cases examined, however, do provide a reasonable sample of the problems that indigenous organizations face and how they are dealing with them. In the South American examples, Indian political organizations confront powerful local elites who are often closely allied with civil and military rulers within national governments, who in turn find powerful international support. These forces are often hostile to the acquisition of political power by any native groups. Here, the indigenous struggle can easily be understood as part of a larger class struggle, although the Indians generally do not regard themselves as part of the class system and are often justifiably suspicious of alliances with leftist groups. In the Canadian and Australian examples, the governments may be supportive, in variable degrees, of native political organizations, but they also have a conflicting interest in encouraging large corporations to extract resources from native lands. Here, however, there is no pronounced class struggle and there may be considerable popular support for native peoples. The Philippine example represents a case in which emerging organizations of indigenous groups faced a hostile dictatorship that was allied with multinational corporations. Meanwhile, the country was divided by a strongly polarized national class system and ongoing armed liberation movements.

The Shuar Solution

A culture that evolves by itself and finds in itself new solutions for new problems, is more alive than ever.[35]

The Shuar are a forest-dwelling people in Ecuador. By their own estimate, they numbered more than twenty-six thousand in 1975. Traditionally, they were self-sufficient cultivators and hunters living in dispersed extended families. Together with other Jivaroan-speaking groups in neighboring Peru, they were widely known as "headhunters" and for their successful resistance to foreign domination since the arrival of the Spanish in 1540. The Shuar still retained control over much of their traditional territory, and their basic culture remained viable well into the twentieth century. However, by 1959 they were outnumbered by colonists and were rapidly losing their most valuable subsistence lands. Their entire way of life was threatened with disintegration.

At that time, the Shuar in the most heavily invaded areas set about developing what they called an "original self-solution" to the crisis. They concluded that their situation had been irrevocably altered by circumstances but felt that they could still make a satisfying adjustment. The basic objective was to retain control over their own future. In other words, they sought self-determination. They realized that the key to self-determination lay in retaining an adequate community land base, which would require effective participation in the government colonization program. If the Shuar sought individual land titles, only a few would succeed, given the procolonist bias in the entitlement process. In the end, the Shuar community would be destroyed. The solution was the creation in 1964 of a fully independent, but officially recognized, corporate body—a federation based on regional associations of many local Shuar communities. The federation became a legal entity, the Federación de Centros Shuar, that as of 1978 contained some 20,000 members organized into 160 local centers and 13 regional associations.[36] According to the federation's official statutes, the basic objectives of the organization are to promote the social, economic, and moral advancement of its members and to coordinate development efforts with official government agencies. Elected officials have carefully specified duties, and five specialized commissions deal with such matters as health, education, and land.

The federation quickly opted for a system of community land titles through the appropriate government body, Instituto Ecuatoriano de Reforma Agraria y Colonización (IERAC), and promoted cooperative cattle ranching as the new economic base. Cattle ranching was especially important because land was titled on the basis of actual use and the legitimate requirement for pastureland was greater than for other forms of land use. The federation obtained financial and technical assistance from various national and international agencies; by 1975, 95,704 hectares were securely in community titles. By 1978 the cattle herd had grown to more than fifteen thousand head and had become the primary source of outside income.

With the approval and support of the Ecuadorian ministry of education, and with the cooperation of the Salesian mission, the federation has developed an education system suited to local needs and supportive of the small-scale culture. Much of the instruction utilizes the Shuar language and Shuar teachers. In order to minimize the family disruption caused by boarding schools and to spread educational opportunities as widely as possible, the federation established its own system of radio-broadcast bilingual education beginning in 1972. The program has successfully reduced the elementary school role of the mission-operated boarding schools, which have now been converted into technical schools for advanced training. The federation has operated its own radio station since 1968, broadcasting in both Shuar and Spanish. In addition, since 1972 it has published a bilingual newspaper, *Chicham*, the official organ of the Shuar federation. The story of the Shuar and their confrontation with the national society is also presented in a motion picture, *The Sound of Rushing Water*, produced by the Shuar themselves.

The federation solution was, in many ways, unique in Amazonia. The Shuar were the first indigenous people to have retained such effective control over their own future. The initiative for the major adaptive changes that have occurred in the Shuar system, as well as the administration of the entire program, have been carried out by the Shuar themselves. Of course, the federation itself was a response to uninvited outside pressures, and its early formation was facilitated by the Salesian missionaries who had been in the area since 1893, but there is no doubt that the Shuar have created a distinctly Shuar solution to the problem. The federation drew on a broad base of financial support so that no single outside interest was able to assert undesired influence.

Technical volunteers from many countries were recruited on a temporary basis, but they did not dominate any programs.

The Shuar are proud of the federation and of the gains they have made. They recognize that they have had to make enormous changes in their culture, but they feel that they are still Shuar. Certainly, many traditional patterns have been abandoned with few regrets, and many material elements are disappearing or have been converted to the tourist trade. But the federation has succeeded in strengthening the Shuar language and cultural identity and in securing a viable resource base. The Shuar are actively promoting selected qualities that they feel represent the essence of their culture and that clearly distinguish them from their non-Indian neighbors. These include communal land tenure, cooperative production and distribution, a basically egalitarian economy, kin-based local communities with maximum autonomy, and a variety of distinctive cultural markers such as hairstyles, body ornamentation, and dress, and the blowgun.

The federation's existence has not been entirely without problems. Understandably, the colonists resented its successes. In 1969 the federation's central office was burned down, presumably by colonists, and federation leaders have been jailed and tortured for crimes for which they were never convicted.[37] Although the Ecuadorian government officially recognizes and cooperates with the federation, actual support for their programs has been sporadic, and outside interests have consistently been favored by government agencies over the needs of the Shuar. The government also forcefully attempted to prevent the Shuar from promoting the political organization of other Ecuadorian Indians and generally seemed opposed to the idea of Ecuador becoming a multiethnic nation.[38] The federation was criticized by leftist organizations for accepting aid from capitalists, whereas some missionaries accused federation leaders of being communists. In the long run, the federation faces other problems as well. Economic differentiation related to cattle ranching and the gradual emergence of an educated and salaried elite may be difficult to contain within the egalitarian ideal to which the federation still aspires. Furthermore, the present Shuar land base, which is broken up into discontinuous islands, may prove in a short time to be inadequate for the needs of a growing population.

The Shuar federation has become a model for other indigenous political organizations. It has itself segmented into other federations of related Shuar and Achuar peoples and has grown and changed since its founding. The Development Council for Ecuadorian Nationalities and Peoples (CODENPE), which was created by Ecuador's 1998 constitution in response to political activism by indigenous people, listed 110,000 Shuar in 2007 organized in 2 major federations, the Interprovincial Federation of Shuar Centers (FICSH) and the Independent Federation of Shuar Peoples of Ecuador (FIPSE). CO-DENPE listed 490 FICSH and 47 FIPSE centers, in addition to 56 centers of the Interprovincial Federation of the Achuar Nationality of Ecuador (FINAE).[39] The Shuar are united with other indigenous groups in the Ecuadorian Amazon by the Confederation of Indigenous Amazonian Nationalities of Ecuador (CONFENIAE) formed in 1980. In 2007 CONFENIAE was composed of 13 confederations and organizations, representing some 880 communities.[40] CONFENIAE is a member of the international Coordinator for the Indigenous Organizations of the Amazon Basin (COICA).[41] This makes it possible for Shuar leaders to confer with indigenous leaders from across Amazonia, thereby facilitating their resistance to international petroleum corporations that are invading their territories.

Indian Unity in Colombia

Without unity we will never have the force to defend our land and the future of our children.[42]

The indigenous peoples of Colombia have made human rights, social equity, and environmental protection the centerpiece of their political struggle for autonomy and self-determination. They emphasize their pre-Columbian ancestry, but their focus is human rights, freedom, and liberty for everyone, and in this respect it is explicitly not racially based. In 2005 there were some seven hundred thousand indigenous people in Colombia representing eighty-four groups and speaking sixty-four languages.[43] They have suffered disproportionately from the civil violence that has engulfed the countryside since the 1960s because, like most indigenous peoples, they occupy remote rural areas that are also rich in natural resources. The National Indigenous Organization of Colombia (Organización National Indígena de Colombia, or ONIC) is the largest indigenous organization in Colombia, coordinating activities and sharing information among some sixty-four other indigenous organizations in the country.[44] The First National Indigenous Congress was held in 1982 near Bogota. It was attended by twenty-five hundred people representing twenty-five indigenous groups from throughout Colombia, plus many international guests, especially from neighboring countries. The congress established the ONIC as the first permanent national-level Indian organization in Colombia, dedicating it to indigenous autonomy and the defense of indigenous communal territory and resources.[45] An official statement issued by the congress's commission on land and settlers defined the most critical issue facing Indian groups in Colombia: "Indian land and all of its resources belong to the community and should be placed totally under the control of the community's internal authority; land should never be divided up as private property."[46]

The Regional Organization of Indigenous Peoples of the Colombian Amazon (OPIAC), formed in 1995, unites some seventy-six thousand individuals in fourteen organizations representing fifty-two distinct ethnic nationalities. The OPIAC is also a member of COICA, the international organization of Amazonian indigenous peoples discussed above.[47] These organizations have effectively raised Indian pride in their own identity, promoted widespread awareness of common problems, and presented realistic proposals to the Colombian government from a position of considerable strength. Significant gains have been made in some areas, but serious opposition also has been aroused. The example of the Regional Indigenous Council of Cauca (CRIC) will be discussed in detail because it was the earliest organization to be established in Colombia, and like the Shuar federation, it became a model for other groups.

The Colombian Department of Cauca, an administrative division in the southwest corner of Colombia, contains one of the densest Indian concentrations in the country. Reliable figures are unavailable, but there were more than two hundred thousand Chibcha-speaking Paez and Guambiano Indians in this department that counted a total population of more than six hundred thousand people in 1968. This is a mountainous region of large coffee plantations, where in 1970, 80 percent of the agricultural land was held by a mere 14 percent of the landowners.[48] The Cauca Indians were conquered by the Spanish in the sixteenth century and were allocated communally held reservations, or *resguardos*, and their own form of internal self-government, the *cabildo* system. The reservations were to be permanently removed from the land market, and it seems that the Indians enjoyed a relatively secure existence in spite of the colonial oppression they faced in the form of labor and tribute payments. However, in the nineteenth century, the reserves began to be invaded by colonists, and the government initiated termination proceedings. Throughout the twentieth century, many reserves have been eliminated entirely and the protesting Indians have been crowded into smaller and smaller reserves that, in many cases, have become inadequate to their needs. The Indians fought protracted legal battles for the defense of these fragmented lands, but little was achieved.

The picture began to change dramatically in 1971 when two thousand Indians from ten reserves held a mass meeting and organized CRIC[48] to coordinate the Indian struggle throughout the Cauca region. The new organization was formed as a federation, and the governing body consisted of representatives from each of the reserves. Annual congresses were convened, and by 1973, forty-five local reserves had joined. CRIC's original objectives were specified in the following seven points, which were the basis of its program:

1. To recuperate the reservation lands
2. To increase the size of the reservations
3. To strengthen the Indian Councils (*cabildos*)
4. To stop the payment of illegal land rents
5. To make known the laws concerning Indians and to insist on their proper application
6. To defend the history, language, and customs of the Indians
7. To train Indian teachers to teach in the Indian language in ways that are applicable to the present situation of the people.[50]

In an unequivocal answer to those who might suggest that they were too heavily acculturated by four hundred years of reservation life to still be considered Indians, they emphatically stated, "We are Indians, and we believe that it is good to be an Indian."[51] The Cauca Indians had much in common with the local peasantry, and indeed both saw the large landowners as enemies, but the Indians were specific about what made them unique. They of course pointed to their ancestry, language, dress, and customs, but they also emphasized their economic egalitarianism: "We are Indians because we believe that the things of the world are made for everyone. It is like saying that since we are all equal, the means of living should also be equal. . . . Because of this, we believe that the land, just as the air, the water, and all the other things which keep us alive, should not be only for the few. The land should not be owned, but should be communal. . . . This is why we like the reservations. Because there, the lands must all be shared out between all the members of the community."[52]

The primary struggle was, of course, over land. The CRIC strategy was to reorganize the councils that were terminated and to campaign for the restoration of the old reserves or for the extension of then existing reserves by legal appeals through the Colombian Institute for Agrarian Reform (Instituto Colombiano de la Reforma Agraria, or INCORA), the government agrarian reform office. When legal means failed, the Indians nonviolently occupied and began to cultivate the lands they claimed. Arrests usually followed, but in many cases their legitimate claims were recognized. Within three years, five thousand hectares had been recovered and the "rents" Indians were charged on lands illegally expropriated from them were eventually abolished.

The early successes of CRIC resulted in countermeasures from the local power structure. At first, the landowners threatened CRIC leaders and attempted to control the *cabildos*. When these measures failed, the government moved to block Indian assemblies. Finally, in 1974, assassinations began and critical areas of the Cauca were militarized. Key CRIC leaders were arrested under the pretext that CRIC was a subversive organization linked to the M-19 leftist guerrillas. By 1979, thirty CRIC leaders, including the CRIC president, were imprisoned. In 1982, CRIC claimed that eighty-two of its leaders had been killed by state, church, and economic interests opposed to its objectives. Leftist, antigovernment guerrilla forces also claimed responsibility for killing seven CRIC members whom they considered "counterrevolutionaries." The violence in Cauca resumed in 1987, when 22 Indian communities were reportedly attacked and 239 people were arrested.[53] These assaults seemed to strengthen their resolve.

The indigenous authorities of Cauca declared in 2005 that they recognized as brothers and sisters all those who understand and fight for the "liberty of Mother Earth," regardless of race, customs, or religion. They found common cause with those of African descent, peasants, and urban inhabitants, most of whom were landless, because in their view private property was largely "in the hands of socio-economic elites who were supported by imperialist foreigners and multinational corporations," and who disregarded their humanity, ignored their rights, and treated them all like slaves.[54]

The indigenous peoples in the Cauca region have suffered enormously from the ongoing Colombian civil war, which they view as a completely separate struggle. According to names and numbers posted by the Association of Indigenous Authorities of Northern Cauca (Asociación de Cabildos Indígenas del Norte del Cauca, or ACIN), the CRIC organization in northern Cauca, in 2005 and 2006 alone thirty-seven people were killed, seventy-four wounded, and thirty were listed as missing.[55] There were seventy-seven cases of arbitrary detentions for weeks and months, fifty-two cases of violent and/or armed transgressions in the territory, legal violations, and unlawful proceedings. More than seven thousand persons were internally displaced because of incursions by the Revolutionary Armed Forces of Colombia (Fuerzas Armadas Revolucionarias de Colombia, or FARC) guerrilla fighters.[56] There were also forced recruitments of indigenous youth by the army as well as FARC, even though the Indians have declared themselves both nonviolent and neutral. CRIC authorities have repeatedly called for dialogue and negotiations among all parties to end the civil conflict and begin rebuilding the country. Thousands of indigenous people conducted marches and mass demonstrations in northern Cauca in 2006, opposing the "neoliberal model" and free trade agreements with the United States and calling for peaceful negotiations with the government. Marchers carried simple wooden batons symbolizing the political autonomy of their *cabildos*, but they were met with tear gas and violence.[57]

The Dene Nation: Land, Not Money

The Dene Indians of Canada's Northwest Territories are one of the best examples of the self-determination revival in North America. These Athapaskan-speaking peoples, who number about 17,000, are scattered throughout some 725,000 square kilometers of the great Mackenzie Valley.[58] In this area, they continue to rely on moose, caribou, and fish for much of their subsistence, just as their ancestors did for thousands of years before them. Since approximately 1790, when they began to be drawn into the fur trade, their economic self-reliance has been gradually reduced. However, their egalitarian regional economy, based on kinship reciprocity, has remained strong. When the world fur market declined after World War II, the Canadian government responded to the "crisis" by attempting to push the Dene into full dependence on the stratified, highly individualistic wage labor economy. To receive their welfare checks and keep their children in school, the Dene were encouraged to settle in towns. This sedentary life made traditional subsistence pursuits more difficult.[59] By the late 1960s, Dene society and culture were showing obvious signs of stress, but even more serious threats loomed when oil was discovered at Prudhoe Bay in Alaska in 1968. The Canadian government immediately proposed converting the Mackenzie Valley into an "energy corridor" for pipelines to move Arctic oil and gas to consumers in the United States and southern Canada. The Dene then had real fears that their entire way of life was in jeopardy.

In 1970, under the slogan "Land and Unity," the Dene formed the Indian Brotherhood of the Northwest Territories, combining all of the scattered tribes into a single political organization capable of mounting an effective struggle for recognition of their rights to the land and an independent existence. Their first major political act, in 1973, was the filing of a legal caveat with the territorial court that registered their prior claim to the land in order to block any further development without approval by the Dene. They were able to demonstrate that the treaties of 1899 and 1921, which supposedly canceled their land rights, were fraudulent, and they obtained a favorable ruling on the caveat. The pipeline companies and the Department of Indian and Northern Affairs were appalled at the decision, which was overturned by the Canadian Supreme Court in 1976 on a technicality, but it did serve to demonstrate the validity of the native claim.

The Dene political movement gradually began to take shape. In 1974 more than 250 native people from throughout the Mackenzie Valley met at Fort Good Hope. They had before them the unfortunate example of the Alaska natives, who had been forced to accept the poorly conceived Native Claims Settlement Act of 1971 to clear the way for the Alaska pipeline. At Fort Good

Hope the Dene agreed emphatically that they wanted their rights recognized, not extinguished; they wanted "land, not money." Their position was clarified the following year at a second assembly of 250 Dene at Fort Simpson, at which a formal Dene Declaration was drawn up. In this eloquent statement, the Dene pointed out that they were a majority within the Northwest Territories, yet they had not been allowed to control their own future. They declared themselves to be a distinct people and a "nation." They also called for recognition of their right to self-determination as native peoples within the Canadian nation. They were not, of course, seeking independent nation-state status. Their proposal was reasonable in terms of the Canadian Constitution,[60] but they were immediately accused of being separatists, racists, or "socialists."

To fully document their claim to the land, in 1974–1976 the Dene carried out an extensive two-year research project into their own land use practices. They interviewed one-third of the Dene hunters and trappers from throughout their territory and plotted on large-scale maps the areas they utilized. This work revealed a maze of trails and traplines in an area that, to outsiders, would look like only wilderness. This demonstrated beyond any doubt that the Dene were indeed still a hunting people. Whether considered in terms of the numbers of people involved, the cash value of the resources obtained, or the actual contribution to the diet, traditional use of the land was absolutely vital for the Dene.[61]

In spite of the mounting native resistance to the proposed pipeline, the major energy companies pressed ahead with their plans. To satisfy all the legal requirements that blocked final approval of the pipeline, the Canadian government commissioned a formal study of the project and its possible implications for the Northwest Territories. The inquiry was conducted by British Columbia Supreme Court Justice Thomas R. Berger, who took the unprecedented step of seeking direct testimony and written documents from the Dene people. For several months in 1975–1976, he visited every major town and settlement in the Mackenzie Valley and heard from nearly one thousand people. In his final report, issued in 1977,[62] Berger expressed strong support for native self-determination and argued that the pipeline should be delayed for at least ten years to allow sufficient time for a just settlement of native claims. The Dene had presented a compelling case.

In fact, the Canadian government was taking seriously the Dene demand for self-determination. In 1976 the minister of Indian affairs asked the Dene to prepare a formal position paper so that negotiations on the Dene land claim could begin. In this "Agreement-in-Principle," the Dene appealed to international law and United Nations declarations in support of their right to self-determination. They listed sixteen principles as a basis for negotiations, including the following:

1. The Dene have the right to recognition, self-determination, and ongoing growth as a People and as a Nation.
2. The Dene, as Aboriginal People, have the right to retain ownership of so much of their traditional lands, and under such terms, as to ensure their independence and self-reliance, traditionally, economically and socially.[63]

The Agreement-in-Principle claimed that it was the Dene's place to define themselves and thereby avoided the divisiveness of a formal definition of who they were. They stated simply, "The Dene know who they are." Who the Dene are is implicit in their concept of self-determination. Self-determination for the Dene means following the Dene system and not the dominant system of southern Canada. As George Barnaby, vice president of the Indian Brotherhood of the Northwest Territories, explained, the Dene system means a co-operative community life based on sharing, joint decision making, and communal land ownership.[63]

In 1981 the Dene struggle for land and political autonomy moved closer to victory with the formation of the Aboriginal Rights Coalition, which brought together all aboriginal groups in Canada, including the various Inuit, Indian, and Métis (mixed French and Indian) organizations to press for explicit inclusion of aboriginal rights in the Canadian Constitution, which was then being rewritten as part of Canada's formal break of its colonial ties to Britain.[65] From 1983 to 1987, four nationally televised conferences were held involving government officials and native leaders to work out the details of a constitutional arrangement for native self-government.[66] These meetings prepared the way for a final agreement in principle, which was signed in September of 1988 by William Erasmus, president of the Dene Nation, and Canadian prime minister Brian Mulroney. Under the terms of this agreement, the Dene would have received full title to some 10,000 square kilometers of land, with both surface and subsurface mineral rights. They received surface rights and significant mineral royalties for another 170,000 square kilometers, as well as traditional land use rights to more than 1 million square kilometers and a 500-million-dollar cash settlement.

In spite of its promise, the Dene agreement suddenly collapsed in 1990 over the government's insistence that all aboriginal rights and claims be extinguished in exchange for "certainty" of land title. Negotiations with the federal government became local and regional, involving five separate Dene nations: the Gwich'in, Sahtu, Dehcho, Tlicho, and Akaitcho. The Gwich'in reached an agreement in 1992, the Sahtu in 1993, and the Tlicho (Dogrib) in 2003. The Sahtu and Métis settled for 41,437 square kilometers, with subsurface rights to 1,813 square kilometers, and a cash settlement of 75 million dollars (Canadian) over 15 years, along with the opportunity to negotiate self-government agreements.[67] In 2000, members of the Sahtu Dene and Gwich'in, together with the Inuvialuit (Inuit) of the western Arctic, formed the Aboriginal Pipelines Group to become one-third business partners with ExxonMobil, Shell, ConocoPhillips, and Esso Imperial Oil to develop, own, and operate a pipeline to move 6 trillion cubic feet of natural gas from gas fields in the Mackenzie Delta to southern Canada and the United States. Commercial business interests seem to have won out over indigenous self-determination in this case. The total cost of the Mackenzie Gas Project is estimated at 7 billion dollars, and it might produce enough natural gas to supply U.S. consumption for one hundred days at 2006 rates.[68] As owners, the Aboriginal Pipeline Group expects to earn between 10 and 20 million dollars per year over twenty years.

Land Rights and the Outstation Movement in Australia

> What is happening is an Aboriginal revival, a reversal—if you like—of frontiers. No longer is the government pushing Aboriginals back. It is Aboriginals who today are pushing Governments back.[69]

Australian Aborigines have refused to either die out or be assimilated. Today they are struggling, with increasing success, to gain legal control over their lands, and they are maintaining traditionally oriented communities in the very remote areas where they can manage their lands, societies, and cultures on their own. The 2006 Australian Census lists an Aboriginal population of 517,000 people.[70] There were more Aborigines than in 1788, but in 2006 they were only 2.5 percent of the total 20 million people in Australia. Approximately one-fourth of the Aboriginal population was living in remote or very remote areas of the country, and nationwide Aborigines owned about 20 percent of the land.[71] Aboriginal lands contain some of the most important biological and environmental resources in the country, and they have been very careful stewards of their land. This gives Aboriginal land management practices enormous significance. Aboriginal ownership is especially important in the Northern Territory, where 66,600 Aborigines constitute one-third of the population and own 44 percent of the land under the terms of the Land Rights (Northern Territory) Act of 1976.[71]

The catalyst for the present revival was the full-scale assault in the mid-1960s by multinational mining corporations on the aboriginal reserves in Arnhem Land and Cape York Peninsula. These regions in the Northern Territory and northern Queensland contained large populations of Aborigines who still lived on their ancestral lands. Unfortunately, the land also contained outstanding bauxite deposits. The Aborigines were opposed to mining because they knew it would mean destruction of their traditional economy and their sacred sites as well as a disruption of their societies. However, the government approved the mining projects, completely disregarding aboriginal protests. Ultimately the mining did proceed, but the Aborigines did not give up. Their resistance attracted the attention of Aborigines and even non-Aborigine supporters throughout Australia and resulted in a major land rights political struggle.

In 1968 the Yirrkala people of the Gove Peninsula in Arnhem Land initiated legal proceedings to establish their aboriginal claim, arguing that the government and the mining companies had illegally appropriated their lands. In 1971 the court finally ruled against them, but this decision only served to draw attention to the blatant injustice of official Australian policies toward aboriginal land claims, which intensified the opposition to those policies.

Aborigines began to organize public demonstrations on an unprecedented scale to demand changes in the law. Early in 1972 an "Aboriginal embassy" was established in a tent in front of the parliament building in Canberra. It was torn down by police, only to be reerected, and remained for six months as an irritating symbol to the Australian government of their injustices to Aborigines. Finally, in December of 1972, the Labour Party came to power on a pro-Aborigine platform, and genuine changes in official policy began to take shape.

The first concrete action on the part of the new government was the establishment in 1973 of an Aboriginal Land Rights Commission, under Justice A. E. Woodward, to determine how to implement a just land policy. The Woodward Commission reports, which came out in 1973 and 1974, strongly recommended that Aborigines in the Northern Territory be given title to their reserved lands and that they be able to prohibit mining on those lands. It also recommended that the Aborigines be allowed to claim unalienated Crown lands outside of the established reserves if they could demonstrate traditional ties, and it called for the establishment of aboriginal-run land councils to implement the new policies. Officially there was at last to be an end to injustice, repression, and the old assimilation policy. According to the new Australian prime minister, E. G. Whitlaw, the primary objective of the new policy would be "to restore to the Aboriginal people of Australia their lost power of self-determination in economic, social and political affairs."[73]

The Labour government did propose a progressive aboriginal land rights bill, but before it could be approved the government was thrown out of office and replaced by a much more cautious government, which proceeded to rewrite and significantly weaken the land rights bill. Angered over the modifications, Aborigines organized a National Aboriginal Land Rights Conference in Sydney in August 1976, where they presented a formal declaration outlining their conditions for a satisfactory land rights settlement as follows:

1. Acknowledgment that all Aborigines, wherever they live, share a claim to land, which was totally the Aborigines' land prior to the arrival of White settlers who stole it from them.
2. That to remedy this injustice, Aborigines must be granted freehold control of all lands they rightfully claim, and total compensation for those lands previously taken away.
3. That the return of all lands to the Aboriginal people must include total control of minerals, forests, fishing, coastal waters, and all other aspects of the land, together with the right to control their own destiny on the land.[74]

When the Aboriginal Land Rights (Northern Territory) Act of 1976 became law in January of 1977, it rejected most of the conditions set forth in the declaration. However, this act still represented at least a partial victory for Aborigines and can be seen as a major concession coming from a government that for nearly two hundred years had stubbornly refused to recognize the legitimacy of any Aboriginal land claims. The act created a legal basis for defending existing reserves and in some cases for extending them. Under the act, the Aborigines organized representative land councils in the Northern Territory and worked vigorously to help local communities document their land claims. The councils have negotiated with mining companies and the government to minimize the detrimental impact of development projects on their lands. Unfortunately, under the terms of the Land Rights Act, state and territorial governments retain considerable control over the administration of Aboriginal land and the Aborigines cannot prevent mining that is considered to be in the "national interest." The two aboriginal land councils in the Northern Territory are officially recognized and are supported by a percentage of the royalties from mining on reserve lands. Aborigines in Queensland and Western Australia have also now organized their own unofficial land councils, and they are pressing for legal control over their lands as well.

After the passage of the Land Rights Act, there were attempts to establish nationally endorsed land rights legislation as a model for the other Australian states, but by 1986 the federal government decided to permit the individual states to continue making their own land policies. At the same time, there were moves by mining and pastoral interests to weaken the Land Rights Act with amendments to reduce aboriginal control over mining and aboriginal benefits from mining royalties and to halt the conversion of pastoral leases to aboriginal lands.[75] Along with these apparent setbacks, however, there have been some positive moves. In anticipation of the 1988 bicentennial year, as early as 1983 the federal government indicated that it was ready to acknowledge that Australia was not in fact *terra nullius* when Europeans arrived—in other words, that Australia was not an unoccupied wasteland in 1788. Throughout 1988, negotiations were under way between the government and Aborigines over the details of a treaty recognizing the pre-European Aboriginal occupation of Australia.

Four years later, in the 1992 *Mabo* decision, the Australian High Court at last rejected the *terra nullius* doctrine. The *Mabo* decision concluded an exhaustively argued case in which the Meriam people of the Murray Islands, located at the top end of Torres Strait off Cape York Peninsula, claimed control of their territory on the basis of their ancestral occupation. This decision provided definitive legal support for all Aboriginal land claims based on prior occupancy. Following *Mabo*, the Native Title Act of 1993 cites the Universal Declaration of Human Rights as well as the International Covenants on Economic, Social, and Cultural Rights as further justification for "the recognition and protection of native title."[76] In the 1996 *Wik* decision, the High Court declared that aboriginal title applied even in areas where grazing and mining leases had been given.

As they have gradually regained some control over the land, and as the government softened its official emphasis on assimilation as the only alternative, Aborigines have begun to reassert their traditional culture and independence in a dramatic way. The most visible manifestation of this revival is the Outstation movement. By 1978, throughout the country there were 148 outstations, or decentralized communities, where small groups of Aborigines were reestablishing the traditional life on their own ancestral lands away from the crowded, dependent conditions of the missions and government posts.[77] In 1986 there were 13,400 Aborigines living in 699 such communities, which were becoming identified as "homeland centres."[78] Estimates for 2001 suggest that about 20,000 people were associated with some 1,000 discrete places with Aboriginal communities of fewer than 100 people.[79] The average population of such outstations was about 20 to 30 people, making them closely resemble the bands of pre-European Aboriginal society. Most are in the Northern Territory, and most are in areas that the census classifies as "very remote." These new communities have sought to be maximally self-sufficient, and wherever possible they rely heavily on wild food resources, but many still receive support from the government and maintain radio and transportation links with central stations. The important thing is that in the outstations, Aborigines can control the conditions of their daily life, and they are securely on their own lands, to which they have profound spiritual bonds. The advantages of life in the outstations were seen immediately in terms of improved health conditions, but the Aboriginal social system is also gaining renewed strength and there has been an enthusiastic revival of ceremonial life. The practical meaning of land rights for Aboriginal people is shown in the following statement from the Northern Territory: "The vision of the Northern Land Council is a Territory in which the land rights of every traditional owner are legally recognized and in which Aboriginal people benefit economically and culturally from the secure possession of their land and sea."[80] However, by 1997 a major shift to the right occurred in Australian national politics, making it more difficult for Aboriginals to implement their newly recognized legal rights to "return to country."

Intense Pressure over Kakadu Uranium

Even before the shift to socially conservative, economically liberal national politics, powerful corporate interests made Aboriginal self-determination difficult. Although under the original terms of the Land Rights Act of 1976, the Aboriginal land councils had the right to negotiate on behalf of traditional owners before mining could proceed on aboriginal land, in practice the Aborigines had limited veto power over mining, subject to national interests, and faced overwhelming pressure to give unwilling "consent." The irony of this situation was that the land councils themselves were ultimately dependent on mining royalties and were thus placed in an ambiguous position as spokespersons for Aborigines opposed to mining. The government attitude was made clear in the 1977 Fox Commission report on the Ranger uranium mine, which declared that Aboriginal opposition "should not be allowed to prevail." In the case of the Jabiluka uranium lease along the eastern border of Kakadu National Park, in 1982 ten aboriginal owners finally gave consent to mining after a ten-day "bargaining session," ending a series of intense negotiations between representatives of the Pancon-Getty Oil consortium and government officials, the land council, and local Aborigines that lasted more than a year. During the negotiations, Aborigines were shuttled by helicopter from their camps to "urgent" meetings and had little choice but to listen to hours of intense haggling. Given that the Jabiluka project was projected to produce 8 billion dollars in uranium yellowcake and 150 million dollars in gold over twenty-seven years, it is hardly surprising that the interested parties were not prepared to accept an Aboriginal veto.[80]

The Howard Government's Radical Paternalism

Under Prime Minister John Howard's pro–free market Labour Party government, which was in power from 1996 to 2007, the focus of Aboriginal policy began to move away from human rights and toward economic performance measures that favored opening Aboriginal lands to outside development interests. The new government suddenly began to characterize Aboriginal self-determination and land rights as "failed policies," and deemphasized constitutional changes that would promote reconciliation over historic damages and injustices suffered by Aborigines. The new focus was on "indigenous economic disadvantage" which was to be overcome by "policy reform" to get Aborigines into the commercial economy and mainstream society more quickly. This was reminiscent of former integration policies. Social support programs that Aborigines managed began to be defunded or eliminated, and local communities were blamed for social problems, justifying the imposition of outside direction. Offering a clear indication of an even more dramatic policy transformation to come, in 2004 the government abruptly abolished the Aboriginal and Torres Strait Islander Commission (ATSIC), an Aboriginal organization founded in 1990 to give Aborigines a political voice in the formulation and implementation of government policies and procedures affecting their social, economic, and cultural development. The ATSIC was a national-level Aboriginal organization composed of thirty-five regional councils, four hundred elected representatives, and eighteen elected commissioners, but it was replaced by decree by a single National Indigenous Council (NIC) with ten appointed commissioners reporting to the minister for families, community services and indigenous affairs. The NIC was asked "to provide expert advice and government on improving outcomes for Indigenous Australians,"[82] but its members served at the will of the prime minister, not the Aboriginal community. The NIC clearly gave the government more direct control over indigenous policies, allowing central government agencies to control policy coordination and deal individually with local Aboriginal groups rather with national Aboriginal organizations interested in self-determination.

"State of Emergency" in the Northern Territory

In June of 2007, Howard, citing a Northern Territory government report that called child sexual abuse in Aboriginal communities "an issue of urgent national significance,"[83] declared a "national emergency" and launched an unprecedented assault on Aboriginal rights that could undo decades of positive policies, legal decisions, and legislation, as well as local and regional political development by Aborigines. The report in question, a government inquiry entitled *Little Children Are Sacred*, was a compilation of anecdotes and "clinical information," not supported by new field research, suggesting that Aboriginal communities in the Northern Territory exhibited conditions commonly associated with child abuse such as family dysfunction, alcohol and drug abuse, poverty, unemployment, and housing shortages. The report's authors noted that it would "be remarkable if there was not [a significant child abuse problem] given the similar and significant problems that exist elsewhere in Australia and abroad."[84] They were also quick to point out that such problems were not restricted to Aboriginal communities, there were few child abuse perpetrators, and there were probably communities with no abuse problems. They did not advocate radical intervention by the state. While child abuse seemed to be an urgent problem, they cautioned, "It is critical that both governments [Australia and the Northern Territory] commit to genuine consultation with Aboriginal people in designing initiatives for Aboriginal communities."[85] This is not what happened.

Within less than two months of the *Children Are Sacred* report, Howard launched his response, requesting an appropriation of 587 million dollars in 2007–2008 to fund what could become a five-year program to "reform community living arrangements" and bring about a "better future for Aboriginal people."[86] The Australian Defence Force (ADF) mobilized NORFORCE, the North West Mobile Force for its Joint Task Force 641, to provide logistic support and build community infrastructure for its "emergency response." A staging area was immediately set up in Alice Springs, and federal and state police, along with teams of doctors, were urgently flown in and began spreading out to the more than seventy Aboriginal communities of one hundred people or more in the Northern Territory that were targeted for immediate intervention. The prime minister set up an eight-person task force to implement the response. The operational commander was a major general who had directed Australia's humanitarian relief after the tsunami hit Southeast Asia in 2004. There were two government officials on the task force, as well as a member of the board of directors of Wal-Mart, the world's largest corporation, and a lawyer who had previously proposed "reforms" to the Land Rights Act that were now being implemented by decree. The two Aboriginal members of the task force, a judge and the principal of a Catholic school, were also appointed members of the National Indigenous Council. By August 2007 a package of emergency legislation had been approved by Parliament giving the emergency response a five-year life span—all justified as protecting children. The primary legislation, the Northern Territory National Emergency Response Act of 2007, is 211 pages of legal language all designed for, but not by, Aborigines.

The first visible emergency action in the Northern Territory was a ban on alcohol and pornography in some fifty-five Aboriginal communities with populations of one hundred or more in "prescribed areas." This ban covered all Aboriginal territories created by the 1976 Land Rights Act and included some 160 community living areas, which were small Aboriginal settlements on Aboriginal lands situated within pastoral leases. Some forty-four town camps in towns such as Alice Springs and Darwin were also designated as "prescribed areas." Virtually all of the sixty-six thousand or more Aborigines in the Northern Territory were living in the prescribed areas or in related out-stations. More importantly, the emergency response also banned the permits that Aboriginal communities required of outsiders entering their Land Rights Act lands, thereby denying them a major means of self-determination. Given the discriminatory manner in which these regulations were being applied, this emergency response would surely constitute a violation of basic human rights, and it is not surprising that the Australian government voted against the adoption of the United Nations Declaration on the Rights of Indigenous People in 2007.

The emergency response declaration also allowed the government to impose leases over Aboriginal settlements for its own improvement projects. It also put in place controls over how welfare recipients spend their money, and imposed new regulations on local Aboriginal shops. Furthermore, the popular Community Development Employment Projects (CDEP) program, which was created in 1977, was to be phased out by June 2008 so that people could find "real work." The CDEP program has proven to be an effective way to provide both employment and services to remote communities and outstations.[87] For example, the Bawinanga Aboriginal Corporation in Maningrida Township, Arnhem Land, is a crucial economic center for thirty-two out-stations and a regional population of twenty-five hundred people. According to its annual reports, in 2005 it turned 12 million dollars in grants primarily from the CDEP program into revenues of 26 million dollars, generating profits of 1.6 million dollars. Its activities include tourism, arts production, resource management rangers, a crab-harvesting and aquaculture project, as well as the West Arnhem Land Fire Abatement Project, using traditional fire management practices to reduce carbon emissions. Surely such activities are "real work."

John Howard and his coalition government were voted out of office in the November 2007 national election, and Howard was replaced as prime minister by Kevin Rudd and the Labour Party. It is too soon to know how the new government will shape aboriginal policy in Australia, but Rudd quickly began meeting with aboriginal leaders. Significantly, one of his first official acts was to sign the Kyoto Protocol to limit carbon emissions in response to global warming.

Philippine Tribals: No More Retreat

Today there are more than 4 million tribal people in the Philippines, representing some forty major groups who seek to maintain their independent identities. Many of these groups have successfully retained their independence by gradually retreating into the mountains, but now, after more than four hundred years of colonial domination, they have nowhere else to go. They are being forced to adopt new forms of self-defense because their final refuges are being invaded by powerful national and international interests. The tribal peoples are strong numerically because they constitute some 10 percent of the total national population. However, they are widely scattered and separated by differences of language and culture, making a common defense difficult. In response to new external threats to their survival, they have begun to bury their internal differences and are mounting a major resistance movement.

The most serious threats facing these groups today are dams, mining, and agribusiness, all of which would displace them from their lands. In 1973 the Philippine government's National Power Corporation (NPC) began attempting to implement its planned construction of twenty-one hydroelectric projects, which would flood tribal lands in Mindanao and northern Luzon. These projects directly support the efforts of multinational companies, such as Del-Monte, which are turning tribal lands into giant pineapple plantations. The tribal peoples quite correctly see their land and their cultures as inseparable. Understandably, they do not want to sacrifice their land and cultures for the benefit of a wealthy few. The official government program for tribal peoples is to crowd them into carefully controlled "Service Centers" in order to free tribal lands for development. Since 1968 this resettlement process has been methodically carried out by the Presidential Assistant on National Minorities (PANAMIN), the special government agency established for that purpose. By 1979 an estimated 2.6 million tribal people were being "assisted" by PANAMIN.[88]

The tribal peoples have used a variety of approaches to prevent the loss of their lands. At first, they sent delegations with petitions directly to Philippine president Ferdinand Marcos. When these appeals were rejected they held organizational meetings, issued formal declarations, and turned to more active resistance. Their basic demands were simple and were eloquently expressed in the formal declaration prepared by the Mangyan people of Mindoro at a meeting of tribal representatives in 1976:

1. We want land for our tribe, enough for all of us, a piece of land that is titled and secure, that others cannot steal. . . . We will not retreat anymore.
2. We want our own way of life. We are willing to live side-by-side with others but we want to live our own culture and traditions.[89]

The five hundred thousand Igorots (Kalinga and Bontoc) in northern Luzon were traditional enemies, but in 1975 they signed a formal peace treaty and combined to fight together against the government's plan to build four major dams on the Chico River in their territory.[90] These dams would have destroyed a highly productive engineering system of terraces to manage water and soil that has been called a "wonder of the world" and that in this case supported some ninety thousand people. The allied Igorot tribes agreed to reject all overtures from PANAMIN and the NPC, and refused all cooperation with the construction effort. At first, the Igorots managed to stall construction by dismantling survey camps, but the workers kept returning. Finally, when antigovernment guerrillas belonging to the New People's Army (NPA) came to the support of the Igorots and began to encourage them to violent action, the Philippine army was called in. The entire zone was militarized and Philippine army units moved to block further protests.

Many tribal leaders were arrested and entire villages were forcibly relocated, but resistance to the dams continued. The Igorots appealed to Marcos and even attempted to prevent funding of the projects by presenting their case to an International Monetary Fund–World Bank conference in Manila, but all of their efforts succeeded only in gaining time while Marcos remained intransigent. Tribal resistance continued to grow, however, and in 1984 more than three hundred representatives of twenty-three local tribal organizations from throughout the mountains of Luzon met together and formed the Cordillera Peoples Alliance to create an even stronger political defense of their homeland. Ultimately, the Igorot resistance contributed to the fall of Marcos in 1986 and opened the possibility of genuine tribal autonomy under the terms of the new constitution sponsored by the Aquino government. However, the uncertain political and military situation in the country makes the long-term prospect for autonomy in the tribal areas problematic. Following the collapse of the Chico project, the World Bank, which had originally funded it, was forced to reassess its view of tribal peoples and development issues; this will perhaps lead it to be more cautious with such projects in the future.

The Cordillera Peoples Alliance continues to be a strong organization. It helped found the International Alliance of Indigenous and Tribal Peoples of the Tropical Forest in 1993, and has participated in the World Commission on Dams (WCD), and the Dams and Development Project of the UN Environment Program (UNEP).[91] The WCD was formed in 1997 by a broad coalition of international organizations supported by the World Bank and the International Union for the Conservation of Nature (IUCN) in response to the obvious difficulties that hydroelectric development were causing worldwide.[92]

The International Arena

International indigenous political organizations, combining related indigenous peoples separated only by national boundaries, have existed for some time. For example, the Nordic Saami Council, uniting the Saami of Norway, Sweden, and Finland, was founded in 1953. However, coordinated large-scale political action by diverse indigenous peoples from many different countries is a recent phenomenon. Since the widespread establishment of regional native organizations, which began in earnest only in the early 1970s, it has been an obvious step for indigenous leaders to convene international conferences of representatives of these national organizations and finally to establish permanent international organizations.

Perhaps the first major multiethnic international conference organized and run by indigenous peoples was the First Circumpolar Arctic People's Conference, held in Copenhagen, Denmark, in November 1973. This conference brought together Indian, Inuit (Eskimo), and Saami (Lapp) representatives from some sixteen indigenous organizations in Alaska, Canada, Greenland, Norway, Finland, and Sweden. In their official resolutions, they agreed to cooperate in the preservation of their cultures and claimed a common identity in their special relationship to the land, which cross-cut their cultural differences. As they declared: "We are autochthonous peoples, that is, we are an integral part of the very lands and waters we have traditionally used and occupied. Our identity and culture is firmly rooted in these lands and waters. It is this relationship which constitutes the very unique features of our cultural identity in contrast to the cultures of other peoples within each of the countries from which we come."[93]

The delegates called upon national governments to recognize and respect their unique claims of collective ownership of their traditional lands and waters, stressing, "There must not be any displacement or interference with our rights by government and/or industry, nor can there be disturbance of our lands."[94]

A few months later, in 1974, another international multiethnic conference, the American Indian Parliament of the Southern Cone, was convened by indigenous peoples in Paraguay for the purpose of defining common problems and proposing solutions. Representatives from fifteen Indian groups from Argentina, Bolivia, Brazil, Venezuela, and Paraguay attended the weeklong conference. The official conclusions of the parliament emphasized the common Indian identity rooted in a cultural heritage that was thousands of years old and had existed independently of any affiliations with present nation-states. Specific statements were issued on a variety of topics, including land, labor, education, language, health, and political organization. The basis of the Indians' position in regard to land closely resembled the view presented earlier by the Arctic peoples and was expressed in their uncompromising statement of principle: "The land is of the Indian. The Indian is the earth itself. The Indian is the owner of the land, with property titles or without them."[95]

More specifically, they stated that Indian land should be recognized as communally held and Indian communities should be legally recognized, self-governing corporate entities. They felt that the natural resources of their lands should be exploited only by themselves for their own benefit. They wanted an educational system that promoted their own cultural values and languages. In regard to their own political mobilization, they stressed the need for greater unity and the rapid formation of more regional federations, but they warned against possible manipulation of their new organizations by alien political interests or by false native leaders who were promoted by government authorities. They felt that any outside aid they accepted should be without ideological preconditions. They also emphasized that divisions promoted by religious sects must not hinder their political unity, and they warned specifically against the dangers of any trend toward the emergence of internal stratification within Indian communities.

Even before the First Circumpolar Arctic People's Conference, preliminary plans were being worked out by the National Indian Brotherhood of Canada for the establishment of a permanent international organization of indigenous peoples having official status as a nongovernmental organization (NGO) of the United Nations. The advantage of such an organization was that it would be in a position to present the case of indigenous peoples before the world community much more effectively than any existing national indigenous organizations. This new organization, the World Council of Indigenous Peoples, was formally inaugurated in 1975 at its first general assembly, hosted by the Sheshaht (Nootka) Indians on their tribal lands on Vancouver Island in British Columbia.[96] Fifty-two delegates representing indigenous organizations from nineteen countries attended. In addition to the numerous Indians from North and South America, there were also indigenous peoples from Australia, New Zealand, Greenland, and Scandinavia. The assembly adopted a formal charter that opened its membership to organizations of indigenous people who were working "to further their economic self-sufficiency and to obtain self-determination."[97] The principal objectives of the WCIP included the following points:

1. To ensure political, economic, and social justice to indigenous peoples.
2. To establish and strengthen the concepts of indigenous and cultural rights.

Policy for the WCIP was formulated by general assemblies and was carried out by an executive council, which was composed of single representatives from major world regions such as Canada, Central America, South America, Europe and Greenland, and the South Pacific. The WCIP obtained financial support from a wide variety of sources including international humanitarian organizations, religious bodies, and national governments. Since gaining NGO status, it also sought funding directly from the United Nations.

The WCIP held its second general assembly in Swedish Samiland in 1977. This assembly issued a final report containing what at that time was the most comprehensive and sophisticated statement of rights and principles yet published by any organization of indigenous peoples. The report, which appeared in the Saami language, Swedish, and English, included a major declaration listing fundamental principles, resolutions, and fourteen basic rights.[98] The fundamental principle stressed at the outset was the just claim of indigenous peoples to their lands. This was followed by the "irrevocable and inborn" right to self-determination. The other rights for the most part amplified these issues of land and self-determination.

The WCIP gradually expanded the scope of its organization to include more and more indigenous groups in various parts of the world. For example, in 1980 the Ainu of Japan joined the council; and the Indian Council of South America (Consejo Indio de Sud America, or CISA) was officially formed as the regional organization for South America with eighteen representatives from nine countries. Some three hundred indigenous representatives from twenty-three countries attended the Fourth Assembly of the WCIP, which was hosted in Panama in 1984 by the Kuna, Guaymi, and Embera Indians. The Fourth Assembly issued a Declaration of Principles of Indigenous Rights. The WCIP participated regularly in UN policy making, along with other indigenous NGOs such as the Aboriginal and Torres Strait Islander Commission, the Grand Council of Crees (Quebec), the Indian Law Resource Center, the Indigenous World Association, the International Indian Treaty Council, the International Organization of Indigenous Resource Development, the Inuit Circumpolar Conference, the National Aboriginal and Islander Legal Services Secretariat, and the Saami Council.

Indigenous Peoples and the Arctic Council

The Arctic Council is perhaps the first international organization to formally include indigenous people in its founding documents and granted the status of permanent participants to organizations of Arctic indigenous organizations. The council was formed in 1996 by the governments of eight countries: Canada, Denmark, Finland, Iceland, Norway, Russia, Sweden, and the United States. It was an outgrowth of meetings that began in 1989 out of "deep concerns" over "threats to the Arctic environment and the impact of pollution on fragile Arctic ecosystems," which led to the adoption of the Arctic Environmental Protection Strategy (AEPS) in 1991.[99] The AEPS stressed "the special relationship and importance of Arctic flora and fauna and their habitats to indigenous peoples" as well as the "unique contribution of indigenous peoples to the stewardship of nature and its resources."[100] Representatives from the Inuit Circumpolar Conference, the Nordic Saami Council, and what was then the USSR Association of Small Peoples of the North all assisted in developing the Arctic Environmental Protection Strategy. The purpose of the Arctic Council is to promote environmental protection and sustainable development in the Arctic in cooperation with indigenous peoples.

Six indigenous peoples' organizations are permanent members of the Arctic Council: The Aleut International Association (AIA), the Arctic Athabaskan Council (AAC), the Gwich'in Council International (GCI), the Inuit Circumpolar Council (ICC), the Russian Association of Indigenous Peoples of the North (RAIPON), and the Saami Council (SC).

Arctic peoples have been at the forefront of international efforts to deal with global warming. For example, Chickaloon Village chief Gary Harrison, as head of the Arctic Athabaskan Council, presented a strong statement to the Council of Parties to the Kyoto Protocol meeting in Montreal, Canada in 2005: "[C]limate change threatens to deprive us of our rights, of our rights to sustain ourselves as we have done for thousands of years," said Harrison, who is also International Chair of Arctic Athabaskan Council. "Arctic Indigenous peoples are threatened with the extinction or catastrophic decline of entire bird, fish and wildlife populations, including species of caribou, seals, and fish critical to our food security," he said. "Changes in habitat, the loss of reindeer pasture, and migration routes for fish, wildlife, and migratory birds are the inevitable consequences of the disappearance of Arctic ice and the warming of the Arctic region. This has the potential for catastrophic damage to millennia-old Arctic indigenous cultures."[101]

The United Nations Declaration on the Rights of Indigenous Peoples

In 1981, 130 indigenous representatives attending the NGO Geneva Conference, "Indigenous Peoples and Their Land," recommended the establishment of a special working group on indigenous peoples as a formal UN mechanism for developing international standards for the treatment of indigenous peoples. In response, the UN Sub-Commission on Prevention of Discrimination and Protection of Minorities promptly established the Working Group on Indigenous Populations, which held its first meeting in Geneva in 1982. It was attended by representatives of the WCIP and indigenous representatives from North, Central, and South America as well as Australia. By 1986 a preliminary draft of ten principles on the rights of indigenous populations was issued, with the tentative objective of having a declaration on the rights of indigenous peoples ratified by the UN General Assembly to mark the five-hundredth anniversary of Columbus's landing in the New World.[102] In 1993, after nearly ten years of work, the Working Group on Indigenous Populations finalized a complete draft of a UN Declaration on the Rights of Indigenous Peoples. Even as a draft, this document was a landmark achievement and a striking demonstration of the increasing political strength of the indigenous peoples movement since its beginnings just twenty years earlier. Hundreds of indigenous organizations participated in the formulation of the draft declaration. It strongly endorsed the right of indigenous self-determination and indigenous control over territory and resources, and condemned all forms of ethnocide and genocide against indigenous peoples. The draft declaration was quickly approved by the UN Sub-Commission on Prevention of Discrimination and Protection of Minorities and was submitted to the UN Commission on Human Rights in 1995. The commission set up a special Open-Ended Working Group to review the draft declaration. The objective was to gain General Assembly approval of the UN Declaration on the Rights of Indigenous Peoples during the UN's 1995–2004 International Decade of the World's Indigenous People, but it was not finally adopted by the UN General Assembly until 2007, when 144 nations voted for adoption, 11 abstained, and 4 nations—Australia, Canada, New Zealand, and the United States—voted against. The key articles include article 3 on the right to self-determination, "to freely determine their political status and freely pursue their economic, social and cultural development"; and article 26, which states that "[i]ndigenous peoples have the right to the lands, territories and resources which they have traditionally owned, occupied or otherwise used or acquired," as well as a right to compensation for resource consfication without their consent (article 28). States are obligated to recognize traditional forms of tenure. The declaration also prohibits forced assimilation (article 8) and forced removal (article 10).[103]

Revision of the ILO's Convention 107

The International Labour Organization (ILO) is a UN-affiliated organization whose members are governments. When member governments ratify particular ILO conventions, it means that they have agreed to abide by the specified standards or face possible censure.

Until the recent political activism of indigenous organizations, the ILO's Convention 107, "Concerning the Protection and Integration of Indigenous and Other Tribal and Semi-Tribal Populations of Independent Countries," which was adopted in 1957, remained as the primary international standard for humane policies toward indigenous peoples. Convention 107 contained positive elements, but it still reflected the integrationist and ethnocentric assumptions typical of the colonial era. Indigenous leaders were especially critical of article 12, which permits the removal of tribals from their territories in the interests of national development. The indigenous delegates to the UN working group, who were in a position to directly influence UN policy, urged revision of Convention 107. In 1986, the ILO agreed that change was in order and convened a committee of experts to begin the revision process. The pro–indigenous peoples experts on the committee wanted the new Convention 107 to endorse self-determination and fought hard to have the rights of indigenous peoples to land and resources strengthened and to reduce the right of national governments to intervene in the name of "national interests."

The debate over the revision of Convention 107 proved contentious. Indigenous peoples were present only as observers and were allowed little direct input, in sharp contrast with the deliberations of the UN working group, which encouraged indigenous involvement. The final document adopted by the ILO in 1989 as Convention 169, "Concerning Indigenous and Tribal Peoples in Independent Countries," improved some of the language of Convention 107 but did not endorse indigenous self-determination. Although it did replace the former phrase *indigenous populations* with the more dignified term *indigenous peoples*, it was careful to specify that the term *peoples* had no special legal standing. Article 16 in the new convention still permits forced relocations of indigenous peoples "when consent cannot be obtained." The UN Declaration on the Rights of Indigenous Peoples provides much stronger support for the human rights of indigenous peoples, but ILO 169 remains important. As of 2003, seventeen countries had ratified Convention 169; in chronological order: Norway, Mexico, Colombia, Bolivia, Costa Rica, Paraguay, Peru, Honduras, Denmark, Guatemala, Netherlands, Fiji, Ecuador, Argentina, Venezuela, Dominica, and Brazil.[104]

Notes

1. Mel Watkins, ed., 1977, *Dene Nation—The Colony Within*. Toronto: University of Toronto Press; Dene Nation, 2007, Dene Declaration, http://www.denenation.com /denedec.html.

2. Unidad Indígena del Pueblo Awá (UNIPA), 2007, *Plan de Vida Awá, Identidad Awá*, www.unipa.org.co/index.htm.

3. World Council of Indigenous People (WCIP), 1977, untitled information leaflet.

4. José Martinez Cobo, 1986, *Study of the Problem of Discrimination Against Indigenous Populations*, UN Document: E/CN.4/Sub.2/1986/7/Add.4, Addendum 4, paragraphs 379–82, cited in United Nations Department of Economic and Social Affairs, 2004, *The Concept of Indigenous Peoples*, background paper, Workshop on Data

Collection and Dissagregation for Indigenous Peoples, Secretariat of the Permanent Forum on Indigenous Issues, PFII/2004/WS.1/3, 2, http://www.un.org/esa/socdev /unpfii/documents/PFII%202004%20WS.1%203%20Definition.doc.

5. United Nations Department of Economic and Social Affairs, 2004, *The Concept of Indigenous Peoples*, background paper, Workshop on Data Collection and Dissagregation for Indigenous Peoples, Secretariat of the Permanent Forum on Indigenous Issues. PFII/2004/WS.1/3, p. 2, http://www.un.org/esa/socdev/unpfii/documents /PFII%202004%20WS.1%203%20Definition.doc (accessed December 14, 2007).

6. Working Paper on the concept of *indigenous people* by Chairperson-Rapporteur Erica-Irene A. Daes, UN Commission of Human Rights, Sub-Commission on the Promotion and Protection of Human Rights (E/CN.4/Sub.2/AC.4/1996/2), June 10, 1996, cited in Rodolfo Stavenhagen, 2002, *Indigenous Issues: Human Rights and Indigenous Issues*, Report of the Special Rapporteur on the situation of human rights and fundamental freedoms of indigenous peoples, United Nations Economic and Social Council, Commission of Human Rights E/CN.4/2002/97.

7. Nunavut Planning Commission, 1993, *Agreement Between the Inuit of the Nunavut Settlement Area and Her Majesty the Queen in Right of Canada*, articles 1 and 35, http://npc.nunavut.ca/eng/nunavut/nlca.pdf.

8. Adam Kuper, 2003, "The Return of the Native," *Current Anthropology* 44(3): 389–402; Michael Asch and Colin Samson, 2004, "On the Return of the Native," *Current Anthropology* 45(2): 261–67; 2006, "More on the Return of the Native," *Current Anthropology* 47(1): 145–49.

9. Julio Carduno, 1980, "Carta abierta a los Hermanos Indios de America," in *Primer Congreso de Movimientos Indies de Sudamerica*, Paris: Ediciones Mitka, 112–13, my translation.

10. Ibid., 120–21, my translation.

11. See, for example, Gerald Berreman, 1978a, "Scale and social relations: Thoughts and three examples," in *Scale and Social Organization*, ed. Fredrik Barth, 41–77. Oslo: Universitetsforlaget; 1978b, "Scale and social relations," *Current Anthropology* 19(2): 225–45; Stanley Diamond, 1968, "The search for the primitive," in *The Concept of the Primitive*, ed. Ashley Montagu, 96–147, New York: Free Press; Robert Redfield, 1953, *The Primitive World and Its Transformations*, Ithaca, NY: Cornell University Press.

12. Pedro Portugal, 1980, "Entrevista con Pedro Portugal," in *Primer Congreso de Movimientos Indies de Sudamerica*, Paris: Ediciones Mitka, 177, my translation.

13. From the brief of the Nunavut Constitutional Forum (NCF) to the Royal Commission on the Economic Union and Development Prospects for Canada, cited in Dennis Patterson, 1984, "Canada: Inuit and Nunavut," *IWGIA Newsletter* 37: 52.

14. *Unidad Indigena*, 1975, 1(1): 4.

15. IWGIA, 1983, *IWGIA Newsletter*, 33: 114

16. Patterson, "Inuit and Nunavut," 39–52.

17. Michael Parfit, 1997, "A dream called Nunavut," *National Geographic* 192(3): 68–91.

18. Nunavut Tunngavik Inc., 2006, *Iniksaqattiarniq, Inuusiqattiarniq: Housing in Nunavut—The Time for Action Is Now*, Annual Report on the State of Inuit Culture and Society 2003/04 and 2004/05, http://www.tunngavik.com/english/pub.html.

19. Nunavut Tunngavik Inc., 2007, Inuit Firm Registry—Approved Businesses as of Sep 07, 2007, http://www.inuitfirm.com/public/pdfreport.php.

20. Sivummut Economic Development Strategy Group, 2003, *Nunavut Economic Development Strategy: Building a Foundation for the Future*, http://edt.gov.nu.ca /docs/nes/NUNAVUTE.pdf, p. I.

21. Sivummut Economic Development Strategy Group, *Nunavut Economic Development Strategy*, VI.

22. The Conference Board of Canada, 2001, *Nunavut Economic Outlook: An Examination of the Nunavut Economy*. http://www.gov.nu.ca/frv21.pdf.

23. Nunasi Corporation, 2005, Operations, Consolidated Balance Sheet, December 31, http://www.nunasi.com/operations.htm.

24. Thomas R. Berger, 2006, The Nunavut Project, Conciliator's Final Report, Nunavut Land Claims Agreement Implementation Contract Negotiations for the Second Planning Period 2003–2013, http://www.ainc-inac.gc.ca/pr/agr/nu/lca/nlc_e.pdf.

25. Ricardo Falla, 1979a, *Historia Kuna—Historia Rebelde*, Serie El Indio Panameno no. 4, Panama: Ediciones "CCS" (Centra de Capacitacion Social).

26. Ricardo Falla, 1979b, *El Tesoro de San Blas*, Serie El Indio Panameno no. 5, Panama: Ediciones "CCS" (Centre de Capacitacion Social); Panamá Contraloría General de la República, 2006, *Panamá en Cifras: Años 2001–05*, Dirección de Estadística y Censo, http://www.contraloria.gob.pa/DEC/main.aspx, Cuardro 211–02; M. Chapin, 2000, *Defending Kuna Yala: PEMASKY, The Study Project for the Management of the Wildlands of Kuna Yala, Panama*, A case study for S*hifting the power: Decentralization and biodiversity conservation*, Washington, DC: Biodiversity Support Program, http://www.worldwildlife.org/bsp/publications/aam/panama/panama.html.

27. Congreso Kuna, *Normas Kunas: Ley Fundamental y Estatuto de Kuna Yala*, http://www.congresogeneralkuna.org/normas%20kunas.htm (accessed September 9, 2007).

28. Harmodio Vivar, *Mensaje de Sailadummaan de la Comarca Kuna Yala*, http//www.congresogeneralkuna.org/mensaje_sailadummagan.htm.

29. Congreso Kuna, *Normas Kunas*, article 28, my translation.

30. Congreso Kuna, *Normas Kunas*, articles 7 and 8.

31. Congreso Kuna, *Normas Kunas*, articles 40 and 41, my translation.

32. Congreso Kuna, *Normas Kunas*, articles 13, 43–49.

33. Marcial Arias, *An Assessment of the Implementation of International Commitments on Traditional Forest Related Knowledge in Panama*, International Alliance of Indigenous and Tribal Peoples of Tropical Forests, http://www.international-alliance.org/documents/Panama-finaledit.pdf (assessed September 2007), 11, table 4.

34. Ibid., 2.

35. Federación de Centros Shuar, 1976, *Solución Original a un Problema Actual*, Sucua, Ecuador: Author, 130, my translation.

36. Jaime Zallez and Alfonso Gortaire, 1978, *Organizarse o Sucumbir: La Federación Shuar*, Mundo Shuar Serie "B," No. 14, Sucua, Ecuador: Centra de Documentación e Investigación Cultural Shuar.

37. Ibid., 78; see also *IWGIA Newsletter*, 1978–1979, nos. 20–23.

38. Norman E. Whitten, 1976, *Ecuadorian Ethnocide and Indigenous Ethnogenesis: Amazonian Resurgence amidst Andean Colonialism*, IWGIA Document no. 23, Copenhagen: IWGIA.

39. Consejo de Desarrollo de las Nacionalidades y Pueblos del Ecuador (CODENPE), 2007, *Nacionalidades y Pueblos Indígenas del Ecuador*, http://www.codenpe.gov.ec/npe.htm (accessed October 1, 2007); FICSH, Federación Interprovincial de Centros Shuar; FIPSE, Federación Independente de Pueblos Shuar de Ecuador; FINAE, Federación Interprovincial de la Nacionalidad Achuar del Ecuador.

40. Confederacion de Nacionalidades Indigenas de la Amazonica Ecuatoriana (CONFENIAE), http://www.ecuanex.net.ec/confeniae/.

41. Coordinadora de las Organizaciones Indígena de la Cuenca Amazónica (Coordinator for the Indigenous Organizations of the Amazon Basin, COICA), http://www.coica.org.ec/index.htm.

42. *Unidad Indigena*, 1975, 1(1).

43. Jean Jackson, 2003, The Crisis in Colombia: Consequences for Indigenous Peoples. American Anthropological Association, Committee for Human Rights, http://www.aaanet.org/committees/cfhr/rpt_crisis_in_columbia.htm; 2005, *Update on the Columbian Crisis for the American Anthropological Association Committee for Human Rights*, American Anthropological Association, http://www.aaanet.org/committees/cfhr/tf_draft_2005_13.pdf, 7.

44. Organización Nacional Indígena de Colombia (ONIC), 2007, *Quiénes Somos*, http://www.onic.org.co/quienes.shtml.

45. IWGIA, 1982, *IWGIA Newsletter* 30: 60–64; 31/32: 30–38.

46. Ibid., 30: 61.

47. COICA, 2007, Miembros, http://www.coica.org.ec/sp/miembros/opiac.html.

48. Departamento Administrativo Nacional de Estadistica (DANE), 1978, *Elementos para el Estudio de los Resguardos Indigenas del Cauca*, Bogota: DANE, 106–107, table 41.

49. CRIC, Consejo Regional Indigena del Cauca, Regional Indigenous Council of the Cauca.

50. Cartilla del CRIC no. 1, cited in Stephen Corry, 1976, *Towards Indian Self-Determination in Colombia*, Survival International Document no. 2, 43–47; see also IWGIA, 1980, *IWGIA Newsletter* 24: 19–26.

51. Corry, *Towards Indian Self-Determination in Colombia*, 43.

52. Cartilla del CRIC no. 1, cited in ibid., 43.

53. IWGIA, 1988, *IWGIA Yearbook 1987*, Copenhagen: IWGIA, 23.

54. Asociación de Cabildos Indígenas del Norte del Cauca (ACIN), 2005, Libertad para la Madre Tierra: El Camino Hacia una Reporma Agraria Popular en Colombia, http://www.nasaacin.net/noticias.htm?x=1612.

55. Asociación de Cabildos Indígenas del Norte del Cauca (ACIN), 2007, Situación de Derechos Humanos y Derecho Internacional Humanitario Zona Norte del Departamento del Cauca, http://www.nasaacin.net/informe_dh_y_dih.htm.

56. Fuerzas Armadas Revolucionarias de Colombia (Revolutionary Armed Forces of Colombia, FARC), a Marxist-Leninist guerrilla army.

57. Asociación de Cabildos Indígenas del Norte del Cauca (ACIN), 2007, Documentos de la Cumbre Nacional Itinerante, http://www.nasaacin.net/documentos _cumbre_nacional.htm.

58. Hugh McCullum, Karmel McCullum, and John Olthuis, 1977, *Moratorium: Justice, Energy, the North, and the Native People*, Toronto: Anglican Book Centre, 40.

59. Michael Asch, 1977, "The Dene economy," in *Dene Nation—The Colony Within*, ed. Mel Watkins, 47–61, Toronto: University of Toronto Press.

60. Peter H. Russell, 1977, "The Dene nation and confederation," on *Dene Nation—The Colony Within*, ed. Mel Watkins, 163–73, Toronto: University of Toronto Press.

61. Phoebe Nahanni, 1977, "The mapping project," in *Dene Nation—The Colony Within*, ed. Mel Watkins, 21–27, Toronto: University of Toronto Press; Scott Rushforth, 1977, "Country food," In *Dene Nation—The Colony Within*, ed. Mel Watkins, 32–46, Toronto: University of Toronto Press.

62. Thomas R. Berger, 1977, *Northern Frontier, Northern Homeland: the Report of the Mackenzie Valley Pipeline Inquiry*, Ottawa: Minister of Supply and Services.

63. Watkins, *Dene Nation*.

64. Georgy Barnaby, George Kurszewski, and Gerry Cheezie, 1977, "The political system and the Dene," in *Dene Nation—The Colony Within*, ed. Mel Watkins, Toronto: University of Toronto Press, 120–21.

65. Peter Jull, 1982, "Canada: A perspective on the Aboriginal Rights Coalition and the restoration of constitutional aboriginal rights," *IWGIA Newsletter* 30: 82–98.

66. Peter Jull, 1987, "Canada: Aboriginal self-government—Assessing the constitutional failure," *IWGIA Newsletter* 50: 69–81.

67. Indian and Northern Affairs Canada, 1993, Sahtu Dene and Metis: Comprehensive Land Claim Agreement, http://www.sahtu.ca/pdf/landclaims/SDMCLA -VOL-1.PDF.

68. Mackenzie Natural Gas Pipeline Project Group, 2007, http://www.mackenziegas project.com/index.asp; The Aboriginal Pipeline Group, 2007, http://www.mvapg .com/page/page/1922394.htm; U.S. Department of Energy, Energy Information Administration, 2007, Annual Energy Review 2006, table 6.5, Natural Gas Consumption by Sector, Selected Years, 1949–2006, http://www.eia.doe.gov/emeu/aer/pdf/pages /sec6_13.pdf.

69. Australia Department of Aboriginal Affairs, 1977, *Address by the Minister for Aboriginal Affairs the Honourable R. I. Viner at the Announcement of the Poll Results for the National Aboriginal Conference Elections*, Perth, November 28, 1977, pamphlet.

70. Australian Bureau of Statistics, 2007, *Population Distribution, Aboriginal and Torres Strait Islander Australians, 2006*, Cat no. 4705.0, 5, http://www.abs.gov.au /AUSSTATS/abs@.nsf/DetailsPage/4705.02006?OpenDocument.

71. J. C. Altman, G. J. Buchanan, and L. Larsen, 2007, *The Environmental Significance of the Indigenous Estate: Natural Resource Management as Economic Development in Remote Australia*, CAEPR Discussion Paper No. 286, Australian National University, College of Arts & Social Sciences, http://www.anu.edu.au/caepr/discus sion.php.

72. Northern Land Council, 2006, Annual Report 2005/2006, 13, http://www.nlc
.org.au/html/files/0506_Annual%20Report_Overview.pdf.

73. A. Barrie Pittock, 1972, *Aboriginal Land Rights*, IWGIA Document no. 3,
Copenhagen: IWGIA, 30. Land rights issues in Australia, Canada, and New Zealand
are also discussed in Marcia Langton, Maureen Tehan, Lisa Palmer, and Kathryn
Shain, eds., 2004, *Honour among Nations: Treaties and Agreements with Indigenous
Peoples*, Carlton, Victoria: Melbourne University Press.

74. National Aboriginal Land Rights Conference, 1976, Sydney, untitled pamphlet.

75. IWGIA, 1987, *IWGIA Yearbook 1986*, Copenhagen: IWGIA, 37.

76. Australia Attorney-General's Office, 2007, *Native Title Act 1993*, part 1.3, Objects, http://www.ag.gov.au/www/agd/agd.nsf/Page/Indigenous_law_and_native_title
Native_title.

77. Australia Department of Aboriginal Affairs, 1978, *Statement by the Honorable
R. I. Viner, M. P., Minister for Aboriginal Affairs, on Aboriginal Policies & Achievements in Aboriginal Affairs, House of Representatives*, November 24, 1978, pamphlet.

78. Australia Parliament of the Commonwealth, 1987, *Return to Country: The
Aboriginal Homelands Movement in Australia*, House of Representatives Standing
Committee on Aboriginal Affairs, Canberra, xvi.

79. J. C. Altman, 2006, *In Search of an Outstations Policy for Indigenous Australians*, Working Paper No. 34, Centre for Aboriginal Economic Policy Research, 3,
tables 1 and 2.

80. Northern Land Council, 2006, Annual Report 2005/2006, 11.

81. Phil Niklaus, 1983, "Land, power and yellowcake," *IWGIA Newsletter* 34:
6–15.

82. Australia Minister for Families, Community Services and Indigenous Affairs,
2007, *National Indigenous Council*, http://www.atsia.gov.au/NIC/default.aspx.

83. Northern Territory Government of Australia, 2007, *Ampe Akelyernemane Meke
Mekarle, "Little Children Are Sacred"*, Report of the Northern Territory Board of Inquiry into the Protection of Aboriginal Children from Sexual Abuse, 7,
http://www.nt.gov.au/dcm/inquirysaac/pdf/bipacsa_final_report.pdf.

84. Ibid., 6.

85. Ibid., 7.

86. Australia Department of Families, Community Services and Indigenous Affairs, 2007, *Northern Territory Emergency Response*, FaCSIA 0635R, http://www
.facsia.gov.au/nter/docs/nter_180807.pdf.

87. J. C. Altman, 2007, *Neo-Paternalism and the Destruction of CDEP*, Centre for
Aboriginal Economic Policy Research, Topical Issue No. 14/2007,
http://www.anu.edu.au/caepr/Publications/topical/Altman_Paternalism.pdf.

88. Joel Rocamora, 1979a, "Agribusiness, dams and counter-insurgency," *Southeast Asia Chronicle* 67: 2.

89. Cited in ibid., 9–10.

90. Charles Drucker, 1985, "Dam the Chico: Hydropower development and tribal
resistance," *Ecologist* 15(4): 149–57 (reprinted in Bodley, 1988a: 151–65); Felix Razon, 1976, *Native Peoples Struggle against U.S. Imperialism in the Philippines*, IW-

GIA Document no. 25, 32–41, Copenhagen: IWGIA; Rocamora, Agribusiness, dams and counter-insurgency; Joel Rocamora, 1979b, "The political uses of PANAMIN," *Southeast Asia Chronicle* 67: 11–21; Martha Winnacker, 1979, "The battle to stop the Chico dams," *Southeast Asia Chronicle* 67: 22–29.

91. Cordillera Peoples Alliance for the Defense of Ancestral Domain and for Self Determination, 2007, http://www.cpaphils.org/.

92. World Commission on Dams, 2007, "Outline of the WCD," http://www.dams .org/commission/intro.htm.

93. Ellen Boye, 1974, "Samarbejde rundt om Nordpolen," in *Gronland*, Copen-hagen, 69.

94. Ibid., 70.

95. Miguel Chase-Sardi and Adolfo Columbres, 1975, *Por la Liberation del In-digena*, Buenos Aires: Ediciones del Sol, 240.

96. Douglas E. Sanders, 1977, *The Formation of the World Council of Indigenous Peoples*, IWGIA Document no. 29, Copenhagen: IWGIA.

97. Ibid.

98. World Council of Indigenous Peoples (WCIP), 1977, *World Council of In-digenous Peoples Second General Assembly, Kiruna, Sweden, August 24–27, 1977*, Report, http://www.cwis.org/fwdp/International/wcip_dec.txt.

99. Arctic Environmental Protection Strategy, 1991, *Declaration on the Protec-tion of Arctic Environment*, Rovaniemi, Finland, http://www.arctic-council.org /Archives/AEPS%20Docs/artic_environment.pdf, 3.

100. Ibid., 39–40.

101. Arctic Athabaskan Council, 2005, *News Release: Arctic Indigenous Peoples Unveil Statement on Climate Change*, http://www.arcticathabaskancouncil.com/press /20051206.php.

102. *IWGIA Yearbook 1987*, 87.

103. United Nations, General Assembly, 2007, Resolution adopted by the General Assembly, United Nations Declaration on the Rights of Indigenous Peoples. A/RES/61/295, http://daccessdds.un.org/doc/UNDOC/GEN/N06/512/07/PDF/N0651207 .pdf?OpenElement.

104. International Labour Organization (ILO), 2003, *ILO Convention on Indige-nous and Tribal Peoples, 1989 (No. 169): A Manual*, http://www.ilo.org/public/english /standards/norm/egalite/itpp/convention/introduction.pdf.

11 Petroleum, the Commercial World, and Indigenous Peoples

THE QUEST TO FIND AND EXTRACT PETROLEUM to support the commercial world's insatiable consumption is at the center of the continuing political conflict between indigenous peoples, governments, and corporations in many parts of the world. This dimension of the conflict directly pits small tribal societies against giant oil companies in some of the world's most remote and environmentally sensitive ecosystems. The petroleum industry highlights the most important contrasts between the tribal and commercial worlds over the material and social basis of human well-being, and tests the ability of indigenous people to mobilize international support for the peaceful defense of their human rights to protect their societies, cultures, ecosystems, and territories. Conflict between oil companies and indigenous peoples is dramatic verification that loss of political control over territory and resources is the primary reason why indigenous peoples become "victims of progress."

When indigenous people assert their human rights to maintain their way of life in opposition to oil development on their territories, they are directly challenging firmly held assumptions about the inevitability of progress in the commercial world as measured by perpetually elevated flows of energy and materials. This conflict highlights the political power of the leaders of countries that are the primary producers and consumers of oil, and who sometimes falsely frame the debate as a stark choice between protecting the interests of a few tribal people versus continued global economic progress and development. The reality is that progress dependent on nonrenewable fossil fuels is not sustainable development, and will only delay the major social and infrastructural changes that must be made to achieve sustainability for the commercial world.

Petroleum: The Unsustainable Foundation of the Commercial World

As is well known, petroleum is the critical foundation of the global commercial system as presently structured. Petroleum is the most desirable fuel in the world. By weight, it has nearly double the energy content of hard coal, and it has the advantage of relative ease of storage and mobility. It is not surprising that approximately 60 percent of the world's primary energy production is now in the form of petroleum and natural gas.[1] The United States is the world's largest consumer of petroleum, accounting for approximately one-fourth of global consumption in 2005. Because American oil production has been declining since 1970, the United States imports more than two-thirds of the crude oil it consumes, making it a dominant influence on the global oil industry. Americans burn about 90 percent of the petroleum they consume as a fuel, thereby contributing significantly to global warming. About two-thirds of American fuel use is in the transportation sector of the economy. The remaining 10 percent is vital material for industrial products such as petrochemicals for plastics, fibers, pharmaceuticals, cosmetics, and as lubricants, and asphalt—all of which seem indispensable for large-scale high-consumption societies like America that are dependent on the global market.[2]

Petroleum matters to indigenous peoples because of the particular way a few financiers and corporate leaders historically chose to develop the industry. Ever since John D. Rockefeller founded Standard Oil in 1870, oil used for transportation has made tribal territories more readily accessible to outsiders, even as it made them targets for oil development. Control over petroleum concentrated power in the hands of a remarkably few people, giving them unprecedented decision-making power over the conditions of daily life for billions of people. Oil elites promoted the development of petroleum-burning internal combustion engines for transportation, to the exclusion of less polluting and more sustainable electric alternatives.[3] Oil elites also used mechanization, pesticides, and synthetic ammonia fertilizer, all based on petroleum and natural gas, to construct large-scale agribusinesses for the global market. These oil-based factory farms have overpowered and displaced small-scale, solar-based local and regional food production systems worldwide.[4] Since 1950 these petroleum-dependent cultural transformations also vastly accelerated global population growth and dramatically increased outside pressure on tribal territories and resources. By the beginning of the twenty-first century, no tribal societies have been unaffected by the commercial world and there are no secure refuge areas for independent tribal peoples.

Petroleum also highlights the human problem of social inequality in the commercial world and the differences between the tribal and commercial worlds in this regard. The reality is that oil is distributed geopolitically in a grossly inequitable manner for a resource that has been made so crucial to so many forms of social power. This makes decision making in the commercial world much less democratic than it could be. Indigenous peoples generally try to organize their societies and cultures democratically, such that everyone contributes to decision making and has access to the key natural resources of land, water, and ecosystems that people need, but this is obviously not the case with oil in the commercial world. The countries of the world are unequal as presently organized, whether viewed by population, military expenditures, GDP, or personal wealth, but countries are most unequal when ranked by their control over oil reserves. This matters because in the commercial world, access to oil now determines all other forms of social power.

The top ten oil countries (about 5 percent of 176 countries in the world) have 84 percent of the world's oil reserves, but only 7 percent of the world's population.[5] The 12 countries in the OPEC cartel control 77 percent of known oil reserves.[6] There are 598 million people living in 115 countries that have no petroleum reserves at all, and are thus totally dependent on a global market over which they have minimal, if any, control. No other form of social power is so concentrated by country. In comparison, the top ten countries ranked by total household wealth have 80 percent of the world's private wealth,[7] but this is distributed among 32 percent of the world's population. World military expenditures, GDP, and personal wealth are all dominated by the United States, and this helps explain both why America is able to consume one-fourth of the world's oil even though it has less than 5 percent of the world's people and directly controls less than 1 percent of world oil reserves.

The oil industry's concentrated economic power is illustrated by the five largest companies, which received 81 percent of the 1.6 trillion dollars in revenues that flowed through the industry in 2005.[8] Exxon Mobil, the world's largest oil company, was also the world's largest publicly traded corporation and received more than 25 percent of worldwide oil industry profits. Oil and oil-related industries dominate the corporate world. Fortune's Global 500 for 2007 lists six oil companies (Exxon Mobil, Royal Dutch Shell, BP, Chevron, ConocoPhillips, and French-based Total), among the world's ten largest companies, along with Wal-Mart and three car companies.[9] These top six oil companies had combined revenues in 2006 of more than 1.2 trillion dollars, which was more than the combined GDPs of the poorest 123 countries — with a combined population of 1.2 billion people — in 2005.

The commercial world's dependence on petroleum makes it a difficult sociocultural system to sustain, given the finite nature of the resource. Global consumption of petroleum has increased from less than 8 billion barrels a year in 1960 to more than 30 billion barrels in 2005.[10] At the 2005 annual rate of consumption the then-known and recoverable global petroleum reserves of

1.2 trillion barrels would be totally gone within just forty-one years.[11] Such projections are, of course, misleading because reserves grow with new discoveries, and it is plausible that twice as much petroleum ultimately remains to be discovered and extracted.[12] However, before new reserves can be developed and consumed, the rate of petroleum consumption is likely to be slowed by the rising financial, social, and environmental costs of exploration and extraction, including the negative impacts of global warming from burning fossil fuels. All of these negative costs will force vast changes on the commercial world. Meanwhile, giant petroleum corporations are seeking to prospect in and develop oil fields in some of world's most vulnerable arctic and tropical forest environments, and other territories occupied by numerous indigenous groups.

All of these petroleum-related scale and power issues help explain why, for example, the Gwich'in peoples in Canada and Alaska, and the Cofan, Siona, Secoya, Shuar, Sarayaku, Huaorani, and other indigenous peoples in Ecuador and Peru are engaged in grossly unequal struggles against oil companies to sustain their ways of life, as discussed below.

The Gwich'in and Oil Development in the Sacred Place Where Life Begins

The Gwich'in are an indigenous people living in 14 villages in Arctic Alaska south of the Brooks Range and adjacent areas of the Canadian Northwest Territory and Yukon.[13] Caribou are their primary subsistence resource, and they claim that they and their ancestors have occupied their territory for 20,000 years. They are the northern-most Athabascan speakers, and their subsistence, social structure, and spirituality centers on the Porcupine River Caribou Herd. The Gwich'in number some 9,000 people and call themselves "people of the caribou." Their territory overlaps almost totally with the year around range of the Porcupine Caribou Herd, except for the herd's calving grounds on the coastal plain north of the Brooks Range. This narrow zone facing the Arctic Ocean is a crucial area that provides the caribou with rich grazing and shelter from insects and predators, and the Gwich'in understandably call it "The Sacred Place Where Life Begins." Much of the Alaskan portion of the Porcupine Caribou Herd range, including their crucial calving area, is in the 76,800 km² Arctic National Wildlife Refuge. The federal government first set aside this region as a protected area in 1960 and later expanded it. The Arctic Refuge includes the largest designated wilderness area in the federal wildlife system and covers three major physiographic zones: tundra, boreal forest, and the Brooks Range, and has the highest biodiversity of any protected area in the circumpolar arctic.[14] Unfortunately from the Gwich'in perspective, the 1002 area, which includes the critical caribou calving area, may also contain 8 billion barrels of technically recoverable oil.[15] This is would supply the approximate equivalent of one year of U.S. petroleum consumption at 2006 rates, but the Gwich'in fear that opening the 1002 area to oil development would irreversibly degrade the caribou herd and their own way of life.

After observing the disruption and displacement that the development of the Prudhoe Bay oil fields in Alaska caused to the neighboring Central Arctic Caribou Herd, the Gwich'in organized to take political action to protect the calving and nursery grounds from oil development. They first convened an international meeting of all Gwich'in leaders from Alaska and Canada in 1988 to adopt a common policy on oil development, and unanimously approved a "Resolution to Prohibit Development in the Calving and Post-Calving Grounds of the Porcupine Caribou Herd."[16] They specifically posed their resolution as a human rights issue, and cited the relevant international resolutions including Article 1 of the International Covenant on Economic, Social and Cultural Rights in affect since 1976, that " . . . in no case may a people be deprived of their own means of subsistence." Their resolution was a political statement that declared: "NOW THEREFORE BE IT RESOLVED: That the United States Congress and President recognize the rights of our Gwich'in people to continue to live our way of life by prohibiting development in the calving and post-calving grounds of the Porcupine Caribou Herd."

More recently the Gwich'in Steering Committee has cited supporting findings in the National Academy of Sciences (NAS) 2003 study of the likely long-term effects of North Slope oil development up to 2025.[17] The Gwich'in noted that their Inupiat neighbors repeatedly told researchers that "a huge industrial complex on the Arctic landscape was offensive to the people and an affront to the spirit of the land."[18] More specifically, the Inupiat reported "that traditional subsistence hunting areas have been reduced, the behavior and migratory patterns of key subsistence species have changed, and that there is increased incidence of cancer and diabetes and disruption of traditional social systems."[19] The Gwich'in were also aware of Inupiat concerns over contamination of their traditional foods, increased risks in hunting, and the increased demands on their time caused by the need to attend constant oil industry related meetings.

In making their case against oil development in Arctic Refuge the Gwich'in also point to the oil industry "History of Wreckage"[20] in Alaska, including the disastrous environmental effects of the 11 million gallon Exxon Valdez spill in Prince William Sound at the terminus of the Trans-Alaska Pipeline. The NAS study that the oil industry created a network of trails, roads, pipelines, and power lines whose effects on the landscape, vegetation, and wildlife extended far beyond their immediate footprints. Industry-related activities left persistent marks on the tundra; disrupted the Bowhead whale migrations; attracted predators, reducing breeding populations of migratory birds; and reduced the reproductive success of the Central Arctic Caribou herd. Cleanup of abandoned sites was minimal and abandoned debris would persist "for centuries." Many of the human and environmental effects are not well understood, including long-term health impacts. The Inupiat peoples find that oil development has made it more difficult for them to hunt whales, which are culturally important subsistence resource, and they are concerned over the possibly catastrophic effects of a major offshore spill.

The most obvious benefit of North Slope oil development is that it produced some 14 billion barrels of oil from 1977 to 2002. This is equivalent to two years worth of U.S. consumption at the 2006 rate. The National Academy report does not leave it to the Inupiat to decide whether or not the oil benefits outweigh the costs, but rather ominously concludes, "Whether the benefits derived from oil and gas activities justify acceptance of the inevitable accumulated undesirable effects that have accompanied and will accompany them is an issue for society as a whole to judge."[21] This conclusion ignores the human rights implications of damage to the traditional subsistence of an indigenous people. The Gwich'in emphatically reject any oil development that would threaten the Porcupine Caribou Herd, but the matter will be decided by the U.S. Congress, the Senate, and the president, who may not be moved the Gwich'in Resolution to Prohibit Development.

In 1999 the Gwich'in formed the Gwich'in Council International as a permanent member of the Arctic Council representing all Gwich'in peoples, together with the other indigenous peoples including the Arctic Athabaskan Council, the Aleut International Association, the Inuit Circumpolar Council (ICC), the Russian Association of Indigenous Peoples of the North (RAIPON), and the Saami Council. One of the primary issues they will deal with in the Arctic Council is the effects of global warming which will be especially acute in the arctic and is discussed below, and which can of course not be separated from the effects of burning arctic oil.

Petroleum Development and Indigenous Rights in Ecuador

The previous example shows how Arctic indigenous peoples organized politically to protect their societies from destructive oil development in their territories. Ecuador is an outstanding example of a similar legal and political struggle by indigenous peoples against petroleum development in the Amazon tropical forest. Indigenous organizations in Ecuador have fought tenaciously, and with some success, to prevent oil development in their territories, and they have sought compensation for damages that have already occurred.

The main oil-producing region of Ecuador is in the forested Amazon drainage, the Oriente Basin section of what geologists call the Putumayo-Oriente-Marañon oil province.[22] The other basins of this oil province are in adjacent parts of Colombia and Peru. Because of its productive potential, this province is ranked by the U.S. Geological Survey as a "priority" oil province in its list of potential global petroleum reserves that could help support America's energy needs for the thirty years between 1995 and 2025.[23] It is also an area of great cultural and biodiversity, and until recently the Ecuadorian Oriente had managed to escape much of the development devastation that Amazonia in general has suffered. Oil exploration began in the province in 1921. The first well was drilled in 1937, and production began in 1963, touching off a major regional oil boom. Between 1963 and 1995 the province produced nearly 3 billion barrels of oil equivalent (gas and oil), mostly from the Oriente. Three billion barrels was enough oil to fuel the United States for 145 days at 2006 consumption rates. If all the 3.9 billion barrels that geologists estimate might ultimately remain to be recovered were extracted, it would fuel the commercial world for only forty-six days. In 2004 Ecuador produced 205 million barrels of petroleum,[24] about twenty days' worth of American consumption at that time. These amounts might seem insignificant from a global perspective, but not when they are concentrated in a few hands as corporate profits. At the historic global market high of 83 dollars (U.S.) per barrel reached in 2007, Ecuador's annual production would generate revenues of some 17 billion dollars, which would equal more than half of Ecuador's 30-billion-dollar 2004 GDP. Oil revenues accelerated Ecuador's total and per capita economic growth, but benefits have not been well distributed, given that 17 percent of the national population was living in "extreme poverty" in 1998.[25] Given the high cost in human, cultural, and environmental destruction that this development has already caused, it might be judged to be a poor exchange. Certainly this is the view of many of the indigenous people and their supporters worldwide.

Many companies secured oil concessions in Ecuadorian Oriente, but from 1964 to 1990 Texaco Oil was the primary developer and operator of the major oil fields.[26] Under the best of circumstances, oil development in the tropical rainforest is a costly and destructive business. Exploration disturbs the wildlife; oil wells and infrastructure cause deforestation; and access trails, roads, and pipelines open otherwise remote areas to outsiders. Texaco's activities amplified all of these problems, because it was effectively able to regulate its own operations in Ecuador without government control. Under these circumstances, rather than following best environmental practices that were standard in the United States, Texaco choose to dispose of wastes from hundreds of wells in open pits, where they contaminated the soil and water. There were also numerous oil spills that were not properly cleaned up. Remediation efforts by the company were apparently inadequate. All of this allowed Texaco to maximize profits by shifting costs to the environment and to the local people. And because of the high levels of poverty in the country, hundreds of thousands of colonists from the Andes followed the oil roads into the rainforest, further disrupting and displacing the indigenous peoples.

Texaco's destructive development practices were an important motivation for indigenous peoples in the Ecuadorian Amazon to organize in self-defense and pursue legal appeals against developers. Various indigenous groups formed the Amazon Defense Coalition (Frente de Defensa de la Amazonia, or FDA) to represent them in legal proceedings against Texaco Oil in 1993.[27] The coalition's "assembly of those affected," includes the Cofán, Huaorani, Kichwa, Secoya, and Siona indigenous nationalities, represented by four different organizations,[28] as well as local settler communities. The specific problems the coalition attributed to Texaco were soil, water, and air contamination; cancer; gastrointestinal illnesses; miscarriages; respiratory illnesses; loss of crops and domestic animals; loss of flora and fauna; loss of indigenous territory; loss of culture; and deforestation. The Amazon Coalition's original legal case was a class-action lawsuit before the U.S. Federal Court in New York,[29] with substantial evidence to support the indigenous claims.[30] After ten years of hearings, the federal court ruled that it was not the appropriate jurisdiction, and in 2003 the coalition brought its case before a superior court in Ecuador, this time against Chevron, the world's seventh-largest corporation and Texaco's new parent company. As of late 2007 the case was still in court, but it has already had widespread impact.[31]

Other indigenous groups closely watched the Texaco case and also began confronting the oil companies. In 2000 the Shuar organization FIPSE accused ARCO (the American-based subsidiary of BP, the giant British energy company) of fraudulently gaining entrance to their territory.[32] The Sarayaku, some one thousand Kichwa-speaking people in five communities south of the areas developed by Texaco, began organized resistance to oil prospecting in their own territory in 1987.[33] The Sarayaku secured a legal title to their territory in 1992, but even so, in 1996 the Ecuadorian government granted a license to an Argentine oil company, Compañia General de Combustibles (CGC) to explore Block 23, a two-thousand-square-kilometer area, 65 percent of which lies within Sarayaku territory.[34] When the Sarayaku protested against the damages being caused by CGC they were threatened by the company and the military. In 2003 the Sarayaku took their case to the Inter-American Commission on Human Rights, which referred it to the Inter-American Court of

Human Rights, which in turn ruled in favor of the Sarayaku in 2005. By late 2007, development in Sarayacu territory was on hold and the Ecuadorian Ministry of Mines and Oil promised that all explosive charges that remained in place for seismic exploration in Sarayacu territory would be removed. The Sarayaku case also had an effect on Burlington Resources, which acquired CGC's Block 23 concession in 2003, when one of its shareholders petitioned it to adopt a policy that respected the rights of indigenous peoples.

Indigenous protests in Ecuador also came to the attention of the United Nations. UN Human Rights Council Special Rapporteur Rodolfo Stavenhagen investigated the human rights situation there in 2006 and received numerous complaints of direct human rights abuses and environmental degradation caused by oil companies. Indigenous peoples accused oil companies and security forces of "acts of persecution, torture, degrading treatment and the illegal detention of opposition organization leaders."[35] Stavenhagen also found that indigenous organizations were resolutely opposed to the Free Trade Treaty the Ecuadorian government was negotiating with the United States, because they feared such international agreements would weaken their control over their natural resources.

The Sarayaku leaders astutely treated their conflict as a human rights struggle. Their rainforest territory was the center of their life, and they clearly understood that it was threatened by the expansion of global capitalism, as Franco Viteri, former Sarayaku community president declared: "[T]he Sarayaku fight has a spiritual connotation, Sarayaku have a very great attachment to Mother Earth, the foundation of our life; it is the source of our cultural development, our history, philosophy, form of life, respect for the earth and the spirituality necessary to be able to overcome any suggestion of the power of capitalism."[36]

Like the motto of the Amazon Defense Coalition—"To Defend the Amazon is to Save the World"—Viteri linked the Sarayaku political struggle to a larger struggle to create a more humane world: "I want to emphasize the dimensions of the fight and the implications the resistance of the Sarayaku has for the process of constructing a pluri-national state and a better world under a new more favorable global social order, with social justice, in which the economic and social rights of all people are respected; mestizos as well as indigenous people, all the residents of Ecuador. In political terms, the fight is a resistance to neo-liberalism. The act of opposing ourselves to an oil company implies that we oppose the Free Trade Area of the Americas and Free Trade Agreements."[37]

The resistance to oil development in the Arctic Refuge by the Gwich'in is paralleled by a similar campaign to protect the Yasuni National Park and a UN-designated bioshphere reserve in Ecuador, which was established in

1989. This is the largest protected area in Ecuador and overlaps with the Huaorani territory, as well as the territory of isolated peoples known as Tagaeri and Taromenane, who have recently killed intruders. The Yasuni park also contains the Ishpingo-Tiputini-Tambococha oil field, the largest undeveloped oil field in the country, which may hold one fourth of Ecuador's oil reserves. The government has not yet moved to protect the entire park, and environmental organizations worldwide and indigenous organizations in Ecuador are conducting an intense campaign to prevent development in this sensitive region. In 2007 Ecuadorian president Rafael Correa declared a moratorium on oil development, proposing to halt all development in exchange for 350 million dollars to compensate for the revenues it would forgo.

Global Warming and Indigenous Peoples

> [T]oday from the Arctic to Mexico, Native Peoples who continue age-old subsistence and cultural traditions intimately woven into the seasonal cycles of plant and animal life, report that the seasons are slipping. These contemporary observations of the shifts in the normal historic range of physical phenomena and bio-behaviors support the conclusions of western scientific observations.[38]

Most governments and international agencies are focused on how to share the burden of reducing greenhouse gas emissions, while paying relatively little attention to how the costs of the actual impact of global warming will be distributed among people and nations. There is already an emerging recognition that the poor will pay. This issue puts indigenous people in the spotlight, because they are already paying extreme costs for climate change impacts they did not cause. The virtually complete loss of an island nation's island would be a dramatic example of the effectively similar loss already suffered by many tribal groups who were forced to surrender control over their physical territory and resources. Some have suggested that the complete loss of small island nations can be taken as a "benchmark" of dangerous climate change, and point out that concepts of justice may be more relevant here than standard economic cost-benefit models.[39] Global warming will be another way in which control over territory may be lost, suggesting that global warming should now be understood as a human rights and social justice issue whose impact will first be felt by indigenous peoples.

The effects of global warming are complex, but they are also very immediate and very visible to indigenous peoples, who are closely attuned with and directly dependent on their local environments. For this reason the primary report of the U.S. Global Change Research Program National Assessment of "Climate Change Impacts on the United States," also called the "Foundation

Report," which was conducted in the 1990s devoted a full chapter to native peoples and their homelands, based on a workshop held with more than 160 representatives of native organizations from throughout the country. To illustrate impacts of global warming on native peoples, the National Assessment cited the example of salmon. Salmon are a critical natural resource and a center of social life of many indigenous peoples in the Pacific Northwest. Salmon are also a key element in the life cycles of many other species. Native peoples in this region were accustomed to climate-related shifts in the migration path of salmon caused by periodic oscillations in ocean temperatures. During El Niño years, salmon return to their spawning grounds by passing north of Vancouver Island, and areas to the south may experience large reductions in returning salmon. It is likely that global warming will cause salmon to completely abandon many of their traditional spawning areas.[40] Increased droughts, forest fires, and glacial retreat are other global–warming-related threats to salmon runs already reduced by dams and industrial pollution.

Signs of global warming are impossible to ignore, and are most visible in the Arctic. In 2007, late summer sea ice reached its lowest recorded historic level, and for the first time ships could navigate the Northwest Passage unaided by ice breakers.[41] The National Assessment prominently featured a case study from the sea–mammal-hunting Yupik Eskimo of western Alaska and adjacent Siberia, where already in the late 1990s warming was disrupting complex ecosystem relationships.[42] Yupik hunters observed a decline in the quality and quantity of walrus fat, as well as a population decline and physical weakening of seals. These trends corresponded to a general thinning and retreat of the sea ice, which made it more difficult for sea mammals to find resting places. As a result, the killer whales, who also preyed on other sea mammals, began eating sea otters; this caused an expansion of the otters' prey, the sea urchins, causing the overabundant sea urchins to overgraze the kelp, which provide food and shelter for fish. The sea ice itself also sheltered fish and accumulated nutrients. Fish, in turn, were food for whales and the Yupik. It is clear that seemingly small changes in temperature can have huge impacts on complex ecosystems. The impact of global warming on indigenous peoples throughout the arctic is discussed in detail in the 2004 Arctic Climate Impact Assessment commissioned by the Arctic Council.[43]

The 2007 Intergovernmental Panel on Climate Change (IPCC) Working Group II contribution to the Fourth Assessment Report[44] discusses many global warming impacts that may well be catastrophic for indigenous peoples and will likely occur before many of the world's large urban centers are affected by storms and sea level changes. The principal impacts for indigenous people include severe melting of Arctic ice, conversion of the Amazon rainforest to savanna, and destruction of coral reefs—all environmental impacts that are likely to involve massive extinctions and loss of biodiversity and will

directly undermine traditional subsistence. Ice melting and tropical deforestation also involve positive feedback effects that may accelerate global
warming. Loss of reefs through coral bleaching and deforestation are also
caused by changes in land use and particular forms of industrial development.
Global warming amplifies all of these impacts. For example, the area in the
Ecuadorian Oriente developed by Texaco Oil is already identified as a "deforestation hotspot" for forest conversion to savanna.[45] The IPCC Working
Group II report discusses indigenous people in several chapters, focusing especially on their traditional knowledge and adaptive capabilities, but separate
chapters on the arctic and small islands are especially relevant. Many small
islands, especially Micronesian coral atolls with mean elevations of only two
meters above sea level, could eventually become uninhabitable due to small
rises in sea level, but they are already highly vulnerable to extreme weather
events such as typhoons, which are likely to increase as oceans heat up.

The Indigenous Response to Global Warming

Indigenous peoples were among the first in the world to experience the negative effects of melting glaciers and sea ice and rising sea levels caused by
global warming. They understand that the commercial world's use of fossil
fuels, together with deforestation and unregulated development, are the primary causes of global warming, and they have been at the forefront in taking
international political action to address these problems.

At least ten indigenous organizations are entitled to attend the annual Conference of the Parties (COP) of the United Nations Framework Convention on
Climate Change (UNFCCC), which since 1994 is the principal international
organization dealing with global warming. The COP is the primary decision-
making body within the UNFCCC. Indigenous organizations are highly democratic structures that foster consensus decision making in small-scale face-
to-face meetings. They are typically composed of a nested hierarchy of
organizations reaching from small local communities of a few hundred people to regional ethnic organizations and national- and international-level bodies, each with elected officials who must directly respond to their con-
stituents. Even seemingly isolated self-sufficient tribal peoples can now have
their say in international forums on global warming, oil development, and deforestation. For example, the 358-member Asháninka (including the Pajonal
Ashéninka) community living at Shumahuani in the relatively remote Gran
Pajonal uplands of the central Peruvian Amazon, whom I visited in 1969 before the beginning of the political mobilization of indigenous peoples in the
Peruvian Amazon,[46] are represented through OAGP,[47] their local Ashéninka
organization (figure 11.1). OAGP is a member of ORAU,[48] a regional organ-

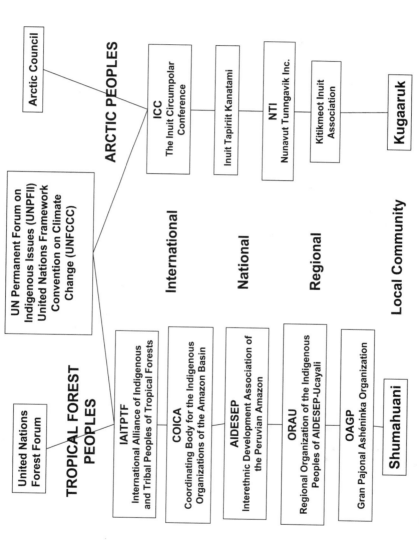

Figure 11.1. Local to Global Hierarchy of Indigenous Political Organizations

ization of ten other local organizations of Ashéninka, Asháninka, Shipbo-Conibo, and Amahuaca peoples. ORAU is a member of AIDESEP,[49] a national-level organization based in Lima and representing six regional organizations that cover the entire Peruvian Amazon. AIDESEP, founded in 1980, coordinates the political activities of fifty-seven ethnic federations and territorial organizations composed of some 1,350 communities with 350,000 people from sixteen language families. At the international level, AIDESEP sends representatives to meetings of COICA,[50] an organization currently headquartered in Quito, Ecuador, and representing indigenous organizations in nine Amazonian countries. COICA is a member of the Thailand-based International Alliance of Indigenous and Tribal Peoples of Tropical Forests (IAITPTF),[51] which has nine regional coordinators representing indigenous organizations in Central and South America, Central and West Africa, South and Southeast Asia, and the Pacific.

A similar hierarchy of indigenous organizations links local communities in the arctic with their respective regional, national, and international organizations, such that the Inuit Nunavut village of Kugaaruk, with just 549 people, sends representatives to the Kitikmeot Inuit Association, which is linked through Nunavut Tunngavik to the Canadian Inuit Tapiriit Kanatami, which sends representatives to the Inuit Circumpolar Conference (ICC). The ICC representatives meet with international nation-state government officials in the Arctic Council, the UNFCCC, and the UN Permanent Forum on Indigenous Issues (UNPFII). In comparison, within the United States, decision making on global warming is a confusing bureaucratic labyrinth that empowers very few people and is easily subverted by powerful lobbies for fossil fuel industries.

Indigenous leaders form networks and alliances with diverse nonindigenous organizations and represent their mutual interests in various international forums. National and international indigenous organizations like COICA, ICC, and IAITPF are often represented at international forums such as the UNFCC, Article 8(j) Working Group-established meetings of the Convention on Biodiversity (CBD), the UN Forest Forum (UNFF), and the UNPFII. ORAU, AIDESEP, and IAITPF participated in an Expert Meeting for the United Nations Forest Forum in 2004 focused on forest issues in the Peruvian Amazon.[52] The IAITPTF presented a declaration to the Eleventh COP of the UNFCCC in Montreal, Canada, in 2005 signed by twenty-three indigenous peoples from throughout the world. The IAITPTF statement specifically linked oil development to global warming and human rights violations, declaring: "The burning of oil, gas, and coal, as fossil fuels, is the primary source of human-induced climate change. Indigenous Peoples have experienced systematic violations by oil, gas, mining and energy industries infringing on our inherent right to protect our traditional lands."[53]

Even more emphatically, the IAITPTF called for "the full phase-out of fossil fuels, with a just transition to sustainable jobs, energy and environment" and declared, "We are against the expansion of and new exploration for the extraction of oil, natural gas and coal within and near Indigenous lands, especially in pristine and sensitive areas, as well as environmentally, socially, culturally, historically and spiritually significant areas." The IAITPTF declaration also called for more support for indigenous participation at climate change forums and specific inclusion of indigenous people on international agendas, and the creation of an adaptation fund to help them adjust to the impacts of global warming.

The ICC is one of the most active indigenous organizations fighting global warming internationally, frequently publicizing their concerns during the COP. Nunavut resident Sheila Watt-Cloutier, ICC chair from 2002 to 2006, presented the Inuit position on this issue at conferences worldwide. Her personal concern as an Inuit grandmother is "that her grandson will not be able to live the Inuit hunting and food-sharing culture that has sustained Inuit physically and spiritually for generations."[54] In 2005 at the UNFCCC Conference of Parties in Montreal, Watt-Coultier unveiled a formal petition to the Inter-American Commission on Human Rights entitled "Seeking Relief from Violations Resulting from Global Warming Caused by Acts and Omissions of the United States." Her petition was supported by the ICC and was signed by sixty-two other Inuit from Nunavut, Newfoundland, Labrador, Northwest Territories, Quebec, and Alaska "on behalf of all Inuit of the Arctic regions of the United States and Canada." The 167-page petition included 796 footnotes and appealed directly to the original American Declaration of the Rights and Duties of Man, which is recognized to be the world's first general international human rights agreement. The American Declaration was adopted by the founding members of the Organization of American States in 1948, including the United States, months before the UN Declaration of Human Rights was issued.

The main points of the Watt-Cloutier ICC petition were that Inuit life and culture are totally dependent on the environment, and every aspect of the environment is being damaged by global warming. The United States is most responsible for this damage, and it is a violation of the Inuit's human rights to enjoy the benefits of their culture, their lands, personal and intellectual property, health, life and security, their means of subsistence, residence, mobility, and inviolability of the home. All of these rights are specified in the Rights and Duties of Man. The petition accused the U.S. government of failing to reduce greenhouse gas (GHG) emissions, failing to cooperate with international reduction efforts, and obscuring the climate science in order to mislead the public on the urgency of the problem of global warming. The petition did not seek a specific cash settlement for damages, instead requesting the Human Rights Commission to conduct its own on-site investigation, hold hearings, and issue a report specifying the responsibility of the United States and calling on the government to take action to limit GHG emissions, cooperate with UNFCC actions, and help the Inuit protect their culture and resources from the effects of global warming and mitigate the damage caused by the United States. Nearly a year later, in 2006, the Inter-American Commission decided not to process the Watt-Coultier petition, suggesting vaguely that it couldn't determine whether the "alleged facts" actually constituted a violation of rights.

Beginning in 2004 the National Congress of American Indians (NCAI) supported efforts to establish a treaty organization linking indigenous peoples throughout the Pacific region, the United States, and Canada to coordinate efforts to fight global warming and deal with its effects. Representatives from eleven indigenous nations met on Lummi Nation territory in the Pacific Northwest in 2007 and signed a treaty establishing the United League of Indigenous Nations.[55] The initial signers included Maori from New Zealand, Australian Aborigines, as well as First Nations peoples from Canada along with various indigenous nations from the Pacific Northwest and Alaska. In addition to developing an indigenous response to global warming, the objectives of the league included cooperation on trade and border crossings between indigenous nations, and protecting cultural properties. A much larger ratification ceremony with many more indigenous nations was scheduled in Denver later in the year. The first of the league's principles was a "shared commitment to care for, conserve, and protect the land, air, water, and animal life within our usual, customary and traditional territories."[56] Principle 5 stressed "our collective rights over the environment consisting of air, lands, inland waters, oceans, seas, sea ice, flora, fauna and all other surface and subsurface resources." Among the documents posted by the league's Working Group on Climate Change is a report by Zoltán Grossman that calls global warming "the biggest threat to the Earth's well-being in history."[57] Grossman notes that indigenous nations are especially suited to respond to global warming because their traditional ecological and environmental knowledge is likely to be strong, they have a local territory to protect, and they have a strong sense of community. This means that environmental protection is unlikely to be a divisive issue, as it frequently is in the United States. Many tribal governments in North America already have environmental departments, and tribal nations are small enough that they can readily involve all tribal members in a coordinated response to climate-related changes.

Notes

1. U.S. Department of Energy, Energy Information Agency (EIA), 2007, *Annual Energy Review 2006*, Report No. DOE/EIA-0384(2006), posted June 27, 2007, table

11.1, World Primary Energy Production by Source, 1970–2004, http://www.eia.doe.gov/emeu/aer/pdf/pages/sec11_3.pdf.

2. U.S. Department of Energy, Energy Information Agency (EIA), 1999, *Petroleum: An Energy Profile 1999*, ADOE/EIA-0545(99), July, http://tonto.eia.doe.gov/FTPROOT/petroleum/054599.pdf.

3. Edwin Black, 2006, *Internal Combustion: How Corporations and Governments Addicted the World to Oil and Derailed the Alternatives*, New York: St. Martin's Press.

4. Richard Manning, 2004, *Against the Grain: How Agriculture Has Hijacked Civilization*, New York: North Point Press; Vaclav Smil, 2005, *Creating the Twentieth Century: Technical Innovations of 1867–1914 and Their Lasting Impact*, Oxford and New York: Oxford University Press, 186–97.

5. EIA, *Annual Energy Review 2006*, table 11.4, World Crude Oil and Natural Gas Reserves, January 1, 2006.

6. Organization of Petrolelum Exporting Countries (OPEC), 2006, OPEC Share of Crude Oil Reserves (2006), http://www.opec.org/home/PowerPoint/Reserves/OPEC%20share.htm.

7. James B. Davies, Susanna Sandstrom, Anthony Shorrocks, and Edward N. Wolff, 2006, *The World Distribution of Household Wealth*, Helsinki, Finland: World Institute for Development Economics Research, appendix V.

8. Robert Pirog, 2006, *Oil Industry Profit Review 2005, CRS Report for Congress*, Report RL33373, Congressional Research Service, The Library of Congress, CRS-1, http://digital.library.unt.edu/govdocs/crs/data/2006/meta-crs-9209.tkl.

9. Fortune Magazine, 2007, "Fortune Global 500," July 23, http://money.cnn.com/magazines/fortune/global500/2007/.

10. EIA, *Annual Energy Review 2006*, table 11.10, World Petroleum Consumption, 1960–2005.

11. EIA, *Annual Energy Review 2006*, table 11.4, World Crude Oil and Natural Gas Reserves, January 1, 2006.

12. Vaclav Smil, 2005, *Energy at the Crossroads: Global Perspectives and Uncertainties*, Cambridge, MA: MIT Press, 210–12.

13. Gwich'in Steering Committee, 2005, *A Moral Choice for the United States: The Human Rights Implications for the Gwich'in of Drilling in the Arctic National Wildlife Refuge*, Fairbanks, AK: Gwich'in Steering Committee, http://www.gwichinsteeringcommittee.org/GSChumanrightsreport.pdf.

14. U.S. Fish and Wildlife Service, Arctic National Wildlife Refuge: Refuge Features, http://arctic.fws.gov/features.htm.

15. U.S. Geological Survey, 2001, *Arctic National Wildlife Refuge, 1002 Area, Petroleum Assessment, 1998, Including Economic Analysis. Fact Sheet 0028–01*, Online Report, http://pubs.usgs.gov/fs/fs-0028–01/.

16. Gwich'in Steering Committee, *Gwich'in Niintsyaa (Resolution)*, http://www.gwichinsteeringcommittee.org/gwichinniintsyaa.html (accessed September 2007).

17. National Research Council, Committee on Cumulative Environmental Effects of Oil and Gas Activities on Alaska's North Slope, 2003, *Cumulative Environmental Effects of Oil and Gas Activities on Alaska's North Slope*, Washington, DC: National Academies Press.

18. Ibid., 138.

19. Ibid., 139.

20. Gwich'in Steering Committee, 2007, History of Wreckage, http://www.gwichinsteeringcommittee.org/history.html (accessed December 16, 2007).

21. National Research Council, *Cumulative Effects*, Executive Summary, 11, http://www.nap.edu/catalogue/10639.html.

22. Debra K. Higley, 2001, *The Putumayo-Oriente-Maranon Province of Colombia, Ecuador, and Peru—Mesozoic-Cenozoic and Paleozoic Petroleum Systems*, U.S. Geological Survey Digital Data Series 63, http://pubs.usgs.gov/dds/DDS-63/DDS-63.pdf.

23. U.S. Geological Survey World Energy Assessment Team, 2000, *U.S. Geological Survey World Petroleum Assessment 2000: Description and Results*, http://energy.cr.usgs.gov/WEReport.pdf.

24. International Energy Agency, 2007, *Oil in Ecuador in 2004*, http://www.iea.org/Textbase/stats/index.asp.

25. World Bank, 2006, *World Development Report 2006. Equity and Development*, New York: Oxford University Press, 294, table 2.

26. Center for Economic and Social Rights, 1994, *Rights Violations in the Ecuadorian Amazon: The Human Consequences of Oil Development*, New York: Center for Economic and Social Rights, http://www.texacorainforest.com/case/Rights_Violations_1.pdf.

27. Amazon Defense Coalition (Frente de Defensa de la Amazonia, FDA), http://www.ecuanex.net.ec/fda/fda.htm, http://www.texacotoxico.org/.

28. Asamblea de Afectados por las Operaciones Petrtoleras de Texaco; La Organización de la Nacionalidad Indígena Siona del Ecuador (ONISE); La Federación de Indígena de la Nacionalidad Cofán del Ecuador (FEINCE); La Organización Indígena Siona del Ecuador (OISE); La Organización de la Nacionalidad Huaorani del Ecuador (ONAHE), http://www.texacotoxico.org/index.

29. *Aguinda v. Texaco*, http://www.texacorainforest.com/case/ComplaintEcuador.pdf.

30. See, for example, Miguel San Sebastián and Anna-Karin Hurtig, 2004, "Oil exploitation in the Amazon basin of Ecuador: a public health emergency," *Pan American Journal of Public Health* 15(3): 205–11.

31. The Amazon Defense Coalition summarizes its case in Amazon Defense Coalition, 2006, *Rainforest Castrophe: Chevon's Fraud and Deceit in Ecuador: An Investigative Report by the Lago Agrio Legal Team of the Amazon Defense Coalition*, http://www.texacotoxico.org/docs/PDF%20Files/rainforest_catastrophe.pdf. Chevon summarizes its defense in Chevon Corporation, 2007, *Plaintiffs' Myths, Distortions and Falsifications*, http://www.texaco.com/sitelets/ecuador/en/plaintiffs_myths.asp.

32. Gina Chávez, Isabela Figueroa, Paulina Garzón, Marioa Melo, Victor López, and Norman Wray, 2002, *Tarimiat Firmes en Nuestro Territorio: FIPSE vs. ARCO*, 2nd ed., Quito: Centro de Derechos Económicos y Sociales, (CDES), Confederación de Nacionalidades Indígenas del Ecuador, (CONAIE), http://www.escr-net.org/usr_doc/FIPSE_Firmes_en_nuestro_territorio_2002.pdf.

33. Gina Chávez, 2005, *Sarayaku: El Pueblo del Cenít Identidad y Construcción*, Informe antropológico-juridico sobre los impactos sociales y culturales de la Com-

pañia CGC en Sarayaku, Quito, http://www.cdes.org.ec/biblioteca/libros/sarayaku-cenit.pdf.

34. Inter-American Court of Human Rights, 2005, *Resolución de la Corte Interamericana de Derechos Humanos de 17 de Junio de 2005. Medidas Provisionales. Caso Pueblo Indígana de Sarayaku*, http://www.corteidh.or.cr/docs/medidas /sarayaku_se_021.pdf.

35. Rodolfo Stavenhagen, 2006, *Report of the Special Rapporteur on the situation of human rights and fundamental freedoms of indigenous people*, Addendum, Mission to Ecuador, Human Rights Council, A/HRC/4/32/Add.2 28 December, 8–10, http://daccessdds.un.org/doc/UNDOC/GEN/G07/100/29/PDF/G0710029.pdf?OpenE lement.

36. Franco Viteri, 2004, "La Lucha de Sarayaku," *Pueblos en Lucha: Casos emblemáticos de defense de derechos indígenas*, IV Congreso latinoamericano de la Red de Antropología Juridica, Quito: Centro de Derechos Economics y Sociales CDES, 21, my translation.

37. Ibid.

38. Robert Gough and Patrick Spears, 1998, "Foreword," in *Native Peoples-Native Homelands Climate Change Workshop: Final Report*, U.S. Global Change Research Program, ii, http://www.usgcrp.gov/usgcrp/Library/nationalassessment/native.pdf.

39. Jon Barnett and W. Neil Adger, 2003, "Climate Dangers and Atoll Countries," *Climatic Change* 61: 321–37.

40. Schuyler Houser, Verna Teller, Michael MacCracken, Robert Gough, and Patrick Spears, 2001, "Potential Consequences of Climate Variability and Change for Native Peoples and Homelands," National Assessment Synthesis Team, *Climate Change Impacts on the United States: The Potential Consequences of Climate Variability and Change, Report for the US Global Change Research Program*, Cambridge: Cambridge University Press, 372, http://www.gcrio.org/NationalAssessment /12NA.pdf.

41. Andrew C. Revkin, 2007, "Scientists report severe retreat of Arctic ice," *New York Times*, September 21, A6.

42. Houser et al., *Climate Change Impacts*, 366.

43. Arctic Climate Impact Assessment (ACIA), 2004, *Impacts of a Warming Arctic: Arctic Climate Impact Assessment*, Cambridge: Cambridge University Press, http://amap.no/acia/.

44. Martin Parry, Osvaldo Canziani, Jean Palutikof, Paul van der Linden, Clair Hanson, eds., 2007, *Climate Change 2007: Impacts, Adaptation and Vulnerability. Contribution of Working Group II to the Fourth Assessment Report of the Intergovernmental Panel on Climate Change*, New York: Cambridge University Press, http://www.ipcc-wg2.org/.

45. Ibid., figure 13.3, 595.

46. John H. Bodley, 2005, *Cultural Anthropology: Tribes, States, and the Global System*, New York: McGraw-Hill, 3–8.

47. Organización Ashéninka del Gran Pajonal (Gran Pajonal Ashéninka Organization, OAGP).

48. Organización Regional de los Pueblos Indígenas de AIDESEP–Ucayali, (Regional Organization of the Indigenous Peoples of AIDESEP–Ucayali, ORAU).

49. Asociación Interétnica de Desarrollo de la Selva Peruana (Interethnic Development Association of the Peruvian Amazon, AIDESEP), http://www.aidesep.org.pe/.

50. Coordinadora de las Organizaciones Indígenas de la Cuenca Amazónica (Coordinator of Indigenous Organizations of the Amazon Basin, COICA), http://www.coica.org.ec/.

51. International Alliance of Indigenous Peoples of Tropical Forests, http://international-alliance.org/.

52. Roberto Espinoza Llanos, 2004, *Forest Privatization and Indigenous Rights and Knowledge in Peru*, United Nations Forestry Forum, http://www.internationalalliance.org/documents/peru_eng_full.doc.

53. International Alliance of Indigenous Peoples of Tropical Forests (IAITPTF), 2005, *Tiohtiá:ke Declaration: International Indigenous Peoples Forum on Climate Change Statement to the State Parties of the COP 11/MOP 1 of the United Nations Framework Convention on Climate Change (UNFCCC)*, http://www.international-alliance.org/documents/TiohtiakeDeclaration.doc.

54. Sheila Watt-Cloutier, 2005, *Peitition to the InterAmerican Commission on Human Rights Seeking Relief from Violations Resulting from Global Warming Caused by Acts and Omissions of the United States*, December 7, 2005, 129, http://www.ciel.org/Publications/ICC_Petition_7Dec05.pdf.

55. Alan Parker, 2007, *Indigenous Nations Treaty Proceedings July 31–August 2, 2007*, Lummi Indian Nation, http://www.indigenousnationstreaty.org/ReportInterimGovAug10.pdf.

56. United League of Indigenous Nations Treaty, http://www.indigenousnationstreaty.org/SignedTreatyAug1.pdf.

57. Zoltán Grossman, 2007, *Possible Climate Change Responses for a United League of Indigenous Nations*, http://www.indigenousnationstreaty.org/ZoltanClimateChange.doc.

12 Human Rights and the Politics of Ethnocide

Not because they are indigenous peoples, but because they are human beings with indigenous cultures, and with unique ways of being human, should their defense and protection be a matter of the highest-priority concern for all people the world over who care about human rights.

—Christian Bay[1]

THE DESTRUCTION OF INDEPENDENT small-scale tribal societies was an immense human tragedy that was brought about by political decisions that were both inhumane and genocidal. Millions died in the hundred years before 1920, when indigenous peoples were forced to surrender nearly half of the globe. Why was this allowed to happen? Was it the inevitable outcome of evolutionary processes with no viable alternatives? What was the role and responsibility of government administrators, missionaries, and anthropologists? This chapter will examine the response of those organizations and individuals within the expanding industrial societies who were most concerned with the fate of indigenous peoples. We will see that ethnocide was caused by political decisions that denied the human rights of indigenous peoples to an independent existence. Those who accepted ethnocide as inevitable were unable to prevent massive depopulation, and humanitarian efforts to minimize the damage diverted attention from the real political issues and delayed the human rights struggle of indigenous peoples.

The problem of tribal destruction was debated by politicians, religious leaders, and scientists for 150 years from the perspective of two conflicting philosophical camps: the "realists," who felt that ethnocide was inevitable, and the "idealists," who argued that tribal survival was possible (see figure 12.1). Realists accepted the "reality" of national expansion. They assumed that indigenous peoples would ultimately be unable to survive as independent peoples and would either become extinct or be integrated into the dominant national society while losing much of their cultural distinctiveness. This was a false choice. Idealists were both more critical of the frontier process and more optimistic about the possibility of indigenous peoples' maintaining their political and cultural integrity.

251

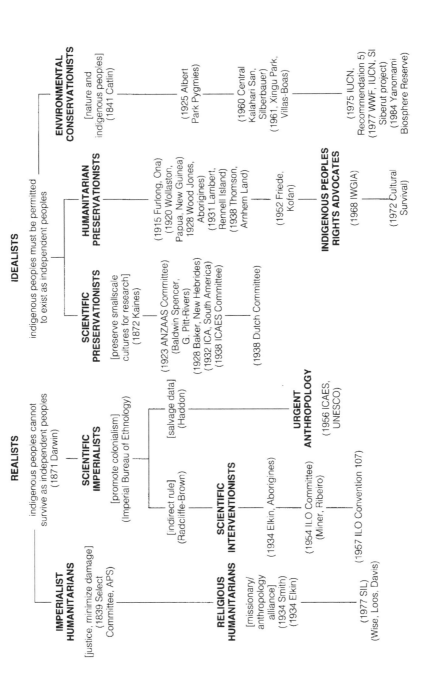

Figure 12.1. Realists and Idealists

The Realists: Humanitarian Imperialists and Scientists

The prevailing realist view that the demise of tribals was inevitable was a self-serving political opinion, not a well-founded scientific judgment. This "myth of inevitability," however, supported government policies of expansion into tribal territories. Unfortunately, the idealist position was largely ignored during the critical early decades of the twentieth century because the debate mistakenly focused on tribal "protection" and "preservation" rather than political self-determination. Realist perspectives dominated policy making until 1968, when idealist organizations began to successfully redefine the tribal survival problem as an issue of community human rights and came to the support of the emerging indigenous political organizations. This shift coincided with global concerns over war, oppression, poverty, and environmental deterioration. Clearly, self-sufficient indigenous peoples would not be the only victims of uncontrolled commercial expansion.

The following sections begin by demonstrating that well into the twentieth century, the scientific community accepted as inevitable the fact that colonial expansion was destroying tribal peoples. We will see that scientists were initially more concerned with the loss of valuable data on indigenous peoples than with the inhumanity of tribal genocide and ethnocide. Next, the rise of applied anthropology will be linked to the efforts by realist anthropologists to minimize the damage to tribal societies while supporting imperialist expansion into tribal areas. Finally, detailed case studies of three realist organizations will be presented: the Aborigines Protection Society, the Summer Institute of Linguistics, and the World Bank.

Vanishing Data and the Reality of Genocide

Regardless of the inherent vitality of indigenous peoples, the overwhelming historical reality, which was well established early in the nineteenth century, was that indigenous peoples died and their cultures disintegrated when Europeans invaded their territory. The British Parliamentary Select Committee on Aborigines acknowledged this fact in their official reports of 1836–1837. Even Charles Darwin included a discussion of the "extinction of savage tribes" in *The Descent of Man* and attributed it to "competition" with civilized races.[2] Anthropologists first saw the impending end of small-scale societies and their cultures in terms of vanishing data to be salvaged and then as an opportunity to make anthropology an applied science.

From the 1870s on, the extinction of tribal societies was a frequent theme in the anthropology section of the British Association for the Advancement of Science and at the meetings of the Royal Anthropological Institute (RAI), where it was assumed that the Pacific Islanders, the Andamanese, the Bushmen, and the Australian Aborigines, among others, all faced "utter extinction" and would soon follow the Tasmanians, who were considered extinct by 1876. Many of these dire predictions proved wrong, however: Not all small-scale cultures died out (even the Tasmanians survived), and the resilience of these cultures and the human capacity for resistance were often vastly underrated, as chapter 10 demonstrated. But the point here is that genocide and ethnocide were occurring on an unprecedented scale, as the physical anthropologist W. H. Flower made clear before the British Association in 1881: "We live in an age in which, in a far greater degree than any previous one, the destruction of races, both by annihilation and absorption, is going on."[3]

Perhaps the most striking demonstration that anthropologists were fully aware of the scope of the destruction of indigenous peoples was their frantic attempt to save the vanishing data, which became a major theme at professional meetings beginning in the 1870s. As Col. A. H. Lane Fox Pitt-Rivers declared in his address to the anthropology section of the British Association in 1871, vital data are "rapidly disappearing from the face of the earth."[4] He joined E. B. Tylor, John Lubbock, and others to prepare the original version of *Notes and Queries* as a guide to salvage anthropology.[5]

Although some authorities attributed the extermination of small-scale cultures to degeneration, most agreed that it was an inevitable result of colonial expansion. It is indeed curious that so few anthropologists challenged the underlying assumption that indigenous groups could not continue to exist as autonomous peoples. Thus, while everyone assumed that unlimited colonialism would doom all indigenous peoples, few anthropologists were willing to urge the obvious step of stabilizing the frontiers and thereby preventing the destruction. The reasons for this failure are complex, but they do not exonerate those involved.

Scientific Imperialists and Applied Anthropology

The realists had their roots in the philosophy of nineteenth-century social Darwinism, which assumed that European expansion was natural and inevitable and would ultimately benefit the whole world. Several realist subgroups can be distinguished: The imperialist humanitarians began with the British Parliamentary Select Committee members, who criticized the destructiveness of tribal policy in the 1830s and founded the Aborigines Protection Society in 1839. These humanitarians wanted justice for dispossessed indigenous peoples and hoped to minimize the harm done to them. This approach eventually led to alliances among anthropologists, missionaries, and governments, such as Brazil's Indian Protection Service (1910) and the Summer Institute of Linguistics (1934).

Another realistic subgroup, the scientific imperialists, dates from the founding of anthropology as a scientific discipline and was exemplified by the unsuccessful nineteenth-century efforts of the Royal Anthropological Institute to establish an Imperial Bureau of Ethnology as a support for the colonial enterprise and to serve as a repository for vanishing data. The scientific imperialists eventually split into two main branches: the scientific interventionists, who were applied anthropologists seeking to combine scientific respect for tribal culture with economic development and integration of the tribals into the national society, and the salvage anthropologists, whose primary concern was to save vanishing data. British anthropologists especially were eager to support the expanding empire and could be labeled *scientific imperialists*.

The response of anthropologists to the crisis of indigenous peoples, aside from the rush to save vanishing data, was to develop the field of applied anthropology. The term *applied anthropology* was coined by RAI president Lane Fox Pitt-Rivers in 1881 to classify a paper entitled "On the Laws Affecting the Relations between Civilized and Savage Life . . . ," which was read before the RAI by colonial administrator Sir Bartle Frere.[6] Frere felt that natural law required "savages" to surrender their political autonomy and become integrated into the dominant society in order to survive.

Some early observers of the extermination of tribal societies recognized that the problem was in the seemingly irreconcilable differences between small-scale and global-scale societies. Although unwilling to condemn colonial expansion itself, they felt that the damage to tribals could be minimized, as Flower expressed in his presidential address to the RAI in 1883: "And when we have to do with people still more widely removed from ourselves, African Negroes, American Indians, Australian or Pacific Islanders, it seems almost impossible to find any common ground of union or modus vivendi; the mere contact of races generally ends in the extermination of one of them. If such disastrous consequences cannot be altogether averted, we have it still in our power to do much to mitigate their evils."[7]

This gloomy optimism was echoed a year later by A. L. P. Cameron in his notes about the vanishing tribes in Australia's New South Wales. He saw the destruction of the tribes as unavoidable: "Experience everywhere proves that races in a state of savagery, and even those races which are beginning to emerge from it, are unable to withstand the advance of European civilization. But it is to be hoped that something will be done without delay to at least ameliorate the condition of the tribes now fading from the earth under the influence of our presence."[8]

Early applied anthropologists were confident that they were doing science, not politics. Reverend Edwin W. Smith, missionary president of the RAI, argued that anthropology should be a "coldly neutral," value-free science when in the service of "practical undertakings," yet it was not to be yoked to "politics, to religion, to nationalism, [or] to philosophy."[9] Value-based policy opinions were not to be passed off as science. However, for Smith anthropology was "not an enemy of progress," and he did not advocate preserving indigenous peoples.

Realist Humanitarians: The Aborigines Protection Society

Throughout the nineteenth century, since its founding in 1839, the Aborigines Protection Society (APS) was the only major humanitarian organization to lobby for just policies toward tribals. The APS favored limited tribal land rights but not the political autonomy of tribal peoples, and it supported the conquest of tribal areas as long as it was carried out justly—although "justice" for the APS apparently only meant protection from direct violence. The motives of the APS were both humanitarian and practical, and although it did not advocate the independent existence of indigenous peoples, this organization set the standard of enlightened policy toward tribals. Operating at the height of the colonial era, the APS did much to reduce the worst abuses against indigenous peoples. However, its benevolent policies were frequently ignored by colonial authorities, and it was unable to prevent the extermination of millions of indigenous peoples. Even if the APS had argued for the right of indigenous peoples to freely follow their own way of life, it probably would have found few supporters in a rapidly developing commercial world that still accepted the legitimacy of imperial expansion by wars of conquest. In 1839 the International Red Cross did not yet exist, and in Europe there was no Geneva Convention to limit the atrocities of war.

The APS was founded by a group of British philanthropists who succeeded in abolishing slavery in the British Empire by 1833 and realized that a similar political struggle was needed on behalf of indigenous peoples to ensure that they were not also victimized by colonial expansion. But unfortunately, at this critical juncture the wrong issue was raised. In 1835 Thomas Buxton, one of the founders of the APS and a member of the British Parliament, succeeded in having the House of Commons Select Committee on Aborigines appointed, with the objective of ensuring that indigenous peoples on the expanding frontiers of empire were treated justly. This attempt to combine colonial expansionism with justice toward indigenous peoples has dominated the realist approach to the "native problem" up to the present time. Over the years, few observers have even suggested that the real question is not how to secure the progress of commercial nations while at the same time extending justice and humanity to indigenous peoples, but rather, whether forcing "civilization" onto indigenous peoples is a just and humane process in and of itself. In retrospect, it is not surprising that in the 1830s the problem of indigenous peoples was not viewed in these terms—the concepts of *human rights* and *self-determination* of peoples had simply not reached such a stage.

The original objective of the APS was to "assist in protecting the defenseless and promoting the advancement of uncivilized tribes." Here again, as with the Select Committee, the right of tribals to maintain their independent existence was not recognized as an issue. The "advancement" of tribes meant that they were to lose their political independence, participate in the economic life of the colonies, and adopt the Christian religion of their conquerors. The primary issue raised by the APS was that this was to occur humanely. The objection was to "unjust invasion," not to the right of political conquest of peoples by states. The right of tribes to maintain control over their lands, often in specially demarcated reserves, was frequently argued by the APS, but the right to remain "uncivilized" was not considered. It is not surprising that the APS merely continued the program of the Select Committee, because Buxton, the first APS president, was also chair of the Select Committee, and four other members of the Select Committee became members of the executive committee of the APS. The religious element in the APS is conspicuous in the fact that several prominent members of the Society of Friends were incorporated in the executive committee.

The APS listed some 281 members in 1839, including 27 religious ministers and representatives from twelve European countries and the United States. Regular public meetings were held in London, and the society's activities were frequently reported in the press. Certainly, the APS was highly successful in focusing public attention on the condition and needs of indigenous peoples, mainly through the publication and distribution of inexpensive pamphlets.

The APS proposed new policies and, by means of written petitions and personal meetings, directly influenced the adoption of legislation, or the intervention of government officials, on behalf of indigenous peoples. It also functioned as a watchdog to see that the laws it helped formulate were followed and that infractions were punished.

One of the primary architects and most active agents of the APS was Thomas Hodgkin, who was also a founder of the society. Under his guidance, the APS attempted with varying degrees of success to intervene on behalf of indigenous peoples in Canada, southern Africa, Australia, and New Zealand. Because colonial rule in Australia had barely begun in 1839, when the APS was founded, the society was in a favorable position to influence policy to benefit the Aborigines. The petitions of the APS and its detailed publications on conditions in Australia were instrumental in the appointment of Protectors of Natives, who were able to buffer the Aborigines from some of the worst types of frontier violence. In 1850, when the extension of the sheep industry was depriving Aborigines of their subsistence and driving them to desperation and ultimate extermination, the APS advocated the establishment of aboriginal reserves, which would combine schools, missions, and farms.

The economic utility of preserving indigenous peoples, but not their cultures, remained a dominant theme for the APS because this was the best way to convince both the public and the government that it made sense to protect Aborigines. If indigenous peoples were to be preserved, they had to become useful farmers, stockkeepers, seamen, and domestic servants. It was thought better to protect than to destroy them, because "self-interest is on the side of justice and mercy."[10]

Throughout the remainder of the nineteenth century, the APS concentrated much of its attention on problems in Africa. It lobbied for international agreements by the colonial nations to reduce frontier abuses as Africa was partitioned at the end of the nineteenth century. But these efforts did not achieve the positive results intended, especially in view of the atrocities committed in the Congo Free State. In Australia the influence of the APS declined as the colonies became more self-governing, and in many areas, such as Tasmania and New South Wales, the Aborigines became less of a problem because so many had been exterminated. In the Pacific the APS attempted, with only limited success, to gain international agreements to limit the availability of guns and alcohol and to regulate the activities of traders and labor recruiters who operated as slavers.

By the end of the century, the APS came to view itself as a combination appellate court for mistreated natives and an advisory body for colonial administrators. In spite of the terrible attrition of indigenous peoples that continued to mark the advance of colonial frontiers, even with the best efforts of the APS to ameliorate conditions, the organization was still not prepared to challenge the legitimacy of colonial expansion. On the contrary, the APS often found it necessary to apologize for its incessant criticism of colonial practice. The APS was, after all, merely setting the standard of humane imperialism— it was not an anti-imperialist organization.

The Aborigines Protection Society eventually merged with the Anti-Slavery Society, which continues to be concerned with indigenous peoples and now can be considered a general human rights organization. As the era of colonial empire building passed, Christian missionary organizations began to play a prominent role as self-styled defenders of the welfare of tribal groups. The following section will examine the realist philosophy of one such organization, the Summer Institute of Linguistics.

Jungle Realities: The SIL Philosophy

The Summer Institute of Linguistics (SIL) is an organization of Bible translators and linguists founded in 1934 by the American missionary-linguist William Cameron Townsend and based on his realist humanitarian philosophy that Christianity, introduced through the Bible in the native language, provides the best means for helping "needy and oppressed" indigenous peoples. The SIL is composed of two corporate entities: the Wycliffe Bible Translators, which presents its religious missionary role to the home churches in the United States and Europe that provide most of the dual organizations' financial support, and the SIL proper, which operates in the field. The SIL has become perhaps the largest organization directly concerned with the welfare of indigenous peoples throughout the world.[11]

With the rise of indigenous self-determination movements in the 1970s, the SIL came under increasing criticism by native groups and their idealist supporters, who objected to the SIL's role in promoting the economic penetration of tribal areas by outsiders while offering Christianity and the promise of economic progress as compensation.[12] In 1976 the SIL defended its intervention philosophy before the 42nd International Congress of Americanists (ICA) meeting in Paris. The SIL's argument was that the introduction of Christianity would help native peoples adapt to the "inevitable contact and change" more easily while retaining their ethnic identities.[13] The implication was that those who condemned missionary intervention were adopting an unrealistic and romantic attitude that apparently ignored the fact that cultures change and that most tribal groups had already experienced either direct or indirect contact with outsiders.

Of course, the reality that culture change is a "normal and inevitable" occurrence is not a matter of dispute. What is at issue is the degree to which contact and change is imposed upon indigenous peoples by the political and economic policies of the dominant society. The SIL accepted the "reality" of existing policies by arguing that "contact and change" was inevitable and that it was the responsibility of Christian missionaries to make it less destructive and to help tribals to adapt to this "reality." The SIL philosophy at that time was clearly not a spirited defense of the self-determination approach.

According to the SIL, native groups faced a wave of outsiders, from oil prospectors and tourists to missionaries and travelers. They also acknowledged the "reality" that these "contacts" were often destructive and that not only was "culture change" occurring, but the natives were being deprived of their territories and resources and were being politically marginalized. However, this was an unavoidable process in the SIL view, because even groups that retreated into remote areas containing nothing of value for the dominant society would eventually be surrounded by civilization. Furthermore, even if they were successful in evading civilization for a time, the natives would eventually seek contact themselves out of a desire to obtain manufactured goods. However, a desire for industrial goods did not necessarily mean that they also sought externally imposed culture change, welcomed missionaries, or were abandoning their political autonomy.

The SIL philosophy also stressed that the natives might not always want to maintain all aspects of their culture and quoted a Candoshi Indian's statement that the Candoshi would not wish to continue headhunting. Furthermore, the natives might be eager to learn about the outside world. Again, this is not the issue. The real point is that these should be internal cultural matters for the tribals to work out themselves, without the pressure of outside intervention, whether from oil companies or missionaries. The SIL may have been unwilling to take a stronger position against intrusion into tribal territories at that time because of its own interest in evangelism. The position it took did support native culture: "Not desiring to force the members of a marginal group to adjust to other forms, nor obligating them to maintain their status quo (if that were possible), it is necessary to find an alternative to help them to retain their identity within a viable, strong, united, and just culture, whose values can survive in the face of culture contact."[14]

This solution assumed that tribals must adapt to externally imposed "culture contact," which meant that the underlying political and economic policies imposing such "contact" went unchallenged. It also implied that something was wrong with the tribal culture that outsiders could, and should, correct. The SIL actually offered guidelines for distinguishing between "positive" and "negative" tribal culture traits. Although official SIL policy was to maintain political neutrality, considering itself a "guest" in each country in which it worked, it argued that intervention in a tribal culture by anthropologists or missionaries for the purpose of reducing "negative" culture traits was appropriate and professionally ethical. Ideally, the SIL argued, this kind of intervention would not destroy the culture; rather, it would judiciously work within the culture.

In response to its critics, the SIL stated that it was not acting paternalistically; it was creating neither dependency nor domination. It was merely providing tools with which the tribals could accommodate themselves in their own way to the "new sociological realities" that they must face. Its role was to promote "fruitful cultural interchange," not cultural domination.

In some respects, the SIL philosophy attempted to represent itself as both realist and idealist. It accepted the inevitability of conquest but denied that ethnocide must follow. Indeed, cultural destruction is not always complete. In the SIL view, ethnocide was not a valid concept, and it would lead to pessimism if one equated ethnocide with culture change imposed by the inevitable progress of civilization. According to Dale W. Kietzman,[15] an SIL member, the term *ethnocide* is ambiguous, because many tribals survive as ethnic groups even though they undergo large-scale cultural change. Kietzman was interested in identifying those factors that make ethnic survival possible, because, in line with the SIL philosophy, he considered the advance of civilization and the consequent transformation of tribal cultures to be unstoppable:

> It will be impossible to divert the sweep of a commercially oriented, energy-deficient civilization through the Amazon basin. Nationalism and pressures of population growth impel exploitation of underpopulated areas.[16]

> The course of Brazilian national development makes it inevitable that all tribes will be brought into permanent contact with Brazilian society.[17]

Of course, Kietzman considered any talk of "isolating" tribals "impractical" and "authoritarian," but he felt that there must be ways of helping threatened Indian groups to adapt "in an orderly manner." Successful adaptation for Kietzman was phrased in terms of *integration*, as Brazilian anthropologist Darcy Ribeiro originally defined it in 1957: "Specifically, tribal peoples adapt by developing greater resistance to disease and divesting themselves of their linguistic and cultural uniqueness."[18]

Kietzman pointed out that many of the "integrated" tribes in Brazil in fact managed to retain their languages and some distinctive cultural traits. In his final list of policy recommendations designed to give the tribals a chance at "gradual and voluntary accommodation to new ways,"[19] Kietzman emphasized the need to safeguard tribal territory and to permit the Indians to determine their pace of change.

Although missionary organizations remain a dominant influence on tribal groups in many parts of the world, since 1960, international lending agencies have come to play a more strategic role by providing financial support for government projects designed to develop tribal areas. The following section examines the realist policy position of the World Bank, the single most influential such agency.

The World Bank: *Operational Manual* 2005 and False Assurances

> How can the government harmonize its interest in the development of a rich ore body or a major hydro potential with the need to safeguard the rights of the tribal people in the project area? These are matters for judgements guided by the principle that Bank assistance should help prevent or mitigate harm, and provide adequate time and conditions for acculturation.[20]

The World Bank, or the International Bank for Reconstruction and Development, a UN affiliate founded in 1945, has had an enormous impact on indigenous peoples because it is one of the world's largest funding agencies for large-scale development programs. For example, in 1983 it approved more than 14 billion dollars in financial assistance to some eighty countries. In 2006 the bank loaned 23.6 billion dollars and had outstanding loans and credits totaling 230 billion dollars.[21] The bank is owned by its 144 member countries and loans money to governments for the primary purpose of promoting economic growth and improving living standards. Unfortunately, many of the projects that it has supported, such as hydroelectric development in India and the Philippines, transmigration in Indonesia, and agricultural development, colonization, and highway construction in Brazil, have forced indigenous populations off their lands and have even led to loss of life. Such programs, as noted in previous chapters, generated armed resistance by tribals and caused international criticism of the World Bank itself. Already under attack for the environmental damage that bank-funded projects had caused, the bank responded to its critics in 1982 by issuing a public document presenting what it considered to be idealistic policy guidelines for funding projects that might affect tribals.[22]

Publication of a formal policy on tribals and development by such a powerful multinational lending agency as the World Bank was a clear measure of the growing strength of indigenous political organizations. However, close inspection of the bank's policy statement at that time reveals serious contradictions. Even though it contained some idealist language, it fell within the realist, albeit humanitarian, perspective. Although the document declared emphatically that the bank would not support projects that tribals rejected, and although it endorsed what it called "cultural autonomy" and "freedom of choice" by tribals in development matters, it was clear that the bank believed that ultimately tribals would be "developed" and would have to surrender their independent existence.

Publicly, the bank acknowledged that national development projects often had disastrous consequences for tribals, but it argued that such failures were due to improperly designed projects, and the bank failed to admit any incompatibility between short-run national development goals and the long-term interests of specific tribal groups. The bank advocated the demarcation of tribal lands, but it also had guidelines for "forced removals" in cases where national interests must override tribal land rights. In reality, the bank seemed unwilling to insist upon special rights for tribal groups that might keep developers out in order to perpetuate their existence as independent communities. Instead, the emphasis was on "interim safeguards" in order to minimize the damage "until the tribe adapts sufficiently" or on the need to "minimize the imposition of different social or economic systems until such time as the tribal society is sufficiently robust and resilient to tolerate the effects of change."[23]

This kind of realism accepted the continuing necessity of national expansion, while proclaiming humanitarian concerns for the people who are harmed in the process. In the bank's view, political self-determination and economic autonomy were not "realistic" goals for tribals, because such goals might give them too much control over their natural resources. The bank's policy stated that the most favorable outcome for tribals was to become "accepted ethnic minorities,"[24] and it carefully avoided linking "ethnicity" to any special community-level human rights or unique political status. These points are significant.

The bank apparently recognized the contradictions between the idealist passages within its policy statement and its actual policy in practice. Bank spokesmen quickly denied that the statement was a "policy statement," preferring instead to call it a "working paper." By 1984, editions of the document began to appear with the disclaimer that it was "unofficial" and did "not necessarily represent the Bank's official policy." In 1986 a spokesman for the World Bank told the Committee of Experts working on the revision of the ILO's Convention 107 that on tribal matters the bank followed secret internal policy guidelines, not its own public policy. In fact, the bank admitted that it did not feel tribals had the right to block development projects because this would give the tribals special privileges. The bank's internal guidelines, which "unofficially" came to light, revealed an underlying realist political philosophy that tribals represented a "stage" of "acculturation," which they would outgrow in time.[25] Conflicts between tribal and national interests were acknowledged, but they were to be resolved in favor of the state, with the harm to tribals "mitigated."

The World Bank became more sensitive to criticism of its lending policies in the 1980s, when environmentalist and pro–indigenous peoples groups mounted a campaign aimed at the U.S. congressional committee that oversees appropriations for the American contribution to the bank.[26] The United States dramatically reduced its support for the bank in 1987, which forced the bank to reassess its policies. An immediate outcome was a reduction in Indonesia's transmigration program, which had negatively impacted indigenous group in Irian Jaya, former Dutch New Guinea.

The bank issued new operational directives for dealing with indigenous people in 1991 to ensure that tribals would benefit from bank-funded projects and that "adverse effects" would be avoided or mitigated.[27] The new key concept was *informed participation* by indigenous people, and the entire process was more formalized, but many obvious problems remained in practice. The bank issued a new indigenous people policy directive in its 2005 *Operational Manual*,[28] this time "ensuring that the development process fully respects the dignity, human rights, economies, and cultures of Indigenous Peoples." The language is somewhat different, but the substance may be the same. The new policy replaces "participation" with "consultation," and retains the possibility of going forward with projects that do cause adverse effects. Under the 2005 manual: "The Bank provides project financing only where free, prior, and informed consultation results in broad community support to the project by the affected Indigenous Peoples. Such Bank-financed projects include measures to (a) avoid potentially adverse effects on the Indigenous Peoples' communities; or (b) when avoidance is not feasible, minimize, mitigate, or compensate for such effects. Bank-financed projects are also designed to ensure that the Indigenous Peoples receive social and economic benefits that are culturally appropriate and gender and intergenerationally inclusive."

The World Bank sets a policy standard, and regional development banks, such as the Inter-American Development Bank (IADB), and major bilateral international development agencies, such as the United States Agency for International Development (USAID), are now likely to take indigenous peoples into account in their projects. However, even when consultation and participation are part of the process, the really large projects these agencies support are often the most damaging to indigenous people. The operation manuals and published guidelines may lend the appearance that all problems will be solved, when the reality for indigenous peoples and the environment still turns out very badly. The contradiction that remains unresolved by even the best set of guidelines is that large-scale projects by their very nature are risky and likely to have adverse affects, and would therefore not have "broad community support" from indigenous peoples.

Massive projects, especially when they involve energy development, still go forward, and massive mistakes are still made. For example, in 2003 the IADB provided 75 million dollars toward the gas pipeline portion of the controversial 820-million-dollar Camisea project, in which an international consortium of energy corporations has developed a natural gas field in the Urubamba region of the Peruvian Amazon.[29] Gas began flowing through the pipeline in 2004, and there immediately were breaks and gas explosions that damaged the rainforest and indigenous subsistence resources. The long-term negative social impacts are only just beginning, but the IADB and the World Bank's International Finance Corporation was already considering an expanded Camisea II project.[30]

The Camisea project throws open a region that was a natural refuge for many independent indigenous groups, including some that have until now managed to remain virtually isolated. Several protected areas, communal reserves, and community lands were designated for indigenous peoples in the process, but how well these lands will be protected is uncertain, and the long-term impacts of oil and gas development in this sensitive area may be catastrophic.

There are bureaucratic safeguards in place for every contingency, but they may prove quite ineffective. In response to the new international concerns for indigenous peoples and the environment, the Peruvian Ministry of Energy and Mines requires that social and environmental impact assessments be conducted before any petroleum development can be carried out. There is even a specific "Management Plan in Case of Contact with Isolated Native Populations" included as an appendix in the community relations guide to protect indigenous groups who are living in "voluntary isolation." Of course, the precautionary principle would suggest that large development projects should not be carried out in territories that are known to be occupied by isolated tribes. Nevertheless, the response plan for a surprise encounter between an oil company worker and a potentially hostile isolated group recommends that the worker should not get too close, but should first find the native interpreter to identify their ethnic affiliation and learn their intentions. Presumably this would be "consultation" and "participation." The worker should also notify their local supervisor, contractor, subcontractor supervisor, or local primary corporate official, who should in turn contact the corporate safety and environment official at the head office in Lima.[31] The encounter could then be appropriately logged as an event for the monthly report.

The more detailed contingency plan recommends that oil exploration teams that cut paths and set off explosive charges for seismic testing need to have well-educated indigenous translators handy who should explain their presence to the natives they might inadvertently encounter as follows: "We are peaceful people, we have not come to fight, or to cause harm to your women and children. We have not come to live on your land, we are only passing through, we are working and we know that these are your lands. We have come to work, to know this land, that is why you hear noises [explosions]. These activities will not hurt the forest, the rivers, or your animals. We have not come to hunt, nor fish, nor to collect forest products. We have our own food."[32]

The drilling rigs, roads, and pipelines that follow might completely negate these reassurances, but at least the official guidelines will have been followed, and the World Bank can properly provide millions of dollars for the project.

The Idealist Preservationists

In contrast to the historically proexpansionist conservatism of the humanitarian and anthropological organizations, a minority of well-informed individuals argued the unpopular and unprofitable position that small-scale self-sufficient cultures were still viable and could be saved—if the appropriate authorities had the will to do so. At least three main groups shared the common theme that indigenous peoples should be left alone, free of outside intrusion: scientific preservationists, humanitarian preservationists, and environmental conservationists (see figure 12.2). Scientific preservationists wanted small-scale cultures preserved for scientific purposes, usually to save the vanishing data. Humanitarian preservationists wanted small-scale cultures left alone because they felt this was the only way to prevent the ultimate destruction of these peoples. Environmental conservationists wanted to preserve both small-scale cultures and their natural environments. The following sections will review the development of each of these approaches.

Human Zoos: The Scientific Preservationists

In 1872 Joseph Kaines, a member of the Royal Anthropological Institute, told the British Association for the Advancement of Science that anthropologists have the "duty" of working to preserve disappearing tribals because the development of their science depended on the survival of tribes.[33] At first the idea of tribal preservation attracted little interest because of the prevailing opinion that tribals were inevitably doomed to extinction. However, between the world wars, from about 1920 to 1938, there were many specific proposals for the preservation of tribals for scientific purposes, although they were seldom implemented because there were few economic advantages in preservation and there was invariably opposition by development interests. This subsection examines several such proposals.

A tribal conservation proposal was presented to the Australian Association for the Advancement of Science (ANZAAS) by a group of anthropologists in 1923. ANZAAS passed a resolution calling for the segregation of certain select, but unspecified, areas in the Pacific containing "uncontaminated" indigenous peoples to preserve them for study. A Committee on Vital Statistics of Primitive Races was set up in order to monitor demographic conditions within designated tribal areas. Vast reserves were created by the Australian government in the 1920s, but these areas were not sanctuaries where Aborigines would be free to live independently.

In 1928 British zoologist John R. Baker[34] proposed a quarantine of the six hundred native residents of the island of Gaua in the New Hebrides to determine if they could escape depopulation and preserve their culture by avoiding European influence. Baker ironically observed that interesting animals were legally protected, whereas "anthropological treasures" were allowed to disappear, but he did not link his proposal directly with environmental conservation. Dr. S. M. Lambert, health officer for the Commonwealth Health Service in the western Pacific, advocated a similar quarantine for Rennell Is-

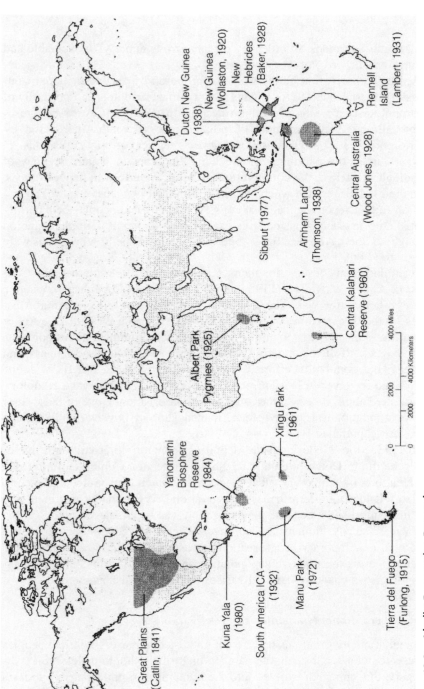

Figure 12.2. Idealist Preservation Proposals

land, in the Solomons, in order to "preserve in its entirety" its valuable and "almost untouched" Polynesian culture.[35]

A tribal conservation policy was also proposed by the International Congress of Americanists (ICA), a scholarly organization composed primarily of anthropologists specializing in the Americas. In 1932 the ICA passed a resolution calling for "conservation" of Indian peoples in South America for scientific purposes. The resolution envisioned the creation of "indigenous reserves," under the patronage of the ICA, "in order to obtain, in view of ethnological interest, the conservation of South American indigenous races, with their languages, and where possible, with their own customs."[36] The resolution further recommended that conservation of tribal peoples be a permanent theme in successive congresses in order to monitor implementation throughout South America, but it appears that none of the ICA proposals were ever carried out.

A similar tribal conservation theme emerged at the 1938 International Congress of Anthropological and Ethnological Sciences in Copenhagen, where a research committee was established "For the Study of Governmental Measures for the Conservation of Aboriginal Peoples Whose Ways of Life Are of Scientific Interest." This committee included such prominent anthropologists as A. R. Radcliffe-Brown, Alfred Kroeber, Paul Rivet, Diamond Jenness, and Donald Thomson, but its efforts were interrupted by World War II. When the committee reconvened in 1946, it shifted its emphasis to salvage ethnology and applied anthropology rather than tribal conservation. None of these early conservation proposals gained any permanent support, however; in fact, some were later repudiated.

In 1938 the Nederlandsche Commissie voor Internationale Natuurbescherming (Dutch International Nature Protection Committee) proposed the creation of a temporary tribal sanctuary in Dutch New Guinea. The committee felt that long-term tribal "preservation" was probably unethical and certainly impossible, because modernization was inevitable, and they specifically rejected any "human zoo" approach. Their final recommendations were presented as temporary "conservation" measures to strictly regulate culture contact in order to minimize depopulation and destabilization and to give anthropologists a chance to study the tribes before they disappeared.[37]

Leave Them Alone: Humanitarian Preservationists

Humanitarian preservationists were not interested in preserving tribal peoples as research objects; instead, they argued that tribals should be left alone. Ultimately, this approach evolved into the humanitarian philosophy of today's advocates for the human rights of indigenous peoples. Initially, scientific organizations were often reluctant to endorse such an approach on purely humanitarian grounds, but many individuals did, and a sampling of their views is presented here.

Charles Wellington Furlong, a lieutenant colonel and resident of Boston who visited the surviving hunting and gathering tribes of Tierra del Fuego in 1907–1908, had great admiration for the ability of the "splendid" Ona tribe to deal successfully with an extremely harsh environment.[38] The Ona's more exposed neighbors, the Alacaluf and Yahgan, were on the brink of extinction due to devastating contacts with civilization. In contrast, Furlong found the outlook for the Ona more hopeful because of the natural protection provided by their remote environment, which held little appeal for outsiders. The Ona occupied the interior of the great island of Tierra del Fuego as well as the coast, and the southern half of the island was blanketed with impenetrable forests, bogs, and snow-covered mountains. Under the disruptive effects of European sheep farming and missionary work, the Ona population plummeted from three thousand in the early 1880s to five hundred by 1910.

As a solution, Furlong recommended that the governments of Chile and Argentina, which divided the island of Tierra del Fuego in two, should permanently reserve the Ona's present natural refuge for their "sole use," especially because it appeared to have little development potential. He also urged that the reserve be restocked with wild guanacos (related to the camel and llama) from the mainland in order to maintain the Ona's primary subsistence resource. Although he realized that this was a "dim hope," Furlong felt that such a policy would be a credit to Chile and Argentina and if it were carried out, "[t]his little remnant of people would be saved and the tribe preserved."[39]

Australian physical anthropologist Frederic Wood Jones took an antimissionary, prohumanitarian preservationist stance toward self-sufficient Aborigines in his 1926 presidential address before the anthropology section of ANZAAS.[40] He quoted the complete text of A. F. R. Wollaston's 1920 plea to the Royal Geographical Society that interior New Guinea be left as an independent tribal area. Wollaston had recommended that the New Guinea interior be left "as a native reserve where these people can live their own life" with no outside interference. [41]

Wood Jones accepted as a scientifically respectable verdict that such reserves would be the only way to guarantee "the racial survival for such people as the Australian Aborigine."[42] He argued that it was land appropriation and prolonged contact with civilization that doomed Aborigines to a "lingering but certain death." Missionary welfare and schooling were inadequate compensation, which he called "euthanasia." Wood Jones rejected the notion that the extinction of the Aborigine was inevitable. In a departure from the reservation system earlier proposed by Baldwin Spencer,[43] which provided for missionaries, schooling, and the interests of settlers, Wood Jones instead advocated "real reserves" that would allow the continuation of tribal culture and traditions.

However, in reviewing the recent history of reserve policy in Australia, Wood Jones was forced to conclude that while the government had bowed to public opinion and pressure from international scientific organizations and established "reserves" for Aborigines in central Australia, in fact these were only "fictions and frauds" because they existed only on paper and were revoked whenever outside economic interests demanded entry. He declared, "There are no real reserves in Australia where the Aborigine is free to live, what everyone is agreed on calling, a life uncontaminated by the white man."[44]

A similar preservation policy was advocated by anthropologist Donald Thomson, who was commissioned by the Australian federal government in 1934 to investigate conditions in the Arnhem Land aboriginal reserve and make policy recommendations after the Aborigines killed five Japanese fishermen and a policeman. Alone and unarmed, Thomson contacted the hostile groups and spent nearly two years with them, from 1935 to 1937. He concluded that the fifteen hundred independent Aborigines who remained in Arnhem Land were "on the road to extinction" and had acted in self-defense in killing intruders. Thomson felt that it was still possible for the Aborigines to remain self-sufficient if given a chance, and that the government would be directly responsible if they were allowed to die. The most remarkable aspect of Thomson's report was the "positive action" he recommended: He felt that the Aborigines should be left in occupation of their own territory and that steps should be taken to "preserve their culture intact." Specifically, Thomson called for (1) "absolute segregation" of the Arnhem Land reserve, (2) complete preservation of the social structure "in toto," (3) complete preservation of the nomadic settlement pattern, (4) protective patrols to prevent outside intrusion, and (5) medical intervention to eliminate yaws, leprosy, and introduced diseases.[45]

Perhaps the most important of Thomson's recommendations was his call for absolute segregation, which would exclude labor recruiters, stockmen, and missionaries from the reserve. He felt this measure was essential because of the cultural and physical vulnerability of the Aborigines. Thomson's proposals were apparently interrupted by World War II and found little support in Australia's anthropological community at the time. However, missionary development was in fact limited, and serious mineral development did not begin in Arnhem Land until the 1960s. The absence of roads and the general remoteness of this region helped maintain a de facto isolation of Arnhem Land from the rest of Australia.

Another statement of support for the right of indigenous peoples to an independent existence was presented by Colombian anthropologist Juan Friede at the 30th ICA meeting at Cambridge in 1952. Friede discussed the situation of the Cofán, a threatened indigenous group living in the upper Amazon of Colombia. At the end of his paper he declared: "The only solution, in my view, would be to recognize for the Cofán, as also for the other indigenous groups of Colombia, their rights as racial minorities, rights to utilize their language and to follow their customs, designating to them at the same time land and rivers with plain guarantees that no whites (settlers, traders, administrators, or missionaries) would establish themselves in their territory."[46]

There was no suggestion in Friede's "solution" that Indians be preserved so that they could be studied. He saw it as simply a matter of ensuring their basic human rights. At the ICA meeting held two years later in Sao Paulo, the human rights approach was strongly endorsed in a resolution on Brazilian Indians. Herbert Baldus, senior Brazilian ethnologist and secretary general of the ICA executive commission, and Paulo Duarte addressed their resolution to the president of Brazil.[47] They noted that the future survival of many Indian groups in Brazil was threatened because their lands were being invaded in complete disregard for their constitutional rights. Baldus and Duarte endorsed proposals placed before the Brazilian Parliament by the Indian Protection Service that were designed to increase the legal protection of Indian lands, requesting funds to demarcate tribal lands and to create the Xingu National Park. The park was created in 1961, but the Indian Protection Service was corrupted and became an agent of Indian dispossession and was disbanded in 1968 (see chapter 3).

The emphasis in this resolution was on "survival of Indian tribes"—there was no mention of their acculturation or integration into the national society as an objective. Likewise, the resolution was not linked to any concern for the scientific value of vanishing data. It was strictly a matter of ensuring human rights. The Xingu project was specifically endorsed because it would permit the maintenance of the intertribal system, which, if broken, "would condemn the tribes to extermination."

Environmentalists and Tribal Sanctuaries

In 1841, after spending eight years traveling through the still uncivilized American West and visiting forty-eight tribes, the American artist George Catlin[48] concluded that there was little hope for the half a million Indians still enjoying "their primitive state." However, he recognized that the government "could shield them from destruction," and he proposed the establishment of a vast national park covering the Great Plains from Mexico to Canada, to preserve both Indian and bison for future generations. In 1872, the year Catlin died, the U.S. government established the first national park at Yellowstone, but by this time nearly all of the tribes had been engulfed by the frontier.

Another link between tribal peoples and nature conservation—perhaps the first such connection since Catlin—involved the Pygmies and Albert Park, Africa's first national park, created in 1925 by the Belgian government. Although the original purpose of Albert Park was to preserve the mountain gorilla, it was enlarged from 92 to 781 square miles in 1929 "to save in their ancestral way of living some of the primitive African Pygmies, a race now threatened by extinction."[49] Subsistence hunting by the Pygmies using "primitive weapons" was permitted in the buffer zones surrounding the gorilla sanctuary in the center of the park. The inclusion of the Pygmies in the park was clearly for the purpose of conserving a vulnerable anthropological resource, not in recognition of their human rights or because the Pygmies were conservationists.

In spite of frequent opposition to sanctuary approaches, at least two large reserves, the 52,347-square-kilometer Central Kalahari Game Reserve in Botswana and the 22,000-square-kilometer Xingu National Park in Brazil, were established in the early 1960s for the dual purpose of nature conservation and the protection of indigenous peoples. However, it was not until Catlin's idealism was revived by conservationists such as Roderick Nash and Raymond Dasmann,[50] and the international environmental movement gained strength, that the concept of tribal sanctuaries became more acceptable.

The 1972 United Nations Stockholm Conference on the Human Environment called for the strict protection of wilderness areas representing diverse biomes, while defending the right of tribal peoples to pursue their traditional activities within such protected zones. As director of the Anthropological Programme of Peru's Manu National Park from 1969 to 1971, Belgian anthropologist Andre-Marcel d'Ans laid the groundwork for the park's present enlightened approach with his policy toward the Machiguenga Indians, who were living in the park.[51] He argued that exploitation of park resources for outside interests should be prohibited and that the Indians should be guaranteed the freedom to hunt, gather, fish, and garden for their own needs.

The American conservationist Raymond Dasmann was a leading figure in drawing world attention to the importance of tribal peoples for environmental planning. In 1973 Dasmann raised the issue of tribals before the International Union for the Conservation of Nature, stressing the importance of preserving human cultural diversity and observing that what the tribals needed was "protection of the opportunity to carry out traditional ways of life."[52] In 1974 he pointed out that tribals were dependent on local resources and tended to manage them for sustained yield and that they were "natural" conservationists living in de facto nature preserves. Dasmann advocated granting tribal groups legal title to, and full control over, their traditional lands, including the right "to exclude all visitors, including missionaries and anthropologists."[53]

Dasmann's perspective was incorporated in recommendation 5, "Protection of Traditional Ways of Life," by the 12th General Assembly of the IUCN, meeting in Zaire in 1975. The assembly stressed the conservation importance of traditional cultural practices and recommended that indigenous groups be allowed to retain ownership and use rights over their traditional lands even when the lands were incorporated into conservation areas. Shortly thereafter, the IUCN World Directory of National Parks and Other Protected Areas included a special classification for "protected anthropological areas" covering "areas set aside to provide for the continuance of ways of life endangered by the expansion of industrial civilization and its technology. They are areas occupied by people practising ways of life of anthropological or historical importance and are intended to provide for the continuance of those ways of life for so long as there are people willing to practice them and capable of doing so."[54]

One of the subcategories of protected anthropological areas included "natural biotic areas" to cover cases in which the impact of human activities on the environment was considered to be minor, as, for example, the San Bushmen in the Central Kalahari Game Reserve of Botswana and the Indians in the Xingu Indian Park in Brazil. Tourism in such areas was to be restricted. *Cultivated landscapes* was a subcategory applied to environments more obviously modified by traditional farming or pastoral peoples. Here the intent was to encourage the continuation of traditional activities, but tourism was considered more acceptable.

Implementation of such proposals was slow. The IUCN's 1977 World Directory lists several parks that were being used by tribal groups, but these were not actually designated as protected anthropological areas and the tribals were often referred to as a "disturbance," as in the case of the Pygmies within the Odzala National Park in Congo-Brazzaville, or the pastoralists in Ethiopia's Awash National Park.

The 1982 United Nations List of National Parks and Protected Areas, also compiled by the IUCN, continued to endorse the possibility of protection of tribal groups and provides Category VII, "anthropological reserves/natural biotic areas," where "the influence or technology of modern man has not significantly interfered with or been absorbed by the traditional ways of life of the inhabitants." Here, tribals are considered to be part of the natural environment and the areas are to be managed to maintain habitat "for traditional societies so as to provide for their continuance within their own cultural mores."[55] The IUCN justified the creation of such anthropological reserves in terms of the uniqueness of tribal cultures and their potential importance for anthropological research and the preservation of genetic diversity in the form of unique local cultigens. Significantly, the 1982 directory listed no existing Category VII reserves, and later lists simply subsumed the interests of indigenous people into existing categories. For example, a Category II national park can "take into account the needs of indigenous people, including subsistence resource use, in so far as these will not adversely affect the other objectives of management."[56]

The UN-endorsed World Conservation Strategy called on development planners to include special provisions for local cultures in their planning and to make use of the specialized environmental knowledge of local cultures.[57] A meeting of the IUCN Commission on Environmental Planning in 1982 recommended that specific material on conservation and tribal peoples be compiled.[58] At about the same time, Gary A. Klee[59] published a survey of conservation, or "resource management," practices by traditional peoples from throughout the world, and the government of Papua New Guinea sponsored a conference on traditional conservation in Papua New Guinea.[60]

Biosphere Reserves

The UN Biosphere Reserve Program, originally proposed in 1971 as part of UNESCO's Man and the Biosphere (MAB) Program, further legitimized the conservation role of tribal peoples and the value of protected tribal ways of life. Biosphere reserves were to constitute a global network of specially protected areas designed to preserve ecosystems, and according to the formal criteria adopted in 1974 by MAB Project No. 8, they were to include "man-modified landscapes." Biosphere reserves were different from standard nature reserves because they were to be used to promote research toward the sustained human use of such ecosystems.

In 1977 the IUCN, the World Wildlife Fund, Survival International, and the Indonesian government began to design a biosphere reserve for Siberut Island, the largest of the Mentawai Islands off the west coast of Sumatra.[61] Siberut was occupied by some eighteen thousand tribal peoples who were maintaining an effective balance with their resource base. It was recommended that the entire island be designated as a biosphere reserve, and forms of development that would not disturb the traditional use of the land were to be promoted. However, it seems that logging and agricultural development were the Indonesian government's highest priority, and more than half of the island was designated as a "development zone" into which the tribals and transmigrants from overcrowded areas of Indonesia were to be moved, over the objections of Survival International. Only one-fourth of the area was designated for traditional use, but not traditional settlement, and the government actually encouraged various forms of disruptive cultural intervention including resettlement. As Effendy A. Sumardja explained, the objective of the Siberut project was to "elevate the people well above the Neolithic level and bring them as gracefully as possible into the 20th century."[62] Thus, the intent of this proposed biosphere reserve was apparently not to maintain an environment where a tribal group could continue a traditional way of life.

One of the most promising applications of the biosphere reserve approach to the protection of a tribal population is Venezuela's Yanomami Biosphere Reserve as proposed by the Instituto Venezolano de Investigaciones Cientificas (IVIC), in 1984.[63] This plan envisioned the creation of a 37,285-square-kilometer biosphere reserve in southern Venezuela in order to protect the Orinoco watershed, the rainforest ecosystem, and ten thousand Yanomami Indians. It was argued that the Yanomami themselves and their unique cultural system were vital to the successful protection of the area because they had utilized the region's natural resources without degrading them. Furthermore, their presence along an otherwise unprotected frontier would discourage potential Brazilian political intervention. The creation of the Yanomami Biosphere Reserve, it was argued, would constitute a definitive exercise of Venezuelan sovereignty in a previously neglected and vulnerable corner of their national territory.

The proposed Yanomami reserve was to be divided into restricted, multiple-use, buffer, and frontier patrol zones. Significantly, especially in comparison with the Siberut plan, some twenty-seven thousand square kilometers of land were to be in the restricted zone, which would be for undisturbed use by the Yanomami. A small multiple-use zone was drawn to contain the various national institutions already present, including missionary, medical, and military posts, and would permit future tourist or recreational use. Any such uses already established within the restricted zone were to be relocated to the multiple-use zone. The buffer zone surrounding the multiple-use area would permit research and restricted public access. The patrol zone paralleled Venezuela's frontier with Brazil and was limited to military security functions. The entire reserve area was to be administered by Venezuela's Ministry of Defense and the Ministry of Environment and Renewable Natural Resources.

When the Yanomami reserve was finally approved by the Venezuelan government in 1991, it was officially called the Upper Orinoco–Casiquiare Biosphere Reserve and covered eighty-three thousand square kilometers. Colonization by outsiders was prohibited and the basic rights of the Yanomami to land and resources within the reserve were recognized in accordance with the original ILO Convention 107. However, the Ministry of the Environment intended to draw up a new management plan that would include provisions to encourage the "ethnodevelopment" of the Yanomami, but any changes in Yanomami culture would not be permitted to damage the environment. Representatives of the Yanomami organized, and the United Yanomami Communities of the Upper Orinoco were included on a management committee set up by the Ministry of the Environment. A portion of the reserve was designated as the National Park of Parima-Tapirapeco and was to be more strictly protected. The long-term prospects for the Yanomami remain unclear, because the government has been unable to prevent the invasion of the reserve by Brazilian miners, who have murdered many Yanomami; in addition, many other Yanomami have died in epidemics. Many other biosphere reserves involving indigenous peoples already exist, such as the Rio Platano Biosphere Reserve in Honduras, La Amistad in Costa Rica and Panama, and the Manu Park in Peru.

The alliance between tribals and environmentalists holds great promise, but many problems remain. Although the two groups have common interests, environmentalists might balk at supporting the increasing demands of tribals for full political autonomy or full entitlement to traditional territory.[64] Such autonomy or entitlement might imply the right of tribals to abandon traditional conservation practices in favor of new technologies and an expanded role in the market economy. Also, if traditional resource management practices have already been abandoned, the environmentalists' assumption that tribals are natural "conservationists" might be misplaced. From the tribal viewpoint, environmentalists and protected areas might be seen as unwelcome intrusions, although in the 1980s the San Blas Kuna proposed a biosphere reserve to protect their borders.

Ideally, such issues might be resolved by placing maximum emphasis on the collective human rights of indigenous peoples to maintain their cultures and giving them full authority to manage their own resources.[65] Some of the options in this regard were discussed by Leslie A. Brownrigg,[66] who noted that protected areas could be established within tribal lands and managed by tribal peoples in their own interests. In other cases, a national conservation agency might control an area occupied by tribals. Here, the tribals would not be legally designated as the owners, but instead could be recognized as "guardians" of the area. Administration would need to allow for population growth and culture change by giving tribals increased access to resources as their needs increased. J. E. Gardner and J. G. Nelson[67] have explored in great detail the different policy options that have been applied to native peoples in national parks by government agencies in Australia, Canada, and the United States. Bernard Nietschmann[68] pointed out that not only are local people often the best managers of their resources, but they are also often the best able to defend their resources against misuse by outsiders if they have the legal authority to do so.

R. F. Dasmann[69] has frequently stressed that reserves in themselves can never be large enough to protect either endangered species or peoples and cultures if they are contained within poorly managed national or global ecosystems. Ideally, the careful management practices of reserved areas would become models of appropriate conservation of natural resources and ecosystems for larger societies. In the long run, only in this way would the future of tribal cultures and the ecosystems sustaining them be secure.

You Can't Leave Them Alone: The Realists Prevail

Of the many conflicts between the proponents of different solutions to the problem of tribal exterminations and ethnocide, the most unfortunate was that in which the realists lumped all of the idealists with the scientific preservationists and accused them of seeking to establish human zoos as a way to preserve their tribal data.

The attack on the idealists was led by Reverend E. W. Smith in his 1934 RAI presidential address when he declared that anthropology did not advocate preserving indigenous people in human zoos, or "refurbishing" disintegrated tribes.[70] He accused the idealists of believing tribals to be racially incapable of progress, but ignored the real political issue of state domination of indigenous cultures. The political opinion Smith passed off as science was that there was no basis for allowing tribals to remain independent. He argued not only that tribals were capable of progress, which was not the relevant issue, but that once tribals came into contact with a "more advanced culture," change was "inescapable." In Smith's view, this was a scientific anthropological law. He cited the renowned British scientist Sir Julian Huxley to support his argument that "human zoos" were impossible. But here again it was obviously a political issue, not a scientific one. Huxley, referring to Africa, had actually stated that tribal preservation was not possible because it was not British policy: "It can never be our aim . . . merely to preserve a human zoo. . . . It cannot be our aim, for it would not work. Our mere presence in Africa makes it in the long run impossible: the fact that we are encouraging native production and native education, permitting the entry of white capital, missionaries, and science into Africa, makes it doubly impossible."[71]

It is significant that Smith also overlooked Huxley's "scientific" observation that many African tribals were being exterminated by civilization and his suggestion that in such cases it made sense to leave them alone. Huxley's qualified opinion on tribal preservation was: "It can never be our aim, save perhaps with a few out-of-the-way peoples whose fate in unrestricted contact with Western ideas would be simply to wilt, degenerate and disappear (the Congo Pygmies seem to be an African example), merely to preserve a human zoo, an Anthropological Garden."[72]

Another central figure in the rejection of idealist approaches was A. P. Elkin, a Sydney anthropologist and Christian minister who followed the functionalist colonial anthropology of Radcliffe-Brown and Malinowski. Elkin was an influential and outspoken advocate of "justice" for Aborigines, but his main concern was to ensure humane treatment for Aborigines as individuals; he was not interested in safeguarding aboriginal lands or maintaining the independence of native peoples. In direct opposition to Thomson, who advocated leaving Aborigines alone, Elkin stressed the need for "raising of the Aborigines in the scale of culture," declaring, "To leave them alone is impossible."[73] Elkin's realism must have stemmed partly from the fact that his research program was supported by the Australian government and the Rockefeller Foundation, both of which supported realist policies. Furthermore, Elkin's immediate predecessor, Radcliffe-Brown, had ominously endorsed the realist position when he declared that "the Australian Aborigines, even if not doomed to extinction as a race, seem at any rate doomed to have their cultures destroyed."[74] Within this context, Elkin's position made good political sense. In his 1934 summary of the "future of Aborigines" written for the journal *Oceania*, Elkin declared: "It should be stated quite clearly and definitely that anthropologists connected with the Department in the University of Sydney have no desire to preserve any of the aboriginal tribes of Australia or of the islands in their pristine condition as 'museum specimens' for the purpose of investigation; this charge is too often made against anthropologists."[75]

The "human zoo" charge, and the related accusations of racism, romanticism, and antiprogress, effectively halted the idealist preservationist movement by 1938. It soon became almost impossible for anthropologists to argue for "preservation" on any grounds, and when the ICAES Committee on the Conservation of Aboriginal Peoples reconvened in 1946, attention was shifted to the dual realist program of data salvage and applied anthropology.

The clearest indication of the political strength of the realist position can be seen in ILO Convention 107, which endorsed integration and development over tribal autonomy.[76] In 1954 the ILO convened a Committee of Experts to debate policy prior to the drafting of Convention 107. According to committee member and anthropologist Horace Miner,[77] the committee was divided between the "protectionists," led by Brazilian anthropologist Darcy Ribeiro, who favored respect for tribal culture and a slow integration of tribals into the dominant society, and Asian representatives who argued for rapid integration.

In the end, the realist position won. As Miner explained, "The realist recognizes the inevitability of increasing encroachment of civilization on the remaining outposts of preliterate culture."[78] The realists battled among themselves over the rate of change, with the applied anthropologists generally favoring greater caution and respect for native culture and the religious humanitarians pushing for more rapid integration, but neither saw any possibility of leaving tribals alone.

Indigenous Peoples' Rights Advocates

> We exist to help tribal peoples protect their rights; the simplest, unarguable rights of all people . . . and, moreover, to support their right to determine, themselves, their own future and that of their children—tribal self-determination.[79]

The idealist perspective had only limited impact as long as it emphasized "preservation" and was represented only by isolated individuals and sporadic resolutions by scientific organizations. However, when it was revealed in 1967 that Brazil's Indian Protection Service, a government organization devoted to realist humanitarian principles, was engaged in a systematic genocidal program, idealist anthropologists were shocked into action. In 1968, at the 38th International Americanist Congress in Stuttgart, Germany, a group of anthropologists led by Norwegian Helge Kleivan formed the International Work Group for Indigenous Affairs (IWGIA).[80] The IWGIA is a human rights organization headquartered in Copenhagen, Denmark, which supports the right of indigenous peoples to maintain their independent existence. Since 1968 a number of similar advocacy organizations have been formed that share the IWGIA's objectives, such as Cultural Survival,[81] founded in 1972 in Cambridge, Massachusetts; Survival International,[82] founded in London in 1969; and the Gesellschaft fur bedrohte Volker (Society for Threatened Peoples) in Germany.[83]

Cultural Survival, one of the most prominent pro-indigenous peoples organizations in the United States, founded and directed by Harvard anthropologist David Maybury-Lewis, seeks to inform the public about the problems of indigenous peoples and to influence policy makers to undertake actions favorable to indigenous peoples. It publishes a journal, the *Cultural Survival Quarterly*, and an extensive series of occasional papers and special reports. It has supported many special assistance projects, often designed by indigenous peoples themselves, to improve their prospects for survival.

The primary objective of such organizations is to help indigenous peoples gain self-determination and international recognition of their human rights.

For example, the IWGIA describes its purpose as "establishing the indigenous peoples' right to self-determination" and "helping to secure the future of indigenous people in concurrence with their own efforts and desires."[84] The overall strategy of these organizations seems to be threefold:

1. To focus international attention on the contemporary situation of indigenous peoples
2. To pressure governments to respect the internationally recognized rights of indigenous peoples
3. To provide financial assistance to indigenous peoples in support of their self-determination struggle

In pursuit of their objectives, these organizations maintain constant communication with each other, with more specialized regional organizations, and with indigenous organizations. Together they form a wide network composed of indigenous leaders, anthropologists, and other field workers, all of whom are in close touch with events that influence indigenous peoples throughout the world. It is now possible to respond almost immediately to any crisis situation, and a powerful coalition of informed opinion can be mobilized to influence government authorities to act responsibly in the expressed interests of indigenous peoples. For example, in 1978 the international organizations learned that the Brazilian government was quietly preparing to "emancipate" Amazon Indians and thereby terminate their legally protected status. An international protest movement was immediately mounted, and the government was forced to withdraw the decree. Since then, the Anthropology Resource Center (ARC) in Boston, the IWGIA, and Survival International coordinated an international campaign, together with other international organizations and twenty-seven pro-Indian organizations in Brazil, in support of a proposal to create a 6.4-million-hectare reserve for the Brazilian Yanomamo Indians to counteract a government plan to isolate them in twenty-one small reserves.

Most international organizations have focused heavily on the issue of protecting tribal land rights. For example, Survival International (SI) lists land rights as its first essential priority. Another organization, Colonialism and Indigenous Minorities Research and Action (CIMRA), like SI based in London, campaigned heavily in favor of Aboriginal land rights in Australia in the 1970s. As part of its campaign, CIMRA offered the following action proposals to concerned individuals who agreed that something should be done to help Aborigines but who ask, "Yes, but what can I do?":

1. Support . . . Aborigine land rights movements.
2. Protest . . . to foreign corporations mining Aborigine land.
3. Lobby . . . the Australian Government.[85]

These recommendations were followed by names and addresses of aboriginal organizations, mining companies, and government officials that could be contacted.

International Development Action (IDA), founded in Australia in 1970 as a research organization, focused on tribal land rights as a development issue. IDA called itself a "development education group" and was funded by Australian religious charities, development aid, and student and educational organizations. One of its early projects was an extended study of the role of multinational mining corporations in the expropriation of aboriginal lands on the Cape York Peninsula of Queensland, Australia. This research was carried out in close cooperation with the Aborigines, and the results were published in a series of monographs.[86] Later, IDA investigated the Purari hydroelectric scheme that would uproot thousands of Papua New Guinea tribal peoples so that massive amounts of electricity could be generated to enable Japanese companies to produce aluminum from the bauxite taken from tribal lands in Cape York Peninsula. The Purari project was not approved as proposed, partly due to the protests raised against it. IDA's New Guinea work was a joint effort between IDA and the Purari Action Group, a native New Guinea organization opposing the development project.

In their efforts to focus world attention on the problems of indigenous peoples, the international organizations arrange press conferences, sponsor lectures, and carry out ambitious publication programs. The IWGIA, for example, has published scores of documents reporting on conditions in Central and South America, Canada, Australia, India, and the Philippines. In addition, it publishes newsletters and yearbooks in English and Spanish. These materials are distributed throughout the world to individuals, indigenous organizations, governments, special UN organizations, and other interested international organizations. Organizations such as the IWGIA operate on small budgets with limited staffs. They support themselves through grants from philanthropic organizations and governments (the IWGIA is heavily supported by Scandinavian governments) and from private donations and subscriptions.

Increasingly, these unique organizations have become important sources of funds to meet requests from indigenous political organizations or to carry out specific projects in support of self-determination for indigenous peoples. Although the total amount of this aid is modest, it represents a significant shift from traditional international aid programs, which often supports massive, inappropriate programs that may adversely affect indigenous peoples. Ideally, the kinds of projects being sponsored by these new organizations are small in scale and are usually initiated and directed by the native peoples themselves. For example, the IWGIA has channeled funds to support conferences organized by indigenous peoples and to help free imprisoned indigenous political

leaders. Together with Survival International, the IWGIA has helped to finance the operation of Indian organizations in Colombia and Ecuador. Most
of the funds ultimately originate from large foundations, charities, and church
aid organizations.

Voluntary Isolation in the Twenty-First Century

As mentioned in the preface, my experience in the 1960s in the Peruvian
Amazon inspired me to write the first edition of *Victims of Progress* to advocate idealist policies that would permit the survival of autonomous tribal peoples without forcing them to either disappear from or integrate with the commercial world. At that time this was not a popular position among
anthropologists, who still primarily took the "realist" position that tribal survival by means of isolation was simply not feasible. As the present chapter
demonstrates, since the early 1970s there has been a major shift in public discourse on this issue. Governments and international agencies now widely af-
firm that tribal peoples have a basic human right to live autonomously, but
this affirmation now needs to be translated into positive action.

The phenomenon referred to in chapter 2 as *direct avoidance* or *active
avoidance* by tribal societies who still lived autonomously is now officially
recognized as *voluntary isolation* by the United Nations;[87] by the governments of Bolivia, Ecuador,[88] and Peru; and by indigenous organizations. This
is a very positive step and a major conceptual change. Many experts on tribal
affairs, including indigenous leaders, anthropologists, and members of
NGOs, are now working together with government agencies to change political realities in order to make tribal survival a realistic possibility.

Voluntary isolation has become an important policy-shaping concept because a few people have raised it to international consciousness. Beginning
with Resolution 3.056, adopted by the World Conservation Congress held in
Bangkok in 2004 by the World Conservation Union, or International Union
for the Conservation of Nature, a group of experts set in motion a promising
new series of actions to protect the world's surviving isolated tribal peoples.[89]
The World Conservation Union brings together 83 governments, 110 government agencies, some 800 NGOs, and thousands of scientists.[90] Resolution
3.056 asked the IUCN director general to promote coordination between
South American governments to "develop and implement proposals aimed at
protecting the lands and territories of indigenous groups living in voluntary
isolation, as part of the respective countries' indigenous peoples policies and
conservation strategies in the Amazon region and Chaco," in cooperation
with regional international organizations, indigenous organizations, and

NGOs. The resolution affirmed as a basic principle that isolated peoples had a right to the protection of their lives, natural resources, and territories, but also stated that "indigenous peoples living in voluntary isolation have the right to freely decide to remain isolated, maintain their cultural values, and to freely decide if, when and how they wish to integrate into national society."

One year later, in 2005, some sixty experts representing a cross-section of organizations and specialists from all over the world attended a special symposium entitled "Isolated Indigenous Peoples of the Amazon and Gran Chaco Region" in Belem, Brazil. They confirmed that numerous groups of uncontacted peoples still existed in more than forty locations in Bolivia, Brazil, Colombia, Paraguay, and Peru, noting that tribal people who intentionally avoid contact constitute part of the "patrimony of humanity," but their physical survival is clearly threatened by even inadvertent contact with outsiders. They reported the existence of far more surviving isolated tribal peoples than many would have expected, because they were able to combine their information on previously unreported contacts. Members of the symposium formed the International Alliance for the Protection of Isolated Indigenous People and pledged to "safeguard the world cultural heritage of these groups." They issued a formal declaration to publicize their recommendations and moved quickly to bring practical proposals for protective actions to prominent international agencies.[91] The group met again in 2006 in Santa Cruz de la Sierra, Bolivia, and issued a new statement, this time stating that there were some two hundred isolated peoples or groups in initial contact in seven South American countries. They urged the national governments involved to immediately implement specific public policies to protect the lives and human rights of these vulnerable peoples.[92]

A member of the alliance network, Alex Rivas Toledo of the Ecuadorian human rights organization, the Center for Economic and Social Rights (Centro de Derechos Económicos y Sociales, or CDES), representing the IUCN's South American branch, presented all of the alliance's findings and specific recommendations in an information document to the Convention on Biological Diversity's (CBD) biodiversity treaty working group on traditional knowledge meeting in Montreal in 2007. The Biodiversity Treaty is an international protocol, like the Kyoto Protocol on global warming, that 189 nations have signed, committing themselves "to achieve by 2010 a significant reduction of the current rate of biodiversity loss at the global, regional and national levels . . . to the benefit of all life on Earth."[93] The alliance's document made the link between saving autonomous isolated tribal peoples and protecting biodiversity, enumerating areas with surviving isolated peoples and urging national governments and international organizations to recognize that voluntary isolation in itself is evidence of negative consent to any form of external intervention. The key principle is that isolated peoples are clearly saying no to either "consultation" or "participation" with outside development interests. Allowing isolation protects people, their traditional knowledge, and biodiversity.

These efforts to promote new policies are clearly having an effect. For example, in 2006, when (as discussed in the previous chapter) it became known that the Ecuadorian government intended to open areas in the Yasuni Biosphere Reserve to oil development, thereby endangering the isolated Tagaeri and Taromenani peoples, the Confederation of Indigenous Nationalities of Ecuador (Confederación de Nacionalidades Indígenas del Ecuador, or CONAIE), issued a formal statement connecting tribal isolation with the human right of self-determination and emphasizing the special vulnerability of isolated peoples: "[I]n the case of peoples in voluntary isolation their self-determination centers on their will to remain free in the forest exercising their territoriality. This very special self-determination condition should not bring with it the risk of death and extermination."[94]

CONAIE was emphatic that the natural resources within the territories of isolated peoples must not be extracted by outsiders: "The territory of Peoples in Voluntary Isolation should be considered absolutely free of any concession over the resources contained there. No area or zone of control of any type, especially for resource extraction, can be constituted over this territoriality."[95] They were referring most obviously to oil and logging concessions, and special classifications such as "buffer zones" that allow any outsider activities in areas occupied by uncontacted peoples. In response to such declarations and campaigns launched by numerous organizations, in April of 2007 the Ecuadorian minister of the environment made a formal presentation to Ecuadorian president Rafael Correa and his cabinet ministers in favor of extraordinary protections for the Tagaeri and Taromenani as isolated peoples, which led to an at least a temporary moratorium on oil development in their territory.

Conclusion

Paradoxically, many self-sufficient small-scale societies were destroyed because global technological evolution outstripped social and political evolution in the twentieth century. A more humanistically evolved global society would control its exploitation of resources while accommodating the existence of autonomous micropolities such as tribes and would permit great ethnic and cultural diversity.

The end of small-scale cultural autonomy is as momentous an event for humanity as is the rise of the commercial age. Yet it has only recently begun to receive much attention. Now, important questions are being raised about the evolving global industrial system: Can the world be made safe for ethnic and cultural diversity, local autonomy, and social equality? Can natural ecosystems be maintained? In many respects, the disappearance of small-scale autonomous societies and their cultures is an early warning device. As these tribal societies have disappeared, the natural ecosystems they occupied have become endangered, and poverty, social inequality, and global insecurity have increased. Today there exist only a few thousand independent tribals enjoying their original cultural autonomy, and the debate goes on over how to deal with them. A broader discussion of these issues will benefit these remnant groups, but will also be significant for the estimated 370 million indigenous peoples who are now struggling to regain control over their lives and resources.

Notes

1. Christian Bay, 1984, "Human rights on the periphery: No room in the ark for the Yanomami?" *Development Dialogue* 1(2): 23–41.
2. Charles Darwin, 1871, *The Descent of Man*, New York: D. Appleton and Company, 228–31. See also Patrick Brantlinger, 2003, *Dark Vanishings: Discourse on the Extinction of Primitive Races*, Ithaca, NY, and London: Cornell University Press.
3. W. H. Flower, 1882, "Chairman's address for anthropology," *Report of the British Association for the Advancement of Science for 1881* 51: 688.
4. A. H. Lane Fox Pitt-Rivers, 1872, "Address to the department of anthropology," *Report of the British Association for the Advancement of Science for 1871* 41: 171.
5. Royal Anthropological Institute of Great Britain and Ireland, 1951, *Notes and Queries on Anthropology*, London: Routledge and Kegan Paul.
6. Sir H. Bartle Frere, 1881, "On the laws affecting the relations between civilized and savage life, as bearing on the dealings of colonists with Aborigines," *Journal of the Royal Anthropological Institute* 11: 313–54.
7. W. H. Flower, 1884, "President's address on the aims and prospects of the study of anthropology," *Journal of the Royal Anthropological Institute* 13: 493.
8. A. L. P. Cameron, 1885, "Notes on some tribes of New South Wales," *Journal of the Royal Anthropological Institute* 14: 370.
9. Edwin W. Smith, 1934, "Anthropology and the practical man," *Journal of the Royal Anthropological Institute* 64: xxxiv–xxxv.
10. Aborigines Protection Society (APS), 1837–1847, *Annual Report*, London: APS, 9:28.
11. Summer Institute of Linguistics, http://www.sil.org/.
12. Søren Hvalkof and Peter Aaby, eds., 1981, *Is God an American? An Anthropological Perspective on the Missionary Work of the Summer Institute of Linguistics*, IWGIA/Survival International Document no. 43; David Stoll, 1982, *Fishers of Men*

or Founders of Empire? The Wycliffe Bible Translators in Latin America, London: Zed Press/Cambridge, MA: Cultural Survival.

13. Dale W. Kietzman, 1977, "Factors favoring ethnic survival," *International Congress of Americanists, Proceedings* 42(4): 527–36; Mary Ruth Wise, Eugene E. Loos, and Patricia Davis, 1977, "Filosofía y Métodos del Instituto Linguistico de Verano," *Proceedings of the 42nd International Americanists Congress, Paris*, 2:499–525.

14. Wise, Loos, and Davis, "Filosfía y Métodos," 502, my translation.

15. Kietzman, "Factors favoring ethnic survival."

16. Ibid., 528.

17. Ibid., 530.

18. Darcy Ribeiro, 1957, *Culturas e Linguas Indigenas do Brasil*, Separata de Educação e Ciêñcias Socais no. 6, Rio de Janeiro: Centro Brasileiro de Pesquisas Educacionais, 21, my translation.

19. Kietzman, "Factors favoring ethnic survival," 535.

20. The World Bank: Operational Manual Statement, cited in IWGIA, 1987, *IWGIA Yearbook 1986*, Copenhagen: IWGIA, 149–53.

21. World Bank, 2006, *World Bank Annual Report 2006*, Operational Summary, frontpiece, http://go.worldbank.org/KQ3OFFED90.

22. Robert Goodland, 1982, *Tribal Peoples and Economic Development: Human Ecologic Considerations*, Washington, DC: World Bank.

23. Ibid., 27, 28.

24. Ibid., 27.

25. *IWGIA Yearbook 1986*, 149–54.

26. For example, John H. Bodley, 1983, "The World Bank tribal policy: Criticisms and recommendations," *Congressional Record*, serial no. 98–37, 515–21 (reprinted in Bodley, 1988a, 406–13).

27. World Bank, 1991, *Operational Directive. OD 4.20: Indigenous Peoples*, http://www.worldbank.org/html/fpd/em/power/wbpolicy/420OD.stm.

28. World Bank, 2005, *Operational Manual. 4.10 Indigenous Peoples OP/BP*, http://wbln0018.worldbank.org/Institutional/Manuals/OpManual.nsf/.

29. See Camisea Project, 2007, http://www.camisea.com.pe/ for a positive view of this giant development project from the developers. For critical perspectives, see Amazon Alliance, 2007, http://www.amazonalliance.org/camisea.html; and Amazon Watch, 2007, http://www.amazonwatch.org/amazon/PE/camisea/.

30. Tom Griffiths, 2007, *Exigiendo Responsabilidad al BID y la CFI en Camisea II: Una Revisión de Estándares Internacionales Aplicables, y Diligencia y Conformidad Debidas*, San Francisco: Amazon Watch, http://www.amazonwatch.org/documents /spanish_camiseaII_report.pdf.

31. Peru Ministerio de Energía y Minas, 2001, *Guía de Relaciones Comunitarias*, Lima: Dirección General de Asuntos Ambientales, Anexo 4, http://www .minem.gob.pe/archivos/dgaae/legislacion/guias/guiaelectrical.pdf.

32. Pluspetrol, 2002, *Plan de Contengencia Antropológico para Poblaciones en Contacto Inicial o en Aislamiento*, Doc-22-02, 5–6, http://www.camisea.com.pe /esp/estados/SGA/Listado/DOC-22.pdf.

33. Joseph Kaines, 1873, "Western anthropologists and extra-Western communities," *Report of the British Association for the Advancement of Science for 1872,* Transactions of the Sections 42: 189–90.

34. John R. Baker, 1928, "Depopulation in Espiritu Santo, New Hebrides," *Journal of the Royal Anthropological Institute* 58: 279–303; 1929, "The Northern New Hebrides," *Geographical Journal* 73(4): 305–25.

35. S. M. Lambert, 1931, "Health survey of Rennell and Bellona Islands," *Oceania* 2(2): 136–73.

36. International Congress of Americanists (ICA), 1932, *Proceedings,* 25: xlv.

37. H. J. T. Bijlmer, 1953, "Protection of native societies," *Proceedings of the Seventh Pacific Science Congress* 7: 131–34; Nederlandsche Commissie voor Internationale Natuurbescherming, 1937, *Conservation of Primitives Still Living in the Stone Age, Especially in New Guinea,* Medeelingen no. 11,1–7. See also abstract of report in Pacific Science Congress, 1953, *Proceedings of the Seventh Pacific Science Congress,* 148–49.

38. Charles Wellington Furlong, 1915, "The Haush and Ona, primitive tribes of Tierra del Fuego," *Proceedings, International Congress of Americanists* 19: 438.

39. Ibid., 444.

40. Frederic Wood Jones, 1928, "The Claims of the Australian Aborigine," *18th ANZAAS, Perth, 1926, Report* 18: 497–519.

41. A. F. R. Wollaston, 1920, "Remarks on 'The opening of new territories in Papua'," *Geographical Journal* (June): 457–58.

42. Wood Jones, "Claims of the Australian Aborigine," 509.

43. Baldwin Spencer, 1913, "Preliminary Report on the Aboriginals of the Northern Territory," Parliament of the Commonwealth of Australia, Northern Territory of Australia, *Report of the Administrator for the Year 1912,* 36–52.

44. Wood Jones, "Claims of the Australian Aborigine," 513.

45. Donald F. Thomson, 1938, *Recommendations of Policy in Native Affairs in the Northern Territory of Australia,* Parliament of the Commonwealth of Australia No. 56.-R2945.

46. Juan Friede, 1952, "Los Cofán: Una tribu de la alta Amazonia Colombiana," *Proceedings, International Congress of Americanists* 30: 218.

47. International Congress of Americanists (ICA), 1955, *Proceedings,* 31(1): lxix–lxx.

48. George Catlin, 1841, *Letters and Notes on the Manners, Customs, and Conditions of the North American Indian,* London: Tosswill and Myers.

49. Mary L. Jobe Akeley, 1931, "Africa's first national park," *Scientific American* (November): 295–98.

50. Roderick Nash, 1968, *The American Environment: Readings in the History of Conservation.* Reading, MA: Addison-Wesley; R. F. Dasmann, 1976, "National parks, nature conservation, and 'future primitive,'" *Ecologist* 6(5): 164–78 (reprinted in Bodley, 1988a, 301–10).

51. Andre-Marcel d'Ans, 1972, "Les tribus indigenes du Parc National du Manu," *International Congress of Americanists* 39(4): 95–100; 1980, "Begegnung in Peru," in *Ist Gott Amerikaner?* ed. Søren Hvalkof and Peter Aaby, 309–51, Gottingen,

Germany: Lamuv Verlag; Hartmut Jungius, 1976, "National parks and indigenous peoples—a Peruvian case study," *Survival International Review* 1(14): 6–14.

52. R. F. Dasmann, 1973, "Sanctuaries for life styles?" *IUCN Bulletin*, n.s. 4(8): 29.

53. R. F. Dasmann, 1975, "Difficult marginal environments and the traditional societies which exploit them," *News from Survival International* 11 (July): 11–15.

54. International Union for the Conservation of Nature (IUCN), 1977, *World Directory of National Parks and Other Protected Areas*, Morges, Switzerland: IUCN.

55. International Union for the Conservation of Nature (IUCN), 1982, *United Nations List of National Parks and Protected Areas*. Gland, Switzerland: IUCN.

56. International Union for the Conservation of Nature (IUCN), 1994, *Guidelines for Protected Area Management Categories*, Gland, Switzerland: IUCN, 19, http://www.iucn.org/dbtw-wpd/edocs/1994–007-En.pdf.

57. International Union for the Conservation of Nature (IUCN), 1980, *World Conservation Strategy: Living Resource Conservation for Sustainable Development*, Gland, Switzerland: IUCN.

58. David Pitt, 1983, *Culture and Conservation: An Action/Research Plan*. Gland, Switzerland: IUCN.

59. Gary A. Klee, 1980, *World Systems of Traditional Resource Management*, New York: W. H. Winston/Halstead Press.

60. Louise Morauta, John Pernetta, and William Heaney, 1982, *Traditional Conservation in Papua New Guinea: Implications for Today*, Monograph no. 16, Boroka, Papua New Guinea: Institute of Applied Social and Economic Research.

61. Jeffrey A. McNeely, 1982, "The people of Siberut: Indonesia's original inhabitants," in *Culture and Conservation*, IUCN/CEP Work in Progress 13, Paper no. 3, Gland, Switzerland: IUCN/CEP.

62. Effendy A. Sumardja, 1984, "Siberut Reserve Impacts on Indigenous People in West Sumatra, Indonesia," paper presented at the First World Conference on Cultural Parks, Mesa Verde, Colorado, 8.

63. Nelly Arvelo-Jimenez, 1984, *La Reserva de Biosfera Yanomami: Una Autentica Estrategia para el Ecodesarrollo Nacional (Borrador de Trabajo)*, Caracas: Instituto Venezolano de Investigaciones Cientificas.

64. James C. Clad, 1985, "Conservation and indigenous peoples: A study of convergent interests," in *Culture and Conservation: The Human Dimension in Environmental Planning*, ed. Jeffrey A. McNeely and David Pitt, 45–62, London: Croom Helm (reprinted in Bodley, 1988a, 320–34).

65. Christian Bay, 1984, "Human rights on the periphery: No room in the ark for the Yanomami?" *Development Dialogue* 1(2): 23–41.

66. Leslie A. Brownrigg, 1985, "Native cultures and protected areas: Management options," in *Culture and Conservation: The Human Dimension in Environmental Planning*, ed. Jeffrey A. McNeely and David Pitt, 33–44. London: Croom Helm.

67. J. E. Gardner and J. G. Nelson, 1981, "National parks and native peoples in Northern Canada, Alaska, and Northern Australia," *Environmental Conservation* 8(3): 207–15 (reprinted in Bodley, 1988a, 334–51).

68. Bernard Nietschmann, 1984, "Biosphere reserves and traditional societies," in *Conservation, Science and Society: Contributions to the First International Biosphere Reserve Congress, Minsk, Byelorussia/USSR*, Paris: UNESCO-UNEP, 2:499–508.

69. R. F. Dasmann, 1982, *The Relationship between Protected Areas and Indigenous Peoples*, paper presented at World National Parks Congress, Bali, Indonesia; 1983, *Biosphere Reserves and Human Needs*, First International Biosphere Reserve Congress, Minsk, Belarus, 6.

70. Smith, "Anthropology and the practical man."

71. Julian Huxley, 1931, *Africa View*, New York: Harper and Row, 137.

72. Ibid.

73. A. P. Elkin, 1935, "Presidential address: Anthropology in Australia, past and present," *Report of the 22nd Meeting of ANZAAS* 22: 207.

74. A. R. Radcliffe-Brown, 1930, "Editorial," *Oceania* 1(1): 3.

75. A. P. Elkin, 1934, "Anthropology and the future of the Australian Aborigines," *Oceania* 5(1): 2.

76. International Labour Organization (ILO), 1953, *Indigenous Peoples: Living and Working Conditions of Aboriginal Populations in Independent Countries*, Studies and Reports, New Series no. 35, Geneva: ILO.

77. Horace M. Miner, 1955, "Planning for the acculturation of isolated tribes," *International Congress of Americanists, Proceedings* 31(1): 441–46.

78. Ibid., 441.

79. Stephen Corry, 1976, *Towards Indian Self-Determination in Colombia*, Survival International Document no. 2, 11.

80. International Work Group for Indigenous Affairs (IWGIA), http://www.iwgia.org/.

81. Cultural Survival, http://www.cs.org/.

82. Survival International, http://www.survival-international.org/.

83. Gesellschaft für bedrohte Völker (Society for Threatened Peoples), http://www.gfbv.de/promis.php.

84. IWGIA leaflet, 1980.

85. Colonialism and Indigenous Minorities Research and Action (CIMRA), 1979, "Yes, but what can I do?" *New Internationalist* 77 (July): 27.

86. J. P. Roberts, ed., 1975, *Mapoon—Book One: The Mapoon Story by the Mapoon People*, Victoria, Australia: International Development Action; Janine Roberts, 1978, *From Massacres to Mining: The Colonization of Aboriginal Australia*, London: War on Want; J. Roberts and D. McLean, 1976, *Mapoon—Book Three: The Cape York Aluminum Companies and the Native Peoples*, Victoria, Australia: International Development Action; J. Roberts, M. Parsons, and B. Russell, 1975, *Mapoon—Book Two: The Mapoon Story According to the Invadors*, Victoria, Australia: International Development Action.

87. Rodolfo Stavenhagen, 2006, *Report of the Special Rapporteur on the Situation of Human Rights and Fundamental Freedoms of Indigenous People*, addendum, Mission to Ecuador, Human Rights Council, A/HRC/4/32/Add.2 28 December, 23, http://daccessdds.un.org/doc/UNDOC/GEN/G07/100/29/PDF/G0710029.pdf?Open

Element; United Nations Permanent Forum on Indigenous Issues, 2007, *Report on the Sixth Session* (May 14–25, 2007), Economic and Social Council Official Records, Supplement No. 23. E/2007/43 E/C.19/2007/12, articles 39–42, http://daccessdds .un.org/doc/UNDOC/GEN/N07/376/75/PDF/N0737675.pdf?OpenElement.

88. Ecuador Ministerio de Ambiente, 2007, *La Política Nacional de los Pueblos en Situación de Aislamiento Voluntario*, http://www.ambiente.gov.ec/paginas_espanol /docs/Politicanacional.pdf.

89. International Union for the Conservation of Nature (IUCN), 2004, *Indigenous peoples living in voluntary isolation and conservation of nature in the Amazon region and Chaco*, RES 3.056, http://www.iucn.org/congress/2004/members/Individual _Res_Rec_Eng/wcc3_res_056.pdf.

90. World Conservation Union (IUCN), http://www.iucn.org/en/about/index.htm.

91. International Alliance for the Protection of Isolated Indigenous People, 2005, http://www.korubo.com/AMAZONDOC/firstpeople.htm (accessed October 2007); Convention on Biological Diversity (Convenio Sobre la Diversidad Biologica), 2007, *Informe de possible medidas para asegurar el respeto de los derechos de comunidades indigenas y locales desprotegidas y voluntariamente aisladas tomando en consideracion sus conocimientos tradicionales y el desarrollo de acceso y participacion en los beneficios*, Grupo de Trabajo Especial de Composicion Abierta Entre Periodos de Sesiones Sobre el Articulo 8(j) y Disposiciones Conexas del Convenio Sobre Diversidad Biologica, UNEP/CBD/WG8J/5/INF/17, June 31, 2007, Anexo II, http://www.cbd.int/doc/meetings/tk/wg8j-05/information/wg8j-05-inf-17-es.pdf.

92. Convention on Biological Diversity, *Informe*, Anexo I.

93. Convention on Biological Diversity, 2007, 2010 Biodiversity Target, http://www.cbd.int/2010-target/default.shtml.

94. Confederación de Nacionalidades Indígenas del Ecuador (CONAIE), 2006, *Pueblos Indígenas en Aislamiento Voluntario en la Amazonía Ecuatoriana: Documento Base*, 6, http://www.sosyasuni.org/files/conaie_taromenani2.pdf, my translation.

95. Ibid., 13, my translation.

Appendix

Human Zoos, Living Museums, and Real People*

I simply desire assurance that the people of Karimui and their lands are free from exploitive encroachment by more sophisticated peoples, and that they are able to retain their social identity.

—Roy Wagner (1971)

It is clear that official attitudes and policies of governments toward tribal peoples have remained basically uniform throughout the world over the past 150 years, and have been overwhelmingly disastrous for tribal peoples and one-sidedly beneficial for industrial civilization. There have been many official investigations of the "plights" of specific peoples over the years, and various proposals have been made for the protection of endangered groups. But most authorities have consistently maintained that progress as defined by industrial civilization is an inevitable and irresistible force, and in the long run they admit no alternative for tribal peoples but their drastic cultural modification or extermination. Those who accept this view consider unworkable, unnatural, and even immoral, any proposals for government policies that would not automatically compromise tribal cultural integrity. Yet there are compelling arguments, both ethical and entirely practical, why native peoples must be given alternatives to progress.

The "Best of Both Worlds" Fallacy

When discussing possible alternatives to the detrimental aspects of progress, anthropologists usually set total *isolation* and no change on one side and complete *assimilation* or loss of cultural identity on the other as the unacceptable extremes, and then support *integration* as a moderate middle position and the only rational alternative. Isolation is vigorously rejected as immoral

---

* This is a reprint of chapter 9 of *Victims of Progress*, 1st ed. Menlo Park: Cummings Publishing Co., 1975. The references cited are included in the present bibliography.

and impossible, while assimilation is considered undesirable only if pressed too fast, and is expected to be the probable outcome of change in the long run. Integration implies merging a people politically and economically with the national society while deliberately encouraging selected, albeit often modified, aspects of traditional culture. In this way the population can be administratively controlled and its resources harvested while enough of the traditional culture will survive to ease the transition to full assimilation. The underlying rationalization for integration is still the familiar ethnocentric assumption that progress will be a certain improvement for all peoples.

The integration approach has been in anthropological favor since at least the turn of the twentieth century when indirect rule began to be advocated as scientifically sound administrative policy. Indirect rule has frequently developed into a policy of *selective emphasis* or *growth from within*, designed to at least temporarily preserve what is thought to be the best from the traditional culture. Through careful direction of the modernization process, it is hoped that progress will bring the best of both worlds to tribal peoples. This aim is clear in the following discussion of native policy in South Africa, where the explicit objective is

> to take from the Bantu past what is "good" and, together with what is "good" for the Bantu in European culture, build up a new distinctive culture. (Schapera 1934:x)

As Elwin (1959:44) explains regarding tribal policy in India:

> We believe that we can bring them the best things of our world without destroying the nobility and the goodness of theirs.

In the northwest frontier areas of India this approach has been applied in its most extreme form to purposefully create pleasing, tailor-made cultures. Very careful modification policies were instituted under Elwin's guidance aimed at improving the "quality of human beings," bringing "*more* colour, *more* beauty," and "a wider and a purer conception of God and man" (Elwin 1959:136, 215–16). Of course at the same time these tribal peoples were urged to become loyal Indian citizens and participants in industrial civilization. Where selective emphasis has been applied in other areas, it has often been justifiably criticized as an attempt to keep the natives backward and subservient and thereby facilitate their exploitation (Keesing 1941:81–95; Mead 1961:369).

The problem with the political and economic integration of tribal peoples, even when ethnic identities are preserved, is that it is really not possible to preserve what is really *best* for them if their well-being in terms of nonethnocentric standards is considered. Integration is not possible unless tribal cultures are made to surrender their autonomy and self-reliance. When these are replaced by dependence on state institutions and the world market economy, a whole series of changes will follow until virtually all the unique features of tribal cultures have been replaced by their contrasting counterparts in industrial civilization. When these features are gone the traditional satisfactions and balances built into most tribal cultures are also lost. If these losses were always compensated for by increased security, health, personal satisfaction, and environmental stability, and the like, then progress might be worth the cost; unfortunately, the exact opposite is usually the case. It appears that the best of both worlds alternative actually takes away what is best in exchange for the worst that industrial society has to offer. Perhaps even more serious is the fact that integration policies disregard the rights of tribal people to choose not to integrate.

The Cultural Autonomy Alternative

It seems that one clear way for a government to protect a tribal people from the detrimental impact of progress is for it to simply allow them to pursue their own way of life undisturbed by outside intervention. If viewed in totally nonethnocentric terms, and considering only the well-being of the people involved, this is not at all an unreasonable proposal. Furthermore, such a course is implicitly supported by the UN-proclaimed rights of self-determination and the right of peoples to freely develop their own cultures.

This alternative to the problems caused by progress departs radically from the best of both worlds or integration approach. It might be called the *cultural autonomy* approach, because the government would actually allow a tribal culture to exist independently of the state and would refrain from policies that would deliberately alter its ecological adaptation. Cultural autonomy would recognize a tribal culture's right to remain permanently outside any state political structure and to reject development or modernization along the lines that would otherwise be forced upon it by outside powers. More specifically, the following three points are involved.

1. National governments and international organizations must recognize and support tribal rights to their traditional land, cultural autonomy, and full local sovereignty.
2. The responsibility for initiating outside contacts must rest with the tribal people themselves: outside influences may not have free access to tribal areas.

3. Industrial states must not compete with tribal societies for their resources.

In a sense, these three points represent the minimal requirements for tribal
survival in the modern world. Where they have been disregarded, tribal cultures disappear and former tribal peoples become peasants. Governments
have systematically ignored all three of these points—contact has been forced
on the tribes; their resources have been exploited; and their rights to land, political sovereignty, and cultural autonomy have been destroyed. If this situation were reversed it would be quite reasonable to assume that tribal cultures
could survive.

Cultural autonomy would perhaps best be implemented through the United
Nations, which would be authorized to designate "tribal autonomous regions"
in parts of the world where autonomous or semiautonomous tribal peoples
still survive. These autonomous regions would be permanently withdrawn
from the sovereignty of the nations that now happen to claim control over
them, and the borders would be secured by international peace-keeping
forces. Health assistance to counteract introduced epidemics could be supplied by the World Health Organization. These proposals are, of course, only
broad outlines, and no attempt is being made to answer specific problems that
might arise if cultural autonomy were implemented in specific areas. The purpose here is to merely raise the issue and to suggest that it is a rational alternative that *should* be considered.

Objections to Cultural Autonomy

Suggestions that the Tasaday, stone-tool-using peoples recently "discovered"
in the Philippines, be left undisturbed have predictably brought charges that
such action would be immoral because it would deny them access to the cultural heritage of Western civilization. Such objections can be disregarded as
simple ethnocentrism, but several other objections are more serious and de-
serve more careful discussion. The cultural autonomy alternative has unfortunately been misunderstood and misrepresented by those who have obscured
it under the misleading category of isolation policies where it could be
ridiculed with false emotional arguments about "human zoos" and "living
museums." As a so-called human zoo policy, cultural autonomy has been criticized as "sheer cruelty" (Williams-Hunt 1952:79) because it would "deny
them the chance to progress"; and has been labeled "inhuman and inefficient"
and "morally wrong" because it would perpetuate famine, disease, and ignorance (Goulet 1971:208, 249); and a "retrograde step" that would stifle "the

right of people to mould their lives according to their light" (Ghurye 1963:193, 172–73). It has also been called simply impossible (Elwin 1959:59) and those who would propose it are accused of not believing the tribals capable of advance or of wishing to keep them in their place, or else their sanity is questioned and they are accused of other inhuman motives.

No reasonable person could suppose that it would be possible; to turn vast areas of the world into preserves for the protection of native cultures. (Metraux 1953:883–84)

No sane, humane and well-informed scientist or scholar could possibly argue that in the interests of the ethnological or cultural record any part of New Guinea should be preserved as a cultural museum or human zoo. (Bulmer 1971:18)

It must be emphasized that cultural autonomy would permit tribal peoples to choose the degree of isolation they wished to maintain; it would not lock them in cages. It would hardly be considered a human zoo approach unless people were deliberately confined against their will for display and scientific observation. Such criticisms might be expected from those who have difficulty viewing different cultures as something other than objects for study and who are too ethnocentric to recognize that other peoples might actually wish to maintain their own lifestyles. Granting a reprieve from progress to the handful of tribal peoples scattered in remote areas with only limited economic potential will certainly not work a hardship on the rest of the world. The resources involved would be insignificant. Even more importantly, it is clear that the industrial world must learn to curtail its rates of resource consumption in any event.

Some will feel that the principle of cultural autonomy may have merit but assume that it is too late to apply because change has already gone too far. This argument about the supposed futility of attempting to "turn back the hands of the clock" (Smith 1934) has been used for years, and was in vogue even when there were still very large populations of essentially untouched tribal peoples. In 1956, Barnett (1956:62) stated that anthropologists "appreciate the futility of advocating a restoration of an extinct way of life." That may be true, but the critical question is: At what point are changes caused by outside intrusion irreversible? It must not be forgotten that there are numerous examples of people reverting to traditional patterns after major changes had occurred. This was the case, for example, in many areas of the Pacific when people were forced to rely on their subsistence economies during the economic depression of the 1930s (Thompson 1940:92); in the Philippines when political upheaval left tribal peoples on their own (Keesing 1934:74); in the Peruvian Amazon when, in 1742, the Campa revolted after intensive Franciscan domination and were left to enjoy more than two hundred years of full autonomy (Bodley 1970:3–7); or the recent case of Canadian Cree "returning to nature" (Anonymous 1972). Judging from these and other similar cases, it might be well to let tribal peoples decide for themselves when their way of life is extinct.

Those who recognize the validity of a cultural autonomy approach, but who argue that it would be impossible or impractical to carry out, may be reminded that it has already been applied to a limited extent in at least a de facto fashion in several parts of the world in recent times. Any areas that have effectively remained outside government control either because they were too remote or because they contained no valuable resources are de facto tribal autonomous regions. Cultural autonomy has with qualifications been temporary official policy in several areas. Modern examples might include the British *inner line policy* in the northeast frontier areas of India (Elwin 1961:43–44); the *closed districts* policy in the Anglo-Egyptian Sudan; the *uncontrolled areas* policy in Australian New Guinea; the *Inini statute* applied to the Indians of interior French Guiana until 1968 (Hurault 1972:360–62); and Rennel and Bellona islands in the British Solomons. Autonomy was also proposed but never implemented for the Aborigines of Arnhem Land in Australia. The Xingu National Park in Brazil has often been described as a human zoo, but it is not a real example of cultural autonomy for several reasons. Even with careful regulation, outsiders have been allowed extensive contacts with the Xingu tribes. Economic dependency on industrial goods has been fostered by both park officials and military officers. Tourists and researchers have been flown in to observe the people, and most significantly, the tribal lands have not proven inalienable. When cultural autonomy has in effect been official policy, it has only been for a limited time and then only for the convenience of the government. These examples demonstrate, however, that tribal autonomy is neither impossible nor impractical when it is thought desirable, but such policies must not be left to the whims of individual states.

Final Arguments

The important point to remember is that tribal societies are not museum pieces to be preserved as curiosities, but they are composed of real people who have developed unique adaptations to unique environments. They have given every indication that they wish to continue pursuing their own life styles, and they should have that alternative.

Perhaps the most important reason for a cultural/autonomy approach is not simply that many tribal peoples have shown repeatedly by their actions that this is what they desire, but rather it may well be that global cultural diversity will be as critical for the long-run survival of mankind as some suggest (Meggers 1971:166; Watt 1972; Dubos 1965; Rappaport 1971). This argument must be taken with special seriousness now that cultures that specifically reject many of the values resulting in our present worldwide environmental problems are themselves about to disappear. We should not forget Tax's recent warning.

> I am certain that there is something for us . . . industrialists to learn from the values associated with the tribal life and with the determination of these peoples to preserve this way of life at all costs. (Tax 1968:345–46)

If industrial civilization cannot exploit tribal cultures without destroying them and degrading their environments, then perhaps it should leave alone those that remain. Anthropologists, at least, might do well to acknowledge their complicity in the destruction of tribal cultures, and to reexamine the question of alternatives. We might remember that even Alan Holmberg came to regret his "adventures in culture change" with the Siriono.

> Today I am frequently disturbed by the fact that I had a hand in initiating some of the changes which probably ultimately overwhelmed them and over which neither I nor they had control. Indeed, when I contemplate what I did, I am not infrequently filled with strong feelings of guilt. Maybe they should have been left as they were. (Holmberg 1954:113)

Given the realities of the present world, it must be admitted that the cultural autonomy solution, while it may be perfectly rational and workable in theory, would be highly unlikely to be implemented. It will undoubtedly remain an intriguing dream of what could have been. In a real sense, it is already too late. Primitive culture, or at least the present generation of primitive culture, is gone—after a very long and successful tenure. If we also realistically assess the present condition of the culture of consumption, it seems likely that this culture, too, will disappear—also a victim of progress, but after a very brief and preposterous career. The important question is: How will the culture of consumption go? Will it be forced to gradually transform itself into a new primitive culture, or will it go out with a total, catastrophic collapse, leaving a shattered world from which a new primitive culture will painfully evolve? In either event, it may be predicted that in the long run if humanity survives, primitive culture will be restored as the most viable human adaptation.

Bibliography

Aborigines Protection Society. 1837–1847. *Annual Report.* Vols. 1–10. London.

Ackermann, F. L. 1964. *Geologia e Fisiografia da Região Bragantina, Estado do Para.* Manaus, Brazil: Conselho Nacional de Pesquisas, Instituto National de Pesquisas da Amazonia.

Aguinda v. Texaco. http://www.texacorainforest.com/case/ComplaintEcuador.pdf (accessed September 2007).

Akeley, Mary L. Jobe. 1931. "Africa's first national park." *Scientific American* (November): 295–98.

Alaska Department of Natural Resources, Division of Forestry. n.d. *Who Owns/Manages Alaska?* Poster. http://plats.landrecords.info/images/who_owns_alaska_poster.jpg (accessed July 7, 2007).

Allan, William. 1965. *The African Husbandman.* New York: Barnes and Noble.

Allard, William Albert, and Loren McIntyre. 1988. "Rondônia's settlers invade Brazil's imperiled rain forest." *National Geographic* 174(6): 772–99.

Altman, J. C. 2006. *In Search of an Outstations Policy for Indigenous Australians.* Working Paper No. 34. Centre for Aboriginal Economic Policy Research, 3, tables 1 and 2.

———. 2007. *Neo-Paternalism and the Destruction of CDEP.* Centre for Aboriginal Economic Policy Research, Topical Issue No. 14. http://www.anu.edu.au/caepr/Publications/topical/Altman_Paternalism.pdf.

Altman, J. C., G. J. Buchanan, and L. Larsen. 2007. *The Environmental Significance of the Indigenous Estate: Natural Resource Management as Economic Development in Remote Australia.* CAEPR Discussion Paper No. 286. Australian National University, College of Arts & Social Sciences. http://www.anu.edu.au/caepr/discussion.php.

Amazon Defense Coalition. 2006. *Rainforest Catastrophe: Chevon's Fraud and Deceit in Ecuador: An Investigative Report by the Lago Agrio Legal Team of the Amazon Defense Coalition.* http://www.texacotoxico.org/docs/PDF%20Files/rainforest_catastrophe.pdf.

Anderson, Douglas D., Ray Bane, Richard K. Nelson, Wanni W. Anderson, and Nita Sheldon. 1977. *Kuunanmiit Subsistence: Traditional Eskimo Life in the Latter Twentieth Century.* Washington, DC: National Park Service, U.S. Department of the Interior.

Andrist, Ralph K. 1969. *The Long Death: The Last Days of the Plains Indian.* New York: Collier Books.

Anonymous. 1945. "Indians shoot at plane." *Life* 18 (March 19): 70–72.

———. 1972. "Back-to-Wild Movement Attracting More Native People in Alberta." *Akwesasne Notes* 4(3): 36.

———. 1972. "Columbia trial reveals life ('Everyone kills Indians') on plains." *Akwesasne Notes* 4(4): 26.

Arcand, Bernard. 1972. The *Urgent Situation of the Cuiva Indians of Colombia*. IWGIA Document no. 7. Copenhagen: IWGIA.

Arctic Athabaskan Council. 2005. *News Release: Arctic Indigenous Peoples Unveil Statement on Climate Change*. http://www.arcticathabaskancouncil.com/press/20051206.php.

Arctic Climate Impact Assessment (ACIA). 2004. *Impacts of a Warming Arctic: Arctic Climate Impact Assessment*. Cambridge: Cambridge University Press. http://amap.no/acia/.

Arctic Environmental Protection Strategy. 1991. *Declaration on the Protection of Arctic Environment*. Rovaniemi, Finland: Arctic Council. http://www.arcticcouncil.org/Archives /AEPS%20Docs/artic_environment.pdf.

Arensberg, Conrad M., and Arthur H. Niehoff. 1964. *Introducing Social Change: A Manual for Americans Overseas*. Chicago: Aldine.

Arhem, Kaj. 1985. *The Maasai and the State: The Impact of Rural Development Policies on a Pastoral People in Tanzania*. IWGIA Document no. 52. Copenhagen: IWGIA.

Arias, Marcial. *An Assessment of the Implementation of International Commitments on Traditional Forest Related Knowledge in Panama*. Chiang Mai, Thailand: International Alliance of Indigenous and Tribal Peoples of Tropical Forests. http://www.international-alliance.org/documents/Panama-finaledit.pdf (assessed September 2007).

Arnold, Robert. 1978. *Alaska Native Land Claims*. Anchorage: Alaska Native Foundation.

Arvelo-Jimenez, Nelly. 1984. *La Reserva de Biosfera Yanomami: Una Autentica Estrategia para el Ecodesarrollo Nacional (Borrador de Trabajo)*. Caracas: Instituto Venezolano de Investigaciones Cientificas.

Asch, Michael. 1977. "The Dene economy." In *Dene Nation—The Colony Within*, edited by Mel Watkins, 47–61. Toronto: University of Toronto Press.

Asch, Michael, and Colin Samson. 2004. "On the return of the native." *Current Anthropology* 45(2): 261–67.

———. 2006. "More on the return of the native." *Current Anthropology* 47(1): 145–49.

Asociación de Cabildos Indígenas del Norte del Cauca (ACIN). 2005. Libertad para la Madre Tierra: El Camino Hacia una Reforma Agraria Popular en Colombia. http://www .nasaacin.net/noticias.htm?x=1612.

———. 2007. Situación de Derechos Humanos y Derecho Internacional Humanitario Zona Norte del Departamento del Cauca. http://www.nasaacin.net/informe_dh_y_dih.htm.

Asociación Interétnica de Desarrollo de la Selva Peruana (Interethnic Development Association of the Peruvian Amazon, AIDESEP). http://www.aidesep.org.pe/.

Australia Attorney-General's Office. 2007. *Native Title Act 1993*, Part 1.3 Objects. http://www.ag.gov.au/www/agd/agd.nsf/Page/Indigenous_law_and_native_titleNative_title.

Australia Commonwealth Bureau of Census and Statistics. 1970. *Official Yearbook of the Commonwealth of Australia*. No. 56. Canberra: Bureau of Census and Statistics.

Australian Bureau of Statistics. 2007. *Population Distribution, Aboriginal and Torres Strait Islander Australians, 2006*. Cat no. 4705.0. http://www.abs.gov.au/AUSSTATS/abs@.nsf /DetailsPage/4705.02006?OpenDocument.

Australia Department of Aboriginal Affairs. 1977. *Address by the Minister for Aboriginal Affairs the Honourable R. I. Viner at the Announcement of the Poll Results for the National Aboriginal Conference Elections*. Perth, November 28, 1977. Pamphlet.

———. 1978. *Statement by the Honorable R. I. Viner, M. P., Minister for Aboriginal Affairs, on Aboriginal Policies & Achievements in Aboriginal Affairs, House of Representatives*. November 24, 1978. Pamphlet.

Australia Department of Families, Community Services and Indigenous Affairs. 2007. *Northern Territory Emergency Response.* FaCSIA 0635R. http://www.facsia.gov.au/nter/docs /nter_180807.pdf.

Australia Department of Territories, Territory of Paupa. 1965. *Report for 1964–1965.* Canberra: Commonwealth Government Printer.

———. 1968. *Report for 1967–1968.* Canberra: Commonwealth Government Printer.

Australia Minister for Families, Community Services and Indigenous Affairs. 2007. National Indigenous Council. http://www.atsia.gov.au/NIC/default.aspx.

Australia Parliament of the Commonwealth. 1987. *Return to Country: The Aboriginal Homelands Movement in Australia.* House of Representatives Standing Committee on Aboriginal Affairs. Canberra.

Awad, Mohamed. 1962. "Nomadism in the Arab lands of the Middle East." In *The Problems of the Arid Zone,* 325–39. Paris: UNESCO.

Bailey, Robert. 1982. "Development in the Ituri Forest of Zaire." *Cultural Survival Quarterly* 6(2): 23–25.

Baker, John R. 1928. "Depopulation in Espiritu Santo, New Hebrides." *Journal of the Royal Anthropological Institute* 58: 279–303.

———. 1929. "The Northern New Hebrides." *Geographical Journal* 73(4): 305–25.

Barber, James. 1967. *Rhodesia: The Road to Rebellion.* London: Oxford University Press.

Barker, Holly M. 2004. *Bravo for the Marshallese: Regaining Control in a Post-Nuclear, Post-Colonial World.* Belmont, CA: Thomson/Wadsworth.

Barnaby, Georgy, George Kurszewski, and Gerry Cheezie. 1977. "The political system and the Dene." In *Dene Nation—The Colony Within,* edited by Mel Watkins, 120–29. Toronto: University of Toronto Press.

Barnett, Homer G. 1956. *Anthropology in Administration.* New York: Row, Peterson.

Barnett, Jon, and W. Neil Adger. 2003. "Climate Dangers and Atoll Countries." *Climatic Change* 61: 321–37.

Barth, Fredrik. 1962. "Nomadism in the mountain and plateau areas of South West Asia." In *The Problems of the Arid Zone,* 341–55. Paris: UNESCO.

Bartolome, Miguel Alberto. 1972. "The situation of the Indians in the Argentine: The Chaco area and Misiones Province." In *The Situation of the Indian in South America,* edited by W. Dostal, 218–51. Geneva: World Council of Churches.

Bascom, William R. 1965. *Ponape: A Pacific Economy in Transition.* Anthropological Records 22. Berkeley and Los Angeles: University of California Press.

Bauer, Peter T., and Basil S. Yamey. 1957. *The Economics of Under-Developed Countries.* Cambridge Economic Handbooks. Chicago: University of Chicago Press.

Bay, Christian 1984. "Human rights on the periphery: No room in the ark for the Yanomami?" *Development Dialogue* 1(2): 23–41.

Bennett, Gordon. 1978. *Aboriginal Rights in International Law.* Occasional Paper no. 37. London: Royal Anthropological Institute of Great Britain & Ireland.

Bennett, Gordon, Audrey Colson, and Stuart Wavell. 1978. *The Damned: The Plight of the Akawaio Indians of Guyana.* Survival International Document no. 7. London: Survival International.

Berger, Thomas R. 1977. *Northern Frontier, Northern Homeland: the Report of the Mackenzie Valley Pipeline Inquiry.* Ottawa: Minister of Supply and Services.

———. 1985. *Village Journey: The Report of the Alaska Native Review Commission.* New York: Hill and Wang.

———. 2006. *The Nunavut Project. Conciliator's Final Report. Nunavut Land Claims Agreement Implementation Contract Negotiations for the Second Planning Period 2003–2013.* http://www.ainc-inac.gc.ca/pr/agr/nu/lca/nlc_e.pdf.

Berkhofer, Robert F. 1965. *Salvation and the Savage: An Analysis of Protestant Missions and American Indian Response, 1787–1862*. Lexington: University of Kentucky Press.

Berreman, Gerald. 1978a. "Scale and social relations: Thoughts and three examples." In *Scale and Social Organization*, edited by Fredrik Earth, 41–77. Oslo: Universitetsforlaget.

——. 1978b. "Scale and social relations." *Current Anthropology* 19(2): 225–45.

Beshir, Mohamed Omer. 1968. *The Southern Sudan: Background to Conflict*. New York: Praeger.

Bijlmer, H. J. T. 1953. "Protection of native societies." *Proceedings of the Seventh Pacific Science Congress*. Christchurch, NZ: Pegasus Press, 7: 131–34.

Billington, Ray A. 1963. "The frontier in American thought and character." In *The New World Looks at Its History*, edited by Archibald R. Lewis and Thomas F. McGann, 77–94. Austin: University of Texas Press.

Birdsell, Joseph B. 1971. "Ecology, spacing mechanisms, and adaptive behavior in aboriginal land tenure." In *Land Tenure in the Pacific*, edited by Ron Crocombe, 334–61. Melbourne: Oxford University Press.

Black, Edwin. 2006. *Internal Combustion: How Corporations and Governments Addicted the World to Oil and Derailed the Alternatives*. New York: St. Martin's Press.

Bodley, John H. 1970. *Campa Socio-Economic Adaptation*. Ann Arbor, MI: University Microfilms.

——. 1972. *Tribal Survival in the Amazon: The Campa Case*. IWGIA Document no. 5. Copenhagen: IWGIA.

——. 1975. *Victims of Progress*. Menlo Park, CA: Cummings.

——. 1976. *Anthropology and Contemporary Human Problems*. Menlo Park, CA: Cummings.

——. 1977. "Alternatives to ethnocide: Human zoos, living museums, and real people." In *Western Expansion and Indigenous Peoples*, edited by Elias Sevilla-Casas, 31–50. The Hague: Mouton.

——. 1978. "Alternatives to ethnocide: Human zoos, living museums, and real people." In *The World as a Company Town*, edited by Ahamed Idris-Soven, Elizabeth Idris-Soven, and Mary K. Vaughn, 189–207. The Hague: Mouton.

——. 1982. *Victims of Progress*. 2nd ed. Menlo Park, CA: Benjamin/Cummings.

——. 1983a. *Der Weg der Zerstörung: Stammesvolker und die industrielle Zivilization*. Munich: Trickster-Verlag. (Translation of *Victims of Progress*.)

——. 1983b. "The World Bank tribal policy: Criticisms and recommendations." *Congressional Record*, serial no. 98–37, 515–21. (Reprinted in Bodley, 1988a, 406–13.)

——. 1985. *Anthropology and Contemporary Human Problems*. 2nd ed. Palo Alto, CA, and London: Mayfield.

——, ed. 1988a. *Tribal Peoples and Development Issues: A Global Overview*. Mountain View, CA: Mayfield.

——. 1988b. "Umweltschutzer unterstutzen Stammesvolker." In *Die neuen "Wilden": Umweltschutzer unterstutzen Stammesvolker—Theorie und Praxis der Ethno-Okologie*, edited by Peter E. Stuben, 54–65. Okozid 4. Giessen: Focus Verlag.

——. 1990. *Victims of Progress*. 3rd ed. Mountain View, CA: Mayfield.

——. 1991. "Indigenous peoples vs. the state: A culture scale approach." Paper presented at Indigenous People in Remote Regions: A Global Perspective. University of Victoria, BC, July 3–5, 1991.

——. 1994a. *Cultural Anthropology: Tribes, States, and the Global System*. Mountain View, CA: Mayfield.

——. 1994b. "A culture scale perspective on human ecology and development." In *Advances in Human Ecology*, edited by Lee Freese, 3:93–112. Greenwich, CT: JAI Press.

——. 1996. *Anthropology and Contemporary Human Problems.* 3rd ed. Mountain View, CA: Mayfield.

——. 1997a. *Cultural Anthropology: Tribes, States, and the Global System.* 2nd ed. Mountain View, CA: Mayfield.

——. 1997b. *Property Inequality, Culture Scale, and Growth in the Palouse.* Unpublished report to the Edward R. Meyer Fund, College of Liberal Arts, Washington State University, Pullman.

——. 1997c. "Comment on 'Revisionism in ecological anthropology' by Thomas N. Headland." *Current Anthropology* 38(4): 611–13.

——. 1999a. "Socioeconomic growth, culture scale, and household well-being: A test of the power-elite hypothesis." *Current Anthropology* 40(5): 595–620.

——. 2001. "Growth, scale, and power in Washington State." *Human Organization* 60(4): 367–79.

——. 2003. *The Power of Scale: A Global History Approach.* Armonk, NY, and London: M. E. Sharpe.

——. 2005a. *Cultural Anthropology: Tribes, States, and the Global System.* New York: McGraw-Hill.

——. 2005b. *The Rich Tribal World: Scale and Power Perspectives on Cultural Valuation.* Presentation to the Society for Applied Anthropology Annual Meeting, Santa Fe, NM.

——. 2008. *Anthropology and Contemporary Human Problems.* Lanham, MD: AltaMira Press.

Bodley, John H., and Foley C. Benson. 1979. *Cultural Ecology of Amazonian Palms.* Reports of Investigations no. 56. Pullman: Laboratory of Anthropology, Washington State University.

Boehm, Christopher. 1993. "Egalitarian behavior and reverse dominance hierarchy." *Current Anthropology* 34(3): 227–54.

Bonilla, Victor D. 1972. "The destruction of the Colombian Indian groups." In *The Situation of the Indian in South America*, edited by W. Dostal, 56–75. Geneva: World Council of Churches.

Bowman, James D. 1965. "They like white men—broiled." (Associated Press.) *Eugene Register-Guard*, October 7, 28.

Boye, Ellen. 1974. "Samarbejde rundt om Nordpolen." In *Gronland*, 65–70. Copenhagen.

Brantlinger, Patrick. 2003. *Dark Vanishings: Discourse on the Extinction of Primitive Races.* Ithaca, NY, and London: Cornell University Press.

Brémaud, O., and J. Pagot. 1962. "Grazing lands, nomadism and transhumance in the Sahel." In *The Problems of the Arid Zone*, 311–24. Paris: UNESCO.

Brokensha, David. 1966. *Applied Anthropology in English-Speaking Africa.* Society for Applied Anthropology, Monograph no. 8. Lexington, KY: Society for Applied Anthropology.

Brooks, Nathan. 2005. *The Alaska Land Transfer Acceleration Act: Background and Summary.* Library of Congress, Congressional Research Service. http://www.lbblawyers.com/RL32734.pdf (accessed July 6, 2007).

Brownrigg, Leslie A. 1985. "Native cultures and protected areas: Management options." In *Culture and Conservation: The Human Dimension in Environmental Planning*, edited by Jeffrey A. McNeely and David Pitt, 33–44. London: Croom Helm.

Buell, Raymond L. 1928. *The Native Problem in Africa.* 2 vols. New York: Macmillan.

Bugotu, F. 1968. "The culture clash: A Melanesian's view." *New Guinea* 3(2): 65–70.

Bulmer, Ralph. 1971. "Conserving the Culture: An Institute of New Guinea Studies. *New Guinea* 6(2): 17–26.

Bunce, George E. 1972. "Aggravation of vitamin A deficiency following distribution of non-fortified skim milk: An example of nutrient interaction." In *The Careless Technology: Ecology and International Development*, edited by M. T. Farvar and John P. Milton, 53–60. Garden City, NY: Natural History Press.

Burger, Julian. 1987. *Report from the Frontier: The State of the World's Indigenous Peoples.* London: Zed Press/Cambridge, MA: Cultural Survival.

Burling, Robbins. 1963. *Rengsanggri: Family and Kinship in a Garo Village.* Philadelphia: University of Pennsylvania Press.

———. 1967. "Tribesmen and lowlanders of Assam." In *Southeast Asian Tribes, Minorities, and Nations*, edited by Peter Kunstadter, 215–29. Princeton, NJ: Princeton University Press.

Cameron, A. L. P. 1885. "Notes on some tribes of New South Wales." *Journal of the Royal Anthropological Institute* 14: 344–70.

Cana, Frank R. 1946. "German South-West Africa." *Encyclopedia Britannica*, 10:230–31.

Capot-Rey, R. 1962. "The present state of nomadism in the Sahara." In *The Problems of the Arid Zone*, 301–10. Paris: UNESCO.

Carduño, Julio. 1980. "Carta abierta a los Hermanos Indies de America." In *Primer Congreso de Movimientos Indios de Sudamerica*, 103–129. Paris: Ediciones Mitka.

Castillo-Cardenas, Gonzalo. 1972. "The Indian struggle for freedom in Colombia." In *The Situation of the Indian in South America*, edited by W. Dostal., 76–104. Geneva: World Council of Churches.

Catlin, George. 1841. *Letters and Notes on the Manners, Customs, and Conditions of the North American Indian.* London: Tosswill and Myers.

Cavalli-Sforza, Luigi Luca, ed. 1986. *African Pygmies*. New York: Academic Press.

Center for Economic and Social Rights. 1994. *Rights Violations in the Ecuadorian Amazon: The Human Consequences of Oil Development. New York: The Center for Economic and Social Rights.* http://www.texacorainforest.com/case/Rights_Violations_1.pdf.

Chagnon, Napoleon A. *1983. Yanomamo: The Fierce People.* New York: Holt, Rinehart and Winston.

Chapin, M. 2000. *Defending Kuna Yala: PEMASKY, The Study Project for the Management of the Wildlands of Kuna Yala, Panama. A case study for Shifting the power: Decentralization and biodiversity conservation.* Washington, DC: Biodiversity Support Program. http://www.worldwildlife.org/bsp/publications/aam/panama/panama.html.

Chapman, Audrey. 1992. *Human Rights Implications of Indigenous Peoples' Intellectual Property Rights.* Paper presented at the American Anthropological Association Annual Meeting, San Francisco.

Chase-Sardi, Miguel. 1972. "The present situation of the Indians in Paraguay." In *The Situation of the Indian in South America*, edited by W. Dostal, 173–217. Geneva: World Council of Churches.

Chase-Sardi, Miguel, and Adolfo Colombres. 1975. *Por la Liberation del Indigena.* Buenos Aires: Ediciones del Sol.

Chatterjee, Suhas. 1967. "Language and literacy in the North-Eastern regions." In *A Common Perspective for North-East India*, edited by Rathin Mittra and Barun Das Gupta, 19–23. Calcutta: Pannalal Das Gupta.

Chaumeil, J. P. 1984. *Between Zoo and Slavery: The Yagua of Eastern Peru and Their Present Situation.* IWGIA Document no. 49. Copenhagen: IWGIA.

Chávez, Gina. 2005. *Sarayaku: El Pueblo del Cenít Identidad y Construcción.* Informe antropológico-juridico sobre los impactos sociales y culturales de la Compañia CGC en Sarayaku. Quito. http://www.cdes.org.ec/biblioteca/libros/sarayaku-cenit.pdf.

Chávez, Gina, Isabela Figueroa, Paulina Garzón, Marioa Melo, Victor López, and Norman Wray. 2002. *Tarimiat Firmes en Nuestro Territorio: FIPSE vs. ARCO.* 2nd ed. Quito: Centro de Derechos Económicos y Sociales, (CDES), Confederación de Nacionalidades Indígenas del Ecuador, (CONAIE). http://www.escr-net.org/usr_doc/FIPSE_Firmes_en_nuestro _territorio_2002.pdf.

Chevon Corporation. 2007. *Plaintiffs' Myths, Distortions and Falsifications*. http://www.texaco.com/sitelets/ecuador/en/plaintiffs_myths.asp.

Chirif, Alberto. 1975. "En torno a la titulacion de las comunidades nativas y a los recursos forestales y de fauna silvestre." In *Marginacion y Futuro*. Serie: Communidades Nativas, 66–76. Lima: Sistema Nacional de Apoyo a la Movilizacion Social, Direccion General de Organizaciones Rurales.

Colonialism and Indigenous Minorities Research and Action (CIMRA). 1979. "Yes, but what can I do?" *New Internationalist* 77 (July): 27.

Clad, James C. 1985. "Conservation and indigenous peoples: A study of convergent interests." In *Culture and Conservation: The Human Dimension in Environmental Planning*, ed. Jeffrey A. McNeely and David Pitt, 45–62. London: Croom Helm. (Reprinted in Bodley, 1988a, 30–334.)

Clark, Grover. 1936. *The Balance Sheets of Imperialism: Facts and Figures on Colonies*. New York: Columbia University Press.

Clastres, Pierre. 1977. *Society against the State: The Leader as Servant and the Humane Uses of Power among the Indians of the Americas*. New York: Urizen Books.

Cleave, T. L. 1974. *The Saccharine Disease*. Bristol, UK: Wright.

Clyde, Paul H. 1935. *Japan's Pacific Mandate*. New York: Macmillan

Cobo, José Martinez. 1986. *Study of the Problem of Discrimination against Indigenous Populations*. UN Document: E/CN.4/Sub.2/1986/7/Add.4.

Consejo de Desarrollo de las Nacionalidades y Pueblos del Ecuador (CODENPE). 2007. *Nacionalidades y Pueblos Indígenas del Ecuador*. http://www.codenpe.gov.ec/npe.htm (accessed October 1, 2007).

———. 2007. Miembros. http://www.coica.org.ec/sp/miembros/opiac.html.

Cole, Monica M. 1966. *South Africa*. London: Methuen.

Collier, George. 1994. *Basta! Land and the Zapatista Rebellion in Chiapas*. Oakland, CA: Food First Books.

Collier, John. 1947. *The Indians of the Americas*. New York: W. W. Norton.

Conference Board of Canada. 2001. *Nunavut Economic Outlook: An Examination of the Nunavut Economy*. http://www.gov.nu.ca/frv21.pdf.

Confederación de Nacionalidades Indígenas del Ecuador (CONAIE). 2006. Pueblos Indígenas en Aislamiento Voluntario en la Amazonía Ecuatoriana: Documento Base. http://www.sosyasuni.org/files/conaie_taromenani2.pdf.

Congreso Kuna. *Normas Kunas: Ley Fundamental y Estatuto de Kuna Yala*. http://www.congresogeneralkuna.org/normas%20kunas.htm (accessed September 9, 2007).

Conrad, Joseph. 1971. *Heart of Darkness*, edited by Robert Kimbrough. New York: W. W. Norton.

Convention on Biological Diversity (Convenio Sobre la Diversidad Biologica). 2007. *Informe de possible medidas para asegurar el respeto de los derechos de comunidades indigenas y locales desprotegidas y voluntariamente aisladas tomando en consideracion sus conocimientos tradicionales y el desarrollo de acceso y participacion en los beneficios*. Grupo de Trabajo Especial de Composicion Abierta Entre Periodos de Sesiones Sobre el Articulo 8(j) y Disposiciones Conexas del Convenio Sobre Diversidad Biologica. UNEP/CBD/WG8J/5/INF/17. June 31, 2007, Anexo II. http://www.cbd.int/doc/meetings/tk/wg8j-05/information/wg8j-05-inf-17-es.pdf.

Cook, Sherburne F. 1955. "The epidemic of 1830–1833 in California and Oregon." *University of California Publications in American Archaeology and Ethnology* 43: 303–26.

Cooper, John M. 1946. "The Patagonian and Pampean hunters." In *Handbook of South American Indians*, edited by Julian H. Steward, 127–68. Vol. 1. Bureau of American Ethnology. Bulletin no. 143. Washington, DC: Smithsonian Institution.

Coppens, Walter. 1972. *The Anatomy of a Land Invasion Scheme in Yekuana Territory, Venezuela*. IWGIA Document no. 9. Copenhagen: IWGIA.

Cornevin, Robert. 1969. "The Germans in Africa before 1918." In *The History and Politics of Colonialism 1870–1914*, edited by L. H. Gann and Peter Duignan. Vol. 1: *Colonialism in Africa 1870–1960*. Cambridge: Cambridge University Press.

Corris, Peter. 1968. *Aborigines and Europeans in Western Victoria*. Occasional Papers in Aboriginal Studies no. 12, Ethnohistory Series no. 1. Canberra: Australian Institute of Aboriginal Studies.

Corry, Stephen. 1976. *Towards Indian Self-Determination in Colombia*. Survival International Document no. 2. London: Survival International.

———. 1993. *"Harvest Moonshine" Taking You for a Ride: A Critique of the "Rainforest Harvest"—Its Theory and Practice*. London: Survival International.

Cowan, James. 1922–1923. *The New Zealand Wars*. Wellington: R. E. Owen, Government Printer.

Crawford, J. R. 1967. *Witchcraft and Sorcery in Rhodesia*. London: Oxford University Press (for International African Institute).

Crocombe, Ron. 1968. "Bougainville! Copper, R. R. A. and secessionism." *New Guinea* 3(3): 39–49.

———. 1971. "Land Reform: Prospects for Prosperity." In *Land Tenure in the Pacific*, ed. R. Crocombe, 375–400. Melbourne: Oxford University Press, 380.

———, ed. 1971. *Land Tenure in the Pacific*. Melbourne: Oxford University Press.

Crocombe, Ron, and Robin Hide. 1971. "New Guinea: Unity in diversity." In *Land Tenure in the Pacific*, edited by R. Crocombe, 292–333. Melbourne: Oxford University Press.

Cunnison, Ian George. 1966. *Bagara Arabs: Power and Lineage in a Sudanese Nomad Tribe*. Oxford: Clarendon Press.

———. 1967. *Nomads in the Nineteen-Sixties*. Hull, UK: Hull University.

Daes, Erica-Irene. 1996. *A Working Paper on the Concept of "Indigenous People."* UN Commission of Human Rights, Sub-Commission on the Promotion and Protection of Human Rights (E/CN.4/Sub.2/AC.4/1996/2) June 10, 1996.

Daly, Herman E. 1993. "The perils of free trade." *Scientific American* 269(5): 50–57.

Departamento Administrativo Nacional de Estadistica (DANE). 1978. *Elementos para el Estudio de los Resguardos Indigenas del Cauca*. Bogota: DANE.

d'Ans, Andre-Marcel. 1972. "Les tribus indigenes du Parc National du Manu." *Proceedings of the International Congress of Americanists* 39(4): 95–100.

———. 1980. "Begegnung in Peru." In *Ist Gott Amerikaner?* Edited by Søren Hvalkof and Peter Aaby, 309–51. Gottingen, Germany: Lamuv Verlag.

Darwin, Charles. 1871. *The Descent of Man*. New York: D. Appleton and Company.

Dasmann, R. F. 1973. "Sanctuaries for life styles?" *IUCN Bulletin*, n.s. 4(8): 29.

———. 1975a. *The Conservation Alternative*. New York: John Wiley and Sons.

———. 1975b. "Difficult marginal environments and the traditional societies which exploit them." *News from Survival International* 11 (July): 11–15.

———. 1976. "National parks, nature conservation, and 'future primitive.'" *Ecologist* 6(5): 164–78. (Reprinted in Bodley, 1988a, 301–10.)

———. 1982. *The Relationship between Protected Areas and Indigenous Peoples*. Paper presented at World National Parks Congress, Bali, Indonesia.

———. 1983. *Biosphere Reserves and Human Needs*. First International Biosphere Reserve Congress. Minsk, Belarus.

Davies, James B., Susanna Sandstrom, Anthony Shorrocks, and Edward N. Wolff. 2006. *The World Distribution of Household Wealth*. Helsinki, Finland: World Institute for Development Economics Research.

Davis, A. E., and T. D. Bolin. 1972. "Lactose intolerance in Southeast Asia." In *The Careless Technology: Ecology and International Development*, edited by M. T. Farvar and John P. Milton, 61–68. Garden City, NY: Natural History Press.

Davis, Shelton H. 1977. *Victims of the Miracle: Development and the Indians of Brazil*. Cambridge: Cambridge University Press.

———. 1980. "Brazilian Indian policy: The present situation." *ARC Bulletin* 3: 2–3.

De'Ath, Colin, and Gregory Michalenko. 1980. "High technology and original peoples: The case of deforestation in Papua New Guinea and Canada." *Impact of Science on Society* 30(3): 197–209. (Reprinted in Bodley, 1988a, 166–80.)

De Marco, Roland R. 1943. *The Italianization of African Natives: Government Native Education in the Italian Colonies 1890–1937*. Teacher's College, Columbia University Contributions to Education no. 880. New York: Columbia University Press.

DeMarrais, Elizabeth, Luis Jaime Castillo, and Timothy Earle. 1996. "Ideology, materialization, and power strategies." *Current Anthropology* 37(1): 15–31.

Denevan, William M. 1976. "Epilogue." In *The Native Population of the Americas in 1492*, edited by William M. Denevan, 289–92. Madison: University of Wisconsin Press.

Dennett, Glenn, and John Connell. 1988. "Acculturation and health in the highlands of Papua New Guinea." *Current Anthropology* 29(2): 273–99.

Diamond, Stanley. 1960. "Introduction: The uses of the primitive." In *Primitive Views of the World*, edited by Stanley Diamond, v–xxix. New York: Columbia University Press.

———. 1968. "The search for the primitive." In *The Concept of the Primitive*, edited by Ashley Montagu, 96–147. New York: Free Press.

Diao, Richard K. 1967. "The national minorities of China and their relations with the Chinese Communist regime." In *Southeast Asian Tribes, Minorities, and Nations*, edited by Peter Kunstadter, 169–201. Princeton, NJ: Princeton University Press.

Dilley, M. R. 1966. *British Policy in Kenya Colony*. New York: Barnes and Noble.

Dobyns, Henry F. 1966. "Estimating Aboriginal American population: An appraisal of techniques with a new hemispheric estimate." *Current Anthropology* 7(4): 395–449.

Docker, Edward W. 1970. *The Blackbirders: The Recruiting of South Seas Labour for Queensland, 1863–1907*. Sydney: Angus and Robertson.

Dostal, W., ed. 1972. *The Situation of the Indian in South America*. Geneva: World Council of Churches.

Drewnowski, Adam, and Barry M. Popkin. 1997. "The nutrition transition: New trends in the global diet." *Nutrition Review* 55(2): 31–43.

Drucker, Charles. 1985. "Dam the Chico: Hydropower development and tribal resistance." *Ecologist* 15(4): 149–57. (Reprinted in Bodley, 1988a, 151–65.)

Dubos, Rene. 1965. *Man Adapting*. New Haven: Yale University Press.

Dyson-Hudson, Neville. 1962. "Factors inhibiting change in an African pastoral society." *Transactions of the New York Academy of Sciences*, ser. 2, vol. 24: 771–801.

Dyson-Hudson, Rada, and Neville Dyson-Hudson. 1969. "Subsistence herding in Uganda." *Scientific American* 220(2): 76–89.

Ecuador Ministerio de Ambiente. 2007. *La Política Nacional de los Pueblos en Situación de Aislamiento Voluntario*. www.ambiente.gov.ec/paginas_espanol/docs/Politicanacional.pdf.

Eder, James F. 1987. *On the Road to Tribal Extinction: Depopulation, Deculturation, and Adaptive Well-Being among the Batak of the Philippines*. Berkeley and Los Angeles: University of California Press.

Edgerton, Robert B. 1992. *Sick Societies: Challenging the Myth of Primitive Harmony.* New York: Free Press.

Eiselen, W. M. 1934. "Christianity and the religious life of the Bantu." In *Western Civilization and the Natives of South Africa,* edited by I. Schapera, 65–82. London: George Routledge and Sons.

Elkin, A. P. 1934. "Anthropology and the future of the Australian Aborigines." *Oceania* 5(1): 1–18.

———. 1935. "Presidential address: Anthropology in Australia, past and present." *Report of the 22nd Meeting of ANZAAS* 22: 196–207.

———. 1951. "Reaction and interaction: A food gathering people and European settlement in Australia." *American Anthropologist* 53: 164–86.

Elwin, Verrier. 1939. *The Baiga.* London: John Murray.

———. 1959. *A Philosophy for NEFA.* 2nd ed. Shillong, India: J. N. Chowdhury.

———. 1961. *Nagaland.* Shillong: P. Dutta.

———. 1969. *The Nagas in the Nineteenth Century.* London: Oxford University Press.

Fabre, D. G. 1963. *Más Allá del Rio das Mortes.* Buenos Aires: Ediciones Selectas.

Falla, Ricardo. 1979a. *Historia Kuna—Historia Rebelde.* Serie El Indio Panameno no. 4. Panama: Ediciones "CCS" (Centra de Capacitacion Social).

———. 1979b. *El Tesoro de San Blas.* Serie El Indio Panameno no. 5. Panama: Ediciones "CCS" (Centre de Capacitacion Social).

Fallows, James. 1993. "How the world works." *Atlantic Monthly* 272(6): 60–87.

Federación de Centros Shuar. 1976. *Solución Original a un Problema Actual.* Sucua, Ecuador: Federación de Centros Shuar.

Fenbury, David. 1968. "Those Mokolkols! New Britain's bloody axemen." *New Guinea* 3(2): 33–50.

Fey, Harold E., and D'Arcy McNickle. 1970. *Indians and Other Americans: Two Ways of Life Meet.* New York: Harper and Row.

Flower, W. H. 1882. "Chairman's Address for Anthropology." *British Association for the Advancement of Science, Report for 1881* 51: 688.

———. 1884. "President's address on the aims and prospects of the study of anthropology." *Journal of the Royal Anthropological Institute* 13: 488–507.

Forde, Daryll. 1953. "Applied anthropology in government: British Africa." In *Anthropology Today,* edited by A. L. Kroeber, 841–65. Chicago: University of Chicago Press.

Formosa Bureau of Aboriginal Affairs. 1911. *Report on the Control of the Aborigines of Formosa.* Taihoku: Formosa Bureau of Aboriginal Affairs.

Fortune. 2007. "Fortune Global 500." July 23. http://money.cnn.com/magazines/fortune /global500/2007/.

Foster, George M. 1969. *Applied Anthropology.* Boston: Little, Brown.

Frere, Sir H. Bartle. 1881. "On the laws affecting the relations between civilized and savage life, as bearing on the dealings of colonists with Aborigines." *Journal of the Royal Anthropological Institute* 11: 313–54.

Friede, Juan. 1952. "Los Cofán: Una tribu de la alta Amazonia Colombiana." *Proceedings, International Congress of Americanists* 30: 202–19.

Fuentes, Hildebrando. 1908. *Loreto—Apuntes Geograficos, Historicos, Estadisticos, Politicos y Sociales.* Vol. 2. Lima: Imprenta de la Revista.

Fundação Nacional do Índio (FUNAI). 2007. Povos Indígenas: As terras-Situação Atual. www.funai.gov.br/index.html (accessed July 8, 2007).

Furlong, Charles Wellington. 1915. "The Haush and Ona, primitive tribes of Tierra del Fuego." *Proceedings, International Congress of Americanists* 19: 432–44.

Furneaux, Rupert. 1963. *The Zulu War: Isandhlwana and Rorke's Drift*. Philadelphia and New York: J. B. Lippincott.

Gardner, J. E., and J. G. Nelson. 1981. "National parks and native peoples in Northern Canada, Alaska, and Northern Australia." *Environmental Conservation* 8(3): 207–15. (Reprinted in Bodley, 1988a, 334–51.)

Garra, Lobodon. 1969. *A Sangre y Lanza*. Buenos Aires: Ediciones Anaconda.

Ghurye, G. S. 1963. *The Scheduled Tribes*. 3rd ed. Bombay: G. R. Bhatkal.

Goldschmidt, Walter R. 1952. "The interrelations between cultural factors and the acquisition of new technical skills." In *The Progress of Underdeveloped Areas*, edited by Bert F. Hoselitz, 135–51. Chicago: University of Chicago Press.

Goodenough, Ward H. 1963. *Cooperation in Change*. New York: John Wiley and Sons.

Goodland, Robert. 1982. *Tribal Peoples and Economic Development: Human Ecologic Considerations*. Washington, DC: World Bank.

Gough, Robert, and Patrick Spears. 1998. "Foreword." In *Native Peoples-Native Homelands Climate Change Workshop: Final Report*. U.S. Global Change Research Program, i–iv. http://www.usgcrp.gov/usgcrp/Library/nationalassessment/native.pdf.

Goulet, Denis. *The Cruel Choice: A New Concept in the Theory of Development*. New York: Atheneum, 1971.

Graburn, N. H. 1976. *Ethnic and Tourist Arts: Cultural Expressions from the Fourth World*. Berkeley and Los Angeles: University of California Press.

Graham, A. C. 1971. "China, Europe and the origins of the modern science." *Asia Major* 16(parts 1–2): 178–96.

Gray, Andrew. 1987. *The Amerindians of South America*. Report no. 15. London: Minority Rights Group.

Gray, Sandra J. 2000. "Memory of loss: Ecological politics, local history, and the evolution of Karimojong violence." *Human Organization* 59(4): 401–18.

Great Britain Parliamentary Papers. 1836. *Report from the Select Committee on Aborigines (British Settlements)*. Imperial Blue Book no. 7, 538.

Greaves, Tom, ed. 1994. *Intellectual Property Rights for Indigenous Peoples, a Sourcebook*. Oklahoma City, OK: Society for Applied Anthropology.

Griffiths, Tom. 2007. *Exigiendo Responsabilidad al BID y la CFI en Camisea II: Una Revisión de Estándares Internacionales Aplicables, y Diligencia y Conformidad Debidas*. San Francisco: Amazon Watch. http://www.amazonwatch.org/documents/spanish_camiseaII_report.pdf.

Grosart, Ian. 1972. "Direct administration." In *Encyclopedia of Papua and New Guinea*, edited by Peter Ryan, vol. 1, 266–69. Melbourne: Melbourne University Press.

Gross, Daniel R., and Barbara A. Underwood. 1971. "Technological change and caloric costs: Sisal agriculture." *American Anthropologist* 73(3): 725–40.

Gross, Daniel R., et al. 1979. "Ecology and acculturation among native peoples of Central Brazil." *Science* 206(4422): 1043–50.

Grossman, Lawrence S. 1983. "Cattle and rural economic differentiation in the highlands of Papua New Guinea." *American Ethnologist* 10(1): 59–76.

Grossman, Zoltán. 2007. Possible Climate Change Responses For a United League of Indigenous Nations. http://www.indigenousnationstreaty.org/ZoltanClimateChange.doc.

Gwich'in Steering Committee. Gwich'in Niintsyaa (Resolution). http://www.gwichinsteeringcommittee.org/gwichinniintsyaa.html (accessed September 2007).

Gwich'in Steering Committee. 2005. *A Moral Choice for the United States: The Human Rights Implications for the Gwich'in of Drillin in the Arctic National Wildlife Refuge*. Fairbanks, Alaska: Gwich'in Steering Committee. http://www.gwichinsteeringcommittee.org/GSChumanrightsreport.pdf.

Hames, Raymond B. 1979. "A comparison of the efficiencies of the shotgun and the bow in neotropical forest hunting." *Human Ecology* 7(3): 219–52.

Hardenburg, Walter E. 1912. *The Putumayo, the Devil's Paradise: Travels in the Peruvian Amazon Region and an Account of the Atrocities Committed upon the Indians Therein.* London: T. F. Unwin.

Harding, Thomas G. 1960. "Adaptation and stability." In *Evolution and Culture*, edited by Marshall Sahlins and Elman Service, 45–68. Ann Arbor: University of Michigan Press.

Harrop, Angus J. 1937. *England and the Maori Wars.* New York: Books for Libraries Press.

Hart, John A., and Terese B. Hart. 1984. "The Mbuti of Zaire." *Cultural Survival Quarterly* 8(3): 18–20.

Hastings, Peter. 1968. "West Irian—1969." *New Guinea* 3(3): 12–22.

Headland, Thomas N. 1997. "Revisionism in ecological anthropology." *Current Anthropology* 38(4): 605–30.

Heilbroner, Robert L. 1963. *The Great Ascent: The Struggle for Economic Development in Our Time.* New York: Harper Torchbooks.

Henry, Jules. 1941. *Jungle People.* New York: J. J. Augustin.

Hewlett, Barry S., and Bonnie L. Hewlett. 2007. *Ebola, Culture and Politics: The Anthropology of an Emerging Disease.* Belmont, CA: Wadsworth/Thompson.

Hickey, Gerald C. 1967. "Some aspects of hill tribe life in Vietnam." In *Southeast Asian Tribes, Minorities, and Nations*, edited by Peter Kunstadter, 745–69. Princeton, NJ: Princeton University Press.

Higley, Debra K. 2001. *The Putumayo-Oriente-Maranon Province of Colombia, Ecuador, and Peru—Mesozoic-Cenozoic and Paleozoic Petroleum Systems.* U.S. Geological Survey Digital Data Series 63. http://pubs.usgs.gov/dds/DDS-63/DDS-63.pdf.

Hippler, Arthur E. 1979. "Comment on 'Development in the non-Western world.'" *American Anthropologist* 81: 348–49. (Reprinted in Bodley, 1988a, 122–24.)

Holmberg, Alan. 1954. "Adventures in Culture Change." In *Method and Perspective in Anthropology*, edited by R. R. Spencer, pp. 103–13. Minneapolis: University of Minnesota Press.

Homewood, K. M., and W. A. Rodgers. 1984. "Pastoralism and conservation." *Human Ecology* 12(4): 431–41. (Reprinted in Bodley, 1988a, 310–20.)

Hooton, Earnest A. 1945. "Introduction." In *Nutrition and Physical Degeneration: A Comparison of Primitive and Modern Diets and Their Effects*, by Weston A. Price. Redlands, CA: Weston A. Price.

Houser, Schuyler, Verna Teller, Michael MacCracken, Robert Gough, and Patrick Spears. 2001. "Potential Consequences of Climate Variability and Change for Native Peoples and Homelands." In *Climate Change Impacts on the United States: The Potential Consequences of Climate Variability and Change, Report for the US Global Change Research Program*, by National Assessment Synthesis Team, 351–77. Cambridge: Cambridge University Press.

Huff, Lee W. 1967. "The Thai Mobile Development Unit Program." In *Southeast Asian Tribes, Minorities, and Nations*, edited by Peter Kunstadter, 425–86. Princeton, NJ: Princeton University Press.

Hughes, Charles C., and John M. Hunter. 1972. "The role of technological development in promoting disease in Africa." In *The Careless Technology: Ecology and International Development*, edited by M. T. Farvar and John P. Milton, 69–101. Garden City, NY: Natural History Press.

Human Security Centre. 2005. *Human Security Report 2005: War and Peace in the 21st Century.* New York: Oxford University Press.

Hunter, Guy. 1967. *The Best of Both Worlds: A Challenge on Development Policies in Africa.* London: Oxford University Press.

Hurault, J. 1972. "The 'Francization' of the Indians." In *The Situation of the Indian in South America*, edited by W. Dostal, 358–70. Geneva: World Council of Churches.

Hutt, W. H. 1934. "The economic position of the Bantu in South Africa." In *Western Civilization and the Natives of South Africa*, edited by I. Schapera, 195–237. London: George Routledge and Sons.

Huxley, Julian. 1931. *Africa View*. New York: Harper and Row.

Hvalkof, Søren. 2004. *Dreams Coming True: An Indigenous Health Programme in the Peruvian Amazon*. Copenhagen: NORDECO.

Hvalkof, Søren, and Peter Aaby, eds. 1981. *Is God an American? An Anthropological Perspective on the Missionary Work of the Summer Institute of Linguistics*. IWGIA/Survival International Document no. 43. Copenhagen: IWGIA/London: Survival International

Hyndman, David. 1988. "Melanesian resistance to ecocide and ethnocide: Transnational mining projects and the Fourth World on the island of New Guinea." In *Tribal Peoples and Development Issues: A Global Overview*, edited by John H. Bodley, 281–98. Mountain View, CA: Mayfield.

International Congress of Americanists (ICA). *Proceedings*. Various locations.

Illich, Ivan. 1970. *Deschooling Society*. Vol. 44: *World Perspectives*. New York: Harper and Row.

Independent Commission on International Humanitarian Issues. 1987. *Indigenous Peoples: A Global Quest for Justice*. London: Zed Press.

Indian and Northern Affairs Canada. 1993. *Sahtu Dene and Metis: Comprehensive Land Claim Agreement*. http://www.sahtu.ca/pdf/sahtulc/SDMCLA-VOL-1.PDF.

Inter-American Court of Human Rights. 2005. Resolución de la Corte Interamericana de Derechos Humanos de 17 de Junio de 2005. Medidas Provisionales. Caso Pueblo Indígana de Sarayaku. http://www.corteidh.or.cr/docs/medidas/sarayaku_se_021.pdf.

International Alliance of Indigenous Peoples of Tropical Forests (IAITPTF). 2005. Tiohtiá:ke Declaration: International Indigenous Peoples Forum on Climate Change Statement to the State Parties of the COP 11/MOP 1 of the United Nations Framework Convention on Climate Change (UNFCCC). http://www.international-alliance.org/documents/TiohtiakeDeclaration.doc.

International Energy Agency. 2007. Oil in Ecuador in 2004. http://www.iea.org/Textbase/stats/index.asp.

International Labour Organization (ILO). 1953. *Indigenous Peoples: Living and Working Conditions of Aboriginal Populations in Independent Countries*. Studies and Reports, New Series no. 35. Geneva: ILO.

———. 2003. *ILO Convention on Indigenous and Tribal Peoples, 1989 (No. 169): A Manual*. Geneva: ILO. http://www.ilo.org/public/english/standards/norm/egalite/itpp/convention/introduction.pdf.

International Union for the Conservation of Nature (IUCN). 1977. *World Directory of National Parks and Other Protected Areas*. Morges, Switzerland: IUCN.

———. 1980. *World Conservation Strategy: Living Resource Conservation for Sustainable Development*. Gland, Switzerland: IUCN.

———. 1982. *United Nations List of National Parks and Protected Areas*. Gland, Switzerland: IUCN.

———. 1994. *Guidelines for Protected Area Management Categories*. Gland, Switzerland: IUCN, 19. http://www.iucn.org/dbtw-wpd/edocs/1994-007-En.pdf.

———. 2004. *Indigenous Peoples Living in Voluntary Isolation and Conservation of Nature in the Amazon Region and Chaco*. RES 3.056. http://www.iucn.org/congress/2004/members/Individual_Res_Rec_Eng/wcc3_res_056.pdf.

IWGIA (International Work Group for Indigenous Affairs). 1983. *IWGIA Newsletter.*
———. 1986. *The Naga Nation and Its Struggle against Genocide.* IWGIA Document no. 56. Copenhagen: IWGIA.
———. 1987. *IWGIA Yearbook 1986: Indigenous Peoples and Human Rights.* Copenhagen: IW-GIA.
———. 1988. *IWGIA Yearbook 1987: Indigenous Peoples and Development.* Copenhagen: IW-GIA.
———. 1994. *The Indigenous World 1993–1994.* Copenhagen: IWGIA.
———. 2007. *Annual Report 2006.* Copenhagen: IWGIA. http://www.iwgia.org/sw17779.asp.
Iyer, L. A. Krishna, and L. K. Bala Ratnam. 1961. *Anthropology in India.* Bombay: Bharatiya Vidya Bhavan.
Jabavu, D. D. T. 1934. "Bantu grievances." In *Western Civilization and the Natives of South Africa,* edited by I. Schapera, 285–99. London: George Routledge and Sons.
Jackson, Jean. 2003. *The Crisis in Colombia: Consequences for Indigenous Peoples.* Arlington, VA: American Anthropological Association, Committee for Human Rights. http://www.aaanet.org/committees/cfhr/rpt_crisis_in_columbia.htm.
———. 2005. *Update on the Columbian Crisis for the American Anthropological Association Committee for Human Rights.* Arlington, VA: American Anthropological Association. http://www.aaanet.org/committees/cfhr/tf_draft_2005_13.pdf, 7.
Jimenez, Nelly Arevalo de. 1972. "An analysis of official Venezuelan policy in regard to the Indians." In *The Situation of the Indian in South America,* edited by W. Dostal, 31–42. Geneva: World Council of Churches.
Johnson, Allen. 2003. *Families of the Forest: The Matsigenka Indians of the Peruvian Amazon.* Berkeley and Los Angeles: University of California Press.
Jones, Garth N. 1965. "Strategies and tactics of planned organizational change: Case examples in the modernization process of traditional societies." *Human Organization* 24(3): 192–200.
Jones, J. D. Rheinallt. 1934. "Economic condition of the urban native." In *Western Civilization and the Natives of South Africa,* edited by I. Schapera, 159–92. London: George Routledge and Sons.
Jull, Peter. 1982. "Canada: A perspective on the Aboriginal Rights Coalition and the restoration of constitutional aboriginal rights." *IWGIA Newsletter* 30: 82–98.
———. 1987. "Canada: Aboriginal self-government—Assessing the constitutional failure." *IWGIA Newsletter* 50: 69–81.
Jungius, Hartmut. 1976. "National parks and indigenous peoples—A Peruvian case study." *Survival International Review* 1(14): 6–14.
Kaines, Joseph. 1873. "Western anthropologists and extra-Western communities." *Report of the British Association for the Advancement of Science for 1872,* Transactions of the Sections 42: 189–90.
Kaplan, David. 1960. "The law of cultural dominance." In *Evolution and Culture,* edited by Marshall D. Sahlins and Elman R. Service, 69–92. Ann Arbor: University of Michigan Press.
Kar, Parimal Chandra. 1967. "A point of view on the Garos in transition." In *A Common Perspective for North-East India,* edited by Rathin Mittra and Barun Das Gupta, 91–102. Calcutta: Pannalal Das Gupta.
Keesing, Felix M. 1941. *The South Seas in the Modern World.* Institute of Pacific Relations International Research Series. New York: John Day.
Keesing, Felix M., and Marie Keesing. 1934. *Taming Philippine Headhunters: A Study of Government and of Cultural Change in Northern Luzon.* London: George Allen and Unwin.
Kelm, Heinz. 1972. "The present situation of the Indian populations in non-Andean Bolivia." In *The Present Situation of the Indian in South America,* edited by W. Dostal, 158–72. Geneva: World Council of Churches.

Kietzman, Dale W. 1977. "Factors favoring ethnic survival." *International Congress of Americanists, Proceedings* 42(4): 527–36.

Kiste, Robert. 1974. *The Bikinians: A Study in Forced Migration.* Menlo Park, CA: Cummings.

Klee, Gary A. 1980. *World Systems of Traditional Resource Management.* New York: W. H. Winston/Halstead Press.

Klima, George J. 1970. *The Barabaig: East African Cattle Herders.* New York: Holt, Rinehart and Winston.

Kloos, Peter. 1972. "Amerindians of Surinam." In *The Situation of the Indian in South America,* edited by W. Dostal, 348–57. Geneva: World Council of Churches.

———. 1977. *The Akuriyo of Surinam: A Case of Emergence from Isolation.* IWGIA Document no. 27. Copenhagen: IWGIA.

Kohr, Leopold. 1978. *The Breakdown of Nations.* New York: Dutton.

Kolarz, Walter. 1954. *The Peoples of the Soviet Far East.* New York: Praeger.

Korwa, Fred. 1983. "West Papua: The colonisation of West Papua." *IWGIA Newsletter* 35/36: 192–97.

Kosokov, K. 1930. *Voprosu o Shamanstve v Severnoy Azii* [On the question of shamanism in northern Asia]. Moscow.

Kroeger, Axel, and Franchise Barbira-Freedman. 1982. *Culture Change and Health: The Case of South American Rainforest Indians.* Frankfurt am Main: Verlag Peter Lang. (Reprinted in Bodley, 1988a, 221–36.)

Kruyt, A. C. 1929. "The influence of Western civilization on the inhabitants of Poso (Central Celebes)." In *The Effect of Western Influence on Native Civilizations in the Malay Archipelago,* edited by B. Schrieke, 1–9. Batavia: Java Royal Batavia Society of Arts and Sciences.

Kunstadter, Peter, ed. 1967. *Southeast Asian Tribes, Minorities, and Nations.* Princeton, NJ: Princeton University Press.

Kuper, Adam. 2003. "The Return of the Native." *Current Anthropology* 44(3): 389–402.

Lambert, S. M. 1931. "Health survey of Rennell and Bellona Islands." *Oceania* 2(2): 136–73.

Lane Fox Pitt-Rivers, A. H. 1872. "Address to the department of anthropology." *Report of the British Association for the Advancement of Science for 1871* 41: 157–74.

———. 1882. "Anniversary address to the Anthropological Institute of Great Britain and Ireland." *Journal of the Royal Anthropological Institute* 11(4): 488–509.

Langton, Marcia, Maureen Tehan, Lisa Palmer, and Kathryn Shain, eds. 2004. *Honour among Nations: Treaties and Agreements with Indigenous Peoples.* Carlton, Victoria: Melbourne University Press.

La Raw, Maran. 1967. "Toward a basis for understanding the minorities in Burma: The Kachin example." In *Southeast Asian Tribes, Minorities, and Nations,* edited by Peter Kunstadter, 125–46. Princeton, NJ: Princeton University Press.

Lee, Richard B. 1984. *The Dobe Kung.* New York: Holt, Rinehart and Winston.

Lehman, F. K. 1963. *The Structure of Chin Society: A Tribal People of Burma Adapted to a Non-Western Civilization.* Illinois Studies in Anthropology no. 3. Urbana: University of Illinois Press.

Levin, M. G., and L. P. Potapov. 1964. *The Peoples of Siberia.* Chicago: University of Chicago Press.

Lévi-Strauss, Claude. 1951. "Social science in Pakistan." *International Social Science Bulletin* 3(4): 825–31.

Lindley, M. F. 1926. *The Acquisition and Government of Backward Territory in International Law.* London: Longman, Green.

Lipkind, William. 1948. "The Caraja." In *Handbook of South American Indians,* edited by Julian Steward, 3:179–91. Bureau of American Ethnology Bulletin 143. Washington, DC: Smithsonian Institution.

List, Friedrich. 1983. *The Natural System of Political Economy*. Translated and edited by W O. Henderson. London: Frank Cass.

Lizot, Jacques. 1976. *The Yanomami in the Face of Ethnocide*. IWGIA Document no. 22. Copenhagen: IWGIA.

Llanos, Roberto Espinoza. 2004. *An Assessment of the Implementation of International Commitments of Traditional Forest-Related Knowledge in Peru*. Chiang Mai, Thailand: International Alliance of Indigenous and Tribal Peoples of Tropical Forests. http://www.international-alliance.org/documents/Peru-finaledit.pdf.

Loh, Jonathan, and Mathis Wackernagel. 2004. *Living Planet Report*. Gland, Switzerland: WWF—World Wide Fund for Nature.

Loram, C. T. 1932. "Native labor in Southern Africa." In *Pioneer Settlement*, edited by W. L. G. Joerg. Special Publication no. 14, 169–177. New York: American Geographical Society.

Louis, Roger, and Jean Stengers. 1968. *E. P. Morel's History of the Congo Reform Movement*. Oxford: Clarendon Press.

Lugard, Sir F. D. 1928. "The International Institute of African Languages and Cultures." *Africa* 1(1): 1–12.

——. 1965. *The Dual Mandate in British Tropical Africa*. London: Frank Cass.

Lurie, Nancy Oestreich. 1957. "The Indian Claims Commission Act." In *American Indians and American Life*, edited by George E. Simpson and J. Milton Yinger, 56–70. The Annals of the American Academy of Political and Social Science (May), vol. 311. Philadelphia: American Academy of Political and Social Science.

Mair, Lucy Philip. 1970. *Australia in New Guinea*. Melbourne: Melbourne University Press.

Malinowski, Bronislaw. 1929. "Practical anthropology." *Africa* 2(l): 22–38.

Manners, Robert A. 1956. "Functionalism, realpolitik, and anthropology in underdeveloped areas." *America Indigena* 16(1): 7–33.

——. 1967. "The Kipsigis of Kenya: Culture change in a 'Model' East African tribe." In *Contemporary Change in Traditional Societies*, edited by Julian Steward, 1:205–359. Urbana: University of Illinois Press.

Manning, Richard 2004. *Against the Grain: How Agriculture Has Hijacked Civilization*. New York: North Point Press

Marks, Nic, and Saamah Abdallah, Andrew Simms, and Sam Thompson. 2006. *The Happy Planet Index: An Index of Human Well-Being and Environmental Impact*. London: New Economics Foundation.

Maunier, René. 1949. *The Sociology of Colonies*. Vol. 2. London: Routledge and Kegan Paul.

Maybury-Lewis, David. 1983. "The Shavante struggle for their lands." *Cultural Survival Quarterly* 7(1): 54–55.

Maybury-Lewis, David, and James Howe. 1980. *The Indian Peoples of Paraguay: Their Plight and Their Prospects*. Special Report no. 2. Cambridge, MA: Cultural Survival.

McCabe, J. Terrence. 2004. *Cattle Bring Us to Our Enemies: Turkana Ecology, Politics, and Raiding in a Disequilibrium System*. Ann Arbor: University of Michigan Press.

McCullum, Hugh, Karmel McCullum, and John Olthuis. 1977. *Moratorium: Justice, Energy, the North, and the Native People*. Toronto: Anglican Book Centre.

McIntyre, Loren. 1988. "Last days of Eden: Rondonia's Urueu-Wau-Wau Indians." *National Geographic* 174(6): 800–17.

McNeely, Jeffrey A. 1982. "The people of Siberut: Indonesia's original inhabitants." In *Culture and Conservation*. IUCN/CEP (International Union for the Conservation of Nature and the Commission on Environmental Planning), Work in Progress 13, Paper no. 3. Gland, Switzerland: IUCN/CEP.

McNeil, Mary. 1972. "Lateritic soils in distinct tropical environments: Southern Sudan and Brazil." In *The Careless Technology: Ecology and International Development*, edited by M. T. Farvar and John P. Milton, 591–608. Garden City, NY: Natural History Press.

Mead, Margaret. 1961. *New Lives for Old*. New York: New American Library.

Meeker-Lowry, Susan. 1993. "Killing them softly: The 'rainforest harvest." *Z* (July/August): 41–47.

Meggers, Betty J. 1971. *Amazonia: Man and Culture in a Counterfeit Paradise*. Chicago: Aldine.

Merivale, Herman. 1861. *Lectures on Colonization and Colonies*. London: Green, Longman and Roberts.

Metraux, Alfred. 1953. "Applied Anthropology in Government: United Nations." In *Anthropology Today*, edited by A. L. Kroeber, pp. 880–94. Chicago: University of Chicago Press.

Mey, Wolfgang E. 1983. "Dammed for progress: About the perversity of state and nation-building in Bangladesh—The Chittagong Hill Tracts Case." Symposium paper, *The Fourth World: Relations between Minority Peoples and Nation-States*. XIth International Congress of Anthropological and Ethnological Sciences, Vancouver, BC.

Miner, Horace M. 1955. "Planning for the acculturation of isolated tribes." *International Congress of Americanists, Proceedings* 31(1): 441–46.

Mittra, Rathin, and Barun Das Gupta. 1967. *A Common Perspective for North-East India*. Calcutta: Pannalal Das Gupta.

Moasosang, P. 1967. "The Naga search for self-identity." In *A Common Perspective for North-East India*, edited by Rathin Mittra and Barun Das Gupta, 51–57. Calcutta: Pannalal Das Gupta.

Monckeberg, F. 1968. "Mental retardation from malnutrition." *Journal of the American Medical Association* 206: 30–31.

Montagu, Ashley. 1972. "Sociogenic brain damage." *American Anthropologist* 74(5): 1045–61.

Morauta, Louise, John Pernetta, and William Heaney. 1982. *Traditional Conservation in Papua New Guinea: Implications for Today*. Monograph no. 16. Boroka, Papua New Guinea: Institute of Applied Social and Economic Research.

Moreira Neto, Carlos de Araujo. 1972. "Some data concerning the recent history of the Kaingang Indians." In *The Situation of the Indian in South America*, edited by W. Dostal, 284–333. Geneva: World Council of Churches.

Morel, E. D. 1906. *Red Rubber*. New York: Nassau Print.

———. 1969. *The Black Man's Burden*. Northbrook, IL: Metro Books.

Mosonyi, Esteban E. 1972. "The situation of the Indian in Venezuela: Perspectives and solutions." In *The Situation of the Indian in South America*, edited by W. Dostal, 43–55. Geneva: World Council of Churches.

Mountjoy, A. B. 1967. *Industrialization and Underdeveloped Countries*. Chicago: Aldine.

Münzel, Mark. 1973. *The Ache Indians: Genocide in Paraguay*. IWGIA Document no. 11. Copenhagen: IWGIA.

Murdock, George P. 1959. Africa: *Its Peoples and Their Culture History*. New York: McGraw-Hill.

Murphy, Robert, and Julian Steward. 1956. "Trappers and trappers: Parallel processes in acculturation." *Economic Development and Culture Change* 4: 335–55.

Nag, Amit Kumar. 1967. "The society in transition in the Mizo District." In *A Common Perspective for North-East India*, edited by Rathin Mittra and Barun Das Gupta, 80–90. Calcutta: Pannalal Das Gupta.

Nahanni, Phoebe. 1977. "The mapping project." In *Dene Nation—The Colony Within*, edited by Mel Watkins, 21–27. Toronto: University of Toronto Press.

Naisbitt, John, and Patricia Aburdene. 1990. *Megatrends 2000*. New York: William Morrow.

Nash, Roderick. 1968. *The American Environment: Readings in the History of Conservation*. Reading, MA: Addison-Wesley.

National Aboriginal Land Rights Conference. 1976. Untitled Pamphlet. Sydney, 1976.

National Research Council, Committee on Cumulative Environmental Effects of Oil and Gas Activities on Alaska's North Slope. 2003. *Cumulative Environmental Effects of Oil and Gas Activities on Alaska's North Slope*. Washington, DC: National Academies Press

Nederlandsche Commissie voor Internationale Natuurbescherming. 1937. *Conservation of Primitives Still Living in the Stone Age, Especially in New Guinea*. Medeelingen no. 11, 1–7.

Netting, Robert M. 1977. *Cultural Ecology*. Menlo Park, CA: Benjamin/Cummings.

New Zealand Department of Statistics. 1960. *The New Zealand Official Year-Book*. Wellington: R. E. Owen, Government Printer.

Niedenthal, Jack. 2001. *For the Good of Mankind: A History of the People of Bikini and their Islands*. Majuro, Republic of the Marshall Islands: Micronitor/Bravo Publishers.

Nietschmann, Bernard. 1984. "Biosphere reserves and traditional societies." In *Conservation, Science and Society: Contributions to the First International Biosphere Reserve Congress, Minsk, Byelorussia/USSR*. 2: 499–508. Paris: UNESCO-UNEP.

———. 1985. "Indonesia, Bangladesh: Disguised invasion of indigenous nations." *Fourth World Journal* 1(2): 89–126. (Reprinted in abridged form in Bodley, 1988a, 191–207.)

———. 1988. "Miskito and Kuna struggle for nation autonomy." In *Tribal Peoples and Development Issues: A Global Overview*, edited by John H. Bodley, 271–80. Mountain View, CA: Mayfield.

Niklaus, Phil. 1983. "Land, power and yellowcake." *IWGIA Newsletter* 34: 6–15.

Nimuendaju, Curt. 1946. *The Eastern Timbira*. University of California Publications in American Archaeology and Ethnology, vol. 41. Berkeley and Los Angeles: University of California Press.

Nishi, Midori. 1968. "An evaluation of Japanese agricultural and fishery developments in Micronesia during the Japanese mandate 1914–1941." *Micronesia* 4(1): 1–18.

Northern Land Council. 2006. *Annual Report 2005/2006*. http://www.nlc.org.au/html/files /0506_Annual%20Report_Overview.pdf.

Northern Territory Government of Australia. 2007. *Ampe Akelyernemane Meke Mekarle "Little Children Are Sacred."* Report of the Northern Territory Board of Inquiry into the Protection of Aboriginal Children from Sexual Abuse, 7. http://www.nt.gov.au/dcm/inquirysaac/pdf/bi pacsa_final_report.pdf.

Nunasi Corporation. 2005. Operations. Consolidated Balance Sheet, December 31. http://www.nunasi.com/operations.htm.

Nunavut Planning Commission. 1993. *Agreement between the Inuit of the Nunavut Settlement Area and Her Majesty the Queen in Right of Canada*, articles 1, and 35. http://npc.nunavut .ca/eng/nunavut/nlca.pdf.

Nunavut Tunngavik Inc. 2006. *Iniksaqattiarniq, Inuusiqattiarniq: Housing in Nunavut—The Time for Action Is Now*. Annual Report on the State of Inuit Culture and Society 2003/04 and 2004/05. http://www.tunngavik.com/english/pub.html.

———. 2007. Inuit Firm Registry—Approved Businesses as of Sep 07, 2007. http://www.inuit firm.com/public/pdfreport.php.

Oliver, Douglas L., ed. 1951. *Planning Micronesia's Future: A Summary of the United States Commercial Company's Economic Survey of Micronesia*. Cambridge, MA: Harvard University Press.

Organization of Petrolelum Exporting Countries (OPEC). 2006. OPEC Share of Crude Oil Reserves (2006). http://www.opec.org/home/PowerPoint/Reserves/OPEC%20share.htm.

Organización Nacional Indígena de Colombia (ONIC). 2007. Quiénes Somos. http://www.onic.org.co/quienes.shtml.

Otten, Mariel. 1986. *Transmigrasi: Indonesian Resettlement Policy, 1965–1985.* IWGIA Document no. 57. Copenhagen: IWGIA.

Pacific Science Congress. 1953. *Proceedings of the Seventh Pacific Science Congress.*

Palacios i Mendiburu, S. 1892. "Conferencia sobre la colonizacion de Loreto." *Boletin de la Sociedad Geografica de Lima* 2: 267–312.

Palmer, George. 1871. *Kidnapping in the South Seas.* Edinburgh: Edmonston and Douglas.

Panamá Contraloría General de la República. 2006. *Panamá en Cifras: Años 2001–05.* Dirección de Estadística y Censo. http://www.contraloria.gob.pa/DEC/main.aspx.

Parker, Alan. 2007. *Indigenous Nations Treaty Proceedings July 31–August 2, 2007. Lummi Indian Nation.* N.p.: United League of Indigenous Nations. http://www.indigenousnationstreaty.org/ReportInterimGovAug10.pdf.

Parry, Martin, Osvaldo Canziani, Jean Palutikof, Paul van der Linden, Clair Hanson, eds. 2007. *Climate Change 2007: Impacts, Adaptation and Vulnerability. Contribution of Working Group II to the Fourth Assessment Report of the Intergovernmental Panel on Climate Change.* New York: Cambridge University Press. http://www.ipcc-wg2.org/.

Patterson, Dennis. 1984. "Canada: Inuit and Nunavut." *IWGIA Newsletter* 37: 39–52.

Peacock, Nadene. 1984. "The Mbuti of Northeast Zaire." *Cultural Survival Quarterly* 8(2): 15–17.

Peoples, James G. 1978. "Dependence in a Micronesian economy." *American Ethnologist* 5(3): 535–52.

Peru Ministerio de Energía y Minas. 2001. *Guía de Relaciones Comunitarias.* Lima: Dirección General de Asuntos Ambientales, Anexo 4. http://www.minem.gob.pe/archivos/dgaae/legislacion/guias/guiaelectrical.pdf.

Pirog, Robert. 2006. *Oil Industry Profit Review 2005.* CRS Report for Congress. Report RL33373. Congressional Research Service, Library of Congress, CRS-1. http://digital.library.unt.edu/govdocs/crs/data/2006/meta-crs-9209.tkl.

Pitt, David. 1983. *Culture and Conservation: An Action/Research Plan.* Gland, Switzerland: IUCN.

Plant, Roger, and Søren Hvalkof. 2001. *Land Titling and Indigenous Peoples.* Sustainable Development Department Technical Paper Series. Washington, DC: Inter-American Development Bank.

Pittock, A. Barrie. 1972. *Aboriginal Land Rights.* IWGIA Document no. 3. Copenhagen: IWGIA.

———. 1975. *Beyond White Australia: A Short History of Race Relations in Australia.* Surrey Hills, New South Wales: Race Relations Committee of the Religious Society of Friends (Quakers) in Australia.

Pitt-Rivers, George H. 1927. *The Clash of Culture and the Contact of Races.* London: George Routledge and Sons.

Pluspetrol. 2002. *Plan de Contengencia Antropológico para Poblaciones en Contacto Inicial o en Aislamiento.* Doc-22-02, 5–6 http://www.camisea.com.pe/esp/estados/SGA/Listado/DOC-22.pdf.

Popenoe, Paul. 1915. "One phase of man's modern evolution." *International Congress of Americanists* 19: 617–20.

Popkin, Barry M. 1998. "The nutrition transition and its health implications in lower-income countries." *Public Health Nutrition* 1(1): 5–21.

Portas, Julio Anibal. 1967. *Malon Contra Malon: La Solución Final del Problema del Indio en la Argentina.* Buenos Aires: Ediciones de la Flor.

Portugal, Pedro. 1980. "Entrevista con Pedro Portugal." In *Primer Congreso de Movimientos Indies de Sudamerica*, 169–80. Paris: Ediciones Mitka.

Posey, Darrell A., and Graham Dutfield. 1996. *Beyond Intellectual Property: Toward Traditional Resource Rights for Indigenous Peoples and Local Communities*. Ottawa: International Development Research Center.

Powell, J. W. 1881. *First Annual Report of the Bureau of Ethnology to the Secretary of the Smithsonian Institution 1879–1880*. Washington, DC: Government Printing Office.

Presland, Anna. 1979. "An account of the contemporary fight for survival of the Amerindian peoples of Brazil." *Survival International Review* 4(1): 14–40.

Price, A. G. 1950. *White Settlers and Native Peoples*. London: Cambridge University Press.

Price, Weston Andrew. 1945. *Nutrition and Physical Degeneration: A Comparison of Primitive and Modern Diets and Their Effects*. Redlands, CA: Weston A. Price.

Prior, Ian A. M. 1971. "The price of civilization." *Nutrition Today* 6(4): 2-11.

Radcliffe-Brown, A. R. 1930. "Editorial." *Oceania* 1(1): 1–4.

Raglan, Lord Fitzroy R. S. 1940. "The future of the savage races." *Man* 40: 62.

Rambo, A. Terry. 1985. *Primitive Polluters: Semang Impact on the Malaysian Tropical Rain Forest Ecosystem*. Anthropological Papers no. 76. Ann Arbor: Museum of Anthropology, University of Michigan.

Rappaport, Roy A. 1971. "The Flow of Energy in an Agricultural Society." *Scientific American* 224(3): 117–32.

Razon, Felix. 1976. *Native Peoples Struggle against U.S. Imperialism in the Philippines*. IWGIA Document no. 25, 32–41. Copenhagen: IWGIA.

Redfield, Robert. 1953. *The Primitive World and Its Transformations*. Ithaca, NY: Cornell University Press.

———. 1962. *A Village That Chose Progress: Chan Kom Revisited*. Chicago: University of Chicago Press/Phoenix Books.

Redfield, Robert, Ralph Linton, and M. J. Herskovits. 1936. "Memorandum on the study of acculturation." *American Anthropologist* 38: 149–52.

Reed, Stephen W. 1943. *The Making of Modern New Guinea*. Philadelphia: American Philosophical Society.

Reinhard, K. R. 1976. "Resource exploitation and the health of western arctic man." In *Circumpolar Health: Proceedings of the Third International Symposium, Yellowknife, Northwest Territories*, edited Roy J. Shephard and S. Itoh, 617–27. Toronto: University of Toronto Press. (Reprinted in Bodley, 1988a, 211–20.)

Reining, Conrad C. 1966. *The Zande Scheme: An Anthropological Case Study of Economic Development in Africa*. Evanston, IL: Northwestern University Press.

Revkin, Andrew C. 2007. "Scientists report severe retreat of Arctic ice." *New York Times*, September 21, A6.

Ribeiro, Darcy. 1957. *Culturas e Linguas Indigenas do Brasil*. Separata de Educacão e Ciências Socais no. 6. Rio de Janeiro: Centro Brasileiro de Pesquisas Educacionais.

Rivers, W. H. R. 1922. *Essays on the Depopulation of Melanesia*. Cambridge: Cambridge University Press.

Roberts, Janine. 1978. *From Massacres to Mining: The Colonization of Aboriginal Australia*. London: War on Want.

Roberts, J. P., ed. 1975. *Mapoon—Book One: The Mapoon Story by the Mapoon People*. Victoria, Australia: International Development Action.

Roberts, J., and D. McLean. 1976. *Mapoon—Book Three: The Cape York Aluminum Companies and the Native Peoples*. Victoria, Australia: International Development Action.

Roberts, J., M. Parsons, and B. Russell. 1975. *Mapoon—Book Two: The Mapoon Story According to the Invaders*. Victoria, Australia: International Development Action.

Roberts, Stephen Henry. 1969. *Population Problems of the Pacific*. New York: AMS Press.

Rocamora, Joel. 1979a. "Agribusiness, dams and counter-insurgency." *Southeast Asia Chronicle* 67: 2–10.

———. 1979b. "The political uses of PANAMIN." *Southeast Asia Chronicle* 67: 11–21.

Rodman, Margaret, and Matthew Cooper, eds. 1979. *The Pacification of Melanesia*. Association for Social Anthropology in Oceania Monograph no. 7. Ann Arbor: University of Michigan Press.

Rossel, Pierre. 1988. *Tourism and Cultural Minorities: Double Marginalisation and Survival Strategies*. IWGIA Document no. 61. Copenhagen: IWGIA.

Rotberg, Robert, and Ali Mazrui, eds. 1970. *Protest and Power in Black Africa*. New York: Oxford University Press.

Rowley, Charles D. 1966. *The New Guinea Villager: The Impact of Colonial Rule on Primitive Society and Economy*. New York: Praeger.

———. 1967. "The villager and the nomad: Aboriginals and New Guineans." *New Guinea* 2(1): 70–81.

———. 1970. *The Destruction of Aboriginal Society*. Vol. 1: *Aboriginal Policy and Practice*. Canberra: Australian National University Press.

———. 1971. *The Remote Aborigines*. Vol. 3: *Aboriginal Policy and Practice*. Canberra: Australian National University Press.

Royal Anthropological Institute of Great Britain and Ireland. 1951. *Notes and Queries on Anthropology*. London: Routledge and Kegan Paul.

Rushforth, Scott. 1977. "Country food." In *Dene Nation—The Colony Within*, edited by Mel Watkins, 32–46. Toronto: University of Toronto Press.

Russell, Peter H. 1977. "The Dene nation and confederation." In *Dene Nation—The Colony Within*, edited by Mel Watkins, 163–73. Toronto: University of Toronto Press.

Ryan, John. 1969. *The Hot Land: Focus on New Guinea*. New York: Macmillan.

Said, Beshir Mohammed. 1965. *The Sudan, Crossroads of Africa*. Chester Springs, PA: Dufour Editions.

Sanders, Douglas E. 1977. *The Formation of the World Council of Indigenous Peoples*. IWGIA Document no. 29. Copenhagen: IWGIA.

San Sebastián, Miguel, and Anna-Karin Hurtig. 2004. "Oil exploitation in the Amazon basin of Ecuador: a public health emergency." *Pan American Journal of Public Health* 15(3): 205–11.

Saussol, Alain. 1971. "New Caledonia: Colonization and reaction." In *Land Tenure in the Pacific*, edited by Ron Crocombe, 227–45. Melbourne: Oxford University Press.

Scarr, Deryck. 1968. "Introduction." In *A Cruise in a Queensland Labour Vessel to the South Seas*, by W. E. Giles. Canberra: Australian National University Press.

Schapera, Isaac.1934. *Western Civilization and the Natives of South Africa*. London: George Routledge and Sons.

Schneider, David. 1955. "Abortion and depopulation on a Pacific island: Yap." In *Health, Culture, and Community*, edited by B. D. Paul, 211–35. New York: Russell Sage.

Schoen, Ivan L. 1969. "Contact with the Stone Age." *Natural History* 78(1): 10–18, 66–67.

Seiler-Baldinger, Annemarie. 1988. "Tourism in the upper Amazon and its effects on the indigenous population." In *Tourism: Manufacturing the Exotic*, edited by Pierre Rossel, 177–93. IWGIA Document no. 61. Copenhagen: IWGIA.

Sinclair, Keith. 1961. *The Origins of the Maori Wars*. 2nd ed. Wellington: New Zealand University Press.

Sivummut Economic Development Strategy Group. 2003. *Nunavut Economic Development Strategy: Building a Foundation for the Future*. http://edt.gov.nu.ca/docs/nes/NUNAVUTE .pdf.

Smil, Vaclav. 2005a. *Creating the Twentieth Century: Technical Innovations of 1867–1914 and Their Lasting Impact.* Oxford and New York: Oxford University Press.

———. 2005b. *Energy at the Crossroads: Global Perspectives and Uncertainties.* Cambridge, MA: MIT Press.

Smith, Adam. 1776. *An Inquiry into the Nature and Causes of the Wealth of Nations.* Vol. 1. London: Strahan & Cadell.

Smith, Edwin W. 1934. "Anthropology and the practical man." *Journal of the Royal Anthropological Institute* 64: xiii–xxxvii.

Smith, V. L., ed. 1977. *Hosts and Guests: The Anthropology of Tourism.* Philadelphia: University of Pennsylvania Press.

Smith, Wilberforce. 1894. "The teeth of ten Sioux Indians." *Journal of the Royal Anthropological Institute* 24: 109–16.

Snow, Alpheus Henry. 1921. *The Question of Aborigines: In the Law and Practice of Nations.* New York: Putnam.

Society for Applied Anthropology. 1963. "Statement on ethics of the society for applied anthropology." *Human Organization* 22: 237.

———. 2007. Statement of Professional and Ethnical Responsibilities. http://www.sfaa.net/sfaaethic.html (accessed July 9, 2007).

Soja, Edward W. 1968. *The Geography of Modernization in Kenya.* Syracuse Geographical Series, no. 2. Syracuse, NY: Syracuse University Press.

Spencer, Baldwin. 1913. "Preliminary Report on the Aboriginals of the Northern Territory." In Parliament of the Commonwealth of Australia, Northern Territory of Australia, *Report of the Administrator for the Year 1912*, 36–52. Melbourne.

Spooner, Brian. 1973. *The Cultural Ecology of Pastoral Nomads.* Modules in Anthropology. Reading, MA: Addison-Wesley.

Starr, Cecie, ed. 1971. *Anthropology Today.* Del Mar, CA: Communications Research Machines.

Stavenhagen, Rodolfo. 2002. *Indigenous Issues: Human Rights and Indigenous Issues. Report of the Special Rapporteur on the Situation of Human Rights and Fundamental Freedoms of Indigenous Peoples.* United Nations, Economic and Social Council, Commission of Human Rights E/CN.4/2002/97. http://daccessdds.un.org/doc/UNDOC/GEN/G02/106/29/PDF/G0210629.pdf?OpenElement.

Stavenhagen, Rodolfo. 2006. *Report of the Special Rapporteur on the Situation of Human Rights and Fundamental Freedoms of Indigenous People.* Addendum. Mission to Ecuador. Human Rights Council. A/HRC/4/32/Add.2 28 December. http://daccessdds.un.org/doc/UNDOC/GEN/G07/100/29/PDF/G0710029.pdf?OpenElement.

Steward, Julian H. 1948. "The Witotoan tribes." In *Handbook of South American Indians*, edited by Julian H. Steward, 3:749–62. Bureau of American Ethnology Bulletin 143. Washington, DC: Smithsonian Institution.

Steward, Julian H., ed. 1967. *Contemporary Change in Traditional Societies.* Urbana: University of Illinois Press.

Stoll, David. 1982. *Fishers of Men or Founders of Empire? The Wycliffe Bible Translators in Latin America.* London: Zed Press/Cambridge, MA: Cultural Survival.

Sturtevant, William C. 1967. "Urgent anthropology: Smithsonian-Wenner-Gren Conference." *Current Anthropology* 8(4): 355–61.

———. 1970. "Resolution on forced acculturation." *Current Anthropology* 11(2): 160.

Suess, Paolo. 1980. "Triplice Aliança na Luta Indigena." *Porantim* 3(17): 8–9.

Sumardja, Effendy A. 1984. "Siberut Reserve Impacts on Indigenous People in West Sumatra, Indonesia." Paper presented at the First World Conference on Cultural Parks, Mesa Verde, CO.

Summer Institute of Linguistics. http://www.sil.org/.

Suret-Canale, Jean. 1971. *French Colonialism in Tropical Africa, 1900–1945.* New York: Pica Press.

Tax, Sol. 1968. "Discussion." In *Man the Hunter*, edited by Richard B. Lee and Irven DeVore, pp. 345–46. Chicago: Aldine.

Thiek, Hrilrokhum. 1967. "An outlook for a better understanding of the tribal people." In *A Common Perspective for North-East India*, edited by Rathin Mittra and Barun Das Gupta, 103–109. Calcutta: Pannalal Das Gupta.

Thompson, Laura. 1940. *Fijian Frontier.* New York: Institute of Pacific Relations.

Thomson, Donald F. 1938. *Recommendations of Policy in Native Affairs in the Northern Territory of Australia.* Parliament of the Commonwealth of Australia No. 56.-R2945. Canberra: Commonwealth Government Printer.

Thornton, Russell. 1987. *American Indian Holocaust and Survival: A Population History since 1492.* Norman and London: University of Oklahoma Press.

Townsend, G. 1933. "The administration of the mandated territory of New Guinea." *Geographical Journal* 82: 424–34.

Turnbull, Colin M. 1963. "The lesson of the Pygmies." *Scientific American* 208(1): 28–37.

———. 1972. *The Mountain People.* New York: Simon and Schuster.

Unidad Indigena. 1975. 1(1).

Unidad Indígena del Pueblo Awá (UNIPA). Plan de Vida Awá, Identidad Awá. http://www.unipa.org.co/index.htm.

United Kingdom House of Commons. 1837. *Report from the Select Committee on Aborigines (British Settlements).* Imperial Blue Book, no. 7, 425. British Parliamentary Papers.

United League of Indigenous Nations Treaty. http://www.indigenousnationstreaty.org/SignedTreatyAug1.pdf.

United Nations Department of Economic and Social Affairs. 2004. *The Concept of Indigenous Peoples.* Background paper, Workshop on Data Collection and Dissagregation for Indigenous Peoples, Secretariat of the Permanent Forum on Indigenous Issues. PFII/2004/WS.1/3. http://www.un.org/esa/socdev/unpfii/documents/PFII%202004%20WS.1%203%20Definition.doc (December 14, 2007).

United Nations Food and Agriculture Organization. 2006. *Global Forest Resources Assessment 2005: Progress towards sustainable forest management.* FAO Forestry Paper 147. www.fao.org/forestry/site/32039/en.

United Nations Permanent Forum on Indigenous Issues. 2007. *Report on the Sixth Session* (May 14–25, 2007). Economic and Social Council Official Records, Supplement No. 23. E/2007/43 E/C.19/2007/12, Articles 39–42. http://daccessdds.un.org/doc/UNDOC/GEN/N07/376/75/PDF/N0737675.pdf?OpenElement.

United States Bureau of the Census. *Census 2000.* Table DP-1. Profile of General Demographic Characteristics: 2000. Wainwright ANVSA, AK. http://censtats.census.gov/data/AK/280027735.pdf (accessed July 2, 2007).

United States Department of Energy, Energy Information Agency (EIA). 1999. *Petroleum: An Energy Profile 1999.* ADOE/EIA-0545(99) July. http://tonto.eia.doe.gov/FTPROOT/petroleum/054599.pdf.

———. 2007. *Annual Energy Review 2006.* http://www.eia.doe.gov/emeu/aer/pdf.

United States Department of the Interior, Office of Territories. 1953. *Report on the Administration of the Trust Territory of the Pacific Islands (by the United States to the United Nations) for the Period July 1, 1951, to June 30, 1952.* Washington, DC.

———. 1954. *Annual Report, High Commissioner of the Trust Territory of the Pacific Islands to the Secretary of the Interior (for 1953).* Washington, DC.

United States Department of State. 1955. *Seventh Annual Report to the United Nations on the Administration of the Trust Territory of the Pacific Islands (July 1, 1953, to June 30, 1954)*. Washington, DC.

———. 1959. *Eleventh Annual Report to the United Nations on the Administration of the Trust Territory of the Pacific Islands (July 1, 1957, to June 30, 1958)*. Washington, DC.

———. 1964. *Sixteenth Annual Report to the United Nations on the Administration of the Trust Territory of the Pacific Islands (July 1, 1962, to June 30, 1963)*. Washington, DC.

———. 1973. *Twenty-Fifth Annual Report to the United Nations on the Administration of the Trust Territory of the Pacific Islands (July 1, 1971, to June 30, 1972)*. Washington, DC.

United States Fish and Wildlife Service. Arctic National Wildlife Refuge: Refuge Features. http://arctic.fws.gov/features.htm.

United States Geological Survey. 2001. *Arctic National Wildlife Refuge, 1002 Area, Petroleum Assessment, 1998, Including Economic Analysis. Fact Sheet 0028–01*. Online Report. http://pubs.usgs.gov/fs/fs-0028–01/.

United States Geological Survey World Energy Assessment Team. 2000. *U.S. Geological Survey World Petroleum Assessment 2000: Description and Results*. http://energy.cr.usgs .gov/WEReport.pdf.

Valcarcel, Carlos A. 1915. *El Proceso del Putumayo y sus Secretos Inauditos*. Lima: H. La Rosa.

Viteri, Franco. 2004. "La Lucha de Sarayaku." In *Pueblos en Lucha: Casos emblemáticos de defense de derechos indígenas*. IV Congreso latinoamericano de la Red de Antropología Juridica. Quito: Centro de Derechos Economics y Sociales CDES.

Vivar, Harmodio. Mensaje de Sailadummaan de la Comarca Kuna Yala. http//www.congreso-generalkuna.org/mensaje_sailadummagan.htm.

Wagley, C. 1951. "Cultural influences on population." *Revista do Museu Paulista* 5: 95–104.

———. 1977. *Welcome of Tears: The Tapirape Indians of Central Brazil*. New York: Oxford University Press.

Wagner, Roy. 1971. "A Problem of Ethnocide: When a Chimbu meets a Karimui." *New Guinea* 6 (June/July): 27–31.

Wallerstein, Immanuel. 1974. *The Modern World-System: Capitalist Agriculture and the Origins of the European World-Economy in the Sixteenth Century*. New York: Academic Press.

Warsh, David. 1984. *The Idea of Economic Complexity*. New York: Viking Penguin.

Watkins, Mel, ed. 1977. *Dene Nation—The Colony Within*. Toronto: University of Toronto Press.

Watt, Kenneth E. F. 1972. "Man's Efficient Rush Toward Deadly Dullness." *Natural History* 81(2): 74–82.

Watt-Cloutier, Sheila. 2005. *Peitition to the InterAmerican Commission on Human Rights Seeking Relief from Violations Resulting from Global Warming Caused by Acts and Omissions of the United States*. December 7, 2005, 129. http://www.ciel.org/Publications/ICC_Petition_7Dec05.pdf.

World Council of Indigenous Peoples (WCIP). 1977. *World Council of Indigenous Peoples Second General Assembly, Kiruna, Sweden, August 24–27, 1977* (report).

Webb, W. E. 1966. "Land capacity classification and land use in the Chittagong Hill tracts of East Pakistan." *Proceedings of the Sixth World Forestry Congress* 3: 3229–32.

Webb, Walter Prescott. 1952. *The Great Frontier*. Boston: Houghton Mifflin.

Weiss, Gerald. 1988. "The tragedy of ethnocide: A reply to Hippler." In *Tribal Peoples and Development Issues: A Global Overview*, edited by John H. Bodley, 124–33. Mountain View, CA: Mayfield.

Wellington, John H. 1967. *South West Africa and Its Human Issues*. Oxford: Clarendon Press/Oxford University Press.

Whitten, Norman E. 1976. *Ecuadorian Ethnocide and Indigenous Ethnogenesis: Amazonian Resurgence amidst Andean Colonialism.* IWGIA Document no. 23. Copenhagen: IWGIA.

Williams-Hunt, Peter Darrell Rider. 1952. *An Introduction to the Malayan Aborigines.* Kuala Lumpur: Government Press.

Winnacker, Martha. 1979. "The battle to stop the Chico dams." *Southeast Asia Chronicle* 67: 22–29.

Wirsing, R. 1985. "The health of traditional societies and the effects of acculturation." *Current Anthropology* 26: 303–22.

Wise, Mary Ruth, Eugene E. Loos, and Patricia Davis. 1977. "Filosofía y Métodos del Instituto Linguistico de Verano." In *Proceedings of the 42nd International Americanists Congress, Paris,* 2:499–525. Paris: Société des Américanistes, Musee d l'Homme.

Wollaston, A. F. R. 1920. "Remarks on 'The opening of new territories in Papua." *Geographical Journal* (June): 457–58.

Wood Jones, Frederic. 1928. "The Claims of the Australian Aborigine." *18th ANZAAS, Perth, 1926, Report of the Australian and New Zealand Association for the Advancement of Science* 18: 497–519. Melbourne.

Woodruff, William. 1966. *Impact of Western Man.* London: Macmillan.

World Bank. 1991. *Operational Directive. OD 4.20: Indigenous Peoples.* http://www.worldbank.org/html/fpd/em/power/wbpolicy/420OD.stm.

———. 2002. *Brazil Rain Forest Pilot Program Success Story 2: Innovative Project Contributes to Regularizing Indigenous Lands in the Amazon.* http://www.worldbank.org/rfpp/docs/SS2%20engl.pdf (accessed July 8, 2007).

———. 2005. *Operational Manual. 4.10 Indigenous Peoples OP/BP.* http://wbln0018.worldbank.org/Institutional/Manuals/OpManual.nsf/.

———. 2006a. *World Development Report 2006. Equity and Development.* New York: Oxford University Press.

———. 2006b. *World Bank Annual Report 2006.* Operational Summary, frontpiece. http://go.worldbank.org/KQ3OFFED90.

World Commission on Dams. 2007. Outline of the WCD. http://www.dams.org/commission/intro.htm.

Wright, R. Michael, Brian Houseal, and Cebaldo de Leon. 1985. "Kuna Yala: Indigenous biosphere reserve in the making?" *Parks* 10(3): 25–27. (Reprinted in Bodley, 1988a, 352–56.)

Zallez, Jaime, and Alfonso Gortaire. 1978. *Organizarse o Sucumbir: La Federación Shuar.* Mundo Shuar Serie "B," No. 14. Sucua, Ecuador: Centra de Documentación e Investigación Cultural Shuar.

Zaman, M. Q. 1985. "Tribal survival in the Chittagong hill tracts of Bangladesh." *Man in India* 65(1): 58–74.

Selected Web Sites

Aboriginal Pipeline Group. http://www.mvapg.com/page/page/1922394.htm.

Amazon Alliance. http://www.amazonalliance.org/camisea.html

Amazon Defense Coalition (Frente de Defensa de la Amazonia, FDA). http://www.ecuanex.net.ec/fda/fda.htm, http://www.texacotoxico.org/.

Amazon Watch. http://www.amazonwatch.org/amazon/PE/camisea/.

Arctic Slope Regional Corporation. http://www.asrc.com/stock/stock.asp.

Asociación de Cabildos Indígenas del Norte del Cauca (ACIN). http://www.nasaacin.net.

Bikini Atoll Web site. http://www.bikiniatoll.com/.

Camisea Project. http://www.camisea.com.pe/.

Coordinator for the Indigenous Organizations of the Amazon Basin (Coordinadora de las Organizaciones Indígena de la Cuenca Amazónica, COICA). http://www.coica.org.ec/index.htm.

Confederacion de Nacionalidades Indigenas de la Amazonica Ecuatoriana (CONFENIAE). http://www.ecuanex.net.ec/confeniae/.

Congreso Kuna. http://www.congresogeneralkuna.org.

Consejo de Desarrollo de las Nacionalidades y Pueblos del Ecuador (CODENPE). http://www.codenpe.gov.ec/npe.htm.

Cordillera Peoples Alliance for the Defense of Ancestral Domain and for Self Determination. 2007. http://www.cpaphils.org/.

Cultural Survival. http://www.cs.org/.

Fédération des Organisations Autochtones de Guyane. http://www.coica.org/en/members/foag.html.

Fundação Nacional do Índio (FUNAI). www.funai.gov.br.

Gesellschaft für bedrohte Völker (Society for Threatened Peoples). http://www.gfbv.de/promis.php.

Gwich'in Steering Committee. http://www.gwichinsteeringcommittee.org

Interethnic Development Association of the Peruvian Amazon (Asociación Interétnica de Desarrollo de la Selva Peruana, AIDESEP). http://www.aidesep.org.pe/.

International Alliance of Indigenous Peoples of Tropical Forests (IAITPTF). http://www.international-alliance.org/

International Work Group for Indigenous Affairs (IWGIA). http://www.iwgia.org/.

Mackenzie Natural Gas Pipeline Project Group. http://www.mackenziegasproject.com/index.asp.

Northern Land Council. http://www.nlc.org.au.

Nunasi Corporation. http://www.nunasi.com.

Nunavut Planning Commission. http://npc.nunavut.ca.

Organización Nacional Indígena de Colombia (ONIC). http://www.onic.org.co.

Survival International. http://www.survival-international.org/.

Unidad Indígena del Pueblo Awá (UNIPA). http://www.unipa.org.co.

United League of Indigenous Nations Treaty. http://www.indigenousnationstreaty.org.

World Bank. http://www.worldbank.org.

Index

About the Author

John H. Bodley is a cultural anthropologist and Regents Professor at Washington State University and author of *Anthropology and Contemporary Human Problems, Fifth Edition.*